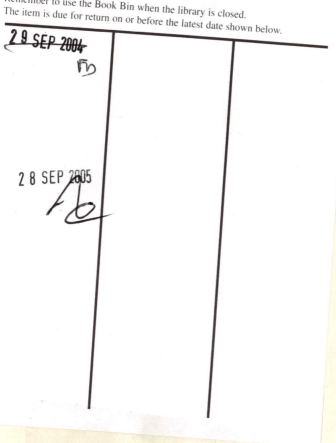

MAIN LENDING   **<u>3 WEEK LOAN</u>**   DCU LIBRARY

Fines are charged **PER DAY** if this item is overdue.
Check at www.dcu.ie/~library or telephone (01) 700 5183 for fine rates and renewal regulations for this item type.
Item is subject to recall.
Remember to use the Book Bin when the library is closed.
The item is due for return on or before the latest date shown below.

2 9 SEP 2004		
2 8 SEP 2005		

OXFORD HISTORICAL MONOGRAPHS

Editors

BARBARA HARVEY   A. D. MACINTYRE

R. W. SOUTHERN   A. F. THOMPSON

H. R. TREVOR-ROPER

CROMWELLIAN IRELAND

English Government and Reform
in Ireland 1649-1660

by

T. C. BARNARD

*Lecturer in History, Royal Holloway College,
University of London*

OXFORD UNIVERSITY PRESS
1975

Oxford University Press, Ely House, London W.1

GLASGOW NEW YORK TORONTO MELBOURNE WELLINGTON
CAPE TOWN IBADAN NAIROBI DAR ES SALAAM LUSAKA ADDIS ABABA
DELHI BOMBAY CALCUTTA MADRAS KARACHI LAHORE DACCA
KUALA LUMPUR SINGAPORE HONG KONG TOKYO

ISBN 0 19 821858 3

© OXFORD UNIVERSITY PRESS 1975

*Printed in Great Britain
by Billing & Sons Limited,
Guildford and London.*

To
Stephen Pratt

PREFACE

This book is not a complete history of Ireland between 1649 and 1660, but a study of certain aspects of English government and policy in Ireland during the Interregnum. My original, tentative suggestions that English policy amounted to more than military reconquest, massacre, and the transplantation of the native Irish 'to hell or Connaught' were greeted by some with incredulity, if not derision. The incredulous may still be unconvinced. However I hope this book will henceforward prevent Cromwellian policy being so easily dismissed. I regret not being able to describe the reaction of lower-class Irish Protestants and Catholics to Cromwellian rule. Lack of evidence is responsible: the surviving material relates to exceptional individuals – the great landowners like Lord Cork or the Catholic priests.

When I first identified this subject, I was surprised that so obvious a gap in the generally well-researched Civil War period had not been filled. I quickly discovered the reason: the destruction of the official records of the period in the fire at the Four Courts, Dublin, in 1922. Originally there must have been at least one hundred and three volumes, of which fifty-five were extant in 1922. The private papers of those involved in Ireland in the 1650s have also suffered either accidental or deliberate destruction. Added to this dearth of public and private papers is the scarcity of contemporary printed material. Whereas historians of the Interregnum in England have the great Thomason collection in which to lose themselves, historians of Ireland have to search for printed books and proclamations in scattered and obscure collections, tracking down unique copies or indeed finding no copies of some recorded publications. To overcome these obstacles I have had to do even more detective work than is usually the lot of the historian. Fragmentary and incomplete as the evidence is, nevertheless there is enough to describe the main lines of policy. At some points I have been forced to conjecture: I have made clear what is speculation.

I am grateful to the trustees of the Bryce studentship for

electing me to the studentship for 1968—9, and also for earlier financial help to travel to Ireland. Similarly I must thank the University of Exeter and the central research fund of London University for grants towards the expenses of research. For permission to use documents in their possession I am indebted to His Grace the Duke of Devonshire, and the trustees of the Chatsworth settlement; Mr. T. Bush; Mrs. D. M. Hare; and the Representative Church Body of Ireland.

Seventeenth-century Ireland has called forth some valuable recent writing from which I have profited: notably that of Aidan Clarke, Hugh Kearney, Terence Ranger, Gerald Simms, and Professor J. C. Beckett. Even so, the period between 1641 and 1660 is still woefully neglected. My sense of isolation has been reduced by the appearance of two valuable studies on themes related to mine: Karl Bottigheimer's *English Money and Irish Land*; and K. T. Hoppen's *The Common Scientist in the Seventeenth Century*. My greatest debt is to two dead writers: to Archdeacon St. J. D. Seymour, whose *The Puritans in Ireland, 1647—1661* (a book strangely neglected by both English and Irish historians) is the only systematic study based on the records destroyed in 1922; and to Robert Dunlop, who collected some of the most important official documents and published them in *Ireland under the Commonwealth*.

While writing this book Anglo-Irish relations have deteriorated. In the main I have only friendship and co-operation to record in my attempts to reconstruct an earlier period of tension. In particular three members of Trinity College, Dublin, have given me expert guidance from the start. William O'Sullivan, as well as making research in the college manuscript room so pleasant and fruitful, has shared with me his wide knowledge of intellectual life in seventeenth-century Ireland. Miss Paul Pollard has put her unrivalled familiarity with seventeenth-century Irish printed material at my disposal, and helped me locate several rare works. Aidan and Mary Clarke have shown me much kindness and hospitality during my visits to Dublin. Among others who have answered questions or given help I must thank: Sir John Ainsworth, Bart., Brother W. P. Allen, Mrs. E. Berry, the Very Revd. F. R. Bolton, Professor D. V. Glass, Dr. K. T. Hoppen, Canon

H. W. Love, Dr. Margaret MacCurtain, the Rt. Revd. H. A.
McAdoo, Lord Bishop of Ossory, Ferns, and Leighlin,
Professor J. A. Murphy, Dr. G. F. Nuttall, Dr. G. D. Ramsay,
Professor Ivan Roots, Mr. Lindsay Sharp, the Most Revd.
G. O. Simms, Lord Archbishop of Armagh, Mr. Quentin
Skinner, the Ven. C. J. Stranks, Mrs. J. Varley, and Dr. D. M.
Woodward. Professor Seamus Pender kindly lent me his
transcripts of the then unpublished parts of the Waterford
corporation books. I have profited from conversations with
Robert Brenner, Patrick Kelly, Valerie Pearl, and Blair
Worden; and from the comments of my examiners, Dr.
Christopher Hill and Professor Hugh Kearney. Charles
Webster, as well as guiding me through the Hartlib collection
at Sheffield, commented on drafts of Chapters VII and VIII;
Professor J. G. Hand and Dr. Wilfrid Prest similarly
commented on Chapter IX.

Finally I thank those people without whom this book
would never have been written. Stephen Pratt first communicated an enthusiasm for history to me. In gratitude for that,
and for many later kindnesses, I dedicate this book to him.
Mrs. Menna Prestwich's teaching revived my interest in the
seventeenth century, and it was she who first made me aware
of the topic covered in this book. Hugh Trevor-Roper has
been a painstaking and vigilant supervisor, in turn critical and
encouraging. I owe much to his guidance and interest.

December 1973   T.C.B.

CONTENTS

Abbreviations   xiii

I. IRELAND IN 1649   1

II. THE GOVERNMENT IN DUBLIN   16

III. THE GOVERNMENT, FINANCE, AND TRADE   26
    i. The financing of Government   26
    ii. The regulation of trade   31
    iii. The character of Irish trade   34
    iv. The volume of Irish trade   42
    v. General effects of government policy   47

IV. THE GOVERNMENT AND THE BOROUGHS   50
    i. Introduction   50
    ii. Official policy   51
    iii. The government of the boroughs   62
    iv. The boroughs and commercial and social policy   71
    v. Dublin   77

V. THE PROPAGATION OF THE GOSPEL   90
    i. The situation in 1649   90
    ii. The Statutory Basis   94
    iii. Fleetwood and the rise of the Baptists   98
    iv. The decline of Baptism under Henry Cromwell   106
    v. The Quakers   109
    vi. Winter and the Independents   112
    vii. Edward Worth and the Cork Association of ministers   117
    viii. The Scottish Presbyterians and Ulster   122
    ix. The Dublin Convention of Ministers in 1658, and its
        effects   126
    x. The Aftermath   132

VI. ECCLESIASTICAL REFORM   135
    i. The Ministers of the Gospel   135
    ii. The approval and control of the clergy   144
    iii. Unauthorized Ministers   150
    iv. The Maintenance of the Ministry   153

    v. The Inquisitions of 1657 and the Church's re-
       organization   160
    vi. The fabric of the church   168
    vii. The conversion of the Irish   171

VII. EDUCATION   183
    i. Education before 1649   183
    ii. The Government and education, 1649—1660   186
    iii. Private efforts   190
    iv. Schools in Dublin   194
    v. Trinity College, Dublin   198
    vi. The second college at Dublin   206

VIII. THE ADVANCEMENT OF LEARNING   213
    i. The background   213
    ii. The Hartlib circle in Ireland   216
    iii. The Land Surveys   226
    iv. Hartlib's Irish Projects   229
    v. Private achievements   237
    vi. The Hartlib circle and the Dublin Philosophical Society   244

IX. THE ADMINISTRATION AND REFORM OF THE LAW   249
    i. The Irish legal system before 1649   249
    ii. The Campaign for law reform   254
    iii. The legal system, 1649—1655   256
    iv. John Cook and the Presidential Court of Munster   262
    v. The administration of the law   276
    vi. The Judges   281

X. CONCLUSION   293

    Bibliography   306

    Index   331

ABBREVIATIONS

The following abbreviations have been used in the text:

Abbott, *Cromwell*	W. C. Abbott, *The Writings and Speeches of Oliver Cromwell.*
Alumni Dublinenses	G. D. Burtchaell and T. U. Sadleir, *Alumni Dublinenses.*
Bodl.	Bodleian Library, Oxford.
Brit. Mus.	British Museum, London.
Cal. Anc. Recs. Dublin	*Calendar of the Ancient Records of Dublin*, ed. J. T. Gilbert and Lady Gilbert.
Cal. S.P. Dom.	*Calendar of State Papers, Domestic.*
Cal. S.P. Ire.	*Calendar of State Papers, Ireland.*
C.B.	Christian Brothers' School, Richmond Street North, Dublin.
C.J.	*Journal of the House of Commons.*
C.J. Ire.	*Journal of the House of Commons of the Kingdom of Ireland.*
Cotton, *Fasti*	H. Cotton, *Fasti Ecclesiae Hibernicae.*
D.N.B.	*Dictionary of National Biography.*
Dunlop	R. T. Dunlop, *Ireland under the Commonwealth.*
Econ. Hist. Rev.	*Economic History Review.*
Eng. Hist. Rev.	*English Historical Review.*
Firth and Davies	C. H. Firth and G. Davies, *A Regimental History of Cromwell's Army.*
Firth and Rait	C. H. Firth and R. S. Rait, *Acts and Ordinances of the Interregnum.*
Hist. MSS. Comm.	Historical Manuscripts Commission.
Irish MSS. Comm.	Irish Manuscripts Commission.
JCHAS	*Journal of the Cork Historical and Archaeological Society.*
JRSAI	*Journal of the Royal Society of Antiquaries of Ireland.*
L.J.	*Journal of the House of Lords.*
L.J. Ire.	*Journals of the House of Lords of the Kingdom of Ireland.*
Nat. Lib. Ire.	National Library of Ireland.
P. and P.	*Past and Present.*
P.R.O.	Public Record Office.
R.C.B.	Representative Church Body Library, Dublin.
R. Ir. Ac.	Royal Irish Academy, Dublin.
Seymour	St. J. D. Seymour, *The Puritans in Ireland, 1647–1661.*
Steele	R. Steele, *Tudor and Stuart Proclamations.*
T.C.D.	Trinity College, Dublin.

Thurloe State Papers	*A Collection of the State Papers of John Thurloe,* ed. T. Birch.
Trans. Royal Hist. Soc.	*Transactions of the Royal Historical Society.*
The Works of Robert Boyle	*The Works of the Honourable Robert Boyle,* ed. T. Birch.

I

IRELAND IN 1649

The combination of the Irish rebellion of 1641 and the English civil war created the problem that had to be dealt with in Ireland in 1649. Rebellion was nothing new in Irish history. Indeed until the beginning of the seventeenth century it had seemed endemic. After 1607, however, there were signs that Ireland was being brought into quiet subjection to English and Protestant authority. The defeat and flight in 1607 of the Northern earls opened the way to what proved the most extensive and successful new plantation — of Ulster. Meanwhile, since the 1580s, Protestant plantation had been progressing in Munster. After 1634 Strafford interested himself in the plantation of Connaught. The extent of these settlements by 1641 is not known: Munster was estimated to have 12,000 Protestant settlers by 1620, dispersed in small communities and isolated in a still predominantly Catholic population;[1] in Ulster there was a higher concentration of new Scottish Presbyterian planters, although they too were a minority;[2] in Connaught little had been achieved by 1641 except to create a feeling of insecurity among the native Irish.[3] In 1641 it was estimated that the new Protestant planters owned 20 per cent of Irish land.[4]

After 1607 English rule was extended in other ways: the country was shired; English justice was imposed throughout the island; determined efforts were made to plant English

[1] D. B. Quinn, 'The Munster plantation: problems and opportunities', *JCHAS* lxxi (1966), esp. pp. 30, 39. See also: R. Dunlop, 'The plantation of Munster', *Eng. Hist. Rev.* iii (1888), esp. pp. 266–7; T. O. Ranger, 'The career of Richard Boyle, first earl of Cork, in Ireland, 1588–1643', Oxford D.Phil. thesis, 1959.

[2] G. Hill, *An historical account of the plantation in Ulster* (Belfast, 1877), p. 589; J. C. Beckett, *The making of modern Ireland* (London, 1966), p. 47. See also: T. W. Moody, *The Londonderry plantation* (Belfast, 1937); J. G. Simms, 'Donegal in the Ulster plantation', *Irish Geography*, vi (1972).

[3] H. F. Kearney, *Strafford in Ireland* (Manchester, 1959), ch. 9.

[4] W. Petty, *The political anatomy of Ireland* (London, 1691), p. 2.

habits and 'civilization'. The peace between 1607 and 1641
and the belief that English authority had taken a firmer hold
made the rebellion of 1641 a shock to English and Irish
Protestants. This feeling was increased by ties of marriage and
social intercourse which had developed between Catholics
and Protestants, and led to the rebellion being represented as
a stab in the back.[5]

Why had the Catholics risen in 1641, bringing to an end
over thirty years of peace? As well as the signs of growing
harmony between the Irish Catholics and the English government, there were still strong forces working against any
assimilation of Ireland. The economic benefits of peace, and
particularly of Strafford's vice-royalty, had been felt by the
numerous Catholic merchants of the sea-ports and towns. In
these quarters a relatively sophisticated constitutional opposition arose, led by Catholic lawyers like Patrick Darcy.
Coalescing with the opposition of the Catholic landed gentry,
it produced in 1640 a campaign against Ireland's subordi-
nation to English interests, against its legal basis in the
operation of Poynings' law, and against the recent erosion of
the Catholics' political power in parliament.[6] Catholic resentment of English rule had been much exacerbated by the
heavy hand of Strafford, which threatened Catholic owner-
ship of land as well as political influence, so that by 1640 the
hitherto discrete elements in the Catholic community — the
Gaelic and the Old English, the descendants of earlier English
settlers — were united against Strafford.[7] It was not only the
specific threats of Strafford's policy that alarmed the
Catholics. Other influences, especially of religion and culture,
stressed the differences between English and Irish. Ireland's

5'A discourse between two councillors of state ...', ed. A. Clarke, *Analecta Hibernica*, xxvi (1970), 162; A. Clarke, 'Ireland and the General Crisis', *P. and P.* xlviii (1970), 86, 90; T. May, *The history of the Parliament of England which began November 3, 1640* (Oxford, 1845), p. 121; J. A. Murphy, 'The politics of the Munster Protestants, 1641–49', *JCHAS* lxxvi (1971), 9.

6Of 256 M.P.s in 1634, 112 were Catholic; of 240 in 1640, 74 were Catholic: A. Clarke, *The Old English in Ireland* (London, 1966), p. 255; Clarke, 'The policies of the Old English in parliament, 1640–1', in *Historical Studies: V*, ed. J. L. McCracken (London, 1965).

7Clarke, *P. and P.* xlviii. 79–99.

continental connections, through trade,[8] and the education of the laity and clergy, were strengthened. The impact of the Counter-Reformation was felt in Ireland in the early seventeenth century and increased Catholicism's hold, especially in the towns.[9] The use of the Irish language in evangelization and in printed devotional books further set the native population apart. Nevertheless the Irish Catholics were not united. The basic tension between Old English and Gaelic remained and showed itself in disagreements over policy, particularly over whether or not to compromise with the English administration.[10] Important though these differences were, Strafford, by ignoring them and treating the Irish Catholics as a homogenous group of doubtful loyalty, helped to create such a group: in 1641 they were temporarily united in opposition to him, if in little else.

Strafford's efforts to increase the state's power in Ireland ignored the local interests of both Catholics and Protestants, leaving him without any substantial body of supporters in 1640.[11] Resentment among Irish Protestants fused with hostility in the English parliament and thus contributed to his downfall. It was Strafford's removal from Ireland, briefly lightening the weight of English rule there, which emboldened Irish Catholics to act to recover their lost influence. In the atmosphere of 1641, overwhelmingly hostile to Strafford, the Catholics' action was intended to be essentially loyalist (like the Long Parliament's in England), freeing the king from the evil councillors and advice which had been

8'The Irish wine trade, 1614–15', ed. H. Kearney, *Irish Historical Studies,* ix (1955).

9J. Brady, 'The Irish Colleges in Europe and the Counter-Reformation', *Proceedings of the Irish Catholic Historical Committee* (1957); P. J. Corish, 'The reorganization of the Irish Church, 1603–41', ibid. (1957); H. Hammerstein, 'Aspects of the continental education of Irish students in the reign of Queen Elizabeth I', in *Historical Studies: VIII,* ed. T. D. Williams (Dublin, 1971); cf. *The Journal of Sir Simonds D'Ewes from the beginning of the Long Parliament to the opening of the trial of the earl of Strafford,* ed. W. Notestein (New Haven, Conn., 1923), pp. 442–3.

10H. F. Kearney, 'Ecclesiastical politics and the Counter-Reformation in Ireland, 1618–1648, *Journal of Ecclesiastical History,* xi (1960).

11T. Ranger, 'Strafford in Ireland: a revaluation', in *Crisis in Europe, 1560–1660,* ed. T. Aston (London, 1965), p. 276; Kearney, *Strafford in Ireland,* pp. 219–20.

imposed on him in Ireland. The rising in Ulster in October 1641 (the area in which the Gaelic population had suffered the greatest dispossession) continued in a new and extreme form the battle that had already been fought in the Dublin parliament.

Two things distinguished the rising of 1641 from earlier Irish rebellions. First, there was its greater political sophistication: shown in the debates of 1640—1 and then continued in the General Assembly of the Confederate Catholics which met at Kilkenny in October 1642 as a representative body for Catholic Ireland.[12] The Catholics insisted on their loyalty to the English crown: their objectives were to remove the recent innovations which had curtailed Ireland's legislative independence and which penalized members of the Catholic church. Furthermore the rebels in Ulster claimed the king's authority for their action, producing a commission under the great seal of Scotland to support their case.[13]

The second difference was that, unlike previous rebellions, the 1641 rising coincided with, and indeed greatly influenced, a protracted political crisis in England. This distracted English attention and resources from the Irish problem, and explained why it was so long before English authority was restored in Ireland. Irish events — the campaign against Strafford and the possible implications of his Irish policies for England, and the rebellion — entered into the Long Parliament's struggle with Charles I. The need to subdue Ireland raised in acute form the mistrust of the king, and the dangers of allowing him control of an army. The Irish rebellion severely damaged the king in England. The rebels' claim to be acting with royal authority seemed plausible to many; news of the rebellion, filtering through in garbled and highly exaggerated accounts, confirmed the widespread fears of a great Catholic design to subvert Protestantism; the king's apparent willingness to use Irish Catholics against the English Parliament suggested that he had been a party to their revolt

[12] P. Darcy, *An argument delivered ... in the parliament of Ireland, 9 Junii 1641* (Dublin, 1764); J. C. Beckett, 'The Confederation of Kilkenny Reviewed', in *Historical Studies: II*, ed. M. Roberts (London, 1959), pp. 33—4.

[13] R. Dunlop, 'The forged commission of 1641', *Eng. Hist. Rev.* ii (1887); Clarke, *The Old English in Ireland*, pp. 165—8.

and that he was prepared to unleash similar horrors on England. The parliamentary leaders, notably Pym, were able to use the Irish situation to confirm and extend their hold over parliament and to press on with their campaign of reform.[14]

The Irish rebellion contributed to the complete breakdown of trust between king and parliament which led to the outbreak of war in 1642; the breach in England in turn caused a deterioration of the position in Ireland. The rebellion had at first involved only the Gaelic Irish in Ulster. Meeting no effective check, the rebellion was joined in 1642 by the Old English of the Pale, and also spread to Connaught and Munster. Furthermore it received the blessing of the Catholic hierarchy. In October 1642 a Catholic rival to the government and parliament in Dublin was set up in Kilkenny. Protestant rule shrank to Dublin, where authority was exercised by lord justices, Ormonde as lord lieutenant (after 1643), and a wholly Protestant parliament; to beleagured garrisons in Ulster, whither a Scottish army was sent in 1642; and to Munster, where a few Protestant strongholds held out.

The Irish struggle was prolonged by the preoccupations of the parties in England and by the disunity of Irish Catholics and Protestants. Among the Confederate Catholics the tensions between Gaelic and Old English quickly reappeared, manifested in a military command unsatisfactorily divided between the Gaelic O'Neill and the Old English Preston, and in divisions over policy. As before 1641 the main contention was whether or not to compromise with the king, securing the best terms rather than persist in the war. Until 1646 it was the more conciliatory attitude, generally favoured by the Old English laity, which prevailed, leading to a cessation of fighting in September 1643 and the 'Ormonde Peace' of March 1646. But then in 1646 the uncompromising clerical

---

[14] *The journal of Sir Simonds D'Ewes*, ed. Notestein, pp. 10–11; R. Clifton, 'The popular fear of Catholics during the English Revolution', *P. and P.* lii (1971); K. Lindley, 'The impact of the 1641 rebellion upon England and Wales, 1641–5', *Irish Historical Studies*, xviii (1972).

party led by the papal nuncio, Rinuccini, gained the upper hand and repudiated the peace.[15]

The Protestant interest was also divided as to how best to preserve its cause. Enthusiastic supporters of the Long Parliament were few in Ireland in 1642, notwithstanding the widespread dislike of Strafford. Most important in linking the Irish discontent with the campaign in the English parliament was John Clotworthy, an Ulster planter who had apparently left the province because of the persecution of the Presbyterians there.[16] Others active in parliament included William Jephson, a planter from Munster: Hardress Waller, recently settled in Limerick, was another important link, who soon became active in the parliamentary army in England and would later be a regicide.[17] But few of the lord justices or members of parliament in Dublin were prepared to side with the English parliament; those who did and who opposed the cessation in 1643 were removed, leaving royalists firmly in control of Dublin. However the Irish Protestants' dilemma was beginning to appear: how to reconcile loyalty to Charles I with the king's apparent willingness to negotiate with the Confederate Catholics, offering them toleration for their religion in return for an army of 10,000 men. If opposition to peace in 1643 had been muted, by 1645 it was much greater. In that year Glamorgan proposed a treaty between Charles and the Catholics, the revelation of which deepened Protestant mistrust of the king.[18] In 1646 Ormonde made peace with the Confederate Catholics on terms similar to those proposed in 1645. A further reason for the ebbing of Protestant royalism was the deterioration of the king's position in England. The victorious parliament offered the

15 On the Confederation: Beckett in *Historical Studies: II*, ed. Roberts; D. F. Cregan, 'The Confederation of Kilkenny: its organization, personnel and history', National University of Ireland Ph.D. thesis, 1947.

16 'Winthrop letters', *Massachusetts Historical Soc. Collections*, 5th series, i (1871), 208; P. Adair, *A true narrative*, ed. W. D. Killen (Belfast, 1866), pp. 218–19; J. H. Hexter, *The reign of King Pym* (Cambridge, Mass., 1941), pp. 43–7; Clarke, *P. and P.* xlviii. 96.

17 M. D. Jephson, *An Anglo-Irish Miscellany* (Dublin, 1964), ch. 2; M. F. Keeler, *The Long Parliament* (Philadelphia, Pa., 1954), p. 234; D. Underdown, *Pride's Purge* (Oxford, 1971), p. 377; Clarke, *P. and P.* xlviii. 96.

18 S. R. Gardiner, 'Charles I and the earl of Glamorgan', *Eng. Hist. Rev.* ii (1887).

best hope of decisive action against the Catholics: increasingly the Irish Protestants turned to it. The most spectacular example of this changing attitude, seeing parliament rather than the king as the best defence against the Catholics, was Ormonde's action in June 1647 in surrendering the city of Dublin to the parliamentary forces rather than let it fall to the Confederate Catholics.

The Protestants in other parts of Ireland had been quicker to desert the king. The Scottish army, which had landed in Ulster under Monro in April 1642, was sent by the Scottish Parliament, bound by the Solemn League and Covenant (which the Dublin parliament condemned in 1644),[19] and spread Presbyterianism wherever it could.[20] So long as the Long Parliament was also formally committed to the Solemn League and Covenant, co-operation was possible. But as the army and the sects began to dictate policy in England, the harmony disappeared and the Scots found themselves pursuing a different policy which was bound to have repercussions in Ulster.[21]

In Munster impatience with the king's conciliatory attitude grew and reached a climax in 1644 when, after Charles's tactless refusal to make Lord Inchiquin lord president of Munster, Inchiquin repudiated the cessation of 1643, turned to the Long Parliament, and resumed the fight against the Catholics. Although this realignment helped Munster to secure such supplies as the Long Parliament provided, that help was too meagre to be decisive. What was worse, the Long Parliament was disunited on policy towards Ireland as on much else. These disagreements prevented action for Ireland. Inchiquin found himself little better treated by the English parliament than he had been by the king, with a lord lieutenant (Lord Lisle) put in over his head in 1646 and his subordinates in Munster, like Broghill and Hardress Waller, apparently more influential with parliament than he was. In

---

19 *C. J. Ire.* i, appendix, pp. 131, 134.

20 H. Hazlett, 'The recruitment and organization of the Scottish army in Ulster', in *Essays in British and Irish history in honour of James Eadie Todd,* ed. H. A. Cronne, T. W. Moody, and D. B. Quinn (London, 1941).

21 On changing Scottish attitudes: D. Underdown, *Pride's Purge*, pp. 65–9.

April 1648 Inchiquin deserted parliament, splitting the Protestant interest in Munster.[22]

The war was prolonged by divisions in England. The king's camp at Oxford contained men willing to compromise with the Confederate Catholics and others who recognized the damage that this would do to the royalist cause in England. Charles, typically, wavered between the two courses.[23] Even more serious for the settlement of Ireland were the cracks which appeared among the parliamentarians. First there were differences between the war and peace parties, then between Presbyterians and Independents in parliament, and between the parliament itself and the more radical army. The appointment of an Irish lord lieutenant, the dispatch of an adequate army to Ireland, and the choice of commanders became issues of contention between the English groups. Although troops were sent in 1643 and again in 1647, under Lord Lisle, they were too few to bring the war to a successful conclusion. It was only when Oliver Cromwell, the army, and their supporters in parliament had gained political control in England that there was vigorous action in Ireland. This did not happen until 1649, when the Long Parliament was purged and the king had been executed.[24] Those political changes, while clearing the way for Ireland's reconquest, lost the new regime some of parliament's previous supporters. Notable among these was Clotworthy, one of the eleven members whom the army wanted impeached in 1647 and who was among the members purged in 1648. Other Irish Protestants secluded included Jephson and Arthur Annesley.[25] In Munster Lord Broghill seriously considered

[22] K. S. Bottigheimer, 'Civil war in Ireland: the reality in Munster', *Emory University Quarterly* (1966); id., *English money and Irish land* (Oxford, 1971), pp. 96–114; J. A. Murphy, 'Inchiquin's change of religion', *JCHAS* lxxii (1967); id., 'The politics of the Munster Protestants', *JCHAS* lxxvi (1971).

[23] J. Lowe, 'Charles I and the Confederation of Kilkenny, 1643–49', *Irish Historical Studies* xiv (1964–5).

[24] For events in England: Underdown, *Pride's Purge*.

[25] Ibid., pp. 69, 81, 168, n., 195, 240–1, 247, 346–7, 366, 370, 377; Adair, *A true narrative*, p. 219; *A full vindication and answer of the XI accused members* (London, 1647), pp. 20–3.

retirement to the continent after the king's execution.[26] In Ulster the Scottish Presbyterians denounced the new English regime, which had repudiated the Solemn League and Covenant and murdered the king.

Between 1646 and 1649 the Irish situation had worsened. The victory of O'Neill over the Ulster forces at Benburb in 1646 and his alliance with the belligerent clerical party of Rinuccini seemed the prelude to a successful assault on Dublin. Divisions delayed the attempt. Fear of it led Ormonde to surrender Dublin to the English parliament in 1647 and to leave Ireland. However the royalist position improved with the defection of Inchiquin and the revulsion among moderates at the king's execution. Ormonde returned to Ireland in September 1648 and attempted to weld together an alliance with Inchiquin and the Confederate Catholics. By January 1649 he had made a treaty with the Confederate Catholics, but it was weakened by the refusal of O'Neill to join. This new royalist offensive was repulsed at the battle of Rathmines on 2 August 1649, which prevented Dublin being recaptured by Ormonde. Later the same month Oliver Cromwell arrived with a large and relatively well-equipped army. Although in October 1649 Ormonde was now able to ally with O'Neill, it was too late. By August 1650 Charles II, having taken the Solemn League and Covenant, repudiated Ormonde's alliance with the Confederate Catholics. Finding his position hopeless, Ormonde left Ireland in December 1650.

The problem of Ireland in 1649 was more complicated than it had been in 1641. In the interval there had been a political revolution in England, and this meant that the English authority which had to be reimposed in Ireland was no longer that of the king but of a new regime, the English Commonwealth established without king or house of lords. In England that regime was unpopular; in Ireland it had virtually no support.

---

[26] R. E. W. Maddison, *The life of the honourable Robert Boyle, F.R.S.* (London, 1969), p. 74; *A collection of the state letters of . . . the first earl of Orrery* (London, 1742), pp. 10–11; *State Papers collected by Edward Hyde, earl of Clarendon* (Oxford, 1767–86), ii. 500; S. R. Gardiner, *History of the Commonwealth and Protectorate* (London, 1903), i. 95, n. 1.

Cromwell's immediate task in 1649 was to reconquer the country. His success in doing that helped overcome some of the opposition among the Irish Protestants. The preservation of the Protestant interest was their prime concern and therefore they gave grudging support to the authority that could do it. The purely military task required vigilance lest the Catholics secure foreign aid and foment a new design; it also required watchfulness of the Irish Protestants who still supported the king and of the Presbyterians in Ulster who had denounced the new regime.

Ireland had also to be made secure against any future rebellion. The manner of resettlement had been decided in 1642 by the Long Parliament and was entirely traditional. The land of the Catholic rebels was to be confiscated. A new plantation of those who had adventured money for Ireland's reconquest would be established. Two and a half million acres were reserved for the adventurers, who originally numbered 1,533. Unlike earlier plantations, this would be spread over Ireland's four provinces.[27] The establishment of this new plantation was an urgent task once the country was subdued. It involved identifying and removing the rebels, measuring and then allocating the lands. These were complex administrative tasks. The new settlement was, however, complicated by the introduction of two new principles after 1649. First it was decided to satisfy the large army of English soldiers in Ireland (between 33,000 and 35,000 men) by grants of Irish land. Immediately the character of the plantation was changed: the civilian settlers (few of whom were in Ireland) were overwhelmed by soldiers (most of whom were already serving in Ireland).[28] The second innovation was the decision to uproot almost the whole Catholic population by adjudging the landless Catholics guilty of rebellion and decreeing their transplantation to the inhospitable province of Connaught.[29] The motive behind this was ideological — to punish the Irish for their part in the massacre

[27] Bottigheimer, *English money and Irish land.*

[28] K. S. Bottigheimer, 'English money and Irish land', *Journal of British Studies,* vii (1967), 13.

[29] S. R. Gardiner, 'The transplantation to Connaught', *Eng. Hist. Rev.* xiv (1899), 700–34; R. C. Simington, ed., *The Transplantation to Connacht, 1654–58,* Irish MSS. Comm. (Dublin, 1971).

of 1641.[30] Unlike the original legislation of 1642 affecting Catholic landowners, this policy was formulated without regard to the economic needs of Ireland and ran counter to the interests of the Irish Protestant proprietors. Promiscuous transplantation could succeed only if there was a massive and immediate influx of Protestant tenants and labourers to replace the Catholics: such an influx did not occur. The transplantation to Connaught proved impossible to implement. The other two parts of the settlement were accomplished. Catholic-owned land was confiscated and given to Protestant adventurers and soldiers. Indeed this was the most dramatic change in Ireland during the Interregnum, which was not undone in 1660. The Catholic share of land fell from 59 per cent in 1641 to 20 per cent in 1660, of which the bulk was in Connaught.[31]

The substitution of Protestant and English landowners for Catholics was the main way in which Ireland was to be secured after 1641. However that policy is not the subject of this book. This is a study of the other methods adopted to re-establish and secure English authority; and also of the methods used to make first the English Commonwealth and then the Cromwellian Protectorate acceptable in Ireland. One was the age-old problem of English rule in Ireland; the other a new difficulty created by the English revolution.

Radicals had been brought to power in England and some of them, deeply committed to far-reaching reforms, came with the army to Ireland.[32] Before 1649 occasional voices had been raised in parliament urging generous treatment of the Irish Catholics (Henry Marten's), and in the sects (Walwyn's voice).[33] Even though Oliver Cromwell himself held out a promise of leniency to the Irish in 1650, such

30 T. C. Barnard, 'Planters and policies in Cromwellian Ireland', *P. and P.* lxi (1973).

31 J. G. Simms, *The Williamite confiscation in Ireland, 1690—1703* (London, 1956), pp. 195—6.

32 *The humble petition of the officers now engaged for Ireland* (London, 1649).

33 [William Kiffin], *Walwins wiles* (London, 1649), sig. A3, p. 21; C. M. Williams, 'Extremist tactics in the Long Parliament, 1642—3' *Historical Studies*, Univ. of Melbourne, xv (1971), 139, n. 17; C. Hill, *The World turned upside down* (London, 1972), pp. 271—2; M.S., *A discourse concerning the rebellion in Ireland* (London, 1642), p. 17; *A discourse concerning the affaires of Ireland* (London, 1650), pp. 2—7.

generosity found no place in the official policies decided in
England between 1649 and 1660.[34] The prevalent view in
the English parliament and army was that the Irish Catholics
were not to be trusted and were indeed racially inferior.[35]
The massacre of 1641 had in part been the result of the
tolerance allowed them by Strafford. The experience of 1641
had revealed the shallow basis of English authority in Ireland,
but it did not discredit the policies followed in the past (with
the exception of Strafford's supposed tolerance). Faith was
still placed in traditional methods, not only new Protestant
settlements, but also Protestant evangelization and education,
the introduction of English customs, language, and dress, the
establishment of English industries, and the thorough imposition of English law. In the past these methods had not
succeeded because they were not pursued with sufficient
vigour: after 1649 that would be remedied. Consequently
there were surprisingly few innovations in English policy
between 1649 and 1660.

Ireland's rulers in the Interregnum also shared with their
predecessors an ambiguous approach to Irish problems.
Native customs and institutions had to be extirpated. Yet
should this be achieved by compulsion or persuasion? Until
1655 the emphasis was on punitive policies which aimed less
at converting the Irish than at bludgeoning them into submission and leaving them too weak to rise again. There were,
however, those who believed that the Irish might be won over
by gentler means, such as preaching to them in Irish and
allowing their different traditions a degree of toleration. In
the past both attitudes had been present in dealings with
Ireland. In the Interregnum policy veered between the two
extremes: on the one hand, corralling the Catholic Irish in
Connaught, where no special efforts were made to enlighten
them; on the other, allowing Catholics to remain outside
Connaught and even in the walled towns, sending preachers
in Irish to them. In general the Draconian policies belonged
to the years of war and their aftermath, when authority
rested with Englishmen unfamiliar with Ireland and schooled

---

34 Abbott, *Cromwell* ii. 196—205.
35 Brit. Mus., Lansdowne, MS. 1228, f. 8; *Thurloe State Papers* ii. 343; iii. 468;
The Speeches and prayers of Major General Harrison (London, 1660), p. 83.

in the legend of the 1641 massacre. After 1655 peace and greater security allowed a relaxation; also there was a change of government in 1655, with Henry Cromwell's arrival, which brought civilians and Irish Protestants to the fore and saw some moderation of earlier severity.

The Cromwellians accepted that to secure Ireland Irish society had to be changed. This was not a new idea. However there was disagreement about the form of these changes. First, there were differences over the treatment of the Irish Catholics; secondly, reforms of English society were in the air which must affect the programme for Ireland. In England there was a ferment of ideas: changes in the church, the law, in corporations and guilds, of education, and of manners were advocated. The cautious suggestions of the members of the Long Parliament in 1641 had been overtaken by more radical proposals by the members of the army and the sects. When the radicals gained power in 1649 it seemed that thorough-going reform must follow: being also the rulers of Ireland that country would be affected too. New divisions between the Rump of the Long Parliament and the victorious Cromwellian army retarded reform and led to fresh political upheavals: the ejection of the Rump in April 1653 and then, after the alarming radicalism of the Barebone's Parliament, the institution of the Protectorate which ushered in Cromwell's restless search for constitutional stability and respectability. Reform, although not forgotten, progressed slowly: Cromwell's apparent retreat from his former radical-ism disgusted old allies and colleagues in arms and so produced new controversies.

The failure to decide what form new church government should take or how the law could be improved delayed settlement in Ireland. Improvisations devised in the immedi-ate aftermath of war acquired a permanence that had not originally been intended. When at length Henry Cromwell replaced the improvisations he was accused of dismantling valuable reforms for which men had fought and died in the civil war. Slow progress in England also increased the import-ance of Ireland for reformers. Summary methods and inno-vations could more easily be tried there, because existing educational, ecclesiastical, and legal institutions had decayed so much during the war. Moreover the circumstances of 1649, with few interests to conciliate, made it much easier to introduce new or simplified machinery. Above all, much of the work of abolition, from which moderates in England shrank, had been accomplished by the war. For these reasons changes in Ireland were regarded as models for action in England.

After 1655 the emphasis changed. Henry Cromwell was primarily interested in securing his father's protectorate before embarking on any more ambitious reforms. This led him to an appraisal of the parties within Ireland, greater efforts to balance them by adopting policies relevant to Irish conditions rather than policies decided on ideological grounds in England, and above all to a cultivation of the Protestant and Presbyterian settlers who had been in Ireland before 1649. This involved loosening ties with the English army radicals and Independents, and adopting policies which they disliked. It did not mean turning his back on reform, although his more ambitious projects had not come to fruition when he was removed in 1659.

The Cromwellians intended to reinvigorate traditional policies with their new spirit, a confident spirit born of victory. The messianism and the feeling of being at the dawn of a new age — of the rule of the Saints or of the Fifth Monarchy — were apparent in attitudes to Ireland. Colonel John Jones, a parliamentary commissioner in Dublin from 1650 to 1654, believed that they had been led by God 'into a strange land and to act in as strange a work, a work that neither we nor our forefathers knew or heard of: the framing or forming of a commonwealth out of a corrupt rude mass . . . ' Similarly Thomas Harrison, chaplain to Henry Cromwell in Dublin from 1655 to 1659, thought that Ireland was 'clay upon the wheele, ready to receive what forme authority shall please to give it'. The chief justice of Munster, John Cook, likened Ireland to 'a white paper'.[36] As time passed some of this heady exhilaration evaporated: Ireland was not *tabula rasa.* There were old institutions; there was a native population, both Protestant and Catholic, whose support was necessary

---

[36] Nat. Lib. Wales, MS. 11440–D, 75; *Thurloe State Papers*, iii. 715; Bodl., Rawlinson MS. A.189, f. 397; Hist. MSS. Comm., *Egmont MSS.* i. 514.

to any regime's permanence. Henry Cromwell took more notice of this existing framework and allowed it to shape his policies.

This book is concerned with the efforts to secure and Anglicize Ireland. The efforts towards new plantation and towards the creation of a chain of Protestant-occupied towns will be considered first, to see how far the existing Catholic population was replaced by Protestants and the effects that this had on the country's security, trade, and prosperity. Attempts to foster trade and industry will also be considered, since they were necessary to any permanent English regime in Ireland. Next, I shall deal with the propagation of the Protestant gospel, a subject central to Cromwellian schemes of settling the country. From religion I shall move to the connected topic of education, in the schools and university, and also to the measures for advancing learning by the introduction and patronage of the new, experimental science. Finally, efforts to alter Irish society by the improvement or reform of the law will be investigated. All these policies had been tried before 1641 and were resumed after Charles II's restoration. Therefore it is necessary to see how far the Cromwellians followed conventional methods and where they broke new ground. The course of reform and policy in Ireland must also be related to contemporary changes in England and Scotland, since the interaction was great. Ireland could be a testing-ground for reforms which might later be applied in England. Also certain reforms attempted in Ireland originated in English conditions and were inappropriate to Irish needs. One theme of this book is the growth in influence of those with direct knowledge of Irish conditions, and the gradual modification of the radical programme of 1649. This book's purpose is twofold: to investigate an important aspect of the policy of the English Commonwealth and Protectorate, throwing light on their methods of government and on the fate of their ambitious plans of reform. The second purpose is to study the perennial problem of English government of Ireland, in this case during a period of flux.

II

THE GOVERNMENT IN DUBLIN

Authority for Ireland's government rested with England after 1649: first with the Rump of the Long Parliament; and then, between 1653 and 1659, with the protector, his councils of state, and the intermittent parliaments. Ultimate decisions about the future settlement of Ireland, the confiscation and redistribution of land, and the policies to be adopted by the governors in Dublin, rested with the Westminster government. Often there was a gulf between decisions taken in England and inspired mainly by English needs and those recommended by the Dublin administration, especially when, under Henry Cromwell, it became increasingly sensitive to Irish Protestant interests. Amongst policies that Henry Cromwell questioned were the imposition of an oath of abjuration on Irish Catholics, the war with Spain (which, like Strafford before him, Henry Cromwell knew would harm Irish trade), and the acquisition of Dunkirk.[1] Although controlled by instructions from England, it was possible to interpret these orders in widely different ways, as Fleetwood and Henry Cromwell showed. In some respects a more serious disadvantage was the extreme dilatoriness with which Irish affairs were treated in England, owing to the protector's indecision and the preoccupation of the council of state and parliaments with English matters. Requests from Dublin for firm action were frequently ignored and bills affecting Ireland were never enacted. The most spectacular example was the failure to pass an act of union.

Changes in the governors at Dublin reflected the shifts of power in England, first from the Rump to the army and Oliver Cromwell, then to Cromwell as protector, and finally in 1659 back in turn to the Rump, the army, and the survivors of the Long Parliament. Since the changes in

---

[1] *Thurloe State Papers*, vii. 217–18.

government in Ireland resulting from the English events greatly influenced Irish policy, they must be catalogued.

In July 1649 the Rump had commissioned Oliver Cromwell as lord lieutenant and commander in chief in Ireland. The following spring Cromwell, having broken Irish resistance, left for Scotland, delegating responsibility to his son-in-law, Henry Ireton.[2] As Ireland was gradually brought under English authority, the want of civil as well as military government was felt. A first step towards meeting the need had been Ireton's appointment as lord president of Munster late in 1649.[3] In June 1650 the English parliament referred consideration of Ireland's future civil government to the council of state. The council of state nominated Edmund Ludlow and John Jones as parliamentary commissioners in Ireland, and parliament appointed them. In October 1650 two more parliamentary commissioners were named: John Weaver and Richard Salwey. Salwey, however, was excused and in November replaced by Miles Corbet.[4] All four — Ludlow, Jones, Weaver, and Corbet — were members of parliament; Ludlow and Jones were also army officers, although only Ludlow served in Ireland, as lieutenant general.[5]

Ireton's death in November 1651 necessitated changes. In January 1652, the council of state, to which the matter had again been referred, recommended John Lambert as the new deputy and acting commander in chief. Since Cromwell's original commission as lord lieutenant, under which the deputy acted, was due to expire in July 1652, Lambert's appointment (at least initially) was for six months.[6]

Consideration of whether or not to renew Cromwell's commission brought into play the growing differences between the Rump and the army. Jealous of Cromwell's and the army's power and prestige, parliament objected to the

---

[2] *C.J.* vi. 435.

[3] *Cal. S.P. Dom. 1649–50* pp. 476, 502; *C.J.* vi. 343.

[4] *C.J.* vi. 432, 435, 480, 499. Their annual salary was £1,000 each: ibid, vi. 486.

[5] *The Memoirs of Edmund Ludlow*, ed. C. H. Firth (Oxford, 1894), i. 248–9. Jones, Ludlow, and Weaver were recruiters. There are lives of all four in *D.N.B.* See also: A. H. Dodd, *Studies in Stuart Wales* (Cardiff, 1952), pp. 131, 191; M. F. Keeler, *The Long Parliament, 1640–1641* (Philadelphia, Pa., 1954), p. 142; *The Memoirs of Edmund Ludlow*, i. 133.

[6] *C.J.* vii. 68, 77, 79.

retention of the office of lord lieutenant, arguing that the title was 'more sutable to a monarchy than a free common-wealth'. On 19 May 1652 the Rump abolished the title, but continued Cromwell in his military command over Ireland. Lambert's post as lord deputy disappeared with the lord lieutenancy. Cromwell as commander was empowered to name an acting commander, and the parliament offered to add his nominee to the parliamentary commissioners for Ireland's civil government. Lambert, however, would not accept this lower position and refused to serve.[7] In this way the Rump emphasized its control over Ireland's government; it did so again by defeating a move by the council of state to remove Weaver, the foremost champion of civil government against the military, from the commission.[8] As acting commander Cromwell and the council of state chose another of Cromwell's sons-in-law, Charles Fleetwood, and he was added to the civil commission. Otherwise the new commission of 24 August 1652 retained the four original parliamentary commissioners. It was to last three years.[9]

Before its expiration there had been changes of government in England which had had repercussions in Dublin. Weaver had been forced out owing to his unpopularity with the army in Ireland early in 1653. Ludlow resigned in 1654 to show his disapproval of the newly instituted protectorate.[10] Not only had the commission been weakened in numbers, reduced from five to three, its surviving members showed no vigour in dealing with mounting political disaffection. Furthermore the parliament from which the commissioners' authority derived had been swept away.

New appointments were made on 27 August 1654, and reflected the wishes of Oliver Cromwell and his council of state. Cromwell revived the title of lord deputy shunned by the Rump and conferred it on Fleetwood. He was to be

---

[7]Lambert never crossed to Ireland. Cf. Lucy Hutchinson, *The Memoirs of Colonel John Hutchinson*, ed. C. H. Firth (London, 1906), p. 188.

[8]*C.J.* vii. 164, 167; Hist. MSS. Comm., *Portland MSS.* i. 644–5, 671–2; *The Memoirs of Edmund Ludlow*, ed. Firth, i. 319.

[9]Ibid. i. 319–20, n. 1; *C.J.* vii. 143, 153, 167; *Fourteenth Report of the Deputy Keeper of Public Records in Ireland* (Dublin, 1882), appendix II, p. 28.

[10]*C.J.* vii. 260, 261; *The Memoirs of Edmund Ludlow*, ed. Firth, i. 373–7; *Thurloe State Papers*, ii. 163.

assisted by a council, to whom six men were appointed.[11] Of
these only one was a survivor from the Rump's commission,
Corbet, and there had been thoughts of laying him aside.[12]
The newcomers were Robert Goodwin, Robert Hammond,
Richard Pepys, William Steele, and Matthew Thomlinson.
Steele and Pepys were included because of their legal qualifications. Neither had sat in the Long Parliament, but Steele
had been active in the parliamentary cause in London and
Pepys in Suffolk.[13] They were typical of those whose
devotion to the parliament in the 1640s brought rewards in
the Interregnum. Goodwin had been an active member of the
Long Parliament and had some experience of Irish business.[14] Thomlinson had risen in the parliamentary army to
the rank of colonel; in 1653 he was appointed to the council
of state.[15] Hammond had also risen rapidly in the army, but
had retired from public life after the events of 1647 and
1648. He died soon after his arrival in Dublin in 1654.[16]
Thus only two of these Cromwellian nominees had been
prominent in the Long Parliament: Corbet and Goodwin.

This new council was less of an improvement than expected. Hammond died, Steele delayed going to Ireland until

[11] The original commission is Brit. Mus., Additional MS. 5014, and is calendared
in Dunlop, ii. 437–43. An earlier version with significant variations is in *Thurloe
State Papers*, ii. 506–8.

[12] Ibid. iii. 145.

[13] Alan Everitt, ed., *Suffolk and the Great Rebellion, 1640–1660*, Suffolk
Record Soc. iii (Ipswich, 1961), 27, 59, 74, 75, 76; Firth and Rait, i. 168, 235,
293, 537, 624, 639, 975, 1093; ii. 43, 309, 478, 675; Shaw, *A history of the
English Church* (London, 1900), ii. 428. Pepys was elected to the Short
Parliament for Sudbury.

[14] Bodl., Rawlinson MS. B.507. ff. 77ᵛ–80; Firth and Rait, i. 32–3; Hist. MSS.
Comm., *Egmont MSS.* i. 271, 299; *Irelands ingratitude to the Parliament of
England* (London, 1643[4]), p. 10; Keeler, *The Long Parliament* p. 191; J. K.
Gruenfelder, 'The elections to the Short Parliament, 1640', in *Early Stuart
Studies*, ed. H. S. Reinmuth (Minneapolis, Minn., 1970), p. 202; MacCormack,
Irish Historical Studies, ix. 49; Bottigheimer, *English money and Irish land*,
pp. 91, 182, 203.

[15] M. Cotterell, 'Interregnum law reform: The Hale Commission of 1652', *Eng.
Hist. Rev.* lxxxiii (1968), 691–2; Firth and Davies, i. 131; Firth and Rait, ii. 702;
The mystery of the good old cause briefly unfolded (London, 1660), p. 26; A. H.
Woolrych, 'The calling of Barebone's Parliament', *Eng. Hist. Rev.* lxxx (1965),
511. Thomlinson's wife, a daughter of Sir William Brooke, was an heiress to the
Cobham estates. Bodl., Rawlinson MS. A.45, f. 192; *Diary of Thomas Burton
Esq.*, ed. J. T. Rutt (London, 1828), i. 184 ff.; *Thurloe State Papers*, ii. 633.

[16] *D.N.B.; Thurloe State Papers*, ii. 633.

1656, and the weak Fleetwood remained in charge. Moreover Pepys, Corbet, and later Steele were distracted by their work as judges. The council was reinforced by Steele's arrival late in 1656, and also by the appointment of William Bury in August 1656. Bury, prominent in the parliamentary cause in Lincolnshire, where he had been treasurer of the County Committee and member of parliament for Grantham in 1654, was evidently chosen for his financial experience, since there was talk (never realized) of making him treasurer in Ireland.[17]

The most important change in the Irish government after 1654 was Henry Cromwell's appointment, on 25 December 1654, as major-general, acting commander of the forces in Ireland, and a member of the Irish council.[18] This appointment ended months of rumour. Even so Henry Cromwell, anticipating conflict between himself and Fleetwood because of his inadequately defined powers, delayed his crossing to Dublin until July 1655.[19] His eventual arrival prompted renewed speculation that he was to replace his brother-in-law, Fleetwood, as lord deputy. However the protector wrote to Fleetwood, 'it's reported that you are to be sent for, and Harry to be Deputy; which truly never entered into my heart.' To avoid humiliating Fleetwood Oliver Cromwell retained him as lord deputy, but suggested, 'if you have a mind', that he leave Dublin. This Fleetwood did in September 1655.[20] Oliver Cromwell's failure to give his son full powers as lord deputy at this critical juncture was one of his least satisfactory compromises. Henry Cromwell had been sent to Ireland to inject firmness into the government and

---

[17] Brit. Mus., Lansdowne MS. 821, ff. 186, 190, 208; Bodl., Tanner MS. 59, ff. 585, 667; *Cobbett's parliamentary history of England* (London, 1808), iii. 1427; A. A. Garner, *Colonel Edward King* (Scunthorpe, 1970), p. 44; Firth and Rait, i. 294, 539, 622, 641, 663, 741, 969, 1086, 1239; ii. 37, 302; *Cal. S.P. Dom. 1656-7*, p. 48; Dunlop ii. 615.

[18] *Fourteenth report of the Deputy Keeper of Public Records in Ireland*, p. 28; Dunlop, ii. 468-9.

[19] The council of state recommended Henry Cromwell's appointment as early as August 1654. *Cal. S.P. Dom. 1654*, pp. 313, 321, 328; Hist. MSS. Comm., *Egmont MSS.* i. 539-40; Brit. Mus., Lansdowne MS. 821, ff. 3ᵛ, 7; *The Clarke Papers*, ed. C. H. Firth, iii, Camden soc., N.S. 61 (1899), 24, 43-4; *Thurloe State Papers*, iii. 581, 614.

[20] Ibid. iii. 572.

halt the disaffection in the army and civil administration. Once Fleetwood left Ireland, Henry Cromwell became its effective governor, yet he lacked sufficient power to quell the Baptist and military opposition quickly. Moreover Fleetwood as lord deputy retained important powers of patronage, was deferred to in the council of state on Irish affairs, and provided a convenient and dangerous focus for Henry Cromwell's opponents.[21] One reason why Oliver Cromwell compromised, allowing Fleetwood to remain titular head of the Irish government, while Henry Cromwell actually governed, was his sensitivity to allegations that he was trying to set up a Cromwellian dynasty. Cromwell indeed said it had been his wish that Richard and Henry Cromwell should 'have liv'd private lives in the country'. A second reason was genuine doubt about Henry Cromwell's suitability for the lord deputyship, owing to his youth, comparative inexperience, but above all 'those passions in you which hee knew you had from your father'. Undoubtedly Henry Cromwell had inherited his father's impulsive temper, and also lacked tact.[22] A third reason was Oliver Cromwell's hope that a balance might be achieved: so long as Fleetwood continued as lord deputy the hostility to the protectorate would be contained, whilst Henry Cromwell's arrival in Dublin would appease the moderates and conservatives alienated by Fleetwood. However the parties in Ireland could not be balanced by such a stratagem.

Fleetwood's commission as lord deputy was due to expire on 1 September 1657. The need for its renewal led to a bitter struggle between Henry Cromwell's and Fleetwood's supporters.[23] Still the protector hesitated to dismiss Fleetwood, for sentimental as well as political reasons. While the wrangling continued, the commission expired and Ireland was left without legal government for two months, an extreme but by no means untypical example of the haphazard

[21] Brit. Mus., Lansdowne MS. 821, f. 103. Henry Cromwell's instructions as lord deputy in 1657 prohibited him from cancelling appointments made by Fleetwood: Huntingdon Record Office, 731 dd Bush, no. 12. This provision is omitted from the version calendared in Dunlop, ii. 672–3.

[22] *Thurloe State Papers*, i. 725–6; iii. 572; Brit. Mus., Lansdowne MSS., 821, f. 246; 823, f. 7ᵛ; J. Nickolls, *Original Letters and Papers* (London, 1742), p. 7.

[23] *Thurloe State Papers*, vi. 446, 632.

processes of Cromwellian government.[24] Reports from Lord
Broghill in Ireland that Henry Cromwell 'is fit to be our chief
governor' evidently swayed the council of state, and on 17
November 1657 Henry Cromwell was commissioned as lord
deputy. The new council was smaller by one member because
Robert Goodwin was dropped.[25] Entrusted at last with full
authority in Ireland, Henry Cromwell pushed ahead with his
more conservative policies. However he now found that his
father had imposed a new check on his power.

The omission of Goodwin from the council, ostensibly on
grounds of age,[26] by removing one of Henry Cromwell's
supporters had left it equally balanced, 'a mere faction of
three against three'.[27] These divisions became apparent when
Henry Cromwell's controversial religious policy was brought
before it: Pepys and Bury supported him; Steele, Corbet, and
Thomlinson opposed.[28] Only Henry Cromwell's casting vote
prevented complete paralysis.[29] As it was he asked in vain
for new councillors to redress the balance; and increasingly
took advice outside the council, from his secretary, William
Petty, and from Lord Broghill.[30]

Oliver Cromwell's death in September 1658 necessitated
the renewal of the Irish commission. In November 1658 the
new protector, Richard Cromwell, made his brother-in-law
lord lieutenant and governor-general. The council remained

---

[24] Ibid. vi. 481, 516. Another example was the failure to change the
requirement that in the lord deputy's absence all the councillors were needed to
constitute a quorum, when Fleetwood returned to England in 1655. Ibid. iv. 23.

[25] Bodl., Carte MS. 73, ff. 143, 156; *Thurloe State Papers*, vi. 447, 493. The
patent and instructions are in Huntingdon Record Office, 731 dd Bush, nos. 12
and 13; cf. Dunlop, ii. 672–3.

[26] *Thurloe State Papers*, ii. 492–3; vi. 506, 599, 648, 650, 661, 665, 683, 724;
vii. 500.

[27] *Thurloe State Papers*, vi. 506.

[28] Bury in 1660 was reputed to be 'a great presbiterian' and was elected to the
General Convention for the Boyle borough of Lismore. Bodl., Carte MS. 31, f. 3;
P. Adair, *A true narrative*, ed. W. D. Killen (Belfast, 1866), p. 236; *An account of
the chief occurrences. . . 12—19 March* [1660] (Dublin, 1659[60]), p. 38;
Thomlinson was willing to intrigue against Henry Cromwell. In 1658 the latter
encouraged him to go to England: Brit. Mus., Lansdowne MS. 823, ff. 170, 204;
Thurloe State Papers, vi. 762, 774; vii. 199, 291, 589.

[29] W. Petty, *Reflections on some persons and things in Ireland* (London, 1660),
p. 39.

[30] Brit. Mus., Lansdowne MS. 1228, f. 8.

the same. Early in January 1659 Pepys, a stalwart supporter of Henry Cromwell, died.[31]

The fall of the protectorate led to Henry Cromwell's dismissal in June 1659 and the triumph of his opponents. The Rump, now reinstated, appointed five parliamentary commissioners. They were Henry Cromwell's three opponents on the Irish council, Steele, Corbet, and Thomlinson, together with Goodwin and John Jones (a commissioner from 1650 to 1654). Until their colleagues arrived Corbet and Steele, who were still in Dublin, were Ireland's effective rulers.[32] Their authority lasted only three months, and was not legally renewed. Nevertheless some of the commissioners continued to act illegally after September.[33] This illegality and the unpopularity of the parliamentary commissioners' policies with Irish protestants led to a *coup* on 13 December 1659 when Dublin Castle was seized and Corbet, Jones, and Thomlinson were imprisoned.[34]

Meanwhile there had been further political upheavals in England. The Rump, having again been interrupted by the army, returned and the members secluded at Pride's Purge were readmitted. Parliament appointed, in January 1660, five new parliamentary commissioners for Ireland's government:[35] Weaver, a parliamentary commissioner from 1650 to 1653; Robert Goodwin, a councillor from 1654 to 1658; Colonel Henry Markham, an English soldier of conservative outlook, connected with Broghill, and who had served the

[31] *Fourteenth report of the Deputy Keeper of Public Records in Ireland*, p. 28; *Thurloe State Papers*, vii. 494, 511, 590.

[32] Bodl., Carte MS. 67, f. 307; *C.J.* vii. 700; *Cal. S.P. Dom. 1658–9*, pp. 372–3.

[33] Brit. Mus., Stowe MS. 185, f. 141; Cambridge Univ. Lib., Baumgartner papers, Strype correspondence, 7, f. 11; Dunlop, ii. 707.

[34] J. Bridges, *et. al., A perfect narrative of the grounds* . . . (London, 1660), pp. 3–4, 15; *The Clarke Papers*, iv, ed. Firth, pp. 202–3; *The Declaration of the Army in Ireland* . . . *Feb. 18 1659[60]* (Dublin, 1659[60]), pp. 2–3; *The Memoirs of Edmund Ludlow*, ed. Firth, ii. 185–200; J. Mayer, 'Inedited letters of Cromwell, Colonel Jones, Bradshaw and other regicides', *Trans. Hist. Soc. of Lancashire and Cheshire*, N.S. i (1860–1), 292–4, 295, 296–7; *Mercurius politicus*, no. 604 (19–26 Jan. 1660), pp. 1040–1. Steele had already returned to England.

[35] *C.J.* vii. 815.

protectorate in Ireland and Scotland;[36] Sir Hardress Waller, a
leading protestant settler who was prominent in the parliamentary cause during the 1640s and seems to have been a
religious Independent;[37] and Sir Charles Coote, the important Old Protestant and lord president of Connaught. These
commissioners were unable to assert the English parliament's
authority in Ireland. Power there had temporarily passed to a
General Convention, representative of the Protestants in
Ireland, which assumed the role of an Irish parliament and
tried to exploit the confusion in England to gain concessions
for Ireland. Once Charles II's restoration in England became
inevitable, the General Convention was unable to take an
independent line and it acquiesced meekly, but unenthusiasti-
cally, in Charles II's return.[38]

Appointment to the Irish government was generally a
reward for political loyalty in England. None of those chosen
between 1650 and 1659 was a Protestant settler in Ireland,
although one or two members of that class, like Sir Robert
King and Coote, were mentioned as possible councillors.[39] In
general those appointed were competent and not without
administrative experience, but most retained assumptions
formed in England and not necessarily relevant to Irish
conditions. Also they kept their English connections, identified with political and religious groups there, and so drew
the Irish government into English political controversies. This
was, of course, nothing new: under Strafford and again after

36 Harvard Univ. Lib., MS. 218, F. 22, T. Cokely to Broghill, 28 Jan. 1658[9];
Dunlop, i. 162, n. 1; ii. 459, 538, 589, 615–16, 648, 665; Hist. MSS. Comm.,
Leyborne-Popham MSS., p. 137; Hist. MSS. Comm., *Various collections*, vi (MSS.
of Lord Brown and Oranmore), pp. 438–9; Firth and Davies, ii. 560; *The
Memoirs of Edmund Ludlow*, i. 261; P. J. Pinckney, 'The Scottish representation
in the Cromwellian parliament of 1656', *Scottish Hist. Rev.* xliv (1967), 99, 104;
W. R. Scott, 'Members for Ireland in the parliaments of the Protectorate', *JRSAI*
5th Ser. iii (1893), 76; *Thurloe State Papers*, vi. 661.

37 Ibid. vi. 774. In February 1660 Waller parted company from the more
conservative settlers of the General Convention: *An account of the chief
occurrences . . . 22–27 February* [1660] (Dublin, 1659[60]), p. 9.

38 Knowledge of the General Convention derives largely from *An Account of
the chief occurrences of Ireland . . . 12–19 March* [1660] which exists in an
apparently unique copy in Worcester College Library, Oxford, and which contains
an unnoticed list of the Convention's members. I hope to publish a separate study
of its policies and membership.

39 Brit. Mus., Lansdowne MS. 821, f. 93; *Thurloe State Papers*, vi. 774; vii. 155.

1660 the Irish government was a battleground for English factions. What was different in the Interregnum was that the lord deputy did not rule on his own, but was assisted by English councillors who often represented different political positions. It may be that Cromwell deliberately kept his son's council balanced, hoping thereby to restrain him from policies unacceptable to the military and commonwealth parties. If this was Oliver Cromwell's calculation, it failed.

The other conspicuous feature of the Irish government was the close relationship between the successive heads of the administration (Ireton, Fleetwood and Henry Cromwell) and Oliver Cromwell. Through his nominees he could keep close watch over Irish policy, but often he did not choose to do this, allowing the deputies considerable freedom.

The chief defects of the government were the division of power between Dublin and Westminster (a constant feature so long as Ireland was under English rule), and between Fleetwood and Henry Cromwell; an insufficient number of councillors; and the serious differences of outlook amongst the members of the government. All made the administration less efficient.

III

THE GOVERNMENT, FINANCE, AND TRADE

i. The Financing of Government

Policy in Ireland changed with the governors, especially when Henry Cromwell replaced Fleetwood. An even greater influence over policy was money. Lack of money was the foremost reason for the failure of much of the Cromwellians' reforming programme, in Ireland as in England. Financial arrangements embittered Anglo-Irish relations during the Interregnum, and proved the most irksome aspect of English government in Ireland, leading the Irish Protestants to re-assert Ireland's legislative independence in 1660.

The main burden was the English army of occupation, an army of perhaps 35,000. Between 6 July 1649 and 1 November 1656 this army cost almost £3,000,000 to maintain.[1] The cost was thereafter reduced by extensive disbanding, but even in 1658 the annual charge was £336,000. Money on this scale was proving increasingly difficult to find, so much so that by 1658 payment was nine months in arrears, and by December 1659 fifteen months.[2] This increased the danger of disaffection in the army and showed the unwillingness of the civilian population to support the army. It made further disbanding of the army even more urgent, and tended to add to the unpopularity of Henry Cromwell's regime with the military party.

In comparison the costs of the civil administration were slight: £46,000 in 1658. Even so Henry Cromwell intended to retrench in 1659, reducing civil expenditure to £35,000, mainly by altering the method of paying official preachers.[3]

---

[1] Dunlop, ii. 638–45; C. H. Firth, 'Account of money spent in the Cromwellian reconquest and settlement of Ireland', *Eng. Hist. Rev.* xiv (1899), 105–9. A copy among Broghill's papers supplies the terminal date: Nat. Lib. Ire., MS. 13,189, item 2. For financing the army before 1649 see: H. Hazlett, 'The financing of the British armies in Ireland, 1641–9', *Irish Hist. Studies*, i (1938–9).

[2] Dunlop, ii. 678; *Thurloe State Papers*, vi. 649, 650, 744, 762, 819, 862; Bodl., Carte MS. 44, f. 677.

[3] Dunlop, ii. 677; *Thurloe State Papers*, vi. 714.

Money came from two main sources: England and Ireland. In the period from 1649 to 1656 £1,566,848 was transmitted from England, and £1,942,548 raised in Ireland itself.[4] The English government, itself faced with bankruptcy, resented the continuing drain of money to Ireland, and wanted to stop it. Pressure grew to make Ireland self-supporting. The subsidy from England was progressively reduced. In July 1655 it was cut from £24,000 to £17,000 per month; and in July 1657 the £17,000 was reduced to a derisory £8,000 per month.[5] Reports of economic recovery and plenty in Ireland were eagerly seized upon to justify the cuts. In 1659 it was said that the subsidy might be ended altogether. Talk of returning prosperity in Ireland had been exaggerated. The reduced revenue was insufficient to cover the costs of government, and in 1658 a deficit of £96,000 was expected.[6] In England there was lack of sympathy for Ireland's condition, and indeed much resentment that the country, far from proving a source of profit, was a financial burden. The Rump had been particularly hostile to Irish requests for assistance.[7]

In Ireland there were four main sources of income: the rents from lands, property, and tithes forfeit by rebellion or already owned by the state; the excise; the assessment; and the customs. A fifth source — forced loans or borrowing from Dublin merchants and Irish landowners — had been valuable before 1649, but tended to dry up once the Protestant interest had been saved, allegedly because of the merchants' poverty, but perhaps because of the administration's increasingly poor credit.[8]

Revenue from land was disappointing. In 1654 quit-rents had been remitted for five years on adventurers' and soldiers' lands to encourage plantation; this concession was extended to the Old Protestant landowners in 1657.[9] The yield from

---

4 Dunlop, ii. 639.

5 Brit. Mus., Lansdowne MSS. 821, f. 224; 822, f. 188; *Thurloe State Papers*, ii. 516, 631, vi. 649, 516, 527; Mayer, *Trans. Hist. Soc. of Lancashire and Cheshire*, N.S., i. 233; cf. M. P. Ashley, *Financial and commercial policy under the Cromwellian protectorate* (Oxford, 1934).

6 *Thurloe State Papers*, vii. 655; Dunlop, ii. 678.

7 *C.J.* vii. 164; Dunlop, i. 265; *The Diary of Thomas Burton*, i. 209, 210, 246.

8 Hazlett, *Irish Hist. Studies*, i. 22; Bodl., Firth MS. c. 5, f. 31ᵛ; Carte MS. 74, ff. 43, 45.

9 Firth and Rait, ii. 727–8; Bodl., Carte MS. 63, ff. 622, 626.

lands was also diminished by too frequent gifts by the protector, against which Henry Cromwell remonstrated. The reluctance of settlers to come to Ireland meant that lands and houses in the walled towns remained empty and untenanted, and the state received no rents.[10]

The excise was introduced into Ireland in 1643 and by 1657 produced £18,000 p.a. Greater stringency in its collection, especially on salt, increased the yield in 1658 but created serious resentment. However dislike of the excise was much less than of the assessment and the customs.[11]

One of the troubles with the assessment and customs was that the level was fixed at Westminster, without (it was thought in Ireland) accurate appraisal of Ireland's ability to pay. The heaviest tax was the assessment. Of the £1,942,548 raised in Ireland between 1649 and 1656, £1,309,695 came from that tax. In December 1650 the maximum monthly total of the assessment to be levied throughout Ireland was fixed at £30,000 by the Westminster government.[12] Once the war was over, that very high figure could be reduced. In 1654 parliament set the monthly total at £10,000 for two years, rising in 1656 to £12,000, £13,000 in 1657, and £14,000 in 1658.[13] In 1657 parliament, after lengthy debate, conceded that Ireland's recovery had been slower than expected in 1654, and set the monthly total at £9,000 rather than £13,000.[14] A reduction of the assessment was the chief reform for which Ireland's members agitated in the protectorate parliaments, having been instructed to do so by their constituents. They met with indifference or hostility from the majority of English members of parliament, and made themselves unpopular by pressing this point, so much so that in 1657 'it was moved yt ye members serving for Ireland

10 *Thurloe State Papers*, vi. 683, 763, 820; Bodl., Carte MS. 74, f. 90; Brit. Mus., Stowe MS. 185, f. 138; Dunlop, ii. 647.

11 *Irelands Excise by the Lords Justices and Councell* . . . (London, 1643); Brit. Mus., Harleian MS. 4706, f. 3; *Thurloe State Papers*, vi. 340; Hazlett, *Irish Historical Studies*, i. 23.

12 Dunlop, i. 4; ii. 639; this limit was exceeded by authorizing separate levies for forage: Nat. Lib. Ire., MS. 11,959, p. 108; Dunlop, ii. 288, 373–4.

13 Firth and Rait, ii. 727–8; cf. *Diary of Thomas Burton*, i. pp. lxxxviii–lxxxix, cvii; Bodl., Carte MS. 74, ff. 90, 90ᵛ.

14 *Diary of Thomas Burton* ii. 200, 208–212, 224, 246; *C.J.*, vii. 554, 557; P.R.O., SP. 63/287, 52–52ᵛ, 70.

might be sent to ye Tower for their contest about pro-
portioning ye assessment twixt England and Ireland.' This
campaign was supported by Henry Cromwell.[15] The failure
to obtain satisfaction led to an increasing eagerness to
withdraw from the Westminster parliament, where the thirty
members for Ireland could never hope to succeed, and to
restore the Irish parliament with the right to tax Ireland. This
step was taken in 1660, with the General Convention, which
substituted a poll-tax for the assessment.[16]

Additional irritations caused by the assessment, apart from
its unrealistically high level, were injustices in its apportion-
ing. The revenue commissioners responsible for its assessment
and collection were usually members of the English army or
administration hostile to the established settlers. Lord Cork
and Lady Ormonde, for example, complained that they were
unfairly assessed.[17] Also the tax fell most heavily on land,
hampering landowners struggling to make good the dep-
redations of war and who had financed resistance since
1641.[18] By 1655 the composition of the revenue commission had changed, giving the old Protestants much more
local control over its apportionment. But so long as the
monthly total was imposed from Westminster, there was
bound to be a feeling of dissatisfaction.[19]

The yield of the customs and water excise, as we shall see,
depended in part on returning prosperity and trade and also
on the efficiency of collection. In 1657–8 the customs

[15]Brit. Mus., Lansdowne MS. 822, f. 92; *Thurloe State Papers*, vi. 862. vii. 72;
P.R.O., SP. 63/287, 131, 147–8.

[16]*Diary of Thomas Burton*, iv. 237–41; Chatsworth, Lismore MS. 31, no. 69;
Mercurius Politicus, no. 612 (15–22 March 1660), pp. 1175–6; *An Account of
the chief occurrences ... 12–19 March* [1660], p. 34; P.R.O., SP. 63/303, 45; *A
'Census' of Ireland*, ed. Pender, pp. 610 ff.

[17]Chatsworth, Lismore MS. 29, Cork's diary, 21 Sept. 1654, 25 Jan. 1654[5],
2 Nov. 1656, 13 July 1657; C.B., Jennings transcripts, I. E. 10. 85, 21 Aug. 1654;
A/II, 24 Dec. 1656; *A declaration of the Lord Deputy and Council for removing
and preventing some mistakes of government in Ireland* (Dublin, 1655), p. 4;
Thurloe State Papers, vi. 623; vii. 649, 650. For the revenue commissions in
Dublin and County Cork in 1651; Nat. Lib. Ire., MS. 11,959, p. 161; *The council
book of the Corporation of Youghal*, ed. R. Caulfield (Guildford, 1878), p. 289.

[18]Hazlett, *Irish Historical Studies*, i. 24; Hist. MSS. Comm., *Egmont MSS.* i.
599.

[19]Chatsworth, Cork's diary, 24, 27, 28, and 30 Apr. 1657; P.R.O. SP. 63/287,
70, 147, 170; *A declaration for the payment of custom and excize* (Dublin,
1654).

produced about £29,000 p.a. This rose sharply in 1658 because the customs were farmed, for £70,000 p.a. This change certainly increased the government's receipts, but created serious political opposition.[20]

There is no doubt that Ireland was heavily taxed during the Interregnum. With no money to spare in England this was a necessity. But there seems also to have been a punitive intention. The 'evil report' of high taxation in Ireland apparently deterred new settlers from coming, and it retarded recovery amongst those already in Ireland.[21] Taxation put an obstacle in the way of a successful new plantation. It also made English rule in Ireland unpopular, as became clear once the sympathetic Henry Cromwell was removed. For Protestant settlers the protectorate seemed responsible for crippling taxation and the denial of concessions, such as Henry Cromwell himself was prepared to make.

Want of money shaped policies. In order to reduce the burden of the army, Henry Cromwell proposed a militia which would be supported on lands. His constructive suggestion was first ignored and then rejected by the English government. It increased suspicions that Henry Cromwell was looking for any pretext to diminish the army's influence.[22] Economy made Henry Cromwell more sympathetic towards the theological arguments in favour of a tithe-supported ministry.[23]

Henry Cromwell wanted to retrench in 1658. Yet he saw that unrelieved austerity would make the protectorate unpopular and prevent it carrying out those constructive reforms essential if Ireland were to be made secure. 'So bitter a pill as an universal retrenchment', he wrote, 'cannot be swallowed without something of sweet to carry it down.' There was an expectation that this new settlement would be accompanied by the realization of new projects. And it is true that the time of proposed economies was also when Henry Cromwell embarked on comprehensive changes in

20 See below, pp. 45–6.

21 Brit. Mus., Lansdowne MS. 1228, f. 1ᵛ; R. Chambre, *Some animadversions upon the Declaration of, and the plea for the army* (Dublin, 1659), p. 26; Dunlop, ii. 484, 513.

22 *Thurloe State Papers*, vi. 405, 505, 516, 527, 569, 657, 661, 681; vii. 401.

23 See below, p. 156.

ecclesiastical organization, the augmentation of Trinity College's revenues, and the establishment of a second college in Dublin.[24]

Henry Cromwell's fall in 1659 and the political confusion of the next year make it impossible to decide just what would have been achieved with more time. But one of the main reasons why more time was necessary, why so little of the promised programme of 1649 and 1650 had been accomplished, was the shortage of money. It was difficult to maintain the basic machinery of government — to pay councillors, judges, preachers, and schoolmasters generously and regularly — let alone embark on more ambitious patronage of the church, the law, education, and learning.

ii. The Regulation of Trade

Closely linked with government finance was official control of trade. The Cromwellians' economic policy for Ireland had two often irreconcilable objects: first, to engineer a recovery so that Ireland would be prosperous and financially self-sufficient; secondly, to restrict Irish trade lest it damage England's, or lest it jeopardize the success of the new plantation. The second, restrictive policy was generally decided in England and was resented in Ireland, contributing to the unpopularity of English rule there.

I shall first describe the official regulation of trade, then the nature and volume of trade, and finally I shall try to assess the over-all effect of policy on Ireland's economic welfare during the Interregnum and later.

In the main the laws restricting Ireland's trade were of two sorts. Some continued a traditional policy of restriction, especially of the wool trade; others were new, prompted by the peculiar circumstances of the Interregnum. In the first category Ireland's wool trade had long been regarded as a potential threat to England, so that the export of Irish wool was strictly controlled to prevent it reaching England's continental rivals. Also measures were taken to ensure that the wool came to England and was not used to start an Irish cloth industry. To impose these controls and to stop smug-

---

[24] *Thurloe State Papers* vi. 819; Sheffield Univ. Lib., Hartlib MS. xv, R. Wood to Hartlib, 8 Apr. 1657.

gling a system of staple ports was introduced, together with licences for export issued by the Irish lord deputy. In 1641 Charles I agreed to the abolition of the licensing system's statutory basis, but the promise was not kept and the statutory ban remained.[25] During the civil war it was impossible to maintain these controls; wool was exported from Catholic-held ports (especially Limerick and Galway) to the continent. As English authority was reimposed the old restrictions were revived. In 1648 and 1658 proclamations repeated the prohibition on foreign export. Moreover the staple system, never formally abolished, was again enforced and operated throughout the 1650s.[26] Because England had for so long exerted a niggardly control over this branch of Irish trade there was no expectation of a more generous policy during the Interregnum. Indeed wool was specifically excepted from Irish requests for free trade with England.[27] Another reason why there was little complaint was the drop in Irish wool production owing to the destruction of flocks during the war. The government acted to preserve lambs to rebuild stocks; new stock was also imported from England and Wales.[28] Only after 1656 were there signs of replenished flocks and reviving wool exports. This improving situation may have prompted the new care for control in 1658 and 1659.[29]

The commodities which could be exported were extremely few before 1655. The need to restock the country was one reason. Another was the expense of importing food and materials to support the English army of occupation. The

25 P. J. Bowden, *The wool trade in Tudor and Stuart England* (London, 1962), pp. 203–12; Kearney, *Strafford in Ireland*, pp. 137–53; G. O'Brien, 'The Irish staple organization in the reign of James I', *Economic History*, a supplement to the *Economic Journal*, i (1926–9), 44–54; *Cal. S.P. Ire. 1660–2*, p. 305.

26 Brit. Mus., Additional MSS. 15,635 and 19,843; Dunlop, i. 243; ii. 715–16; Firth and Rait, i. 1061; Steele, ii. no. 599 (Ireland).

27 Brit. Mus., Lansdowne MS. 1228, f. 19.

28 *The Herbert Correspondence*, ed. W. J. Smith, Irish MSS. Comm. and Board of Celtic Studies (Cardiff and Dublin, 1963), p. 142; Bristol Archives Office, Bristol deposition book, 1654–57, f. 40ᵛ; Steele, ii. nos. 464, 471, 500 (Ireland).

29 P.R.O., SP. 63/287, 172, 290; Brit. Mus., Stowe MS. 185, f. 138. Recorded wool imports from Ireland to Bristol were: 22 bags (1654), 8 bags (1655), 24 bags (1656), 53 bags (1657), 147 bags (1658), 259 bags (1659), 408 bags (1660), 581 bags (1661); Society of Merchant Venturers, Bristol, Wharfage books i and ii (henceforward Bristol wharfage books).

prohibited goods included butter, hides, beef, pork, cattle, tallow, and leather. Wool, as already mentioned, was controlled; so too was timber.[30] Indeed the only commodity in which there was any substantial export trade before 1655 was fish. Scarcity had made these controls necessary. As produce became more plentiful, the restrictions became a source of revenue, with the government granting licences. This certainly happened with the export of hides and brass, but perhaps not with foodstuffs. This policy was criticized for favouring prosperous merchants who could pay for the privilege.[31]

Other restrictions were the result of the political situation or of war. Trade with Scotland was forbidden until 1653, owing to the risk of infection by royalist disaffection. The Anglo-Dutch war interrupted what had been an important branch of Irish trade.[32] The removal of these foreign dangers and the evidence of returning prosperity (at least in some areas of Ireland) made possible the return to more normal trade in 1655. The government was also influenced by financial arguments (the benefits to customs and excise receipts) and perhaps by pressure from merchants. Thus in September 1655 the government allowed freedom of trade in tallow, butter, hides, beef, pork, and cattle.[33] Henceforward the official emphasis was on reviving Ireland's traditional trade rather than protecting the new plantation. This policy accorded with Henry Cromwell's concern to put the protectorate in Ireland on a secure foundation by conciliating the established Protestant settlers.

Even after 1655 Irish trade suffered from disadvantages.

[30] Nat. Lib. Ire., MS. 11,959, pp. 105, 108; Steele, ii, no. 464, 471, 476, 500 (Ireland).

[31] C.B., Jennings transcripts, A/6, 17 Feb. 1654[5], 8 Mar. 1654[5]; A/7, 22 Feb. 1654[5]; A/9, 27 July 1655; P. H. Hore, *History of the town and county of Wexford: the town of Wexford* ... (London, 1906), p. 306; Hore, *History of the town and county of Wexford: Old and New Ross* (London, 1900), p. 335; H. E. Nott and E. Ralph, eds., *The deposition books of Bristol, ii. 1650–54*, Bristol Record Soc. (Bristol, 1948), pp. 34, 62; Steele, ii, no. 527 (Ireland); Brit. Mus., Lansdowne MS. 1228, f. 16.

[32] Firth and Rait, ii. 69–70; Dunlop, i. 135, 211–12, 230; ii. 370; *Thurloe State Papers*, ii. 149, 163; R. M. Young, *Historical notices of old Belfast* (Belfast, 1896), pp. 77, 96–7.

[33] Brit. Mus., Lansdowne MS. 1228, ff. 3v–4; Steele, ii, no. 569 (Ireland); Dunlop, ii. 539.

Wool exports were still restricted; Ireland had to pay customs duties on goods sent to England, so that Irish goods could not compete with English ones. Moreover the English Book of Rates had been introduced which ignored the special character of Irish trade. Irish trade also came within the compass of the Navigation Act of 1651.[34] Above all the absence of free trade, such as Scotland and the American colonies had received and which Ireland had expected after its union in the commonwealth and protectorate, became a major political grievance, as was the customs administration after 1658 when it was farmed to English contractors.[35] Thus Irish trade after 1655 was not free from obstructions.

iii.   The Character of Irish Trade

Let us now look at the principal commodities exported from Ireland to see if any significant changes in the character of trade occurred. Fish was the main export before 1655. The principal catches were herrings, salmon, and pilchards, and the trade was centred on Wexford. Dublin, Waterford, Dungarvan, Youghal, Cork, and Limerick were other important fishing ports. The season attracted fishermen from Scotland, England, and Holland. In particular the Coopers' Company of Bristol was deeply involved in the trade.[36] Oliver Cromwell had recognized the fisheries' importance in 1649, and the regime tried to foster it. However this encouragement was counteracted by another official measure, the introduction of the excise, which fell heavily on salt essential to the preservation of fish. Those involved in the trade sought, and obtained, a remission of the excise used in salting fish.[37] During the decade the Coopers of Bristol

34 Brit, Mus., Lansdowne MS. 1228, f. 2; P.R.O., Dublin, Ferguson MS. xiii, 67; *Thurloe State Papers*, ii. 404.

35 Barnard, *P. and P.* lxi. 63.

36 Bristol Archive Office, Deposition book, 1654–57, ff. 166–72[v]; Nat. Lib. Ire., MS. 11,961, pp. 288–9; Sheffield Univ. Lib., Hartlib MS. lxii (45); Brit. Mus., Egerton 1762, f. 170; *Archivium Hibernicum*, viii. 86; Kearney, *Strafford in Ireland*, p. 130; *Cal. S.P. Ire. 1647–60*, p. 328; H. O'Grady, *Strafford and Ireland* (Dublin 1923), i. 134.

37 Nat. Lib. Ire., MS. 11,959 pp. 6–7, 11, 12–13; Abbott, *Cromwell*, ii. 143; *A declaration for the payment of custom and excize*, p. 4; Dunlop, i. 66; ii. 461, 477; Hore, *The town of Wexford*, pp. 308, 311, 314; Bodl., Carte MS. 52, f. 420; Steele, ii, no. 482 (Ireland); Young, *Historical notices of old Belfast*, p. 77.

found themselves liable to new taxes and met unparalleled competition from Irish merchants anxious to exploit the fisheries. Probably the most important step towards more vigorous exploitation was the interest taken by Martin Noel, who acquired property in Wexford and was anxious to improve the trade. There was even talk of organizing a Fisheries' Company to put the trade on a better basis, but nothing was achieved.[38]

In 1654 there was said to have been a record catch of 80,000 to 120,000 barrels of herrings taken off Wexford. The importance of the trade is suggested by the fact that of 58 vessels recorded as trading between Ireland and Bristol in 1655, 33 came from Wexford and carried cargoes of herring. In 1656, 27 of the 54 Irish ships coming to Bristol sailed from Wexford with herrings. Until 1659 exports of herrings to Bristol remained constant, declining in 1660. However the proportionate part played by fish in Irish exports fell as the other branches of trade were freed from restrictions and revived: in 1659 of the 123 Irish vessels recorded as trading with Bristol only 30 carried cargoes which included herrings.[39] Much of the fish was for domestic or English consumption. However there is also evidence of fish exports from Wexford to French ports, including Marseilles, in the 1650s.[40]

The reopening of trade in other goods after 1655 brought no immediate upsurge. In 1657 Henry Cromwell admitted that Ireland, like other reviving plantations, 'receives many imported goods, but exports little . . .' Exports were 'coarse commodities', like hides, tallow, and pipestaves.[41] Only

[38]Brit. Mus., Lansdowne MS. 1228, f. 5; R. Lawrence, *The Interest of Ireland in its trade and wealth stated* (Dublin 1682), i, sig. C4; Nat. Lib. Ire., MSS. 8535, letter of F. Harvey, 24 Sept. 1659; 14910; *Cal. S.P. Dom. 1658–9*, p. 120; and below, p. 59.

[39]Total exports of herrings in 1641 were 23,311 barrels and in 1669, 12,893 barrels. Recorded imports into Bristol were 2,820 barrels (1655), 2,271 (1656), 3,050 (1657), 2,479 (1658), 3,130 (1659), 1,082 (1660) and 1,447 (1661). Bristol wharfage books, i and ii; R. Dunlop, 'A note on the export trade of Ireland in 1641, 1665, and 1669', *Eng. Hist. Rev.*, xxii (1907), 755; H. F. Hore, 'Particulars relative to Wexford . . .'. *Journal of the Kilkenny and South East of Ireland Archaeological Soc.*, N.S. iv (1862–3), 88.

[40]Bristol Archives Office, Bristol deposition books, 1654–7, f. 33ᵛ; 1657–61, f. 146.

[41]*Thurloe State Papers*, vi. 789.

gradually were exports of wool, beef, and pork increased.
Furthermore the profits from livestock could be uncertain. In
Ulster in November 1657, for example, cattle yielded no
profits; butter was the only product to bring good returns.[42]

The traffic in hides was one which the government had
licensed before 1655, and had formed an important element
in trade with Bristol. The administration was much less eager
to allow the manufacture and export of pipestaves. Pipestaves
had been exported in large quantities in the 1630s. The trade
was regarded as a harmful one 'which as it brought great
profit to the proprietaries, so the felling of so many thou-
sands of trees ... did make great destruction of the
woods'.[43] From one point of view the clearance of woods
served the government well, by removing shelter for the
native Irish. For that reason Lord Cork had justified his
massive destruction of woods in County Cork as 'commonwealth work'. The Cromwellians, although eager to root out
the papists, had stronger reasons for protecting the woods.
Timber, essential for building new planters' homes and
rebuilding the old, was in desperately short supply. Irish
shipping, notoriously weak, also needed timber.[44] The
government in the Interregnum tried hard to conserve
Ireland's woods, but was hampered by grants of many woods
to the adventurers and soldiers.[45] The government tried to
discourage the manufacture of pipestaves, and in 1656 the
Irish council considered whether or not to ban 'the disposure
of wood for making pipestaves ..., which usually are made
of the best timber ...' No prohibition seems to have been

---

[42] Bristol wharfage books, i and ii; Chatsworth, Lismore MS. 31, item 62;
P.R.O., SP. 63/287, 112v, 169, 172.

[43] G. Boate, *Irelands naturall history*, pp. 120, 122; Sheffield Univ. Lib., Hartlib
MS. xlii (45); J. H. Andrews, 'Notes on the historical geography of the Irish iron
industry', *Irish Geography* iii (1958), 140; H. O'Grady, *Strafford and Ireland*, i.
296–8; T. Ranger, 'The career of the first earl of Cork', Oxford D.Phil., 1959, pp.
128–33.

[44] Somerset record office, DD/BR/ely, 3/5, letter of R. Needler, 9 Aug. 1655;
The council book of the corporation of Cork, ed. R. Caulfield (Guildford, 1879),
p. 550; Brit. Mus., Lansdowne MS. 1228, f. 20; Dunlop, ii. 441, 564; Steele, ii,
no. 468 (Ireland); *The Works of Sir William Temple, Bart.* (London, 1770), iii. 29.

[45] Brit Mus., Additional MS. 5014, clause 13; Dunlop, i. 268; ii. 441, 459,
483–4, 491, 564–5, 601, 712; Nat. Lib. Ire., MS. 11,959, pp. 163–4;
Nat. Lib. Ire., MS. 2325, p. 255; *C.J.* vii. 164; C.B., Jennings transcripts, A/10, 12
May 1656.

imposed. However from 1657 there was a sharp drop in the numbers reaching Bristol, which may have reflected official policy.[46]

An unusual element in Ireland's trade in the 1650s was the startling increase in grain exports (at least to Bristol) in 1659 and 1660. There were two reasons. A series of poor harvests in England had created dearth and high prices. By contrast Ireland had abundant harvests, certainly in 1657 and 1659, which led to a glut and extremely low prices.[47] Irish producers exported their crops, not so much from hope of abnormal profits as from a wish to find any market. In past crises Ireland had acted as England's granary.[48] In 1659 3,836 quarters of wheat entered Bristol from Ireland; and in 1660 3,035 quarters of wheat and 1,328 quarters of oats arrived there.[49] How exceptional this was is shown by a comparison of the total exports of wheat from Ireland to England at other times: none was recorded in 1641; 875 quarters in 1665 and 1,667 quarters in 1669.[50] Ireland had agricultural plenty at the end of the Interregnum, but it may have been regional, and it did not necessarily produce prosperity as well.

If trade was to expand, the customs receipts rise, and the native Irish be cured of their supposedly endemic idleness, Ireland had to export more than coarse commodities. Manufacturing and industrial ventures were needed. Earlier schemes, such as the iron-works of the first earl of Cork, had been embraced not only because they offered personal profit, but because they also showed the way in which communities of industrious and God-fearing Protestants could be created in place of the rebellious Irish.[51] The secure settlement of

[46] Dunlop, ii. 565; Bristol Wharfage books, i and ii; cf. M. F. Cusack, *A History of the Kingdom of Kerry* (London, 1871), p. 284.

[47] Ashley, *The commercial policy of the commonwealth and protectorate*, p. 177; W. G. Hoskins, 'Harvest fluctuations and English economic history, 1620–1759', *Agricultural History Review*, xvi (1968), 16, 21; Bristol Archives Office, Deposition book, 1657–61, f. 155ᵛ; Chatsworth, Lismore MS. 31, item 17; Somerset record office, DD/BR/ely, letter of W. Parkinson, 11 Nov. 1659; P.R.O., SP. 63/287, 94.

[48] Kearney, *Strafford in Ireland*, pp. 25, 130.

[49] Bristol wharfage books, i and ii.

[50] Dunlop, *Eng. Hist. Rev.* xxii. 755.

[51] T. Ranger, 'The career of the first earl of Cork', Oxford D.Phil., ch. v; H. F. Kearney, 'Richard Boyle, ironmaster', *JRSAI* lxxxiii (1953), 156–62.

Ireland in the Interregnum, it was felt, depended on the creation of more industry. This work, unfortunately, conflicted with English interests. In particular the development of a strong Irish woollen industry could not be allowed. Before 1641 the main industrial ventures had been the making of iron and glass, linen manufacture, tanning, and brewing. These ventures continued, with few innovations, during the 1650s.

At least eleven iron-works had been destroyed during the war, including those of Sir Charles Coote.[52] However Coote and the son of another of the earlier owners, Lord Cork, resumed production during the Interregnum. Coote received official encouragement, with contracts to supply the Irish army with ordnance.[53] He, and other owners, were allowed to retain native Irish labour at their works.[54] Lord Cork revived his father's ventures more slowly. In 1653 he was obliged to import iron from Bristol to repair Lismore Castle. By 1659 he was selling iron at £18 per ton, and exporting it to Minehead.[55] A new centre of manufacture was at Enniscorthy, County Wexford, where Timothy Stampe (who was alleged to have lost money in England) said that he had spent £30,000 by 1662 erecting several iron-works and other buildings, 'making thereby a very considerable plantacon'. The Enniscorthy works, in which Colonels Phaire and Ingoldsby were also engaged, imported ore from the Forest of Dean and skilled labour from England: in the 1680s the works' employees had a reputation of religious nonconformity.[56] A weakness of earlier schemes, as indeed of those of

52G. Boate, *Irelands naturall history*, pp. 130; E. McCracken, 'Charcoal-burning ironworks in seventeenth and eighteenth century Ireland', *Ulster Journal of Archaeology*, xx (1957), 125, 131.

53In 1654 Coote was entrusted by the government with the repair of Irish ordnance: Bodl., Rawlinson MS. A.208, p. 396.

54Bodl., Firth MS. c.5, f. 82; King's Inns, Dublin, Prendergast MS. ii. 328, 687; Nat. Lib. Ire., MS. 11,959, p. 198; Dunlop, ii. 327, 657.

55Chatsworth, Cork's diary, 28 Oct. 1653, 31 Jan. 1654[5], 6 Dec. 1655, 2 Nov. 1656, 8 Nov. 1659; Lismore MS. 31, no. 62; *The Works of Robert Boyle*, v. 241.

56The Enniscorthy scheme originated in 1656 and was functioning before 1660: Nat. Lib. Ire., MS. 30, items 1, 5, 11, 12, 15; P.R.O., Dublin, MS. 368 a; Andrews, *Irish Geography*, iii. 144—6; Hore, *The town of Wexford*, pp. 323, 324; Hore, *History of the town and county of Wexford: Enniscorthy* (London, 1911), pp. 508, 518; McCracken, *Ulster Journal of Archaeology*, xx. 126, 134; Bodl., Clarendon state papers, 88, ff. 261—4.

the 1650s, was that while they aimed at giving useful
employment to the native Irish, they had to rely on labour
imported from England and so contributed little to the
civilization of the native population.[57]

There were similar drawbacks in the making of glass. The
glasswork started by the Frenchman, Philip Bigoe, on the
Parsons's estate at Birr in King's County, was revived in the
1650s and allowed to employ Irish papists. Evidently the
domestic industry could not satisfy Irish needs, and special
care was taken to preserve glass.[58] Soap, potash, and steel
were also produced in small quantities.[59] Mining, because of
the technical problems involved, interested members of the
Hartlib circle. In Ireland the venture which attracted most
attention in the Interregnum was the lead and silver mine in
County Tipperary, which had earlier been granted to William
Webb who acted as a government surveyor in the 1650s.[60] In
1655 the mine was exempted from the excise, and granted to
two Cromwellian colonels, Abbott and Prettie. Abbott
brought over workmen from England: again skilled labour
was not available locally.[61]

Tanning had been under government control before 1649,
when the right to grant licences was vested in the lord
deputy.[62] Government control continued after 1649. One

[57] Cf. *The works of Sir William Temple*, iii. 28.

[58] King's Inns, Dublin, Prendergast MS. ii. 379—80; Boate, *Irelands naturall
history*, p. 162; Sheffield Univ. Lib., Hartlib MS. lxii (45); E. McCracken, *The
Irish woods since Tudor times: distribution and exploitation* (Newton Abbott,
1971), pp. 87—8; *Letters of denization and acts of naturalization for aliens in
England and Ireland*, ed. W. A. Shaw, Huguenot Soc. of London, xviii
(Lymington, 1911), 336; M. S. D. Westropp, 'Glassmaking in Ireland', *Proceedings, Royal Irish Academy*, xxix, section C, no. 3 (1911), pp. 34—5.

[59] Bristol Archives Office, Deposition book, 1657—61, f. 16; Bristol wharfage
book, ii. p. 111 recte 103; P.R.O., SP. 63/287, 27[v], 46, 113[v], 176; *Cal. S.P. Ire.
1647—60*, pp. 604, 620.

[60] Webb said he had spent £4,000 opening the mine: Dutch and English workers
were said to have been employed there. *Cal. S.P. Ire. 1633—47*, pp. 4—5, 86;
Boate, *Irelands naturall history*, p. 141; G. O'Brien, *Economic history of Ireland
in the seventeenth century* (Dublin, 1919), p. 53; Brit. Mus., Egerton MS. 1762,
ff. 152[v], 153; P.R.O., Dublin. Ferguson MS. xiii. 138; *The Works of Robert
Boyle*, v. 241.

[61] Brit. Mus., Lansdowne MS. 823, f. 233[v]. For the mine's later history: D. F.
Gleeson, *The last Lords of Ormond* (London, 1938), p. 162; O'Brien, *Economic
history*, p. 148.

[62] Clarke, *The Old English in Ireland*, p. 50; McCracken, *The Irish woods*, pp.
79—82; O'Brien, *Economic history*, p. 84.

reason was to prevent tanners from stripping bark from living trees and so destroying woods. Another was to encourage tanning in the English manner rather than the production of Irish brogues. This attempt to eliminate Irish dress did not succeed.[63] Tanyards certainly existed throughout the decade, but the leather which they produced was generally used in Ireland and not exported. It was the raw skins which were sent to England.[64]

Brewing was also regulated periodically. Again ideological and economic reasons were mixed. The suppression or control of alehouses was a necessary step in the reformation of manners, particularly those of the native Irish, supposedly the main keepers of alehouses and the worst drunkards. A system of licensing was introduced by the Cromwellians, and corporations tried to limit the number of alehouses within particular towns.[65] Purely economic controls included setting maximum prices for beer and wine in September 1652, and regulating the measures in which alcohol was sold.[66] Few traders seem to have specialized in brewing: it was not until 1670 that a guild of brewers was incorporated in

63 *Analecta Hibernica*, xv. 248; Boate, *Irelands naturall history*, pp. 120–2; *The council book of the corporation of Youghal* ed. R. Caulfield (Guildford, 1878), pp. 295–6; Chatsworth, Lismore MS. 31, no. 62; *Cal. Anc. Recs. of Dublin*, ed. Gilbert, iv. 175–6; Dunlop, i. 177; Pender, 'Studies in Waterford', *JCHAS* lv (1950), 39; Hore, *The town of Wexford*, p. 307; Steele, ii, nos. 478, 498.

64 Bristol wharfage books, i and ii; Bristol Archives Office, Deposition books, 1657–61, ff. 146–146ᵛ; *The Deposition books of Bristol*, ii, ed. Nott and Ralph, p. 120; Hore, *Old and New Ross*, p. 340; McCracken, *The Irish woods*, p. 82; cf. D. M. Woodward, 'The overseas trade of Chester, 1600–1650', *Trans. Lancashire and Cheshire Hist. Soc.* cxxii (1971), 40; O'Brien, *Economic history*, p. 197. In December 1658 the Irish glovers and white tanners asked that all sheep fells and other fells be manufactured in Ireland. Whether or not the request was granted we do not know. C.B., Jennings transcripts, A/14, 6 Dec. 1658.

65 H. O'Grady, *Strafford and Ireland* (Dublin, 1923), i. 307–13; P.R.O., Dublin, MS. I.a.52.42, p. 52; Brit. Mus., Egerton MS. 2122, f. 176ᵛ; Steele, *Tudor and Stuart proclamations*, ii, nos. 519, 529, 530, 537, 585; Kilkenny Municipal archives, White book, f. 6; Pearse St. Public Library, Dublin, Gilbert MS. 78, p. 122; *The council book of the corporation of Youghal*, ed. Caulfield, p. 299; Pender, *JCHAS* lv. 43; Dunlop, ii. 351.

66 Brit. Mus., Egerton MS. 1762, ff. 109ᵛ, 203ᵛ, 205ᵛ; 'Extract from the papers of Sir Henry Butler . . . delivered at the Quarter-Sessions held at Londonderry, 21 January 1655[6]', *Anthologia Hibernica*, i (Dublin, 1793), 414; P.R.O., Dublin, Ferguson MS. xiii. 101; Nat. Lib. Ire., MS. 11,961, p. 313; Hore *The town of Wexford*, pp. 307, 314. For similar measures in England: G. D. Ramsay, 'Industrial *laisser-faire* and the Policy of Cromwell', *Econ. Hist. Rev.* xvi (1946), 103.

Dublin. However leading merchants, like Aldermen Tighe and Hutchinson, were deeply involved in the trade.[67] Brewers came into conflict with the Cromwellian regime owing to the heavy excise on beer: large arrears were still unpaid in 1660.[68]

The development of cloth manufacture in Ireland posed problems. Fears in England of Irish competition had prevented the establishment of woollen manufacture. This English hostility seems to have been slightly moderated through the exceptional circumstances of the war. An acute shortage of clothing for the soldiers in Ireland led to a toleration of cloth manufacture in Ireland. Some proposals later in the decade received official support because they offered a way of employing and Anglicizing the Irish. Such manufactures were few, producing inferior cloth, and unable to satisfy domestic needs: very little cloth seems to have been exported.[69] In 1655 William Barton, an adventurer and important London clothier, asked for his lands to be granted in Connaught so that he might establish a manufacture there and provide work for many poor. The request was not acceded to: later, in 1658, Barton was involved in the Irish customs farm.[70]

As an alternative to woollens, Strafford had fostered linen making, and that policy continued during the Interregnum. However it had no remarkable results. In the immediate aftermath of the war there was a shortage of flax seed.[71] No linen is recorded as arriving in Bristol from Ireland between 1654 and 1660, but this is hardly conclusive evidence as the

---

[67] *Cal. S.P. Ire. 1669–70*, p. 277; T.C.D., Mun. P/I/455; *Cal. Anc. Recs. of Dublin*, ed. Gilbert, iv. 90; Bodl., Rawlinson MS. B.508, f. 37.

[68] Bodl., Carte MS. 154, ff. 19ᵛ, 20ᵛ, 21, 29ᵛ, 30, 32ᵛ, 33ᵛ–34; *C.J. Ire.* ii. 20.

[69] King's Inns, Prendergast MS. i, pp. 8, 431; Brit. Mus., Egerton MS. 212, ff. 3ᵛ, 4, 4ᵛ, 7; Nat. Lib. Ire., MS. 11,961, pp. 113, 267; *Cal. S.P. Ire. 1647–60*, pp. 21, 26, 27, 28; Dunlop, i. 72, 85, 111, 122; ii. 578, 628. Only two bundles of freize are recorded as entering Bristol from Ireland between 1654 and 1660: Bristol wharfage books, i and ii; cf. Brit. Mus., Harleian MS. 4706, f. 42; *Cal. S.P. Ire. 1660–2*, pp. 691–2.

[70] Bottigheimer, *English Money and Irish Land*, pp. 176, 199; V. Pearl, 'London's Counter-Revolution', in *The Interregnum*, ed. G. E. Aylmer (London, 1972), p. 41; *Cal. S.P. Ire. 1647–60*, p. 679.

[71] R. Child to S Hartlib, 11 Mar. 1651[2], 13 Nov. 1652: Sheffield Univ. Lib., Hartlib MS. xv.

bulk of Bristol's Irish trade was not with linen-producing Ulster. On the other hand, there is no sign that linen production increased in the 1650s.[72]

In the past Irish trade and industrial enterprises had been strictly controlled: similar restrictions continued throughout the Interregnum, and trade remained in the same channels as before. Similarly the Cromwellians' attitude towards internal trade was traditional (as I shall show), relying on municipal corporations and guilds to enforce regulations.

iv The Volume of Irish Trade

War, scarcity, and the need to protect the new plantation led to tight government control over trade and economic life. However there were ample precedents for such close regulation, and there was little innovation in Cromwellian policy. We have now to assess the effect of government policy on Ireland in the 1650s.

Contemporaries suggested that the numerous inhibitions had brought trade to a standstill. A detailed petition of the mid-1650s spoke of 'little or noe manufactures at present in the country, nor any to be rationally expected untill the country doe growe to be more fully peopled, planted and stocked'. It also complained that the 'trade outward . . . is wholly discouraged'. The want of good coin and Irish products had caused the merchants of Bristol and Chester to stop trading with Ireland.[73] Another obstacle was the lack of Irish shipping: Dublin was said to have only two ships fit for trade, the owners of the others having removed either to England or, if Catholic, to the continent.[74] Henry Cromwell confirmed the truth of these laments in 1657: Ireland received imports, but had little to export except hides, tallow, and pipestaves.[75] Ireland's languishing condition during the Interregnum was described even more forcefully by a twentieth-century economic historian: in these years

---

[72] *Cal. S.P. Ire. 1647—60*, p. 826; W. H. Crawford, 'The rise of the linen industry', in *The formation of the Irish economy*, ed. L. M. Cullen (Cork, 1968), pp. 23—5.

[73] Brit. Mus., Lansdowne MS. 1228, ff. 2, 3^v—4.

[74] Brit. Mus., Lansdowne MS. 1228, f. 18.

[75] *Thurloe State Papers*, vi. 789.

tillage all but ceased; and the cattle of the country was insufficient to supply even the Irish demand. The woods were felled; the promising mines were neglected and let fall into decay; and the tracts of bog and mountain, which were being reclaimed with so much labour, were suffered to fall back into their original condition of infertility. Trade and industry languished; the shipping of Ireland disappeared from the seas; and the wealth derivable from the fisheries was again abandoned to foreigners.[76]

Almost every detail in that onslaught can be attacked. Tillage was deliberately fostered and by 1654 corn was again cheap and plentiful;[77] cattle stocks improved; the woods were protected by the government, if not always effectually; land reclamation continued;[78] Irish shipping, although depleted, still entered English ports;[79] the fisheries were exploited for Irish gain, the Coopers of Bristol were denied their customary share. Yet, if in detail these charges can be refuted, is the essential point — that trade languished — untrue?

In the earlier seventeenth century the bulk of Irish exports had been either agricultural produce or the coarse products mentioned by Henry Cromwell. The absence of manufactured goods in the 1650s was nothing new.[80] The real problem was that in the years immediately after 1649 the staple products of Ireland were in desperately short supply and had indeed to be imported into the country. Is it possible to be more precise about the volume of trade in the decade; and about the date and scale of recovery?

The whole of this study is beset by shortage of sources. In relation to trade the darkness is almost total. No Irish port-books of the period are known to survive; and those for England during the civil war are lacking.[81] The only detailed evidence is the wharfage records of the Bristol Merchant

76 O'Brien, *Economic history of Ireland in the seventeenth century*, p. 115.

77 Nat. Lib. Ire., MS. 11,959, pp. 148–9, 150–1; *Analecta Hibernica* xv. 245; Dunlop, ii. 309; Steele, *Tudor and Stuart proclamations*, ii, no. 462a.

78 R. Child to S. Hartlib, 29 Aug. 1652; Sheffield Univ. Lib., Hartlib MS. xv.

79 Bristol wharfage books, i and ii.

80 On the nature of Irish trade: *Cal. S.P. Ire. 1647–60*, pp. 327–8; Kearney, *Strafford in Ireland*, ch. II; W. B. Stephens, 'The overseas trade of Chester in the early seventeenth century', *Trans. Hist. Soc. of Lancs. and Cheshire*, cxx (1968), esp. pp. 24–5; Woodward, 'The overseas trade of Chester, 1600–1650', ibid, cxxii (1971).

81 Except for some stray survivals of 1648–9 mentioned in Woodward, *Trans. Hist. Soc. Lancs. and Cheshire*, cxxii. 38–40.

Venturers, which begin in 1654. Valuable as these are, too much dependence on them is obviously unwise, and they offer no chance of comparison between trade in the Interregnum and Bristol's earlier or later Irish trade. In general the wharfage books show trade in the traditional commodities, with fish particularly important before 1655 and corn between 1659 and 1661.

Another possible index of Irish trade is the customs receipts. But here too there are formidable obstacles. Owing to the imposition of the English Book of Rates, the levies before 1641 differed from those in the 1650s.[82] Another difficulty is that the rise in customs revenue during the Interregnum probably owed more to greater efficiency in collection than to rapidly reviving trade. A third distortion was the exemption from customs of imported goods necessary to Ireland's resettlement.[83] Bearing these difficulties in mind, it is nevertheless worth seeing how much the customs produced.

Between July 1649 and November 1656 the combined yield of the customs and excise was £252,474: an annual average of about £35,000.[84] By 1657 there had been an undoubted improvement, the customs and water excise yielding £29,000 and the inland excise a further £20,410.[85] In 1658 Henry Cromwell expected the customs to produce a profit of £25,000, once the costs of administration were paid. At the same time, he believed the customs administration was unsatisfactory, because Ireland had many small ports, which meant employing and paying numerous collectors, and because trade was 'so small for want of exportable commodities'.[86] Henry Cromwell favoured farming the customs, a course which had already been adopted by Strafford with spectacular success and in England during the Inter-

82 *A Declaration for the Payment of Custom and Excize* (Dublin, 1654); *Diary of Thomas Burton*, iv. 241.

83 Firth and Rait, ii. 735.

84 Dunlop, ii. 639.

85 Bodl., Carte MS. 73, f. 72. For the yield between May 1656 and May 1657: *Thurloe State Papers*, vi. 340.

86 *Thurloe State Papers*, vi. 404.

regnum.[87] In 1658 the Irish customs and excise were farmed at £70,000 p.a. to three Englishmen, already involved in the management of the English revenues.[88] Although he had favoured the principle of farming, Henry Cromwell believed that this farm was unrealistically high. It would mean increasing the customs's yield threefold. This could be done only if there was far greater severity, or 'some miraculous increase of trade'.[89] As he expected, the first course — of greater stringency — was adopted, and it soon created serious political opposition. A test case was brought by Alderman Ridgley Hatfield, a former mayor of Dublin and warden of the city's Merchant Guild, to challenge the legal basis of the customs: it was halted after government intervention.[90] In June 1660 the farmers' contract was brought to a premature end, after twenty-six months instead of the stipulated seven years. In that time almost £160,000 had been collected, of which £123,000 were paid to the English and Irish governments.[91] Although the farmers had not fulfilled their obligation to pay £70,000 p.a., they had come much closer than Henry Cromwell anticipated. How much this was the result of greater efficiency and how much of brisker trade, we do not know. Judging from contemporary English experience and Strafford's in Ireland, improved administration was largely responsible.

How did this revenue compare with receipts before 1641 and after 1660? Farming dramatically increased the customs in Ireland between 1613 and 1641. A peak was reached in 1637—8 with receipts of £57,387, followed by £55,582 in 1638—9 and £51,874 in 1639—40.[92] Superficially the receipts between 1658 and 1660 seemed to have reached the same level. But it must be remembered that the customs rates

[87] Customs receipts rose from £140,000 in 1643 to £502,000 in 1659; an increase out of proportion with the growth in trade. Charles Wilson, *England's Apprenticeship* (London, 1965), p. 130.

[88] The contract is in Brit. Mus., Sloane MS. 972, ff. 25—8v. The farmers were Thomas Morrice and William Dodson, both of Westminster, and John Drury of London. For their other activities: *C.J.* vii. 783, 784; *Cal. S.P. Dom. 1657—8*, p. 113.

[89] Brit. Mus., Lansdowne MS. 822, f. 200v.

[90] *Cal. S.P. Ire. 1647—60*, pp. 678—9.

[91] A copy of the farmers' accounts is in T.C.D., MS. F.2.1, ff. 163—70, summarized in Bodleian Library, Carte MS. 52, f. 420.

[92] Kearney, *Strafford in Ireland*, pp. 159—68.

were higher in 1658; that the totals included the new tax of the inland excise, which accounted for about 40 per cent of the total. If allowance is made for those distorting factors, the yield was surprisingly high, perhaps 80 per cent of what it had been in 1638. Between 1660 and 1667 the customs and excise fluctuated from £40,000 to £55,000, averaging about £50,000 p.a. Between 1663 and 1667 the inland excise produced from £30,000 to £38,000, averaging £36,000 p.a.[93] This was an improvement on the yield between 1658 and 1660, but not a startling one; and suggests a growing recovery of internal and external trade which had started before 1660.

The traditional trade with England was certainly resumed, even if its scale was smaller than in the past. There was coastal trade: in 1654 corn imported into Dublin was then shipped to Cork and Dingle in boats belonging to Chester, London, and Barnstaple.[94] But what of Ireland's continental trade, especially with Spain, Holland, and France, which had been of great importance before 1641? The expulsion of Catholic merchants damaged this more than trade with England. England's wars with Holland and Spain also interfered with important branches of Irish trade.[95] We know of vessels trading from Bristol to Ireland and then to Marseilles and Leghorn; from Bristol to Carrickfergus and Marseilles; from Carrickfergus to La Rochelle; of trade between Rouen and Cork, and between Middelburg and Ross.[96] In 1659 it was reported from Lisburn that there was shipping between Ulster and Bordeaux almost every month.[97] Research in continental archives would probably yield more details of this part of Ireland's trade. It seems probable that continental trade declined most sharply during this period and recovered much less quickly; and that this contributed to the decay of ports like Limerick and Galway, whilst helping Dublin and its

[93] Brit. Mus., Harleian MS. 4706, ff. 7—8; ibid., Additional MS. 18,022, ff. 47ᵛ—48; Bodleian Lib., Carte MS. 52, ff. 407, 408; Hist. MSS. Comm., *Ormonde MSS.*, N.S. iii. 373.

[94] Bodl., Rawlinson MS. A.208, pp. 396, 397, 400, 417.

[95] Dunlop, i. 230; *Thurloe State Papers*, ii. 404.

[96] Bristol Archives Office, Deposition books, 1654—7, ff. 104, 215ᵛ; 1657—61, ff. 22, 27, 102, 146.

[97] P.R.O., SP. 63/287, 290; cf. *The town book of the corporation of Belfast*, ed. R. M. Young (Belfast, 1892), p. 76.

merchants, advantageously placed for trade with England, to a greater share.

Ireland was well placed for trade with the American and West Indian colonies, the first landfall between the American continent and England. Contacts were strengthened through the brisk traffic in Irish deported from their homeland to America, one of the few cargoes available in Ireland before 1655. Tobacco was imported directly into Ireland, but in general this trade was in English hands, owing to the lack of Irish shipping and the operation of the Navigation Act.[98] It may be found that the London merchants who showed most interest in Ireland during the decade were those involved in the West Indies and American trade.[99]

v. General Effects of Government Policy

In conclusion, although official inhibitions on Irish exports reduced trade and the admission of goods free of customs meant low revenue returns, these policies did help to restock Ireland. The high level of cattle and sheep exports in the 1660s was made possible by the recovery in the 1650s.[100] More damaging were the policies decided in England which ignored the special character of Ireland. The failure to grant free trade discriminated against Irish goods and also made goods imported in Ireland (unless exempted from customs) expensive.[101]   Critics of the 1658 customs farm claimed that it too was economically harmful. But most immediately apparent was the political opposition that these fiscal measures excited amongst the powerful merchants and settlers, and which undermined the popularity of English rule as represented by Henry Cromwell.[102]

In two other respects the Westminster government was seriously negligent. It failed to regulate the debased coinage in Ireland, despite repeated and desperate requests from Dublin. The lack of good coin and presence of much foreign

[98] C.B., Jennings transcripts A/10, 14 Nov. 1656; P.R.O., Dublin, Ferguson MS. xiii, pp. 61–2; Bristol Archives Office, Deposition books, 1654–7, ff. 19, 75, 86^v, 132^v, 156^v, 1657–61, ff. 7, 10^v, 57^v.

[99] Cf. Brenner, *P. and P.* lviii.

[100] L. M. Cullen, *Anglo-Irish trade* (Manchester, 1968), pp. 29–30.

[101] In 1657 imported goods were said to cost a third more than in London: R. Wood to Hartlib, 27 May 1657, Sheffield Univ. Lib., Hartlib MS. xxxiii.

[102] Barnard, *P. and P.* lxi.

and adulterated money interfered with trade and the collection of taxes and rents, made English merchants reluctant to trade with Ireland, and led to popular disturbances.[103] At a local level some of the difficulties were overcome by the use of trading tokens, but it did nothing to help foreign trade.[104] Ireland also suffered grievously from piracy. Again the Dublin administration pressed for action, but to no avail.[105] Thus in commercial matters English rule during the Interregnum brought Ireland few benefits and serious disadvantages. However the Interregnum was not exceptional in this respect. Traditionally Irish interests were rigorously subordinated to England's: it had been the case during Strafford's government; it would be intensified after 1660 with the Cattle Acts and the ban on wool exports in 1697.[106]

Having catalogued much that was damaging and little that was new, it is pleasant to end by mentioning an innovation: the introduction of a committee for trade. During the Interregnum three men deeply interested in commercial and fiscal questions served the Irish government: Petty, Worsley (who had been secretary to the English council of trade in 1650), and Robert Wood (who had written on currency reform before coming to Ireland in 1656).[107] Given their known interests and expertise, it is surprising that (so far as we know) none of them was asked to recommend how Ireland's trade might be improved. They may, of course, have had an unrecorded influence. Wood, in Henry Cromwell's

---

103Brit. Mus., Lansdowne MS. 1228, ff. 2ᵛ–3, 18.

104Brit. Mus., Additional MS. 19,859, f. 38; S. Hayman, 'The local coinage of Youghal', *Journal, Kilkenny and S.E. of Ireland Archaeological Soc.*, N.S. iii (1858–9), 224–31; T. B. Costello, 'Trade tokens in the County of Galway in the seventeenth century', *Journal, Galway Archaeological and Hist. Soc.*, vii (1911–2), 31–40; P. Seaby, *Coins and tokens of Ireland* (London, 1970); W. A. Seaby, 'A bond for issuers of Youghal tokens', *JRSAI*, ci (1972), 161; 'The tradesmen's coinage of Waterford in the seventeenth century', *Journal, Waterford and S.E. of Ireland Archaeological Soc.*, viii (1902).

105*Cal. S.P. Dom. 1656–7*, p. 219; ibid., *1659–60*, pp. 25–6; Barnard, *P. and P.* lxi. 64.

106C. A. Edie, *The Irish Cattle bills*, Transactions, American Philosophical Soc., N.S. lx, part 2 (Philadelphia, Pa., 1970).

107See below, p. 224.

household, and Petty, his secretary, were well placed to advise.[108]

Matters of trade were referred to the multifarious committees established by the parliamentary commissioners in Ireland after 1650. For example, the important Cork House committee, set up on 1 August 1653, was to consider trade and its improvement, as well as the transplantation of the Irish.[109] In June 1655 a committee specifically for trade was appointed by the Irish council, which considered how normal conditions could be re-established and recommended the lifting of some trade restrictions.[110] In 1656 the Irish administration was authorized to appoint a committee of trade 'of so many experienced persons . . . for the better carrying on and ordering of trade in Ireland'.[111] The members of the committee are unknown; its recommendations had to be approved at Westminster, so that it had no chance to innovate. The appointment of specialist trade committees continued after 1660. The General Convention of that year had an active trade committee, and in 1661 the Irish government established a new committee which included gentlemen, merchants, and privy councillors. Robert Wood was a member, and Petty served on its successors.[112] The limited powers of the Irish government to regulate the country's economic life reduced the value of this specialized body. Nevertheless it did show a growing professionalism in government, and a greater interest in collecting information and formulating policies for commerce.

---

108 Petty prepared 'a catalogue of such particulars as more neerly concerne the present trade of Ireland', but this was a private enterprise: R. Wood to S. Hartlib, 8 Apr. 1657, Sheffield Univ. Lib., Hartlib MS. xxxiii.

109 Nat. Lib. Ire., MS. 11,959, pp. 240–1; Dunlop, ii. 369–70.

110 Ibid. ii. 525–6.

111 Brit. Mus., Lansdowne MS. 1228, f. 19; Dunlop, ii. 578.

112 *An Account of the chief occurrences . . . 12–19 March* [1660], p. 3; R. Lawrence, *The Interest of Ireland in its trade and wealth stated* (Dublin, 1682), sig. [C6].

IV

THE GOVERNMENT AND THE BOROUGHS

i. Introduction

Official policy towards the Irish corporations during the Interregnum had three objects: strategic, political, and economic. Unfortunately one policy could not simultaneously secure all three ends. The government wanted not only to debar Catholics from the civic government and trading guilds, but also to expel them from the boroughs' physical confines. The boroughs were thought to have a special strategic importance. By placing them all in Protestant and English hands, the country would be protected against any future Catholic rising. The Cromwellians differed from their predecessors in remodelling existing towns rather than incorporating new ones.[1]

The boroughs were politically important because the execution of the Dublin and Westminster governments' orders depended on the municipalities' co-operation. Magistrates and aldermen obedient to, if not enthusastic about, Cromwellian policy were needed. Also the corporations' composition would affect the outcome of parliamentary elections.

The towns as centres of both internal and external trade had a key role in Ireland's economy. In large measure the government's revenue receipts depended on their trade and prosperity. The government by expelling Catholic merchants, for political and strategic reasons, retarded the towns' economic recovery. The failure to find adequate replacements for the Catholic merchants, with their ships, stocks, and continental contacts, was a major cause of the Cromwellian settlement's failure and the languishing state of Irish trade throughout the Interregnum.

The removal of Catholic property owners from the towns was of an equal importance with the transplantation of

[1] R. J. Hunter, 'Towns in the Ulster Plantation', *Studia Hibernica*, xi (1971).

Catholic landed proprietors, yet it has received little attention. In this chapter I shall describe the legislation which
affected the boroughs; then its application in particular
towns, seeing how effective the policy was and who the new
rulers were. The economic, social, and political implications
of the policy will then be considered, together with the
attempts to reverse it in 1660. Finally, I shall deal with the
city of Dublin, the treatment of which, although illustrating
many of the general trends, differed in its consequences.

ii. Official Policy

Two sorts of enactment affected the Irish towns: one dealt
with property; the other with the towns' inhabitants. In
1643, in an attempt to improve trade and establish the
Protestant interest, the towns of Limerick, Waterford, and
Wexford were offered for sale by the English parliament.
They were not sold, but this was the start of official schemes
to take the key towns from Catholic control.[2] Property in
the boroughs which belonged to the rebels was (like land)
confiscated and used as security for the adventurers' loans.
The government wanted to control schemes for the towns'
resettlement and to avoid piecemeal alienation. However the
wish conflicted with the need to raise money by disposing of
the houses. As early as March 1651 leases on these houses for
a maximum of seven years were permitted; in 1657 thirty-
one-year leases were allowed.[3] Rents from houses produced
£7,400 in the year 1656–7.[4] This policy was criticized; not
only because it allowed haphazard settlement, but also,
because it damaged the towns' prosperity. On the one hand
the yield from the houses was thought disappointingly low;
on the other, the rents were regarded as too high, discouraging would-be tenants. As a result property stood empty,

[2] Firth and Rait, i. 192–7. The prices were: £30,000 for Limerick, £25,000 for
Waterford, and £7,500 for Wexford. In 1653 half the houses in Limerick,
Waterford, and Clonmel were reserved for sale: ibid. ii. 728.

[3] Steele, ii. no. 466 (Ireland); Dunlop, ii. 665–6.

[4] Thurloe State Papers, vi. 340. In 1654 house rents produced £6,000; in
1659–60, £7,800. The regional yields in the latter period were; Wicklow, Dublin,
Kildare, Meath, and Louth, £2,484; Wexford, Waterford, and Tipperary, £1,739;
Kilkenny, Carlow, King's and Queen's Counties, £730; Cork, Kerry, Limerick, and
Clare, £2,574; and Westmeath, Leitrim, Longford, Roscommon, Mayo, Galway,
and Sligo, £333. The counties of Ulster produced nothing: Bodl., Carte MS. 74, f.
90; Nat. Lib. Ire., MS. 2701, pp. 62–3.

especially in Cork, Galway, Limerick, and Waterford, and decayed.[5]

New inhabitants of any condition were difficult to find. It was even more difficult to attract prosperous newcomers able to support the trade previously driven by the Catholics. Ambitious schemes of resettlement (as I shall show) failed. Nevertheless it remained official policy to expel Catholics from the walled towns.[6] As an administrative undertaking the eviction of all Catholics proved impossible. Also the wisdom of this indiscriminate policy was gradually questioned. On 27 December 1654 the Irish Council asked a committee to consider whether or not the Catholic merchants' presence in the walled towns was to the state's advantage.[7] The recommendations of this, and of a second committee, are unknown, but to judge from the policy adopted the restrictions on Catholics living and trading in the boroughs remained technically in force.[8] There were frequent attempts to make the policy effective; and ample evidence exists of widespread evasion, so that Catholics continued to live within the boroughs. However their exclusion from the municipal governments and from trade was apparently much more successful.

The scale of the Catholic exodus from the towns was suggested by petitions circulating after 1660. It was argued then, and Charles II accepted the contention, that the Catholics' removal had depressed Irish trade, causing 'lessening of our revenews, and impoverishing our subjects . . . , most of the merchants of abilities formerly residing there [in Ireland] being inforced to keep their stocks and traffique in forrain parts to the inriching of forrain princes'. We know that a group of sea captains from Wexford had removed themselves and their ships to the continent.[9] Many of Waterford's leading merchants also went overseas during

---

5 Brit. Mus., Stowe MS. 185, f. 138; Dunlop, ii. 646–7; T. J. Westropp, 'Cromwellian account books, Limerick', *JRSAI* xxxvi (1906), 203.

6 Steele, ii. no. 587 (Ireland); Hore, *The town of Wexford*, p. 320.

7 C.B., Jennings transcripts, I.E.10.87, 27 Dec. 1654.

8 Except in Galway: Brit. Mus., Additional MS. 19,843, ff. 143ᵛ, 157; C.B., Jennings transcripts, A/7, 22 Feb. 1654[5].

9 Charles II to the lord justices of Ireland, 22 May 1661, in P. Gale, *An Inquiry into the ancient corporate system of Ireland* (London, 1834), p. cxxx; *Cal. S.P. Ire. 1660–2*, pp. 335–7, 339.

the Interregnum. Most settled at St. Malo, where they already had strong ties; others went to Calais, Ostend, La Rochelle, Nantes, St. Sebastian, and even to Mexico. Petitioning for readmission to Waterford after 1660, they claimed to have acquired by their industry not only 'a reasonable stock, but much more experience in traffique and commerce, theire insight therein being such as . . . do exceede that of all theire predecessors in that cittie and equall to that of all the merchants now in Ireland'.[10]

The departure of these Catholic merchants would have been less serious had substantial Protestant planters taken their place. The Catholics in 1660 said that this had not happened: the Irish towns 'never had less trade, or manufactures, nor in mans memory have been so poor and decayed as at present; the reason being plain, for that most of those transported thither [to Ireland] on hopes to have dwelling houses without rent . . .'[11] This picture is confirmed from less hostile sources.

Some towns formerly dominated by Catholics were singled out for special projects of resettlement, notably Waterford and Galway. Oliver Cromwell hoped to colonize Waterford with New England Protestants. The potential colonists considered the idea, asking for liberty of worship and land for a free school and college, but never came.[12] In 1651 the town's military governor, Colonel Richard Lawrence, proposed colonization by 1,200 soldiers from England: a proposal that was accepted by Ireton and the English parliament. The first steps towards the realization of this scheme was an order of 1 March 1651 for Catholics to leave Waterford within three months.[13] Undoubtedly some settlers did arrive

---

[10] Bodl., Carte MSS. 33, ff. 587, 589, 591, 593, 594; 34, f. 29; Bristol Archives Office, Deposition books, 1654–7, f. 176; Cal. S.P. Ire. 1660–2, pp. 245, 251; ibid., 1669–70, pp. 317, 568–70; S. Pender, Waterford Merchants Abroad (Tralee, 1964); The Civil Survey, VI, ed. R. C. Simington, Irish MSS. Comm. (Dublin 1931–), pp. 174, 175, 182; Thurloe State Papers, i. 620; J. Mathorez, 'Notes sur les prêtres irlandais refugiés a Nantes aux xviie et xviiie siècles', Revue d'histoire de l'Église de France, iii (1912), 165–6, n. 1.

[11] Pearse St. Library, Gilbert MS. 219, pp. 263–4.

[12] Nickolls, Original letters and papers, pp. 44–5.

[13] Propositions approved of and granted by the Lord Deputy of Ireland to Colonel Richard Laurence, 26 Feb. 1650[1] (London, 1650[1]); Whitelocke, Memorials of the English Affairs, iii. 291; Steele, ii. no. 465 (Ireland).

under Lawrence's scheme.[14]   Waterford also benefited from
its close trading links with Bristol, some of whose merchants
now settled there.[15]   The religious radicalism of Waterford's
new inhabitants seriously disturbed the authorities, so much
so that after 1660 it was suggested that the Cromwellian
settlers there be treated as the Catholics had been in the
previous decade: removed from the town and planted in the
surrounding county.[16]

Protestant settlers were attracted to Waterford, but
Catholics remained. In May 1655, for example, the
Protestants petitioned against the Catholics' 'subtlety' which
enabled them to retain the greater part of Waterford's trade.
Particular grievances were the Catholics' foreign trading connections and their evasion of customs, enabling them to
undersell Protestants.[17]   Although renewed efforts were
made to enforce the earlier orders and remove all Catholics,
complaints continued after 1656 of Catholics being accepted
as apprentices and freemen.[18]   Although there clearly was
some evasion of prohibitions by the Catholics, the bulk of
Waterford's trade passed to Protestants. A change in the
town's population was discernible. In the three central wards
Protestants formed a majority in 1660. There an English
enclave had been created. The Catholics had retired outside
the city walls: in the suburbs of Waterford Catholics still
outnumbered Protestants.[19]   Comparison with the rest of
County Waterford showed what special efforts had been
concentrated on the town: in the county Protestants were a
very small minority.[20]   This tendency persisted. In 1672 the

14 C.B., Jennings transcripts, A/6, 28 May 1655.

15 Alderman Thomas Noble and Alderman John Heavens, a skinner, both came
from Bristol. Friends' Library, Swarthmore MS. i, item 26; Bristol wharfage
books, i, pp. 2, 13, 28, 42, 85, 170; ii, p. 86 *recte* 88; Bristol Archive Office,
Deposition book, 1657–61, f. 20ᵛ; *The Deposition books of Bristol, ii, 1650–54*,
ed. Nott and Ralph, pp. 55–6; 'The tradesmen's coinage of Waterford', *Journal,
Waterford and S.E. of Ireland Arch. Soc.* viii. 3.

16 Bodl., Carte MS. 32, f. 290; Clarendon state papers, 79, f. 183ᵛ. Cf. *The
Bishop of Waterford's Case* (Dublin, 1670).

17 C.B., Jennings transcripts, A/6, 28 May 1655.

18 C.B., Jennings transcripts, A/8, 10 Oct. 1655; A/16, 29 Oct. 1659; Pender,
JCHAS liv. 41–2.

19 There were 637 English and 1,647 Catholics: *A 'Census' of Ireland, c. 1659*,
ed. Pender, p. 348.

20 In the county 11,639 Irish and 712 Protestants were recorded: ibid.

Catholic bishop of Waterford commented that 'the Catholics are far more numerous than others; this particularly holds good for those living outside the cities, but in the cities the heretics are of equal number with the Catholics'.[21]

Galway was also singled out for special schemes of resettlement. Its geographical advantages were extravagantly praised: 'for situation . . . voisinage and commerce it hath with Spain, the Straits, West Indies, and other places, no towns nor port in the three nations, London excepted . . . is more considerable, nor in all probability would more encourage trade abroad or manufacture at home . . . if well improved . . .'[22] Galway had a special strategic importance, having been the the last Irish city to fall to the Cromwellians in 1652, and because of its strong continental links was regarded as the most likely landing-point for a foreign invasion. Particular care was needed. Yet such care seemed to have been precluded by the lenient terms on which Galway surrendered to Sir Charles Coote, which had included confirmation of its civic rights. These terms had eventually to be set aside by the English parliament. But until that was done, it was impossible to proceed with Galway's settlement, and the Catholic corporation survived alongside (although often in conflict with) the military government. In 1655 Oliver Cromwell's breach with Spain and the reports of a projected invasion made the security of Galway a vital concern.[23]

In 1655 Catholics were expelled from Galway's government and trade. Replacing them was difficult. In 1657 it was said of Galway's Protestant inhabitants, 'they are poor and have no trading at all'. A similar impression was gained when Henry Cromwell visited the town.[24] The contrast between its former prosperity and its sunken condition after 1655 prompted a Protestant minister to apply the Lamentations of Jeremiah to it: 'her merchants were princes among the nations, but now the city which was full of people is solitary and very desolate'.[25]

[21] P. Power, *A Bishop of the penal times* (Cork, 1932), p. 29.

[22] *Thurloe State Papers*, vi. 209.

[23] King's Inns, Prendergast MSS. i, p. 569; ii, p. 513; *Archivium Hibernicum*, vi. 186–7; Dunlop, ii. 431–2, 546–7, 548–50, 576, 620; *Thurloe State Papers*, iv. 198; v. 317, 349, 505, 545.

[24] *Diary of Thomas Burton*, ii. 110; *Thurloe State Papers*, vi. 483.

[25] R. Easthorp to H. Cromwell, Galway, 17 July 1657: Brit. Mus., Lansdowne

How were 'new princes among the nations' to be tempted to Galway? Henry Cromwell realized that substantial merchants were essential and hoped to attract some from London. Irish members of parliament vainly solicited in London for such planters.[26] In 1657 there was talk of a merchant from Rotterdam, 'of vast estate, and divers other merchants in Holland and other provinces in Germany, being Protestants and freinds to the common wealth of England', bringing their stock and ships to Galway. Although Dutch traders already had a strong interest in the port, the scheme came to nothing. Similarly approaches made to America for settlers were fruitless.[27]

Eventually a different expedient was tried, by which the repopulating of Galway was combined with settling part of the state's debt. The money spent by the towns of Gloucester and Liverpool was to be repaid, in Gloucester's case by a grant of property worth £1,518 p.a. in Galway.[28] This solution had been devised in England: in Ireland it was deplored. 'Few of them will dwell here', it was predicted, 'and few of them ar fyt to carry on trade'. Gloucester's agent, having viewed the corporation's newly acquired property, returned a gloomy report.[29] These forebodings were brushed aside, and the scheme extended to settle Liverpool's debt as well.[30] The Irish council, faced with a *fait accompli*, tried to make the best of the scheme, insisting that Liverpool's and Gloucester's representatives meet and discuss 'improving and reviving that place by manufacture there and trade abroad'.[31] Some Protestants from Gloucester and Liverpool did come to the area, but they were not of the type to

MS. 822, f. 154; cf. *The Memoirs of Ann Lady Fanshawe* (London and New York, 1907, pp. 59, 60.

[26] *Thurloe State Papers*, vi. 483; R. Easthorp to Sir H. Waller, Galway, 17 July 1657: Brit. Mus., Lansdowne MS. 822, f. 156.

[27] Lansdowne MS. 822, f. 154. These merchants wanted freedom to trade as denizens, and leases for thirty-one or forty years. It was said, they will 'bring over ten thousand pounds a man, some more, some lesse': ibid. 822, f. 156.

[28] J. Hardiman, *The history of the town and county of Galway* (Dublin, 1820), pp. 138—9, appendix vi, pp. xxxiv—xlii.

[29] Brit. Mus., Lansdowne MS. 822, f. 156; *Diary of Thomas Burton*, ii. 110.

[30] *Thurloe State Papers*, vii. 39; Dunlop, ii. 436—7, 676, 684; James Picton, *Selections from the Municipal Archives and Records of Liverpool* (Liverpool, 1883), i. 148—50.

[31] Dunlop, ii. 684.

restore Galway's trade quickly. One contemporary dismissed them as 'a few mechanick barbers and taylers', 'mean persons unfit to carry on the trade of soe great a porte'; they also acquired a reputation for Baptist sympathies.[32]

The damage from depopulation (caused as much by the plague as by expulsions)[33] had a lasting effect on Galway. The port's decline began in the Interregnum, when its trade with the continent was interrupted and its new settlers lacked the resources for extensive trading.[34]

Galway and Waterford were exceptional in being the objects of special plans: they were, however, typical in illustrating the Cromwellians' major problem — of attracting prosperous newcomers able to trade and to whom municipal government could be entrusted. There were other official schemes to procure settlers. Attempts were made to persuade New Englanders to come. A few arrived, but there was no general response.[35] Oliver Cromwell's utopian and philanthropic proposal to settle refugees from Bohemia in Ireland also failed.[36] There were hopes that more Huguenot and Dutch families would emigrate to Ireland, joining their compatriots there. In 1656 the Irish government wooed them with offers of denization.[37] Few came, and those who did were mainly artisans, useful enough once industries had been

[32]R. Easthorp to ? Sir Charles Coote, Galway, 11 June 1657: Brit. Mus., Lansdowne, MS. 822, ff. 86, 156; Cal. S.P. Ire. 1660–2, pp, 325, 423, 554.

[33]Hist. MSS. Comm., Tenth report, appendix V, p. 500. The plague was believed to have started at Galway, having been introduced there from a Spanish ship.

[34]Catholics were able to regain trading privileges after 1660, and in 1667 Galway was still Ireland's third port with 7 per cent of trade. Brit. Mus., Harleian MS. 4706, ff. 7–8; Cullen, Anglo-Irish trade, p. 14; J. Hardiman, The history of the town and county of Galway (Dublin, 1820), p. 147; Hist. MSS. Comm., Ormonde MSS., N.S. vii. 115–16; M. D. O'Sullivan, Old Galway (Cambridge, 1942), p. 348; J. G. Simms, Jacobite Ireland (London, 1969), pp. 230–1. The only substantial Cromwellian settler known to me was John Eyres, mayor in 1660–1: D. F. Gleeson, The last lords of Ormond (London, 1938), p. 250; The economic writings of Sir William Petty, ed. C. H. Hull (Cambridge, 1899), ii. 616.

[35]King's Inns, Prendergast MSS. i, pp. 308–9, 362; ii, pp. 38–9, 360; C.B., Jennings transcripts, A/10, 14 Nov. 1656; A/11, 30 July 1656, 26 Jan. 1656[7]; A/12, 5 May 1656; A/28, 24 Jan. 1654[5]; Brit. Mus., Egerton MS. 212, f. 3ᵛ.

[36]R. Vaughan, The Protectorate of Oliver Cromwell (London, 1838), ii. 447; Sheffield Univ. Lib., Hartlib MSS. 1 (16) and liii (6); Thurloe State Papers, iii. 710. In 1567 it had been proposed to settle Protestants from Flanders in Ireland; Dunlop, i. xlv, n. 2.

[37]Brit. Mus., Lansdowne MS. 1228, ff. 4ᵛ, 16; Dunlop, ii. 582–3.

established but little help in revitalizing trade.[38] Only one substantial Dutch merchant is known to have settled during the decade: Isaac van Hoegarden, at Kilrush, in County Clare. Nothing of his activities is known. However, in 1665 his son, Abraham van Hoegarden, was Laurence de Geer's agent and partner in Limerick. Any participation by de Geer, son of Louis de Geer 'the Krupp of the seventeenth century', was a hopeful sign for Ireland.[39]

Attempts to interest the four English boroughs which had adventured money for Ireland's reconquest in communal colonization failed. Some of these lands were quickly sold;[40] others let to Irish tenants. They were not settled by substantial citizens. Oliver Cromwell tried to efface the London Companies' unhappy experiences in Ulster before 1641 by granting the Irish Society a new charter. Because their Irish lands had yielded little or no profit during the war, the Companies quickly sold the new lands acquired in settlement of their debts.[41] Occasional important London merchants who had gained lands through the adventure, like William Barton,[42] William Hawkins,[43] and Alexander Bence,[44] settled or interested themselves in Ireland, but they were extremely few.

38R. Child to S. Hartlib, Lisburn, 11 March 1651[2]: Sheffield Univ. Lib., Hartlib MS. xv; Friends' Library, Swarthmore MS. 3, item 132. For the few recorded acts of denization in the 1650s: *Letters of denization and acts of naturalization for aliens in England and Ireland, 1603–1700*, ed. W. A. Shaw, Huguenot Soc. of London, xviii (Lymington, 1911), 337.

39Bodl., Carte MS. 68, f. 549; Clarendon state papers, 84, f. 9; R. Hayes, 'Some old Limerick wills' *N. Munster Antiquarian Journal*, i (1936–9), 165–6; *Cal. S.P. Ire. 1663–5*, pp. 673–4; ibid., *1669–70*, pp. 2–3, 115–16, 391; J. E. Elias, *De Vroedschap van Amsterdam, 1518–1795* (Haarlem, 1903), i. 60; *Letters of denization*, ed. Shaw, pp. 61, 86, 338; H. R. Trevor-Roper, *Religion, the Reformation and social change* (London, 1967), p. 8.

40Bottigheimer, *English money and Irish land*, pp. 157–60; Exeter City Record Office, Dartmouth borough archives, DD 62700 A; J. B. Pearson, 'Corporation of Exeter estate in Ireland', *Transactions, Devonshire Association*, xliv (1912), 431–7.

41P.R.O., Dublin, Lodge's records of the Cromwellian rolls, p. 453; Guildhall Library, London, MS. 11,588/4, Grocers' Co. orders of the court of assistants, 1640–88, pp. 322, 339, 382, 429, 450; A. H. Johnson, *The history of the worshipful Company of the Drapers of London* (London, 1922), iii. 220; Raymond Smith, *The Irish Society, 1613–1963* (London, 1966), pp. 38–9.

42For Barton, see above p. 41.

43Hawkins's lands were set out in Co. Down, yet he settled in Cork, of which county he was high sheriff in 1656. It was he who tried to interest New

Apart from Laurence de Geer's connection with Limerick through Abraham van Hoegarden, the most hopeful event in the midst of vain talk of attracting English or continental traders was the interest Martin Noel acquired in Ireland. Noel, who has been called Oliver Cromwell's right-hand financier, was involved in many of the commercial enterprises of the period. A debt of £3,697 owing to Noel was discharged by the grant of two hundred houses in Wexford.[45] Wexford was the centre of the Irish herring fisheries, and Noel soon interested himself in the trade, greatly improving it. In April 1658 Noel said he had 'transplanted much of my interest, and affaires, and relations into Ireland'.[46] Exploitation of the Irish fisheries fitted in well with Noel's other interests. Salt, essential to the herrings' preservation, could come from his Cheshire salt-pans.[47] Noel was also indirectly involved in the Irish customs farm of 1658: its treasurer was a kinsman of his, advised by Noel to participate. He retained these Irish interests after 1660, being returned to the Irish parliament in 1661 as member for the borough of Wexford and advising the government on Irish fiscal measures.[48]

Englanders in settling at Galway. Brit. Mus., Lansdowne MS. 822, f. 196; T. C. Barnard, 'Lord Broghill, Vincent Gookin and the Cork elections of 1659', *Eng. Hist. Rev.* lxxxviii (1973), 364, n. 4.

[44] Bence, son of Alexander Bence, M.P. for Aldeburgh in the Long Parliament, settled his father's considerable estate in Tipperary about 1655. Bristol Archives Office, Deposition book, 1654–7, f. 40ᵛ; Bottigheimer, *English Money and Irish Land*, pp. 176, 199; D. Brunton and D. H. Pennington, *Members of the Long Parliament* (London, 1954), pp. 76–7; Keeler, *The Long Parliament*, pp. 106–7; V. Pearl, *London and the outbreak of the Puritan Revolution* (Oxford, 1961), p. 194, n. 139.

[45] J. P. Prendergast, 'The clearing of Kilkenny, anno 1654', *Journal, Kilkenny and S.E. of Ireland Archaeological Soc.*, N.S. iii (1860–1), 336, n. 1. Noel's partner in this property was Capt. John Arthur, mayor of Wexford in 1661. Brit. Mus., Lansdowne MS. 822, ff. 162, 164; Hore, *The town of Wexford*, pp. 323–4, 325, 335, 337, 382. For Noel's importance: Wilson, *England's apprenticeship*, p. 130; M. P. Ashley, *The financial and commercial policies of the Cromwellian Protectorate* (Oxford, 1934), pp. 2, n. 1, 4, n. 1, 8, 12, 54, 65, 87, 100, 102, 135, 162.

[46] R. Cromwell to H. Cromwell, 29 July 1657; M. Noel to H. Cromwell, 24 Nov. 1657 and 9 April 1658: Brit. Mus., Lansdowne MSS. 822, ff. 162, 280; 823, f. 33.

[47] For salt being shipped from Chester to Ireland: Chester City Record Office, CB 166/ ff. 56ᵛ–57.

[48] Nat. Lib. Ire., MS. 30, item 16; P.R.O., Northern Ireland, D.1618, no. 24; P.C.C., Hyde 120; *Cal. S.P. Ire. 1660–2*, pp. 590, 591; ibid., *Dom. 1666–7*, p. 421; Hist. MSS. Comm., *Ormonde MSS.* N.S. iii. 143, 144; Ashley, op. cit., p. 102.

Noel and van Hoegarden were undoubtedly exceptional. The impression, based on dangerously scanty evidence, is of small men, often those who had failed in England, moving to Ireland in the hope of doing better. Lord Deputy Fleetwood averred that those who received Irish lands 'are poor, and not able to go over into Ireland'.[49] This prediction was inaccurate: new settlers did go to Ireland, but often they arrived in a state of such indigence that they received relief at the quayside.[50] Their condition did not augur well for the speedy replacement of the expelled Catholics by a new class of entrepreneurs. Indeed the adventurers had little impact on either the political or commercial life of Ireland. This was shown, for example, in the Irish house of commons of 1661, to which only sixteen adventurers were elected. Of these some were absentees or only temporarily in Ireland.[51]

The motives impelling immigrants to settle in Ireland in this period (as indeed in earlier ones) are a matter of conjecture, and likely to remain so in the absence of information about the economic and religious condition of these men. Thus only tentative reasons can be offered for the failure of the ambitious Cromwellian plantation. Obvious inducements to come to Ireland in the Interregnum were the cheapness of land and the reports of plenty.[52] Against those attractions had to be set uncertainties in the title to lands,

49 *Diary of Thomas Burton*, ii. 240.

50 King's Inns, Prendergast MS. i, pp. 377—8; P.R.O., Dublin, Ferguson MS. xiii, p. 68; C.B., Jennings transcripts, A/10, 14 Nov. 1656; *Cal. S.P. Dom.*, 1658—9, p. 321.

51 K. S. Bottigheimer, 'The restoration land settlement in Ireland: a structural view', *Irish Historical Studies*, xvii (1972), 7.

52 The cost of Irish land in the 1650s was estimated at five years' purchase. This compared with eight or ten years' betwen 1622 and 1630; and ten to fifteen years' in Charles II's reign. Petty put the price of an English estate at 20 years' purchase in the 1650s. R. Wood to ɔ. Hartlib, 20 Apr. 1659: Sheffield Univ. Lib., Hartlib MS. xxxiii; R. Needler to A. Pym, 9 Aug. 1655; J. Chambre to W. Parkinson, 5 June 1658; P. Curwen to R. Needler, 16 June 1658; Somerset Record Office, DD/BR/ely, 3/4 and 3/5; *Cal. S.P. Dom. 1658—9*, pp. 56—7; R. Lawrence, *Englands Great Interest in the well planting of Ireland* (Dublin, 1656), p. 33; W. Petty, *A treatise of taxes and contributions* (London, 1662), sig. A3, pp. 27—8; *Trevelyan Papers*, iii, ed W. C. and C. E. Trevelyan, Camden Soc. 105, (1872), p. 282. For earlier and later estimates: *Calendar of the Salusbury Correspondence, 1553—circa 1700*, ed. W. J. Smith, Board of Celtic Studies, Univ. of Wales, History and Law Series, xiv (Cardiff, 1954), 64, 69; Petty, loc. cit.; Simms, *Jacobite Ireland*, pp. 10—11.

heavy taxation, the reputation of religious extremism before 1655 and of rigorously enforced uniformity after 1655, and fears that the Catholics might once again overwhelm the Protestant communities. For men of substance there was no powerful incentive to settle in Ireland. For humbler men there were no longer motives like severe economic distress or land hunger in England,[53] or the wish to escape oppressive political or religious systems.

Wealthy adventurers generally did not come to Ireland, preferring either to sell their newly acquired estates or to leave their management to agents, indifferent to the nationality and religion of tenants so long as rents were paid. The other element in the Cromwellian settlement — the soldiers — bulked much larger. Usually without lands in England, already in Ireland and with their estates allocated more quickly than the adventurers', the soldiers were more likely to stay. However before the settlement of their lands officers had tended to buy up their men's debentures, thereby acquiring large estates.[54] The former officers who devoted themselves to these new estates were quickly assimilated into Irish Protestant planter society, becoming indistinguishable in outlook and interest from the older Protestant settlers.

A plantation on the scale intended by the legislation of 1642, 1652, and 1653 did not occur. It had been intended to settle 1,043 adventurers and perhaps 35,000 soldiers on Irish lands. In 1670, 500 adventurers and 7,500 soldiers had their estates confirmed. In comparison with the earlier plantations of Ulster and Munster these were still large numbers.[55] They were, however, more widely dispersed throughout Ireland than in the earlier settlements, and failed to have an influence commensurate with their numbers. The historian of American plantations in the seventeenth century, A.P. Newton, contrasted the settlement of Massachusetts with unsuccessful schemes, concluding that the Massachusetts

53 *The Agrarian History of England and Wales: IV*, ed. J. Thirsk (Cambridge, 1967), pp. 757—60, 789.

54 P.R.O., Dublin, M.3149; D. F. Gleeson, 'An unpublished Cromwellian document', *N. Munster Antiquarian Journal*, i. 78—81; J. P. Prendergast, *The Cromwellian settlement of Ireland* (London, 1865), appendix iii, pp. 211—17.

55 Bottigheimer, *English Money and Irish Land*, p. 140; Barnard, *P. and P.* lxi. 32—4.

colony succeeded because 'it was never a plantation financed in the main by adventurers remaining at home in England and bound by their English ties and interests . . . '[56] A similar explanation may well apply to the failure of the Cromwellian plantation of Ireland. Without a massive influx of new settlers from England, the Cromwellians had to rely on the existing Protestant inhabitants in Ireland or the soldiers who settled there to replace the Catholics. This dependence is apparent in the settlement of the boroughs.

iii. The Government of the Boroughs

Most Irish corporations were suspended after 1649, and had to submit to military rule until 1656. Only a few exceptional boroughs – Dublin, Belfast, Carrickfergus, and Youghal – hung on to their charters throughout the Interregnum. Even these towns found their rights curtailed, and functions assumed by the military. In Youghal, for example, the military governor tried to intrude his nominee into the posts of clerk of the market and saymaster, posts customarily in the mayor's gift.[57] The military party, which flourished under Fleetwood, wanted to bring all towns under military rule, especially because civilian magistrates opposed the army's political and religious radicalism. Dublin was the most important corporation to retain its independence: in 1654 the Baptist and military party hoped to have it suppressed, a threat which made the municipality put its support behind Henry Cromwell's more sympathetic policies.[58] Throughout Ireland there was serious friction between 'sword and mace' until 1656.[59]

Returning prosperity, Henry Cromwell's known preference for civilian government, and the growing extremism of the military, emboldened the inhabitants of several towns to petition in 1656 for their charters' restoration. Henry

56 A. P. Newton, *The Colonizing Activities of the English Puritans* (New Haven, Conn., 1914), pp. 49, 123.

57 The validity of Youghal's charter was in doubt, and the governor agreed to withdraw his nominee pending a decision: *The council book of Youghal*, ed. Caulfield, pp. 291, 292.

58 *Thurloe State Papers*, ii. 163.

59 William Wright, *A preparative to a pacification betwixt the south and north suburbs of Corke* [Cork, 1656], p.3.

Cromwell and his council, willing enough to meet these requests, lacked power to do so. The deficiency was soon made good by instructions from England. The re-establishment of the Dublin court of chancery, under whose seal charters were issued, removed the final obstacle.[60] Cork,[61] Kilkenny,[62] Waterford,[63] Limerick,[64] Wexford,[65] Ross,[66] Derry,[67] and Cashel[68] were among the towns to have their charters restored.

To whom did the Cromwellians give local power? The only Cromwellian charter to survive is that for Derry: an untypical document granted to the city of London for a new society to continue the plantation in Ulster. It also differed from municipal charters in being granted by the lord protector at Westminster.[69] It nominated twelve aldermen, twenty-four burgesses, and other officers. It is reasonable to assume that the other Cromwellian charters named the corporate body. Unfortunately we do not have the names of these nominees in other boroughs, and is is impossible to compile lists of aldermen. For most of the leading boroughs we have only the mayors' names. Examination of those names offers some clues as to the sort of men entrusted with the towns' government. Three main sorts of borough can be distinguished. First, there were those whose corporations had been dominated by Protestants before 1649, like Dublin and

[60] Dunlop, ii. 567, 578, 652; *Thurloe State Papers*, iv. 545.

[61] The Cork charter was dated at Dublin, 27 Apr. 1656: Hist. MSS. Comm., *Appendix to the first report*, p. 128. Unfortunately neither the charter, nor the other records calendared there, survive.

[62] St. Patrick's College, Maynooth, Renehan MS. ii, p. 556; *Cal. S.P. Ire. 1647—60*, pp. 561—2.

[63] Pender, *JCHAS*, liii. 153.

[64] Dunlop, ii. 631; J. Ferrar, *The history of Limerick* (Limerick, 1787), p. 281; M. Lenihan, *Limerick: its history and its antiquities* (Dublin, 1881), p. 191. An *inspeximus* of James I's charter was granted in 1657. This document has disappeared from its last recorded location. Hist. MSS. Comm., *Appendix to the first report*, p. 131; R. Herbert, 'The antiquities of corporation of Limerick', *N. Munster Antiquarian Journal*, iv (1945), 93.

[65] Nat. Lib. Ire., MS. 11,961, p. 216; Bristol Archives Office, Deposition book, 1654—7, f. 172ᵛ; Hore, *The town of Wexford*, pp. 314, 316.

[66] Brit. Mus., Egerton MS. 212, f. 3ᵛ; Hore, *Old and New Ross*, p. 343.

[67] *The bishopric of Derry and the Irish Society of London, 1602—1705, i, 1602—1670*, ed. T. W. Moody and J. G. Simms, Irish MSS. Comm. (Dublin, 1969), pp. 246 ff.

[68] Brit. Mus., Egerton MS. 212, ff. 4, 4ᵛ.

[69] *The bishopric of Derry and the Irish Society*, ed. Moody and Simms. p. 281.

Belfast. Secondly, there were the boroughs previously controlled by Catholics which passed to established Protestant
settlers after 1649. A notable example was Cork. Finally,
there were corporations dominated by Catholics before 1649
and without sufficient established Protestant inhabitants to
replace them. In these towns — like Waterford, Kilkenny,
Galway, and Limerick — new settlers (either civilians or
soldiers) took over.

Boroughs of the first two types were concentrated in the
areas of earlier Protestant plantation. Before 1649 the
Munster Protestants had controlled only the smaller, recently
created boroughs, but not Cork itself or Kinsale and Youghal.
In the 1650s the Old Protestants gained control of the older
boroughs. Favoured by Henry Cromwell, the corporations'
new rulers proved reliable supporters of his administration.[70]
In Ulster special care had to be taken to prevent Scottish
Presbyterians with royalist sympathies from governing the
boroughs. Thus between 1651 and 1653 the mayors of the
important garrison of Carrickfergus were army officers,
settled there before 1649.[71] After 1653 the mayors were
civilians resident in the town before 1649.[72] The majority of
the twelve aldermen nominated in Derry had been there
before 1641.[73] In Belfast the pattern was the same: the
Cromwellian sovereigns and burgesses had been prominent in
the town before the war.[74]

Outside Munster and Ulster conditions were different, as

[70] Kearney, *Strafford in Ireland*, pp. 239, 261; Barnard, *Eng. Hist. Rev.* lxxxviii.
355–6. For reaction to the restoration of the Cork charter: Brit. Mus.,
Lansdowne MS. 821, f. 188; 'Corks Jopean', appended to William Wheeler, *To the
honorable commissioners of assessments* [Cork, 1656], p. 4.

[71] They were Capt. Roger Lyndon, deputy recorder in 1639 and commander in
1641, and Capt. John Dalway, P.R.O., Northern Ireland, T.707, pp. 61, 70;
Bodl., Rawlinson MS. A.482, f. 4ᵛ; Dunlop, ii. 634, n. 2; *The town book of the
corporation of Belfast, 1613–1816*, ed. R. M. Young (Belfast, 1892), p. 46.

[72] S. McSkimmin, *The history and antiquities of the town of Carrickfergus*, ed.
E. J. McCrum (Belfast, 1909), p. 415.

[73] Apart from Ralph King and Charles Coote, members of Old Protestant
families of more than local importance, Simon Pitt, Henry Osborne, Luke Ashe,
and John Elwyn had earlier held office in the town. George Carey was the son of
a recorder and M.P. for Derry. T. W. Moody, *The Londonderry plantation*
(Belfast, 1937), pp. 448–50; Dunlop, ii. 633, n. 10.

[74] *The town book of the corporation of Belfast*, ed. Young, esp. pp. 11, 20, 25,
26, 37, 73–4, 76, 82, 83.

can be shown by a study of four corporations — Galway, Limerick, Waterford, and Kilkenny. Galway, as has been seen, was a special case. Because of the terms of its surrender a Catholic corporation survived until 1655. The Protestants in the town petitioned for its suppression. Even before it was suppressed in 1655 the military government had shown scant respect for the town's privileges, imprisoning the mayor and some aldermen.[75] Galway's strategic importance meant that after 1655 soldiers were chosen as mayor. Three were men of rank: Sir Charles Coote, Colonel Peter Stubbers,[76] and Lieutenant-Colonel Humphrey Hurd.[77] The three other Cromwellian mayors were humbler soldiers who had settled in Galway: two of them were probably Baptists.[78]

Limerick's position was similar to Galway's, having previously been ruled by Catholic merchants.[79] Limerick had also been a centre of determined resistance to English reconquest. Remote from the centre of English rule, it was dangerously exposed on the western seaboard. The old corporation was easily extinguished. After its restoration in 1656, the mayors were army officers, the first indeed being the town's military governor, Henry Ingoldsby.[80]

[75]*Archivium Hibernicum*, vii. 22; Hist. MSS. Comm., *Tenth report*, appendix v, p. 501; Hardiman, *The history of Galway*, p. 135 n.

[76]In 1660 it was proposed that Stubbers be excepted from the act of indemnity: an indication of extreme views. Hist. MSS. Comm., *Tenth report*, appendix v, p. 501; Firth and Davies, ii. 660—3.

[77]Hurd was conservative in outlook and supported Charles II's restoration. During the Interregnum he migrated to Kilkenny, where his land had been allocated, and became an alderman there. Kilkenny Municipal Archives, White book, f. 18; Hist. MSS. Comm., *Ormonde MSS.* ii. 245; *The Memoirs of Edmund Ludlow*, ed. Firth, ii. 193; Prendergast, *The Cromwellian settlement of Ireland*, pp. 215—17; *A 'Census' of Ireland, c. 1659*, ed. Pender, pp. 413, 620, 640.

[78]Paul Dod and John Matthews, for whom see: Society of Antiquaries, London, MS. 138, f. 238; Bodl., Clarendon state papers, 73, f. 264; Martin J. Blake, *Blake family records, 1600—1700* (London, 1905), p. 77. The third was Gabriel King, possibly a member of the Old Protestant family of Abbey Boyle, Roscommon.

[79]Jordan Roche, mayor of Limerick in 1639, mentioned real estate worth £2,000, as well as considerable personal estate: J. G. Barry, 'The Cromwellian settlement of the County of Limerick', *Journal, Limerick Field Society*, i, part iv (1897—1900), 25. For Limerick's continental trade: E. P. Shirley, 'Extracts from the journal of Thomas Dineley', *Journal, Kilkenny and S.E. of Ireland Archaeological Soc.*, N.S. v (1864—7), 439—40.

[80]Ferrar, *The history of Limerick*, p. 281. Limerick's other mayors were Capt. Ralph Wilson, William Yarwell, commissary of stores there, and Capt. William Hartwell.

Waterford and Kilkenny resembled Galway and Limerick in that they had had few Protestant settlers before 1649; they differed because Protestants did settle in Waterford and Kilkenny in considerable numbers after 1649. Waterford's mayors, although they had served in the Protestant army, were following civilian occupations by 1656.[81] Kilkenny's mayors had also seen military service, but some had earlier connections with Ireland, and by 1656 were preoccupied with settling their new estates.[82] In contrast with the military governor of Kilkenny, Daniel Axtell, who was a Baptist, the town's mayors seem to have been political moderates.[83]

[81] The mayors were George Cawdron, Andrew Richards, Thomas Watts, and John Houghton. Cawdron, a Baptist, was receiver of revenue in the town, and harried Lord Cork. In 1661 he was imprisoned for debt. He ceased to be a member of the corporation after 1660. Brit. Mus., Additional MS. 19,833, f. 8ᵛ; Nat. Lib. Ire. MS. 2701, pp. 62–3; Chatsworth, Lismore MS. 29, Cork's diary, 2 Nov. 1656; Friends' Library, Swarthmore MS. i, item 26; *Cal. S.P. Ire. 1660–2*, pp. 304, 325; J. Ivimey, *A history of the English baptists* (London, 1811), i. 240. Richards was a merchant, who supported the Restoration, was maligned as a traitor in 1662, and again served as mayor in 1667: Devon County Record Office, 1262 M/Irish deeds, indenture of 3 June 1681; *Cal. S.P. Ire. 1647–60*, p. 601; ibid., *1660–2*, p. 495; *A 'Census' of Ireland, c. 1659*, p. 349; *Council books of the corporation of Waterford, 1662–1700*, ed. S. Pender, Irish MSS. Comm. (Dublin, 1964), pp. 13, 23, 77, 133, 196–200, 201–3, 282; Houghton was described as a gentleman in 1660. He too supported the Restoration: in 1669 he was removed from the aldermanic bench after an absence of three years. *Council books*, ed. Pender, pp. 13, 60–1; *Cal. S.P. Ire. 1647–60*, pp. 707–8. Watts was removed from office as an alderman and a justice of the peace in 1662 for alleged sedition: in 1669 he was reinstated. *Council books*, ed. Pender, pp. 6–7, 9, 61, 87, 92, 125, 262. See also J. O'Hart, *Irish landed gentry when Cromwell came to Ireland* (Dublin, 1883), pp. 378, 392, 403, 410.

[82] The mayors were Capt. Thomas Evans, Major Thomas Adams, Capt. John Jeonar, and Capt. Abel Warren. Warren was the son of a dean of Ossory. Thomas Warren, *A history and genealogy of the Warren family* (London, 1902), pp. 274–7.

[83] Jeonar, a cook in Charles I's household before joining the army, helped seize Dublin castle in 1659. G. D. Burtchaell, *Genealogical memoirs of the members of parliament for the county and city of Kilkenny* (Dublin and London, 1888), p. 48; Hist. MSS. Comm., *Ormonde MSS.*, N.S. iii. 422; *The Memoirs of Edmund Ludlow*, ii. 185. Evans represented the town in the 1661 parliament. Burtchaell, op. cit., pp. 51–2; F. O'Donoghue, 'Parliament in Ireland under Charles II', M.A. thesis, University College, Dublin, 1970, pp. 150, 159, no. 2. Warren had a narrow escape from the Baptists, after which he became a religious and political moderate. Dr. Williams' Library, Baxter letters, 3, f. 234; Brit. Mus., Lansdowne MS. 823, f. 118; J. Bridges, *A perfect narrative* (London, 1660); *The Memoirs of Edmund Ludlow*, ed. Firth, ii. 202, 471. Adams may have been more radical: the Baptists, Axtell and Lawrence, were overseers of his will. C.B., Waterford Prerogative wills, 1582–1675, p. 81.

This bald analysis reveals variations between the corporations dominated by Old Protestants, by new settlers, and those kept under a form of military government even when their charters had been restored. These variations were less important than the one common factor: that the government of all Irish boroughs had become a Protestant monopoly. This was something new, and of lasting importance. In 1660 it was acknowledged that 'the corporate towns are now mostly inhabited by English and Protestants and governed by them, whereas before the war, it was difficult for a Protestant to get office in any town'.[84] Exactly how this domination — the root of the Protestants' political ascendancy — had occurred demands closer attention.

I have assumed that the Cromwellian charters named the corporate body; it is also reasonable to assume that these nominees were Protestants. We do not know whether tests to exclude Catholics and malignants were written into the charters. What little evidence survives suggests that entry into municipal office was controlled by other methods. In December 1650 the parliamentary commissioners in Ireland were authorized to introduce the English ordinance for imposing oaths on mayors.[85] Subscription to the Engagement of loyalty to the new English Commonwealth was certainly demanded from the mayors of Dublin and Drogheda. Steps were taken to extend the Engagement to freemen in other Irish corporations: such a test was already required in English boroughs.[86] Later in the decade the mayor of Dublin was sworn in the court of exchequer; certificates for the swearing of provincial mayors were returned to chancery.[87] In England corporations failed to impose the Engagement on its officers as required; possibly there was similar non-compliance in Ireland.[88] After 1653

[84] *Cal. S.P. Ire. 1660–2*, p. 174. Cf. *Letters written by . . . Earl of Essex . . . in the year 1675* (London, 1770), pp. 185–6.

[85] Firth and Rait, ii. 495.

[86] Nat. Lib. Ire., MS. 11,959, p. 15; Brit. Mus., Egerton MS. 1779, f. 39ᵛ. The oaths are printed in Firth and Rait, ii. 2, 242–3.

[87] P.R.O., Dublin, Ferguson MS. xiii, p. 51; *The council book of Drogheda,* ed. Gogarty, pp. 20, 35–6.

[88] A. M. Johnson, 'Politics in Chester during the Civil Wars and Interregnum, 1640–62', in *Crisis and order in English towns 1500–1700,* ed. P. Clark and P. Slack (London, 1972), pp. 221, 222–3.

the Engagement lapsed and was replaced by a less demanding oath of loyalty to Oliver Cromwell as lord protector.[89] Probably (but not certainly) it was enforced in Ireland. It was in any case a test of political and not religious reliability.

Catholics and rebels were specifically excluded from national political life by the constitutional settlements of the Interregnum. Theoretically the proclamations expelling Catholics from the walled towns and the later oath of abjuration prevented any papists remaining in the boroughs to claim civic rights. Yet many Catholics did stay, and some retained their rights. Specific by-laws had to be made to remove them. Thus, in January 1653, the Dublin corporation ruled that no Catholic should be admitted as a freeman or apprentice.[90] Elsewhere corporations acted more slowly and equivocally. It was not until January 1657 that Drogheda corporation decreed that no papist in future should become a freeman, adding that 'every respective inhabitant which is papist and now resident within this towne shall by this present act be disenfranchized.'[91] Although removed from the town's freedom, there was no attempt to expel Catholics altogether. The borough of Trim, in Meath, waited until September 1659 before disenfranchizing those who could not speak English, and whose wives and children did not attend Protestant worship.[92] In Waterford after 1656 there were still complaints of Catholics becoming freemen: the corporation there also considered whether or not Catholics should be admitted to trade.[93]

If the Catholics' local position rested on by-laws, obviously their treatment would be influenced by the temper of particular corporations. Government policy put the Irish boroughs in Protestant hands during the 1650s. These Protestants, although they tolerated the presence of Catholics within the towns, would resist any attempt by the Catholics to regain power. Such efforts occurred after 1660, especially

89 Firth and Rait, ii. 830–1; D. Underdown, 'Settlement in the Counties, 1653–1658', and A. H. Woolrych, 'Last quests for settlement, 1657–1660', in *The Interregnum*, ed. G. E. Aylmer (London, 1972), pp. 172, 186–7.

90 *Cal. Anc. Recs. Dublin*, ed. Gilbert, iv. 38.

91 *The council book of Drogheda*, ed. Gogarty, pp. 42–3.

92 Nat. Lib. Ire., MS. 2992, f. 1.

93 Pender, *JCHAS* lv. 43; lii. 174.

when Charles II's first pronouncements seemed sympathetic towards the Catholics.[94] Seriously alarmed, the Protestants organized themselves to defend their recently won privileges.[95] In August 1661 Charles II reassured the Protestants by amplifying his original, alarming statement: his intention was to restore Catholics to the towns' trade, not to the magistracy or the corporations' government.[96] Execution of the king's wishes still rested on the boroughs' co-operation: Dublin corporation kept out Catholics by by-laws imposing religious tests; other boroughs refused to readmit Catholics to trade.[97] Gradually it became clear that the Catholics could be reinstated only if the corporations were taken from Protestant control. This James II started to do. His incautious reversal of the recently established Protestant domination aroused fierce indignation which hastened his overthrow.[98]

One argument used by Protestants after 1660 for caution in readmitting the Catholics was its effect on the composition of the Irish house of commons.[99] Government policy

---

[94]Gale, *An inquiry into the ancient corporate system,* p. cxxx; *Cal. S.P. Ire. 1660–2,* pp. 356–7.

[95]Lord Anglesey to Orrery, 24 Sept. 1661: Nat. Lib. Ire., MS. 13,217, (2); Brit. Mus., Egerton MS. 2537, ff. 345–5ᵛ; Egerton MS. 2618, ff. 98, 100; Bodl., Clarendon state papers, 74, f. 460ᵛ; Carte MS. 59, ff. 491–6; Gale, *An inquiry,* pp. cxxxii–cxxxvi; Hist. MSS. Comm., *De L'Isle and Dudley MSS.* vi. 510–11, 512–13.

[96]Sir E. Nicholas to the lords justices of Ireland, 13 Aug. 1661: Gale, *An Inquiry,* pp. cxli–cxlii; *Cal. S.P. Ire. 1660–2,* p. 396.

[97]Bodl., Clarendon state papers, 89, f. 26; *Cal. Anc. Recs. Dublin,* ed. Gilbert, v. 198, 528; P. D. Vigors, 'Extracts from the books of the old corporation of Ross', *JRSAI* 5th Ser. ii. 173. The 'New Rules' of 1672 were an attempt to solve this problem. Office holders in the boroughs were required to take the oaths of allegiance and supremacy (from which they could be dispensed by the lord lieutenant and the Irish privy council). Freemen, however, could be admitted without taking the oaths. Gale, *An inquiry,* p. cxlix; Victoria and Albert Museum, Forster collection, Orrery letters, f. 36ᵛ; *Letters written by . . . Earl of Essex,* pp. 187–8; 'Galway Corporation Book B', ed. M. J. Blake, *Journal, Galway Archaeological and Hist. Soc.* v (1907–10), 72–80; H. F. Hore, *Journal, Kilkenny and S.E. of Ireland and Arch. Soc.,* N.S. iii.452–3; iv. 88.

[98]James II's *quo warranto* proceedings against Irish boroughs are listed in Nat. Lib. Ire., MS. 8644 (5); and Bodl., Clarendon state papers, 89, f. 100. In the eighteenth century Catholics were debarred from the boroughs by by-laws, not by statute: M. Wall, 'The rise of a Catholic middle class in eighteenth century Ireland', *Irish Historical Studies,* xi (1958), 92, n. 3; J. G. Simms, 'Irish Catholics and the parliamentary franchise, 1692–1728', ibid., xii (1960–1), 28–37.

[99]Gale, *An inquiry,* p. cxxxv; *Letters written by Essex,* pp. 188–9; *State letters of Orrery,* pp. 48, 59.

towards the corporations, creating new ones or remodelling the old, had aimed at reducing Catholic power in the Irish parliament. This had been the motive behind James I's lavish incorporations of Irish boroughs.[100]   In England during the Interregnum new charters were issued as a means of exercising political control.[101]   But in Ireland in the 1650s this motive was less apparent, largely because of the dramatic decline in the Irish boroughs' political importance. The *de facto* union of England and Ireland had reduced Ireland's parliamentary representation to thirty: only seven of these members sat for boroughs.[102]   Furthermore, the electors' qualifications were established by legislation, so that even if Catholics crept into the freedom of towns, they were debarred from voting by other restrictions.

The restoration of the Dublin parliament in 1661 revived the political importance of the boroughs. The Protestants were alarmed lest Catholics, emboldened by the promise of royal favour, were returned. In the event these fears proved groundless. Protestants still dominated the corporations in 1661, and only one Catholic was elected to the commons.[103] Catholics were not legally debarred from membership of the lower house. However, because of the survival of the Cromwellian and Protestant corporations, Catholics were denied the local foothold which was the necessary basis of national dominance. Protestants, although entrenched in power, wanted to guard against Charles II's possible generosity which would flood the boroughs with Catholic freemen and in turn affect the house of commons.[104]   They asked

100 Kearney, *Strafford in Ireland*, pp. 223–5; House of Commons papers, 1835, xxviii, First report into the municipal corporations in Ireland, pp. 10–11.

101 B. L. K. Henderson, 'The Commonwealth Charters', *Trans. Royal Hist. Soc.*, 3rd Ser., vi (1912), 129–62; G. D. Ramsay, 'Industrial *laisser-faire* and the policy of Cromwell', *Econ. Hist. Rev.* xvi (1946).

102 Firth and Rait, ii. 932–3.

103 This was Geoffrey Browne at Tuam. A new election was ordered at which Browne was defeated, so no Catholic sat in the 1661 house of commons. Orrery suggested that Catholics had been candidates at many places. Catholics were not debarred from the house of lords: the Protestant majority there was dependent on the bishops, a powerful reason for upholding episcopacy. Bodl., Clarendon state papers, 74, ff. 385–5ᵛ; *Cal. S.P. Ire. 1660–2*, p. 355; O'Donoghue, 'Parliament under Charles II', p. 42.

104 *Cal. S.P. Ire. 1660–2*, pp. 224, 445, 679; ibid., *1663–5*. pp. 65, 85, 91, 115, 232; *Letters written by Essex*, pp. 188–9; *State letters of Orrery*, p. 19.

that the oath of supremacy be imposed on all members of the commons. In June 1642, in the wake of the rebellion, the oath had been applied in the Irish commons; and a bill was prepared to put this action on a secure legal foundation. The bill had never received the royal assent.[105]   Charles II wanted no such test applied to the Irish members of parliament; Ormonde, the lord lieutenant, was placed in an awkward position, his obedience to the king conflicting with the need to conciliate the worried Protestants. By stalling he was able to uphold the king's tolerant policy, and the oath was not imposed.[106]

The Protestant monopoly in the Irish house of commons was the most spectacular sign of the great advance in Protestant power which had occurred between 1649 and 1661.[107]   Yet it was more important as a symbol than for its direct consequences. After 1661, the Irish parliament was little better than a cipher, and met infrequently. A more constant and acute grievance was the cause of the Catholics' exclusion from the commons: the Protestants' continuing hold over the boroughs' government. This proved to be one of the most enduring Cromwellian contributions to Ireland.

iv. The Boroughs and Commercial and Social Policy

Many of the radicals who came to power in England in 1649 supported greater freedom of trade and an end to the monopolies of the great chartered companies. Expectations

---

[105]*C.J. Ire.* appendix to vol. i, pp. 31, 34—5, 40; *An ordinance of the commons assembled in Parliament, for a bill ordered to be sent to the Kings Maiesty to be transmitted under the Great Seale of England. Concerning the qualifications of the Knights, Citizens and Burgesses who shall be admitted to sit in Parliament for the Kingdome of Ireland* (Dublin, 1647).

[106]For a different view: M. MacCurtain, *Tudor and Stuart Ireland* (Dublin, 1972), p. 163.

[107]The General Convention of 1660, in which most of the Irish boroughs were represented, first showed the new Protestant ascendancy. Probably the only Catholic member was Nicholas Everard, representing Fethard, Co. Tipperary, a borough which had survived in Catholic hands (through the terms of its surrender in 1649) until suppressed in 1659. Abbott, *Cromwell*, ii. 209—10; *An Account of the chief occurrences . . . 12—19 March* [1660], p. 36; Dunlop, ii. 713; Thomas Laffan, 'Fethard, County Tipperary; its charters and corporation records, with some notice of the Fethard Everards', *JRSAI* xxxvi (1906); F. X. Martin, 'The Tirry Documents in the Archives de France, Paris', *Archivium Hibernicum*, xx (1957), 89, n. 1.

of major changes were disappointed: new men were installed in the old, privileged positions.[108] In Ireland official policy after 1649 strengthened municipal and guild control, and did nothing to increase commercial liberty. Heavily dependent on local agents to execute its policies, the Dublin administration secured co-operation by confirming the powers of these agents.

The decay of trade and scarcity of tradesmen during the war led to temporary reforms. In 1651 the freedom of Dublin was offered to Protestant tradesmen and handicraftsmen for £1 if they settled there before September 1652.[109] In Novermber 1651 there was an attempt to curtail the power of the Dublin municipal and mercantile hierarchy. The mayor, aldermen, and officers of the guilds were ordered to produce their charters, to stop restraining or imprisoning freemen for lawfully exercising their trades. At the same time the parliamentary commissioners fixed maximum fines for freedom.[110] Faced with a severe trade depression, the leading Dublin merchants had tried to exploit their position and engross what little trade there was. The acute shortage of skilled men and commodities forced a relaxation of traditional regulations until 1656.[111] By April 1656 there had been sufficient recovery in Dublin for the leading guild, the Merchant Guild, to restore its old entry fine of £40.[112] Returning prosperity was obviously a main cause of this reviving power: it may also have owed something to the greater sympathy of Henry Cromwell's conservative regime, anxious to conciliate men of substance.

108 For policy in England: J. P. Cooper, 'Social and economic policies under the Commonwealth', in *The Interregnum*, ed. Aylmer, esp. pp. 124, 130, 131–2, 137–8; R. Brenner, 'The civil war politics of London's merchant community', *P. and P.* lviii (1973); M. James, *Social problems and policy during the Puritan Revolution* (London, 1930); Ramsay, 'Industrial *laisser-faire* and the policy of Cromwell', *Econ. Hist. Rev.* xvi.

109 Steele, ii, no. 480 (Ireland).

110 Brit. Mus., Egerton MS. 1762, ff. 12–13.

111 In 1646 and 1648 the Guild had been unable to stop non-freemen trading. In 1652 there was an attempt to distribute the small trade more equitably by reviving the regulation that each member should keep only one shop or tavern: Pearse St. Library, Gilbert MS. 78, pp. 118, 122, 127; *Cal. Anc. Recs. Dublin*, ed. Gilbert, iii. 440–1.

112 By 1656 it had at least seventy-seven members: Pearse St. Library, Gilbert MS. 78, pp. 131, 132.

In Dublin and the other boroughs the government was content to leave control of economic life to the merchant staple, which was dominated by the mayor and aldermen. This policy seems to have worked best in Dublin, where there was a recovery after 1655: other corporations were slower to revive and used their privileges to keep the small trade in the hands of the inner circle. There were frequent complaints about the breakdown of regulations, the intrusion of strangers and papists, and insistence that the rules be obeyed.[113] The government supported the guild system, which functioned in the leading Irish towns during the Interregnum. In Dublin, for example, there were sixteen guilds; at least ten in Drogheda and Cork; and four in Kilkenny.[114] Their authority was not always effective. In particular, the withdrawal of papists outside the town walls into the suburbs often made it difficult to control their activities.[115] At Kilkenny and Carrickfergus there are indications that the officers of the guilds and corporations abused their power to engross the reduced trade at the expense of the commonalty. At Waterford, where 220 freemen had been admitted when the corporation was restored in 1656, there were complaints that too many had been enfranchised.[116] Evidently there was a conflict between the wish to attract new traders and the small volume of trade at Waterford. To overcome it the Waterford corporation proposed setting up a joint stock, with the mayor and sheriffs distributing the goods available for sale amongst the free-

113 P.R.O., Northern Ireland, T.707, p. 76; Brit. Mus., Egerton MS. 212, f. 31; *Cal. Anc. Recs. Dublin*, ed. Gilbert, iv. 70, 108; *The council book of the corporation of Youghal*, ed. Caulfield, p. 295; 'Manuscripts of the old corporation of Kinsale', *Analecta Hibernica*, xv (Dublin 1944), pp. 174, 175; *The council book of Drogheda*, ed. Gogarty, pp. 42, 44, 46, 51; Pender, *JCHAS* liii. 109; liv. 26; lv. 33, 36—7.

114 *Cal. Anc. Recs. Dublin*, ed. Gilbert, iv. 183—4; Cork University Library, Caulfield MSS., Cork D'Oyer Hundred Court Book, 1656—1729, pp. 6, 9; E. M. Fahy, 'The Cork Goldsmiths Company, 1657', *JCHAS* lvii (1953); *The council book of Drogheda*, ed. Gogarty, pp. 39, 52; Kilkenny Municipal Archives, White Book, f. 11.

115 Ibid., f. 6; Brit. Mus., Egerton MS. 212, f. 35^v; C.B., Jennings transcripts, A/6, 11 May 1655, 16 June 1655; A/13, 26 Sept. 1658; King's Inns, Prendergast MS. ii, pp. 402, 465; Nat. Lib. Ire., MS. 11,961. p. 392.

116 P.R.O., Northern Ireland, T.707, p. 76; Kilkenny Municipal Archives, White book, f. 14; Pender, *JCHAS* lv. 37, 40.

men.[117]   In general it seems that the insistence on maintaining customary privileges was a symptom of the depressed state of trade.

In return for the confirmation of their powers, the corporations and guilds were expected to enforce the Dublin government's orders. Not only were by-laws made to exclude Catholics from freedom and efforts made to expel them, the corporations were active in trying to keep the towns clean, to prevent a recurrence of the plague.[118]   The apprenticeship laws were enforced.[119]   Attempts were also made to control prices, weights, and measures.[120]   Another serious problem with which the boroughs had to deal was the poor, much increased in numbers by the war.

In May 1653 the Dublin administration evoked a grim picture: of 'great multitudes of poor swarming in all parts of this nation', some 'feeding on carrion and weeds', and of orphans exposed to wolves and birds of prey.[121]   The government maintained the conventional distinction between idle vagrants, who were to be set to work in houses of correction, 'until they be broken from their idle course of life, and made willing to betake themselves to some honest calling'; and the impotent poor. To relieve the latter the government invited subscriptions throughout Ireland.[122] Resources were inadequate to cope with this enormous problem. One solution, eagerly adopted, was to round up vagrants and ship them overseas, especially to the West Indies.[123]   However this did not solve the problem: bands of

117 Ibid. lii. 172; liv. 26.
118 Pender, *JCHAS* lii. 162, 163; liii. 111; liv. 29; lv. 41−2; Kilkenny Municipal Archives, White book, f. 16ʳ−ᵛ; *Analecta Hibernica*, xv. 172−3.
119 Pearse St. Library, Gilbert MS. 78, p. 128; P.R.O., Northern Ireland, T.707, pp. 71, 72; Pender, *JCHAS* lii. 150−3; lv. 41−2.
120 Nat. Lib. Ire., MS. 11,961, p. 196; Brit. Mus., Egerton MSS. 212, f. 4ᵛ; 1762, f. 170; *The council book of Youghal*, ed. Caulfield, p. 289; *Analecta Hibernica*, xv. 175.
121 Dunlop, ii. 340−1.
122 Ibid.; Steele, ii, nos. 475, 478, 515 (Ireland).
123 Dunlop, ii. 341, 354−5, 384, 399−401, 421−2, 430−2, 434, 444, 655; Chatsworth, Lismore MS. 29, Cork's diary, 18 Jan. 1657[8]; J. W. Blake, 'Transportation from Ireland to America, 1653−60', *Irish Historical Studies*, iii (1943); Steele, ii, no. 520 (Ireland).

vagrants continued to roam the coutryside, threatening security. The government was particularly alarmed by the number
of poor in Dublin, and made determined efforts to remove
them.[124]

Before 1649 the state's care had been supplemented by
corporations and private benefactors: this continued in the
1650s. On the one hand the state provided money: in 1649
half the profits from the sequestrated lands of the Church of
Ireland were reserved for the relief of widows, orphans, and
maimed soldiers.[125]   Commissioners for almshouses and hospitals were appointed to administer the money.[126]   On the
other hand much was left to the boroughs and parishes. In
1652 Dublin corporation authorized a monthly levy of £30
for poor relief. The corporation also maintainted an alms-
house. However the hospital in the city, for wounded
soldiers, was financed by the state.[127]   Other boroughs
supported hospitals and almshouses. In the Cork precinct a
surgeon's services were provided for the poor free by the
state.[128]   A levy of £200 was authorized to establish a
workhouse at Abbey Boyle, County Roscommon; and the
state agreed to provide an additional £100. At Bandon, in
County Cork, £100 was used to buy stocks for the poor to
work.[129]   Efforts were made to relieve the poor and the state
accepted some responsibility. Nevertheless relief tended to be
piecemeal and was vitiated either by lack of money or by a
hostile attitude towards the Catholic poor, so that the limited
resources were concentrated on the Protestants. It is true that
the situation faced by the Cromwellians had been much
aggravated by war, plague, and famine, but the Cromwellians
had no new solutions.

124Brit. Mus., Egerton MS. 212, f. 5ᵛ; Cal. Anc. Recs. Dublin, ed. Gilbert, iv.
156; Dunlop, ii. 707.
125Steele, ii, no. 477 (Ireland).
126P.R.O., Dublin, Ferguson MS. xiii, p. 135.
127Cal. Anc. Recs. Dublin, ed. Gilbert, iv. 19, 29, 60, 98, 150, 166; and see
below, pp. 214, 241–2.
128Nat. Lib. Ire., MS. 11,961, pp. 111–12, 127; The council book of
Drogheda, ed. Gogarty, pp. 29, 40, 58; Hore, The town of Wexford, p. 314; Hore,
Old and New Ross, p. 340; Pender, JCHAS lii. 163.
129C.B., Jennings transcripts A/11, 11 July 1655; Brit. Mus., Egerton MS.
1762, f. 174.

In its instructions from England the Dublin government had been enjoined to enforce the English ordinances for the reformation of manners. In turn the government asked the judges on assize, the justices at the quarter-sessions, and the magistrates in the boroughs to apply these laws. Thus in January 1656 the justices of the peace at Derry were to present those who profaned the sabbath, cursers, common swearers, drunkards, adulterers, fornicators, keepers of gaming houses, gamesters, disorderly alehouse-keepers, those who ploughed by the tail, burnt corn in the straw, or pulled wool off live sheep, idle wanderers, and cosherers. Efforts were also made to suppress superstitious holidays and to ban maypoles.[130] Many, but not all of these measures were Cromwellian innovations, introduced from England. But even before 1649 there had been laws aimed at reforming the manners of the Irish, eradicating customs like coshering, the wearing of Irish dress, or the use of the Irish language. Not only Protestants, but also some Catholic clergy had agreed on the need to reform Irish manners.[131] These earlier efforts were intensified after 1649. The boroughs tried to enforce the laws, they kept houses of correction, whipping-posts, ducking-stools, and stocks.[132] Yet there is no sign that this policy was any more successful than it had been in the past. The punitive policy had to be accompanied by positive measures to create enthusiasm for English ways, and such efforts were generally lacking. Also corporations, with numerous calls on their limited resources, could prove lethargic and half-hearted agents of the government.

---

130 *Anthologia Hibernica*, i. 414; Dunlop, ii. 496–7, 598; King's Inns, Prendergast MS. i, pp. 192, 209; Firth and Rait, ii. 1298–9; Hist. MSS. Comm., *Portland MSS.* i. 503; Steele, ii, no. 589 (Ireland).

131 J. Bossy, 'The Counter-Reformation and the people of Catholic Ireland, 1596–1641', in *Historical Studies: VIII*, ed. T. D. Williams (Dublin, 1971), pp. 164, 166.

132 King's Inns, Prendergast MS. ii, 467; Kilkenny Municipal Archives, White book, f. 6; Nat. Lib. Ire., MSS. 2992, p. 66; 11,959, p. 61; 11,961, pp. 115–16; Pearse St. Library, Gilbert MS. 78, p. 128; *The council book of Youghal*, ed. Caulfield, pp. 294, 299; *The council book of Drogheda*, ed. Gogarty, p. 50; *Cal. Anc. Recs. Dublin*, iv. 119; Pender, *JCHAS*, lv. 43.

v. Dublin

Cromwellian policy aimed at establishing a Protestant monopoly in Dublin. The effects of this policy were rather different in the capital, owing to its special character. Dublin, and especially its ruling group, benefited as no other Irish town from the official policy of favouring Protestants. I shall suggest that Dublin's prosperity and pre-eminence after 1660 can be traced to the 1650s.

It is difficult to establish Dublin's position before 1649. The city's history in the seventeenth century has yet to be written.[133] We know that in the first half of the century Dublin, as the capital, was the centre of administration; the seat of the law courts, of an inn of court, of a university, and of two cathedral chapters. It was also an important port. The size of Dublin is impossible to estimate with any exactitude. One statement in 1647 spoke of a male and female population over fifteen of 24,000, indicating a total population of 40,000.[134] An unreliable estimate in 1660, almost certainly too low, set the total at 17,000.[135] After 1660 there was a rapid growth, so that by 1680 Dublin's population was perhaps 60,000.[136] As well as population increase, there was considerable physical expansion after 1660, and a growth in Dublin's proportionate share of Irish trade.[137] Not only was Dublin by far the largest city in Ireland, it was indisputably the second city of the British Isles: by 1700 its rivals, Norwich and Bristol, numbered 30,000 and 20,000 respectively.[138]

---

[133] J. T. Gilbert, *History of the City of Dublin*, 3 vols. (Dublin, 1861), is almost exclusively topographical.

[134] Hist. MSS. Comm., *Ormonde MSS.*, N.S. i. 113; cf. W. G. Hoskins, *Local history in England* (London, 1959), p.145.

[135] Pender, *A 'Census' of Ireland, c. 1659*, pp. 363–73; R. A. Butlin, 'The population of Dublin in the late seventeenth century', *Irish Geography*, v (1965), 57; J. G. Simms, 'Dublin in 1685', *Irish Historical Studies*, xiv (1965), 212

[136] Butlin, *Irish Geography*, p. 57.

[137] On growth after 1660: Brit. Mus., Harleian MS. 4706, ff. 7–8; P.R.O., SP. 63/351, 319–20; Butlin, *Irish Geography*, v. 51–9; N. T. Burke, 'An early modern Dublin suburb: the estate of Francis Aungier, earl of Longford', ibid. vi (1972); M. Craig, *Dublin, 1660–1800*, 2nd ed. (Dublin, 1969); Simms, *Irish Historical Studies*, xiv. 212 ff.

[138] In 1676 Norwich's population was estimated at 20,000 and at 30,000 by 1700: P. Corfield, 'A provincial capital in the late seventeenth century: the case of Norwich', in *Crisis and Order in English towns*, ed. Clark and Slack, pp. 263–7;

Contemporaries suggested that there had been a meteoric rise of Dublin after 1660, connected with the benign political atmosphere.[139] This impression of dramatic change comes partly from ignorance about the city's condition before 1660. There were, I believe, changes which included an accelerated pace of growth, but they started in the 1650s and not with Charles II's restoration.

During the rebellion Dublin enjoyed the double-edged advantage of being the only major town to escape capture by the Catholics. It became a refuge for Protestants from all parts of Ireland; but it had also to bear a disproportionate share of financing the war. In return for lending money, merchants sometimes profited from government and army contracts. When the parliamentarians took over Dublin in 1647, some royalists departed. Much more serious in reducing the population was the plague which broke out in 1650. At its height Petty estimated that 1,300 were dying each week.[140] Undoubtedly this was the main cause of the city's sharp drop in population.

In 1651 the city's common council convincingly described Dublin as 'exceedinglie depopulated, at least one halfe of the number of houses that were therein pulled downe and destroyed'. At the same time it was said that 'the number of

W. E. Minchinton, 'Bristol: the metropolis of the west in the eighteenth century', *Trans. Royal Hist. Soc.,* 5th Ser. iv (1954), 75. London's population in 1660 has been put at 400,000: E. A. Wrigley, 'A simple model of London's importance in changing English society and economy, 1650–1750', *P. and P.* xxxvii (1967). In 1683 St. George Ashe, having visited Amsterdam, estimated that Dublin was one-tenth larger in area, and smaller only than London and Paris. However Amsterdam's population at the time, 185,000, was much larger: 'Sir Thomas Molyneux, Bart., M.D., F.R.S.', *Dublin University Review,* xviii (1841), 472; E. Hélin, *La Démographie de Liège aux XVIIe et XVIIIe siècles,* Académie Royale de Belgique, classe de lettres, memoires, collection in-8° 2nd Ser., lvi, fasc. 4 (Brussels, 1963), 64.

139In 1672 Lord Essex thought that Dublin had increased by half; in 1691 Dr. Charles Willoughby put the increase since 1660 at a third: *Cal. S.P. Dom., May–Sept. 1672,* pp. 153–4; K. Dewhurst, 'The genesis of state medicine in Ireland', *The Irish Journal of medical science,* 6th Ser., no. 368 (Aug. 1956), pp. 370, 372.

140Petty, *Political Anatomy,* p. 19. Whitelocke repeated details from the newlsetters that in the week ending 24 Aug. 1650, 797 died of plague in Dublin; and 200 died in the week ending 27 June 1650: *Memorials of the English Affairs,* iii. 212, 231–2. The prosperous were able to leave Dublin to escape the contagion: *Cal. Anc. Recs. Dublin,* ed. Gilbert, iv. 10.

tradesmen [and] manufacturers are growen verie fewe, and of some callings there are scarce any left.'[141] Repopulation and the revival of trade were urgent needs. The traditional guild restrictions had to be relaxed to admit non-freemen, first in 1646 and again in 1650.[142] As we have seen, at the corporation's request the parliamentary commissioners offered the freedom of the city to all artificers settling there before September 1652.[143] These concessions had some effect, but mainly in replenishing the merchant body at its humbler levels. In 1652 the corporation complained that those who had recently arrived 'to sett upp theire trades . . . have but small stockes'.[144] Dublin, like the other Irish towns, suffered an influx of the indigent. However the failure of substantial merchants to settle in Dublin mattered less than in the other towns, because Dublin already had a well-established community of Protestant merchants, willing to support Cromwellian policy for the city. The removal of Catholics was vigorously prosecuted in Dublin; in 1647 common councilmen sympathetic to the Confederate Catholics were expelled. This policy seems to have been more effective than in many parts of Ireland: by 1660 the proportions of English to Irish were 6,459 to 2,321, with the Irish concentrated in the suburbs.[145] These expulsions of Catholics brought no revolution in Dublin's municipal government: before 1649 Protestants had had a large share in Dublin's government and trade.

Dublin suffered in the Interregnum less because Catholics were removed than because Protestant merchants' trade had been damaged by the war and by the restrictions which continued after 1649. In 1646 the Protestant merchants had complained of their lack of money and shipping; in 1644 the inhabitants of Dublin had petitioned the Irish parliament about their hardships in the hope of a remission of rents.[146]

[141] Ibid. iv. 3.

[142] *Cal. Anc. Recs. Dublin*, iii. 440–1; Pearse St. Library, Gilbert MS. 78, p. 130.

[143] Steele, ii, no. 480 (Ireland). Originally the corporation had asked that the concession last for three years.

[144] *Cal. Anc. Recs. Dublin*, iv. 23.

[145] Ibid. iii. 451; Steele, ii, nos. 556, 558 (Ireland); Pender, *A 'Census' of Ireland, c. 1659*, p. xiii.

[146] *Cal. S.P. Ire., 1633–47*, p. 473; *C.J. Ire.* i, appendix, p. 139.

In 1652 Dublin's citizens were said to be 'much disabled in theire estates by the decay of tradinge, and by the greate chardge that hath lyen uppon this cittie, and by loane monneyes for the supplie of the armie'.[147]   Often the loans were not repaid.[148]   Strict government controls inhibited trade until 1655. Dublin merchants were to the fore in petitioning for an end to the restriction.[149]   After 1655 the absence of free trade with England, the rigours of the customs administration (in the hands of Englishmen), and the generally unsympathetic attitude of the Westminster government provoked new protests.[150]   The commercial policy imposed from England prevented the Dublin merchants benefiting as much as they had hoped from Cromwellian rule. In April 1655 it was reported that the Dublin merchants were unable to lend to the government, as they had earlier, 'being generally so poore and standing in need of their own stocks for carrying on their owne trade'. There may also have been a spirit of non-cooperation, resulting from the harshness of economic policy and dislike of the political and religious complexion of Fleetwood's government.[151]   Poverty was certainly not universal among the Dublin merchants. By 1656 the Merchant Guild was sufficiently recovered to insist once more on its monopoly.[152]   Individual aldermen were prospering, buying lands and gaining profitable positions.[153]

Economic life began to return to normal after 1655, although it was hit by depression in 1659. How was Dublin's municipal government affected by the new regime? The changes resembled those in English corporations during the period: a Catholic corporation was not replaced by a Protestant one; instead in the critical period between 1647

[147]*Cal. Anc. Recs. Dublin*, ed. Gilbert, iv. 23.
[148]Ibid. iv. 23, 54, 170; *Cal. S.P. Ire. 1647–60*, pp. 643–4.
[149]P.R.O., SP. 63/286, 57–8, calendared with some signatures given inaccurately in *Cal. S.P. Ire., 1647–60*, pp. 572–3.   .
[150]Barnard, *P. and P.*, lxi.
[151]Bodl., Carte MS. 74, f. 43.
[152]Pearse St. Library, Gilbert MS. 78, p. 130.
[153]Guildhall Library, MS. 11,588/4, pp. 322, 334; A. H. Johnson, *The history of the worshipful Company of the Drapers of London*, iii. 220; Nat. Lib. Ire., MS. 2323, p. 201.

and 1652 leadership passed to men able to lend to and supply the English army, enthusiastic about the political and religious programme for which it stood. Some of these men, notably Daniel Hutchinson and Thomas Hooke, had hitherto been outside the governing élite, and in this sense were helped to power by the political changes of the Interregnum. Even among the most fervent supporters of the parliamentarian cause, not all had previously been outside the governing circle, and none was a complete newcomer to Dublin. Moreover committed political and religious radicals were too few in Dublin for power to be monopolized by them: the majority of Cromwellian aldermen had a more neutral attitude, supporting the regime because it offered the best defence against the Catholics and the best hope of stability.[154] None of the aldermen was enthusiastic about military rule. Thus between 1653 and 1655 there was serious friction between the corporation and the military party which wanted to suppress the Dublin corporation: as a result the aldermen were unenthusiastic about Fleetwood and eagerly rallied to Henry Cromwell when it seemed that he might replace Fleetwood.[155]

The most prominent members of the Cromwellian 'party' which took the lead in the corporation were Thomas Hooke, Daniel Hutchinson, John Preston, and Richard Tighe. Religion formed their common bond: all were members of Dr. Winter's Independent congregation at St. Nicholas's church, of which Hooke and Hutchinson were elders.[156] Their nonconformist sympathies persisted after 1660.[157] None was a newcomer to Dublin in the 1650s. Hutchinson had been admitted to Dublin's freedom (as a chandler) in 1634.[158] Tighe was a first-generation settler who had prob-

---

154 *Cal. Anc. Recs. Dublin*, ed. Gilbert, iv. 181.

155 Hist. MSS. Comm., *Egmont MSS.* i. 553; Brit. Mus., Lansdowne MS. 821, f. 46; *Thurloe State Papers*, ii. 163; v. 477; vi. 493.

156 Nickolls, *Original letters and papers*, p. 138; *Reliquiae Baxterianae*, ed. M. Sylvester (London, 1696), i. 172; *Thurloe State Papers*, v. 477.

157 *Cal. S.P. Ire. 1663–5*, p. 499. Hutchinson, Tighe, and Preston were involved with Erasmus Smith's schools: a project with a nonconformist aura. See below, pp. 191–2.

158 *Cal. Anc. Recs. Dublin*, ed. Gilbert, iii. 290.

ably arrived before 1641 and certainly before 1649.[159] Hooke was living in Dublin in 1637 when he was described as a merchant.[160] Preston, also a first-generation settler, had arrived in Dublin before 1649.[161]

Dublin's trade in the seventeenth century was too small to allow merchants to specialize in particular branches as they did in London.[162] There is no sign that the trading interests of the committed 'Cromwellian' aldermen differed from their more moderate colleagues': it is possible, however, that they were more deeply involved in government contracts. Hutchinson was particularly active in this sphere, serving as deputy treasurer at Dublin shortly after the Cromwellians' arrival.[163] Hooke helped to provision the Protestant army and was still owed money in 1657: both Tighe and Preston had also advanced money.[164] One difference of importance was that neither Hutchinson nor Hooke had been a member of the leading Dublin Merchant Guild, whose members had tended to dominate the city's government: it was in this respect that they were outsiders.[165]

Hutchinson, Hooke, Tighe, and Preston all served as mayor of Dublin in the Interregnum. They were compensated for

159 He was the son of William Tighe of Market Deeping, Lincolnshire. Genealogical Office, Dublin, MSS. 96, p. 199; 178, p. 369; J. B. Burke, *A genealogical and heraldic history of the landed gentry of Ireland*, 9th ed. (London, 1899), p. 442; H. F. Berry, 'The Goldsmiths' Company of Dublin', *JRSAI*, xxxi (1901), 127; O'Hart, *Irish landed gentry when Cromwell came to Ireland*, p. 408.

160 *The Registers of S. Catherine, Dublin, 1636–1715*, ed. H. Wood, Parish Register Soc. of Dublin, v (Exeter and London, 1908), 234.

161 His father was Hugh Preston of Bolton, Lancashire: his eldest son married Tighe's third daughter: Genealogical Office, MS. 87, p. 111; *The Economic Writings of Sir William Petty*, ed. Hull, ii. 616.

162 Brenner, *P. and P.* lviii.

163 Nat. Lib. Ire., MS. 11,961, p. 7; Bodl., Carte MS. 63, f. 624; Brit. Mus., Additional MS. 19,845, ff. 30–30ᵛ; *Analecta Hibernica*, xv. 246; *Cal. S.P. Dom. 1649–50*, pp. 173, 233, 381, 384; ibid., *1650*, pp. 90, 572, 574; ibid., *1651*, pp. 4, 11, 466, 537, 540, 567; ibid., *1652–3*, pp. 106, 157; ibid., *1653*, p. 455; ibid., *1654*, pp. 32, 180, 197; Firth and Rait, ii. 1133; Mayer, *Trans Historic Society of Lancs. and Cheshire*, N.S. i. 198; Dunlop, i. 88–9; Hist. MSS. Comm., *Egmont MSS.* i. 424.

164 Brit. Mus., Additional MS. 19,845, f. 31; Bodl., Carte MS. 63, f. 624; *Analecta Hibernica*, xv. 246; *Cal. S.P. Ire. 1647–60*, pp. 643–5, 733, 736, 742, 848; ibid., *1660–2*, pp. 78, 84; ibid., *Dom. 1650* p. 576; ibid., *Dom. 1652–3*, pp. 106, 157; ibid., *1653*, p. 455; ibid., *1655*, p. 590; Dunlop, i. 110; *Thurloe State Papers*, vi. 405.

165 Pearse St. Library, Gilbert MS. 78, r 120.

the slow repayment of their loans by other official positions. Hutchinson, as well as being deputy treasurer, was a justice of the peace, a revenue commissioner for the Dublin precinct, high sheriff of Dublin and Wicklow, and member of parliament in 1653 and 1654.[166] Hooke too was a justice of the peace and revenue commissioner. More lucrative was his appointment as a commissioner for the probate of wills and as farmer of the petty customs of Dublin.[167] Similarly Preston and Tighe served as justices of the peace, and Tighe represented Dublin in the 1656 parliament.[168] All four men acquired substantial estates outside Dublin: Hutchinson established a cloth manufacture at Athy in County Kildare; Alderman Preston was singled out by Petty as one of the principal beneficiaries of the land transfers of the period.[169]

At least three other aldermen were members of Winter's Independent congregation.[170] If the Cromwellian aldermen were bound together by their religious outlook, there were other aldermen less enthusiastic about the religious innovations of the Interregnum. Two of the trading guilds defied the government by appointing known episcopalians as their chaplains.[171] At least two of the aldermen who continued in office during the 1650s were known to be unsympathetic to the Cromwellians. Daniel Bellingham, a goldsmith able to command large resources, served the returning royalists in 1660 as Hutchinson had the Cromwellians. During the Interregnum Bellingham was in touch with the exiled

166 Nat. Lib. Ire., MS. 11,959, p. 161; T.C.D., MS. F.3.1.18, f. 110; Comerford, *Collections relating to the dioceses of Kildare and Leighlin*, i. 320; *Cal. Anc. Recs. Dublin*, ed. Gilbert, iv. 47; Dunlop, ii. 632; *Thurloe State Papers*, ii. 445; iii. 133.

167 Nat. Lib. Ire., MS. 11,959, pp. 136–7, 161; T.C.D., MS. F.3.18, f. 139^v; *Cal. Anc. Recs. Dublin*, ed. Gilbert, iv. 53; R. Lascelles, *Liber munerum publicorum Hiberniae* (London, 1824–30), i, part ii, p. 80.

168 T.C.D., MS. F.3.18, f. 139^v; Genealogical Office, MS. 96, p. 199; Comerford, *Collections relating to the dioceses of Kildare and Leighlin*, i. 320; Gale, *An Inquiry into the ancient corporate system*, p. cclxiii; *Thurloe State Papers*, v. 477.

169 Brit. Mus., Additional MS. 36,786, f. 292; *Cal. S.P. Dom. Dec. 1671–May 1672*, p. 72; Lawrence, *The Interest of Ireland*, part ii, p. 189; *The Economic Writings of Sir William Petty*, ed. Hull, ii. 616; House of Commons papers, 1835, xxviii. 229.

170 William Bladen (the government printer), Thomas Richardson, and William Cliffe: Nickolls, *Original letters and papers*, p. 138. Bladen was said to have spent £2,000 in the Protestant cause: Bodl., Tanner MS. 36, ff. 158, 202.

171 See below, p. 152.

Ormonde.[172]   William Smith was already regarded as the city's elder statesman before 1649, having served three times as mayor. He was the city's choice to wait on Charles II in 1660, and was elected to the General Convention in 1660 and to the Parliament of 1661. As late as 1675 Smith was again made lord mayor in an attempt to compose serious differences in the corporation.[173]

Because Dublin's government before 1649 had been Protestant, conditions there were closer to those in English towns than in any other Irish town; and what happened in Dublin during the 1650s resembled contemporary changes in English boroughs. From his study of Newcastle Mr. Howell concluded that 'the Civil War had no real effect on the structure of Newcastle politics; it had only a temporary effect on its composition by substituting one oligarchy for another'.[174]   In Dublin Hutchinson and Hooke, outsiders in not belonging to the Merchant Guild, advanced in power. However the traditional governing group was not altogether eclipsed. Especially after Henry Cromwell's arrival in 1655, Dublin's government was in the hands of members of the Merchant Guild and Hutchinson's influence seems to have declined.[175]

172 Nat. Lib. Ire., MSS. 2323, pp. 201, 306; 2326, p. 219; T.C.D., MS. F.2.1., f. 163; Bodl., Carte MS. 68, f. 602; Brit. Mus., Stowe MS. 1008, f. 181; Berry, *JRSAI* xxxi. 126, 127; Berry, 'The Merchant Tailors' Gild', *JRSAI* xlviii. 28; *Cal. S.P. Ire., 1660–2,* pp. 61, 188, 398, 638, 693–4; Hist. MSS. Comm., *Ormonde MSS.,* N.S. iii. 405.

173 He was a nephew of Ald. Thomas Evans of Dublin, and described as a gentleman. Sheriff in 1637 and also an alderman in that year, he served as mayor in 1642, 1644, and 1645; *Cal. Anc. Recs. Dublin,* ed. Gilbert, iii. 316, 321, 345, 395, 423, 433. In 1645 he was master of St. Audeon's Guild, which sheltered an episcopalian chaplain throughout the 1650s. Smith is also said to have attended vestry meetings of St. John's Church, of which the Presbyterian Patrick Kerr was incumbent. Ibid. iv. 181; Royal Irish Academy, MS. 12.0.13, ff. 1, 4ᵛ, 9, 20ᵛ, 21, 21ᵛ, 22ᵛ; *An Account of the chief occurrences . . . 12–19 March* [1660], p. 36; *Cal. S.P. Ire. 1660–2,* p. 71; S. C. Hughes, *The Church of St. John the Evangelist, Dublin* (Dublin, 1889), p. 23; *Letters written by Essex,* pp. 342, 344–5, 396.

174 Howell, *Newcastle upon Tyne and the Puritan Revolution* p. 343.

175 The mayors of Dublin between 1656 and 1660 had all served as masters of the Merchant Guild: Berry, 'The Records of the Dublin Gild of Merchants, known as the Gild of Holy Trinity, 1438–1671' *JRSAI* xxx (1900), 67. Hutchinson's closeness to the Independents and his connection with John Weaver (whose son had married his daughter) may have associated Hutchinson with the Independents' fall from Henry Cromwell's favour in 1658; Genealogical Office, MS. 141, p. 137; Brit. Mus., Additional MS. 15,635, f. 60 ᵛ.

All Protestant merchants in Dublin had virtually the same interest, as trade was not greatly diversified: to uphold the Protestant cause, to secure peace, and to free trade from restrictions. The effective choice of aldermen was narrow so that there was a high degree of continuity, royalists serving in the 1650s and the Cromwellian aldermen remaining in office after 1660.[176] This was similar to the situation which has been observed in Chester, where the Cromwellians' zealous supporters were few, making a thorough purge of the corporation impossible.[177]

Apart from the distinct Cromwellian and royalist groups, a third group is identifiable among the aldermen: the Dutch and Huguenot traders. This important element in Dublin still awaits close investigation. Members of the group who were aldermen during the Interregnum included Lewis and John Desminières,[178] Peter and Daniel Wybrants,[179] Hubert

[176]In 1660 there had been an attempt to exclude Hooke from pardon, and there were later, unsuccessful objections to the continuing presence of Cromwellian aldermen on the bench: Bodl., Clarendon state papers, 73, f. 264; *Cal. S.P. Ire. 1663–5,* p. 499.

[177]Johnson, 'Politics in Chester', in *Crisis and Order in English Towns,* ed. Clark and Slack, pp. 217, 220, 229–30.

[178]John Desminières of Rouen was naturalized in 1639, appointed sheriff in 1654, and an alderman in 1656. He was warden of the Merchant Guild in 1655–6, and its master from 1661 to 1663. Lewis Desminières of Utrecht was first naturalized in 1655 and again in 1662. A Robert Desminières was one of the Dutch merchants trading in Dublin who petitioned Charles I in 1631: in 1637 he lived in Dublin. P.R.O., SP. 63/286, 57ᵛ; Berry, *JRSAI* xxx. 67; Brit. Mus., Add. MS. 23,688, f. 89; *Cal. Anc. Recs. Dublin,* ed. Gilbert, iii, appendix vii, pp. 550 ff.; iv, pp. 69, 107; *Fifty-seventh report of the deputy keeper of public records in Ireland,* appendix iv, pp. 555, 561; *The Registers of S. Catherine, Dublin,* ed. Wood, p. 234; Nat. Lib. Ire., MS. 11,961, p. 86; *Letters of denization and acts of naturalization for aliens,* ed. Shaw, pp. 336, 337; W. B. Wright, *Records of the Anglo-Irish families of Ball* (Dublin, 1887), p. 19.

[179]Peter and Daniel Wybrants were among the Dutch merchants who petitioned the king in 1631. Daniel Wybrants was naturalized in 1624, became an alderman in 1641, and served as sheriff the following year. Peter Wybrants was elected to the Irish parliament in 1646. He fined to avoid being mayor in 1654. He was warden of the Merchant Guild twice during the Interregnum and a justice of the peace. In 1660 he waited on Charles II, together with Alderman William Smith, on the city's behalf. Daniel Wybrants, the younger, became a freeman in 1651. T.C.D., MS. F.3.18, f. 139ᵛ; Brit. Mus., Stowe MS. 202, f. 325; P.R.O., SP. 63/286, 57ᵛ; Royal Irish Academy, MS. 12.O.13, ff. 1, 12ᵛ, 13ᵛ, 20ᵛ, 22ᵛ; *Cal. Anc. Recs. Dublin,* ed. Gilbert, iii. 374, 391, 550 ff.; iv. 66–7; *Cal. S.P. Dom. 1651–2,* p. 568; ibid., *May–Sept. 1672,* p. 552; ibid., *Ire. 1660–2,* p. 71; *C.J. Ire.* i, appendix, p. 209; Gale, *An Inquiry into the ancient corporate system,* p. cclxiii; *Fifty-seventh report,* appendix iv, pp. 555, 562; *Letters written by Essex,* p. 414; *Letters of denization,* ed. Shaw, p. 330.

Adrian,[180] and Sankey Sulliard.[181] Others who had been prominent in the city's life before 1649 included the van den Hovens from Amsterdam,[182] the Cremers,[183] William Verschoyle,[185] and Theodore Schoute.[185] Their importance was increased by the war, when their overseas contacts were used to finance the struggle. Theodore Schoute, a member of the Dublin Parliament, and the Wybrants were particularly active in this matter.[186] During the Interregnum, although there was some resentment of their share of Irish trade, it was hoped that more foreign Protestants might be tempted to Dublin. Warner and Derrick Westenra and Lewis Desminiéres were the only important merchants to settle in Dublin and to

---

180Adrian, an apothecary, was naturalized in 1640. An alderman in the 1650s, he was knighted after 1660. Brit. Mus., Additional MS. 19,843, f. 131; Berry, *JRSAI* xxxi. 127; *Cal. Anc. Recs. Dublin*, ed. Gilbert, iii. 369; 'Hearth money roll for County Dublin, 1664', *Journal County Kildare Archaeological Soc.* xi (1930—3), 449; *Letters of denization*, ed. Shaw, p. 336.

181Sulliard became an alderman in 1645; he had been made apothecary-general to the army in 1642. He died in 1659. Genealogical Office, MS. 76, p. 23; *Cal. Anc. Recs. Dublin*, ed. Gilbert, iii. 438; iv. 179; *Cal. S.P. Ire. 1633—47*, p. 782; *C.J. Ire.* i, appendix, pp. 196, 197, 198—9.

182Peter van den Hoven was an original member of the Dublin Goldsmiths' Company in 1637. He was sheriff in 1647—8. Garret van den Hoven was naturalized in 1646 and served as sheriff in 1652 and 1654. T.C.D., Mun. P/1/339, 362—6; Brit. Mus., Sloane MS. 1731 B, f. 19ᵛ; Berry, *JRSAI* xxxi. 123; *Analecta Hibernica*, xv. 316; *Cal. Anc. Recs. Dublin*, ed. Gilbert, iii. 345, 449; iv. 26, 62, 67; *Letters of denization*, ed. Shaw, p. 337; Bodl., Rawlinson MS. A.208, p. 408.

183Balthazar Cremer, from Geissen in Germany, was naturalized in 1620 and died in Dublin in 1659. Tobias Cremer, naturalized in 1639, was sheriff in 1653. Thomas Cremer, a merchant, became a freeman in 1651. Genealogical Office, MS. 76, p. 33; *Cal. Anc. Recs. Dublin*, ed. Gilbert, iv. 16, 51; J. H. Hessels, *Epistolae et tractatus cum reformationis tum ecclesiae Londino-batavae historiam illustrantes* (Cambridge, 1897), iii, part 2, p. 2911 (no. 4360); *Letters of denization*, pp. 329, 336; *Cal. S.P. Ire. 1633—47*, pp. 767, 772, 775; *Registers of S. Catherine, Dublin*, ed. Wood, p. 234.

184Ibid., p. 234; *Cal. Anc. Recs. Dublin*, ed. Gilbert, iii. 553.

185A freeman in 1637, Schoute was naturalized in 1638. By 1654 he was dead and Peter Wybrants was his executor: Brit. Mus., Additional MS. 19,843, f. 157ᵛ; *Cal. Anc. Recs. Dublin*, ed. Gilbert, iii. 364; *Letters of denization*, ed. Shaw, p. 336.

186*Cal. S.P. Ire. 1633—47*, pp. 385, 605, 607, 686—7, 766; *History of the Irish Confederation*, ed. J. T. Gilbert (Dublin, 1882—91), iii. 171; *The corporation book of Youghal*, ed. Caulfield, p. 548; *C.J. Ire.*, i, appendix, pp. 36, 67, 96; Hist. MSS. Comm., *Ormonde MSS.*, N.S. ii. 258; *L.J.* x. 135—54.

be naturalized in the 1650s.[187] The records, although defective, suggest that in comparison with the periods before 1640 and after 1660 few foreign merchants came to join those already in Dublin. There were also hopes that the Dutch in Dublin might encourage skilled artisans to settle there. Daniel Wybrants was involved in a scheme to bring cloth workers from Leyden to Dublin. However that was after 1660: again the Interregnum seems to have been barren.[188]

The foreign Protestants in Dublin increased in importance during the 1650s, but did not grow greatly in numbers. So far as we know they stood for no distinctive policy, merging with the moderates who moved easily from support of the Cromwellians to acceptance of Charles II. None of these merchants appears to have been a religious Independent or among the Cromwellians' conspicuous supporters.

The political changes in Dublin during the 1650s were minor: with few exceptions the character of the corporation was as it had been before 1649. There was no appreciable broadening in the social composition of the city's government. The administration was content to uphold the traditional authority of the guilds. Popular reaction within Dublin to the Protectorate is difficult to detect. Only in 1659 is there evidence of lower-class unrest, which was directed not against the municipality but against the radical governors who replaced Henry Cromwell.[189]

The two permanent effects on Dublin of Cromwellian rule were religious and economic. The Protestant community in Dublin proved receptive, once conventional authority had

[187]P.R.O., Dublin, Lodge MSS., 1.a.52.42. pp. 5, 10; *Letters of denization and acts of naturalization*, ed. Shaw, p. 337. The Westenras came from Haarlem: see also: Royal Irish Academy, MS. 12.0.13., f. 21ᵛ; Nat. Lib. Ire., MS. 8535, item 15; Berry, *JRSAI* xxx. 67; *Cal. S.P. Ire. 1660–2*, p. 649; *Fifty-seventh report of the deputy keeper of public records in Ireland*, p. 555; G.E.C., *Complete Peerage*, xi. 181, n.c.

[188]Violet Barbour, *Capitalism in Amsterdam in the seventeenth century*, 2nd. ed. (Ann Arbor, Mich., 1963), pp. 121–2, n. 78; N. W. Posthumus, ed., *Bronnen tot de Geschiednis van de Leidsche textielnijverheid*, v, 1651–1702, Rijks Geschiedkundige publicatiën, 39 (The Hague, 1918), pp. 570–2. Daniel Wybrants kept strong links with Holland: one of his sons settled there and his daughters married Dutchmen: Brit. Mus., Stowe MS. 202, f. 3?5; *Cal. S.P. Ire. 1647–60*, pp. 591, 620; W. C. Stubbs, 'The Weavers' Guild', *JRSAI* xlix (1919), 66.

[189]C.B., Jennings transcripts, A/16, 23 Nov. 1659; *A Sober Vindication of Lt. Gen. Ludlow*, pp. 3, 11.

been shattered, to religious Independency. As we have seen, the 'Cromwellian' aldermen were Independents, separated from their neutral colleagues by their religion. Before 1641 no Protestant nonconformity had been recorded in Dublin; after 1660 dissent was a serious problem, not least because it enjoyed covert aldermanic support.[190]   In 1662 an alderman was discovered at a coventicle; in 1670 the lord mayor elect was among those urging Dr. Thomas Harrison (formerly Henry Cromwell's chaplain) to return to an Independent congregation in the city.[191]   The possible scale of the problem is shown in a report of the funeral of Joseph Teate, a government preacher during the Interregnum and subsequently ejected for nonconformity. An eye-witness in 1666 was 'amazed at ye number yt accompanied his herse, the lord mayor and aldermen, lord chief baron,[192] judges, both men of great and small rank made him followers, no lesse (as some think) than 3000'.[193]   Again in 1675 Lord Essex complained that some of the Dublin aldermen were 'notorious nonconformists' and were lay elders of congregations.[194] Protestant dissent had established itself during the 1650s and remained a serious feature of Dublin life after 1660.

In economic life the impact of Cromwellian policy was still felt after 1660. Dublin merchants had protested against the government's commercial policy, and with good cause. Yet there had been a return to more normal trade after 1655, from which Dublin was uniquely placed to benefit. The capital already contained the Protestant merchants on whom the Cromwellians now conferred a monopoly of trade. The expulsion of Catholic traders and the failure of substantial newcomers to arrive from England were less damaging to Dublin. The established merchants of the capital suffered from depleted stocks, lack of money, and the government prohibitions, so that the full benefits of their privileged position were not felt until after 1660. However in the

190 *Cal. S.P. Ire. 1663—5*, p. 499.

191 Bodl., Carte MS. 45, f. 458; *The Autobiography of Henry Newcome, M.A.*, ed. R. Parkinson, Chetham Soc. xxvii (1852), ii. 185, 190.

192 John Bisse, recorder of Dublin during the Interregnum.

193 T. Bonnell to J. Johnson, 23 Oct. 1666; Cambridge Univ. Library, Baumgartner papers, Strype correspondence, 4, f. 42.

194 *Letters written by Essex*, p. 104.

Interregnum Dublin gained from the fact that the bulk of its trade was with England.[195] This was the branch of Irish trade most encouraged in the 1650s, while the Spanish and French trades (carried on from the ports of the southern and western seaboard) were severely curtailed. After 1660 it was apparent that Dublin's share of Irish trade had increased since 1641. So far as the wool and linen trades were concerned, Dublin had had no clear ascendancy before 1641.[196] In 1663–4, 44 per cent of Irish imports passed through Dublin, but only 32 per cent of exports.[197] By 1668, 40 per cent of Ireland's total trade belonged to the capital.[198] Obviously the import trade was stimulated by Dublin's growing population; in the Interregnum it was increased by the need to restock the country. Dublin's importance had been emphasized by the centralizing tendencies of the Interregnum which continued after 1660: the suppression of provincial government in Connaught and Munster left Dublin as the unrivalled centre of administration and law; its importance as an educational, medical, and social centre also grew. But as well as these factors in Dublin's rapid expansion account must be taken of Cromwellian policy. The insistence that the boroughs' government and trade should be Protestant monopolies often depopulated and impoverished Irish towns. In Dublin, however, the policy accorded better with the city's composition and involved less interruption of the traditional pattern of trade and government.

[195]Kearney, *Strafford in Ireland*, p. 131.

[196]Ibid. pp. 157–8.

[197]Bodl., Carte MS. 52, f. 407. Based on customs receipts, these figures may reflect variations in the efficiency of collection. Dublin's share of imports fluctuated: 36 per cent in 1660–1, 44 per cent in 1661–2, 46 per cent in 1662–3: Ibid., f. 410.

[198]Brit. Mus., Harleian MS. 4706, ff. 7–8. There was still a disparity between the share of imports (nearly half the country's total) and exports (a third): ibid., f. 6v.

V

THE PROPAGATION OF THE GOSPEL

i. The situation in 1649

Since the Reformation the spread of English Protestantism had been seen as a method of securing English rule: 'a powerfull and able ministry, the only best way to promote plantation'.[1] The rebellion of 1641 discredited the Church of Ireland, showing that its efforts at evangelization had failed. The Church of Ireland's weaknesses were easily diagnosed: clerical poverty; pluralism, and non-residence; a poorly educated or ignorant clergy, usually unable to speak Irish; an outmoded parochial organization; few churches fit for use. There was general agreement that when English authority was re-established in Ireland, there must be reforms to make the Church of Ireland more effective. Those who reviewed the century since the Reformation agreed that there had been an almost total neglect of the spiritual welfare of 'the poor Irish'.[2]

Not until 1649 was it possible to repair the earlier neglect, and by that time there were further reasons to belittle the work of the Church of Ireland. It suffered from the same corruptions as the Church of England and so must be swept away. Ireland's true reformation would date from 1649.[3] A unique opportunity was offered by parliament's victories in Ireland to introduce purified institutions, in church and state. Where episcopalians had been negligent, Ireland's new ministers would vigorously evangelize the country.[4] In practice this ardour was diminished by two facts. First, there was doubt as to whether the native Irish were capable of spiritual

[1] *The Humble Petition of the Protestant Inhabitants of the Counties of Antrim, Downe, Tyrone, etc.* (London, 1641).

[2] *Two Biographies of William Bedell, Bishop of Kilmore*, ed. E. S. Shuckburgh (Cambridge, 1902), pp. 124, 167; [V. Gookin], *The Great Case of Transplantation in Ireland Discussed* (London, 1655), p. 19; P. Heylyn, *Aerius Redivivus* (Oxford, 1670), p. 392.

[3] Brit. Mus., Lansdowne 1228, f. 8; Abbott, *Cromwell*, ii. 107, 201, 203.

[4] *Thurloe State Papers*, ii. 118.

regeneration. Here the legend of the 1641 massacre and the general guilt of the Irish nation had a powerful influence.[5] It was only gradually that a more generous approach to the native Irish, admitting of attempts to convert them, took hold.[6] Until 1655 Protestant evangelization was concentrated on the English soldiers and garrisons. A second reason for neglect was uncertainty as to what doctrines should be taught. Anglicanism and Presbyterianism were proscribed. The religion that was to replace those forms in Ireland had not been defined in 1649 (and was not throughout the Interregnum), and had to await a decision in England. In this period of uncertainty sects proliferated in the army and administration, producing bitter contentions. These controversies distracted energies from evangelization.

Indiscriminate condemnation of what had gone before, because associated with the episcopalian church, meant that the close parallels between the preoccupations and methods of Bishops Bedell and Bramhall in the 1630s and those of the puritan reformers were ignored. In the same way after 1660, bishops anxious to reform the re-established Church of Ireland refused to acknowledge that their objectives were the same as those of the Cromwellian clergy. During the Interregnum only one member of the Church of Ireland escaped this hostility: 'the no less good then great Bishop Ussher'.[7] Indeed Ussher's reputation was deliberately fostered in the 1650s, both in England and in Ireland. There was a hope (misguided) that Ussher might be annexed to the Cromwellian church settlement, and his authority used to gain general acceptance for the national church constantly under discussion. Ussher's known interest in reforming ecclesiastical government to bring it closer to its antique prototype led to his name being invoked indiscriminately in

[5] Ibid. ii. 343; iii. 468; Brit. Mus., Lansdowne 1228, f. 8; *Rebels No Saints* (London, 1661), p. 119; Dunlop, i. 178–9; ii. 308; 'The petition of officers of the precincts of Dublin, Carlow, Wexford and Kilkenny', in *Mercurius politicus*, no. 251 (29 Mar.–5 Apr. 1655), p. 5236.

[6] M.S., *A Discourse concerning the Rebellion in Ireland* (London, 1642), p. 17; *A Discourse Concerning the Affaires of Ireland* (London, 1650), pp. 2–7; Gookin, *The Great Case of Transplantation* p. 3; W. Perkins, *The Christian Doctrine*, translated into Irish by G. Daniel, (Dublin, 1652), sig. [2].

[7] E. Worth, *The Servant doing, and the Lord blessing* (Dublin, 1659), p. 31.

many schemes of reform.[8] Ussher was also admired for his firm anti-Catholicism, his uncanny prophecy of the 1641 massacre, and for his alleged resistance to the Laudian Bramhall.[9] He was looked to by Lord Broghill and the Protestant gentry of Munster, as well as by moderates in England. In Ireland Ussher was praised by Baptists, Ulster Presbyterians, and former episcopalians: his example inspired· proposed religious settlements for Ireland.[10] The most solid effort to install Ussher as the presiding genius of Cromwellian policy (the ecclesiastical counterpart of Bacon) was the purchase of his library in 1657 for the use of the projected second college at Dublin.[11]

Ireland's rulers in 1649 disavowed the episcopalian church and promised more vigorous evangelization, although the institutional and doctrinal framework in which it was to occur was undecided. What was the attitude of the Protestants already in Ireland to this policy? Certainly they favoured better care for propagating Protestantism. However they were less eager for fundamental reforms.

The Church of Ireland enjoyed general support amongst the Protestant laity, except in Ulster. This acceptance was temporarily obscured when changes introduced by Bramhall and Strafford provoked resistance similar to that to the Laudian innovations in England.[12] With the fall of Strafford

8Two pirated versions of Ussher's scheme appeared, in 1641 and 1656. The latter forced Ussher's chaplain and executor, Nicholas Bernard, to publish the authentic text: *The Reduction of Episcopacie* (London, 1656). Cf. M. J. Mendle, 'Politics and political thought, 1640—42', in *The Origins of the English Civil War* ed. Conrad Russell (London, 1973), pp. 236, 278 n. 23.

9N. Bernard, *The Life and Death of the Most Reverend ... Dr. James Usher* (Dublin, 1656), pp. 39—40, 60—1, 86—7; *Thurloe State Papers*, v. 121.

10Bodl., Carte MS. 45, f. 10; Lawrence, *The Interest of Ireland*, part ii, p. 77; Worth, *The Servant doing*, p. 31; Hist. MSS. Comm., *Egmont MSS.* i. 554; *The Tanner Letters*, ed. C. McNeill, Irish MSS. Comm. (Dublin, 1943), p. 389; G. F. Nuttall, *Richard Baxter* (London, 1965), p. 78. For his contacts with St. John and other M.P.s in 1651: D. Underdown, *Pride's Purge* (Oxford, 1971), pp. 20—1; Brit. Mus., Add. MS. 10,114, ff. 27, 27ᵛ, 28ᵛ, 29, 29ᵛ, 30, 30ᵛ, 31, 31ᵛ, 32, 32ᵛ, 33, 33ᵛ.

11On this: T. C. Barnard, 'The purchase of Archbishop Ussher's Library in 1657' *Long Room*, Bulletin of the Friends of Trinity College Dublin Library, iv (1971), and below, p. 211.

12Clotworthy complained in 1635, 'ye church heere is tenderly p[ro] vided for, and hath fine new clothes. We want no addition yt the witt of man can invent to make ye worship off God pompous in outward, butt penurious in the inward part': *Collections of the Massachusetts Historical Soc.*, 5th Ser. 1 (Boston, Mass., 1871), 208.

and Bramhall and with the very existence of Protestantism
jeopardized in 1641, the laity rallied to the Church of
Ireland. The character of the church and the nature of Irish
society explained the absence of dissatisfaction. The Canons
of 1615 (Ussher's work) had entrenched Calvinist doctrine in
the Irish church.[13] One of Bramhall's offences had been to
replace those Canons with the English Canons of 1604.[14]
Reform, for Irish Protestants, meant the restoration of the
1615 Canons. Lay control over the Irish church was strong
and remained so, despite Bramhall's efforts to reduce it. So
long as the church was Erastian, Calvinist, and firmly anti-
Catholic, it served the Protestant settlers' purposes. Only in
Ulster, where Presbyterianism had taken strong root along
with the Scottish settlers, was there Protestant dissent from
the established church.

In general Ireland lacked urban communities of Protestants
similar to those in which religious radicalism developed in
England. Dublin was the only sizeable Protestant centre:
smaller towns had been established in the recent plantations
of Munster and Ulster. It was in these areas that the first faint
stirrings of sectarianism occurred, in Munster and Dublin
only after 1641.[15] The clergy generally followed where the
gentry led. Only when the Protestant cause in Ireland was
divided between supporters of Charles I and of the English
parliament did divisions appear amongst the clergy. As with
the laity, few of the clergy had been enthusiastic supporters
of the English parliament in 1642. But by 1647 and even
more so in 1649 the best hope for Protestantism in Ireland
was clearly the victory of the English parliament. Two factors
still deterred many clergy from throwing in their lot with the
conquering English: loyalty to Charles I, and dislike of the
religious changes to which the new rulers were committed.

[13]Heylyn *Aerius Redivivus*, p. 394; R. B. Knox, *James Ussher Archbishop of
Armagh* (Cardiff, 1967), pp. 12—23; R. Parr, *The Life of ... James Usher*
(London, 1686), p. 15; *The Works of ... Bramhall*, ed. J. Vesey (Dublin, 1676),
sig. [i2].
[14]F. R. Bolton, *The Caroline Tradition of the Church of Ireland*, (London,
1958), pp. 10—14; Knox, *Ussher*, pp. 48—52.
[15]T.C.D., MS. F.2.3., f. 283; Hist. MSS. Comm., *Ormonde MSS.*, N.S. i. 92; F.
Teate, *Nathanael, Or an Israelite Indeed*, (London, 1657), sig. A2—A2ᵛ; *State
Papers collected by Edward, earl of Clarendon*, ed. R. Scrope and T. Monkhouse,
3 vols. (Oxford, 1767—86), i. 252.

Many former ministers of the Church of Ireland preferred the privations of exile to collaboration; others held fast to episcopalian forms in private. Yet some overcame their reluctance and accepted employment from the Cromwellians as official preachers: at least sixty-seven ministers previously beneficed in the Church of Ireland did this.[16] It is easy to dismiss them as Vicars of Bray, anxious to avoid poverty or harassment. However, their behaviour can be defended. In theory they had to forsake the Book of Common Prayer and renounce episcopacy, but the authorities were not always able to enforce these renunciations. The Cromwellian church in Ireland need differ little from the Church of Ireland in doctrine, even if its organization was different. So long as the state church's doctrine was undefined (as it remained throughout the period), it might accommodate with ease a wide variety of ministers. Moreover public employment under the Cromwellians did enable ministers principally interested in spreading Protestantism and combatting Catholicism to continue this work.

Moderate reform had been in the air before 1649, and not all Irish Protestants were averse from changes.[17] But there had been very little pressure for the far-reaching reforms introduced in 1649, which reflected English interests and desires. Finding the ecclesiastical policy of the new rulers between 1649 and 1655 repugnant, Irish Protestants formulated policies of their own, which, whilst accepting the Cromwellian framework of no Common Prayer Book or bishops, would secure their traditional objectives. It was a weakness that that policy in 1649 took little interest in Irish Protestant wishes: it introduced a further division into the Protestant camp which hindered effective evangelization.

ii. The Statutory Basis

The importance of a better provision for the Protestant

16 They accounted for about 17% of the official preachers in Cromwellian Ireland. There were undoubtedly more than Seymour recorded. Seymour, pp. 206–24.

17 Apart from Ussher's interest in modified episcopacy, Ormonde in 1648 promised a church settlement 'according to the example of the best Reformed Churches', a formula which permitted possible changes. *A Declaration of the Lord Lieutenant Generall of Ireland* (Cork, 1648), sig. [A3].

gospel was widely accepted by 1649. What legislation was passed to achieve this?

The Long Parliament's legislation of 1642 for Ireland's resettlement reserved a proportion of the confiscated land for building and endowing new churches. Similar provision had been made in the plantation of Ulster.[18] In 1643 the English parliament authorized reforms of existing parochial organization through the union and division of parishes.[19]

There were no changes in Ireland until parliament gained control of Dublin in 1647, when the parliamentary commander introduced the religious changes ordered in England by the Long Parliament. On 24 June 1647 the use of the Book of Common Prayer and Anglican ceremonies was forbidden. The Directory of Worship was substituted. Outraged protests came from the Church of Ireland clergy who had flocked to the capital as a place of refuge.[20]

Earlier in 1647, before Dublin's surrender, the Long Parliament had introduced a Presbyterian system of church government into England. A parliamentary committee was asked to prepare similar changes for Ireland, but it never made any recommendations.[21]

Only in 1649 were the changes already enforced in Dublin extended to other parts of Ireland. Where English authority was imposed, the existing church was dismantled. Comprehensive legislation to replace the episcopal hierarchy and parochial system was expected now that parliament had started Ireland's actual resettlement. The 'dark corners of the land', to which Ireland's needs were often likened, were tackled by the Rump early in 1650.[22] Commissions for the

[18]16 Car. 1, c. 33, xi (England); G Hill, *An historical account of the Plantation in Ulster* (Belfast, 1877), pp. 91 ff., Moody, *The Londonderry plantation*, pp. 34–5, 454–6.

[19]R.C.B., MS. Libr. 27, Armagh Inquisition, p. 35.

[20]C. W. Russell and J. P. Prendergast, *The Carte Manuscripts in the Bodleian Library, Oxford* (London, 1871), p. 104; Seymour, pp. 3–4; Bodl., Carte MS. 21, f. 275; D. Wilkins, *Concilia Britanniae et Hiberniae* (London, 1737), iv. 555–6.

[21]*C.J.* v. 40.

[22]C. Hill, 'Puritans and "the Dark Corners of the Land" ' *TRHS*, 5th Ser. xiii (1963); and 'Propagating the Gospel', in *Historical Essays 1600–1750*, ed. H. E. Bell and R. L. Ollard (London, 1963). For direct comparisons of Wales's and Ireland's needs: M. Poole, *A Model for the maintaining of Students of choice abilities at the University* (1658), sig. [A3]; J. Tillinghast, *Generation–Work* (London, 1655), pt. i, p. 44.

propagation of the Gospel in Wales and in the north of England were established.[23] These offered useful precedents for Ireland, which seemed to have been adopted in March 1650. On 8 March an ordinance for the propagation of the Gospel in Ireland was passed. Its date and those concerned in its passage suggested that it was similar to the measures for Wales and the north: its contents showed that it was not.

The Irish ordinance was read first on 30 November 1649.[24] Before the measure was passed, the Rump had to be goaded into action by Cromwell in Ireland through three of the chaplains who had accompanied him there. His three agents were Hugh Peter, John Owen, and Jenkin Lloyd. To Peter was attributed authorship of the Welsh ordinance. Throughout the 1640s Peter had also interested himself in the fate of Protestantism in Ireland, twice visiting the country to invigorate the Protestant cause. The second of his visits was with the Cromwellian army in 1649.[25] Having so recently seen Ireland's condition at first hand, we may assume that Peter urged the Rump to legislate for Ireland as well as Wales.

John Owen also went with Cromwell to Ireland in 1649. Early in 1650 he returned to represent Irish needs to the parliament: he did so in a sermon preached before the house of commons on 28 February 1650.[26] Owen's sermon breathed new life into the ordinance first read the previous November. The following day the committee to which the ordinance had been referred was authorized to receive propositions as to how the Gospel might be propagated in Ireland.[27]

---

23 On the Welsh commission: Hill, *Historical Essays; An Act for the Propagation of the Gospel in Wales, 1649[50]* ..., Cymdeithas Llên Cymru, 2nd Ser. 2 (1908); T. Richards, *A History of the Puritan Movement in Wales, 1639–1653* (London, 1920); for the north: Howell, *Newcastle and the Puritan Revolution*, pp. 234–6.

24 *C.J.* vi. 374.

25 Christopher Hill, *Historical Essays*, p. 43; Richards, *A History of the Puritan Movement in Wales*, pp. 78–80; *A Declaration of the gallant service performed by ... H. Peters in the West of England* (London, 1646); *A Letter from Ireland ... From Mr. Hugh Peters* (London, 1649).

26 J. Owen, *The Stedfastness of Promises, and the Sinfulness of Staggering* (London, 1650); *C.J.* vi. 248.

27 *C.J.* vi. 374.

The third chaplain, Jenkin Lloyd, is less well known than Peter or Owen, yet was more important in preparing the ordinance. It was Lloyd who framed the ordinance, acting no doubt on Oliver Cromwell's instructions.[28] Lloyd had accompanied Cromwell to Ireland, and was later employed by him on several missions.[29] Lloyd's key role, as well as the character of the trustees who were mainly Cromwell's rather than the Rump's nominees, showed that Cromwell was the driving force behind the measure.[30]

The ordinance of 8 March 1650 was not a comprehensive act to supply Ireland with a preaching ministry.[31] Indeed it contained no provisions directly connected with propagating the Gospel. Its main effect was to increase the endowments of Trinity College Dublin, which in the long term would help train more ministers in Ireland but offered no immediate contribution. Standing alone, this ordinance provided no authority for the proscription of the Church of Ireland and its ministers, or for erecting an alternative. Clearly it was not meant to stand alone. On the day of its passage, 8 March, preparations started for another ordinance to abolish the Anglican hierarchy and to outlaw the Anglican prayer-book.[32] This ordinance was never passed, so that the absence of any legal basis for ecclesiastical changes had to be made good by the instructions issued to successive governors of Ireland between 1650 and 1659.[33] Thus the parliamentary commissioners in October 1650 were empowered to enforce the English ordinances abolishing the hierarchy and Common Prayer Book, and those against delinquent or malignant clergy.[34]

[28] Nat. Lib. Ire., MS. 11,959, pp. 124–5.
[29] Bodl., Rawlinson MSS. A.328, pp. 21, 95, 163; A.24, f. 146; *Cal. S.P. Dom., 1650*, pp. 75, 533; ibid., *1651*, pp. 90, 91, 117, 118; ibid., *1655*, p. 160; King's Inns Dublin, Prendergast MS. i, p. 176; T.C.D., MS. F.3.18, f. 139ᵛ; B. M. Egerton MS. 1762, f. 207; *Thurloe State Papers*, ii. 162–4; Whitelocke, *Memorials*, iii. 189. Lloyd had also been connected with the Welsh ordinance: *C.J.* vii. 258–9; Firth and Rait, ii. 345; *L.J.* ix. 108; Richards, *A History of the Puritan Movement in Wales*, pp. 85, 271, 330.
[30] The trustees are considered below at pp. 198–9.
[31] Firth and Rait, ii. 355–7.
[32] *C.J.* vi. 379; Whitelocke, *Memorials*, iii. 159.
[33] Dunlop, i. 2, 5, 264; ii. 437–43, 615; Brit. Mus., Add. MS. 5014; *Thurloe State Papers*, ii. 506–8; Bodl., Carte MS. 67, f. 307; Firth and Rait, ii. 1298.
[34] Dunlop, i. 2, 5.

In this way the destructive part of Cromwellian policy was sanctioned. But was there legislation to encourage Protestant ministers to work in Ireland? In 1647 a parliamentary committee was asked to propose ways of advancing and maintaining a preaching ministry there. No proposals were made.[35] In March 1650, in response to Owen's sermon, the parliamentary committee's scope was widened to consider methods of improving the ministry in Ireland.[36] Two expedients were devised to supplement the ordinance.

First, on 8 March the Rump resolved to send six ministers to Dublin. Owen had singled out the capital's pressing needs.[37] Secondly, financial baits were offered to ministers removing to Ireland. An ordinance of 23 June 1654 established a grant of £50, but the practice was by then well established.[38] Compared with Ireland's needs, and with treatment of Wales and the north, the Rump's legislation was meagre, and had been achieved only at Cromwell's and his entourage's prompting. One explanation of the failure to do more was the expectation of an act of union which would give clear definition and a solid legal foundation to the relationship between England and Ireland. Anticipating such an act, parliament tended not to legislate separately for Ireland. When no act was passed, much English policy towards Ireland remained on an informal basis throughout the Interregnum, including important religious changes. This explanation hardly exculpates either the Rump or its successors from their almost complete failure to fulfil their promises and justify English rule in Ireland by spreading the Protestant Gospel. Another unfortunate consequence of the absence of legislation was that much room for improvisation was left to the governors in Ireland. Between 1649 and 1655 religious policy reflected their unorthodox tastes.

iii. Fleetwood and the rise of the Baptists

Ireland itself had produced few sectaries before 1649. Novel doctrines — religious Independency and Baptism — were in-

35 *C.J.* v. 40. Parliament occasionally acted to supply Ireland with ministers before 1649: Brit. Mus., Sloane MS. 4769, ff. 9, 46ᵛ; Sloane MS. 4771, f. 17.

36 *C.J.* vi. 374; Owen, *The Stedfastness of Promises*, p. 46.

37 *C.J.* vi. 379; Owen, *The Stedfastness of Promises*, p. 44.

38 Firth and Rait, ii. 929; R.C.B., Seymour MSS., pp. 1, 5, 6, 7, 8, 75, 76.

troduced from England by soldiers and their chaplains, and made little headway outside the garrisons. The chaplains to Lord Lisle's army in Munster were said to have introduced Independency in 1647; in 1649 there was more widespread activity.[39] Initially arrangements were dangerously informal, soldiers preached as well as chaplains. There was no machinery for vetting preachers' qualifications or opinions. Many came at the invitation of army officers. As early as 1650 Owen had warned of the dangers of this situation: that ministers ejected in England might go to the greater freedom of Ireland.[40] Precisely these dangers were illustrated by one of the first ministers appointed to preach in Dublin: Andrew Wyke. Wyke had twice been in trouble in England for his unorthodox beliefs, and in 1650 had been imprisoned at Coventry for Ranter beliefs. Yet in Ireland in 1651 he was welcomed and given a government salary.[41]

By 1651 more formal arrangements for preaching were being made. By October 1651 there were at least two gathered congregations of Independents in Dublin. One, established by Samuel Winter who had come to Dublin as chaplain to the parliamentary commissioners, met in St. Nicholas's church, and flourished throughout the decade.[42] The other, gathered in Christ Church cathedral, had John Rogers as its pastor.[43] A difference in the membership of these distinct congregations was discernible. Rogers's congregation included Dublin's military governor, Hewson, and other Cromwellian officers. In contrast the leading members of Winter's church were civilians, and included the

---

[39] Hist. MSS. Comm., *Egmont MSS.* i. 374. For evidence of Owen preaching in Ireland: J. Rogers, *Challah*, in *Ohel or Bethshemesh* (London, 1653), with separate pagination, p. 3, *recte* 415.

[40] Owen, *The Stedfastness of Promises*, pp. 44–5; Abbott, *Cromwell*, ii. 108.

[41] A. L. Morton, *The World of the Ranters* (London, 1970), p. 119; *Cal. S.P. Dom, 1650*, pp. 133, 143, 517, 550; Hist. MSS. Comm., *Leyborne-Popham MSS.*, pp. 57–9; Seymour, pp. 20–1, 224; Whitelocke, *Memorials*, iii. 163; W. T. Whitley, *A Baptist Bibliography* (London, 1916), i. 26.

[42] *C.J.* vi. 486; Dunlop, i. 172; *Mercurius politicus*, no. 72 (16–23 Oct. 1651), p. 1148; Mayer, *Trans. Historic Soc. of Lancashire and Cheshire*, N.S. i. 172; *Several proceedings of Parliament* (26 June–3 July 1651), p. 1412.

[43] E. Rogers, *Some account of the life and opinions of a Fifth-Monarchy man* (London, 1867), pp. 27–30.

Cromwellian aldermen of Dublin.[44] These differences were not important in 1651. They became so in 1653 when Rogers, confronted with an offensive by the Baptists, returned to England.[45] Many of his former congregation, including the important officers, embraced Baptism and became bitter opponents of the Independents led by Winter, who increasingly sided with civilian rule. By 1653 religious extremism — Baptism, in particular — was identified with the oppressions of Ireland's military government.

The rise and spread of Baptism was swift. It led to violent contentions which turned Ireland's new rulers in upon themselves and left them little energy to tackle the country's problems. We have to explain how Baptism took this hold. Contemporaries blamed the lord deputy, Fleetwood, alleging that he was an active patron of the sect.[46] This was not so, but Fleetwood's weakness was a major cause of the Baptists' strength. It is, therefore, necessary to sketch his character.

Fleetwood was a religious Independent. He borrowed Calvin's works from the library of Trinity; his personal chaplain was an Independent.[47] Like Oliver Cromwell he set great store by liberty of conscience, regarding it as a chief gain of the wars. He was reluctant to act against any man who could lay claim to godliness.[48] Though he might wring his hands at the spectacle of saint contending against saint in Ireland, he could not curtail religious freedom. Admirable though these principles were, his forbearance was exploited by 'politick men . . . to further their sinful practices'.[49]

44 Rogers, *Challah*, pp. 395–6, 398–9, 2–9 *recte* 414–21; *Reliquiae Baxterianae*, i. 171–2; Nickolls, *Original Letters and Papers*, p. 138; *Thurloe State Papers*, v. 477.

45 Rogers, *Challah*, pp. 300–8; Rogers, *Some account*, p. 30; B. S. Capp., *The Fifth Monarchy Men* (London, 1972), p. 261.

46 *The Mystery of the Good Old Cause Briefly Unfolded*, (London, 1660), p. 11; J. S. Reid, *History of the Presbyterian Church in Ireland*, ed. W. D. Killen (Belfast, 1867), ii. 175; Robert Ware, *The Hunting of the Romish Fox* (Dublin, 1683), p. 229; *Your Servant Gentlemen. Or what think you of a Query or two more* (London, 1659[60]), pp. 7–8.

47 T.C.D., MS. D.1.2., unfoliated. The chaplain was Nathanael Partridge, for whom see below, pp. 136, 137, 141.

48 *Thurloe State Papers*, iii. 70, 112, 136; 'Letters etc., of early Friends', ed. A. R. Barclay, in *The Friends' Library* ix, ed. W. Evans and T. Evans (Philadelphia, Pa., 1847), 404.

49 P. Adair, *A True Narrative*, pp. 207, 222; R. Chambre, *Some Animadversions*, p. 7; *Thurloe State Papers*, ii. 150.

Fleetwood was warned that he would be used by the Baptists as Major-General Harrison had been by the Fifth-monarchists in England.[50] But he did nothing to curb the Baptists, allowing them to dominate his government. A contemporary judgement was harsh but true: quite simply Fleetwood was 'not fit for government, especially of an army so difficult to rule, and of a whole kingdom in such reeling times'.[51]

Fleetwood's tolerance would have mattered less had his fellow councillors been firm. Ludlow, having resigned from the civil government in 1654, was immediately admitted to a Baptist congregation in Dublin.[52] Of the other councillors Corbet was prepared to connive at Baptism;[53] John Jones, although he lamented the ferocious controversy, did nothing to quieten it;[54] only Richard Pepys openly opposed the Baptists and as a result found his position in the council weakened.[55]

Fleetwood's and the council's attitude helped Baptism to spread: it was not responsible for its introduction into Ireland. Like religious Independency it came with the English army. In particular two ministers who arrived after 1649 bore much responsibility for spreading Baptism. They were Thomas Patient and Christopher Blackwood. Patient had begun to question episcopacy before the civil war in England. Dissatisfied, he emigrated to New England.[56] Between 1644 and 1650 he was in London, active among the Baptists there. By April 1650 he was at Kilkenny.[57] His preaching had great effect in Waterford and Kilkenny, where the military governors (Lawrence and Axtell respectively) were converted.

50 *Thurloe State Papers*, iv. 406.
51 Adair, *A True Narrative*, p. 222.
52 *Thurloe State Papers*, ii. 163.
53 Bodl., Carte MS. 63, ff. 618, 620.
54 Mayer, *Trans. Historic Soc. of Lancashire and Cheshire*, N.S. i. 235–6, 238.
55 Bodl., Carte MS. 63, ff. 618, 620.
56 T. Patient, *The Doctrine of Baptism* (London, 1654), sig. A4–A4ᵛ; B. R. White, 'Thomas Patient in England and Ireland', *Irish Baptist Historical Society Journal*, ii (1969–70).
57 *A confession of faith of seven congregations or churches in London . . . called Anabaptists* (London, 1646), sig. [A4]ᵛ; *Heart-bleedings for professors abominations* (London, 1650), p. 16; D. King, *A Way to Sion sought out and found* (London, 1649), sig. [A4]ᵛ; Nickolls, *Original letters and papers*, pp. 6–7; B. R. White, 'The organisation of the Particular Baptists, 1644–1660', *Journal of Ecclesiastical History*, vii (1966), 220.

From Waterford Baptist doctrines were taken to Dublin, and by December 1652 Patient had himself moved to the capital.[58] Christopher Blackwood, rector of Staplehurst in Kent before the war and then an army chaplain, had already expressed Baptist opinions in print before coming to Ireland. In 1653 he was appointed official preacher at Kilkenny.[59]

By 1653 Baptism had made great headway in Ireland, with congregations in the main towns: Bandon, Carrickfergus, Clonmel, Cork, Dublin, Galway, Kilkenny, Kinsale, Limerick, Waterford, and Wexford.[60] Baptist activity was confined to the English garrisons: no interest was shown in the native Irish. As a result the English Protestants were bitterly divided.[61] Why was it that what appeared to be a narrow theological controversy — over infant baptism — provoked so strong a response, dividing English soldiers from the existing Protestant settlers? The spread of Baptist tenets owed less to the work of official preachers (Baptists paid government salaries numbered no more than a dozen) than to the enthusiasm of lay converts.[62] Above all it was the sect's success in the English army which transformed it from a minor nuisance into a major political danger.

At the highest level, as we have seen, the Dublin government adopted a tolerant attitude. Patient was employed as preacher to Fleetwood and the general officers: he was allowed to preach at Christ Church in Dublin.[63] The conversion of leading officers helped the sect's spread. In January

---

[58] B.M., Egerton MS. 1762, ff. 182–183ᵛ; Rogers, *Challah*, pp. 300–8; Seymour, p. 33.

[59] C. Blackwood, *Apostolicall Baptisme* (London, 1645); Seymour, p. 60; Whitley, *A Baptist Bibliography*, i. 212; W. T. Whitley, 'The plantation of Ireland and the early Baptist Churches', *The Baptist Quarterly* N.S. i. (1922–3), 279.

[60] Ivimey, *A History of the English Baptists*, i. 240–1. The manuscript of this account is in Nat. Lib. of Wales, Deposit 409 B, pp. 30–2.

[61] Dr. Williams' Library, London, Baxter letters, 3, f. 234; Mayer, *Trans. Historic. Soc. of Lancashire and Cheshire*, N.S. i. 235–6, 238.

[62] Seymour identified ten, one of whom (Tandy) was perhaps not a Baptist. In addition John Draper, Edward Hutchinson, and John Chambers were. Ivimey, *A History of the English Baptists*, i. 240–1; Rogers, *Challah*, p. 306.

[63] Patient's salary (£11 4s. per month) was part of the military establishment, and unlike that of other ministers, not included in the civil list. Bodl., Rawlinson MS. A.208, pp. 379, 390, 410, 420, 421, 427, 434, 439, 441, 453; Seymour, pp. 35, 218, n. 2; Blackwood acknowledged Fleetwood's favour to him: Blackwood, *An Exposition* (London, 1659), sig. A3. His book, *Some Pious Treatises* (London, 1654), was dedicated to Fleetwood's wife.

1652 it was Captain John Vernon and Adjutant-General William Allen (who will reappear) who brought the Baptists' message from Waterford to Rogers's congregation in Dublin. In 1653 it was noted that most of the Irish Baptists 'have relation to the Armie and therefore are subject to be called away'.[64] Tours of duty by Baptist soldiers allowed a thorough evangelization of the country.

In many garrisons the sect was patronized by the governor. In 1655 twelve military governors, as well as members of the civil administration, were said to be Baptists.[65] Furthermore these sympathetic officers had power over religion, being asked to procure ministers for Ireland. The settlement of Baptist preachers at Kilkenny, Waterford, Maryborough, and Naas can be traced to the initiative of governors.[66] Once converted to Baptism, governors withdrew from Independent services: Colonel Robert Barrow did this at Carrickfergus; in Galway Colonel Thomas Sadler threatened to do the same.[67] Ministers at New Ross and Trim were discouraged when moderate governors were replaced by Baptists. Rather than do battle they returned to England.[68] Baptist sympathizers acquired other offices with influence over ecclesiastical affairs, becoming justices of the peace and (in Galway)

[64] Ivimey, *A History*, i. 240; Rogers, *Challah*, pp. 300, 302; Bodl., Rawlinson A.13, f. 105. For soldiers preaching: Petty, *Reflections*, pp. 75–6; *Thurloe State Papers*, iv. 328; *The Bishopric of Derry*, ed. Moody and Simms, p. 346.

[65] *Thurloe State Papers*, iv. 91.

[66] Blackwood was settled at Kilkenny through Axtell's influence. Colonel Lawrence invited James Knight to Waterford, but Knight preferred to settle at Limerick and instead Patient officiated at Waterford. John Hunt, formerly assistant to Blackwood, was settled at Maryborough on the recommendation of Blackwood and Axtell. Peter Row, a member of Patient's Waterford congregation, was installed at Naas thanks to Colonel Hewson. Nat. Lib. Ire., MS. 11,961, pp. 221–2, 311–12; R.C.B., Seymour MSS., p. 1; Capp, *The Fifth Monarchy Men*, pp. 253–4; Ivimey, *A History of the English Baptists*, i. 240; Rogers, *Challah*, p. 306; Seymour, p. 215; *Thurloe State Papers*, iv. 90. The Baptist Colonels Sankey, Barrow, Prettie, and Sadler were all asked by the government to find ministers. R.C.B., Seymour MSS., pp. 2, 68; Nat. Lib. Ire., MS. 11,961, p. 409; Ivimey, op. cit. i. 240; Seymour, p. 58.

[67] Brit. Mus., Lansdowne MS. 822, f. 261; *Thurloe State Papers*, iii. 29.

[68] Brit. Mus., Lansdowne MSS. 821, f. 222; 823, f. 143; R.C.B., Seymour MSS., p. 205; J. B. Leslie, *Ferns Clergy and Parishes* (Dublin, 1936), p. 221; A. G. Matthews, *Calamy Revised* (Oxford, 1934), p. 375.

mayor.[69] The military government which prevailed in most Irish towns until 1656 gave Baptist officers unique opportunities to advance the sect. By 1654 it was felt that membership of the sect was the key to advancement: this feeling brought more converts, so that 'the officers . . . bowed down to the idol baptism, for promotion'. In May 1654 Sir Archibald Johnston heard that 'the officers in Irland were al Anabaptists'.[70]

Support in high places explained how the Baptists took so firm a hold between 1652 and 1654. Yet we have still to explain why highly placed officers so readily embraced the sect. There were two main reasons, one religious, the other political. The Baptists' exclusive doctrine attracted soldiers anxious to retain their distinctive identity as the elect in a country of unregenerate papists. Propaganda about the English mission in Ireland had encouraged chiliastic fervour in the army. Discouragements — Ireton's death, the slower than expected progress of the reconquest, and the spread of plague to English quarters[71] — made the soldiers fearful of spiritual backsliding. These set-backs could be interpreted as signs that reformation had not yet been accomplished; that it could not be through the 'official' religion of the army, Independency; and that a new sect would achieve it. The greater leisure after 1653, when the war was won, allowed religious speculation in a force whose members were already celebrated for their religious radicalism.

Many of those sent to Ireland in 1649 had had a record of political radicalism in England. One of the early converts to Baptism was William Allen, who had been an army Agitator in 1647.[72] The sect attracted political radicals, and as a result acquired a political importance. This became clear in

[69] The County Wexford commission of the peace for 1655 contained at least four Baptists: Ivimey, *A History of the English Baptists*, i. 241; Nickolls, *Original Letters and Papers*, p. 149; J. P. Swan, 'The Justices of the Peace for the County of Wexford', *JRSAI*, 5th Ser. iv (1894), 67. The mayors of Galway were Paul Dod and Lt. John Mathews, for whom see above, p. 65, n. 78.

[70] *The Friends' Library*, ix. 406; *Diary of Sir Archibald Johnston of Wariston*, II, 1650—1654, ed. D. H. Fleming, Scottish History Soc., 2nd Ser. xviii, (1919), 249.

[71] For the plague's impact on Baptists: National Lib. of Wales, Deposit 409 E, p. 32.

[72] Rogers, *Challah*, pp. 300, 302; Ivimey, *A History of the English Baptists*, i. 240. For his earlier career: W. Allen, *A Faithful Memorial of that remarkable*

1654 when widespread dissatisfaction developed in the Irish army about the creation of the protectorate. The leaders of that opposition, Allen, his brother-in-law, Vernon, and Axtell, were conspicuous members of the Baptist church. They used its organization to further their political campaign, so that the Baptist churches in Ireland served the same political function as the Fifth-monarchist congregations in England. Moreover, through Vernon and Allen, there were close links between the English and Irish movements.[73] Also John Rogers, whose Dublin congregation had become a centre of Baptism, had himself become a Fifth-monarchist after his return to England. Rogers retained connections with Ireland, and perhaps co-ordinated Fifth-monarchist opposition with Irish discontent.[74] From 1654 the Baptist churches gained converts amongst the politically disaffected. Fleetwood failed to see that these churches were being used as a cover for opposition which aimed at the overthrow of his father-in-law's protectorate.

Oliver Cromwell, however, appreciated the political dimension that Baptism had now acquired, and was alarmed by Fleetwood's laxity. He sent his younger son, Henry Cromwell, to assess the situation in Ireland in March 1654. Henry Cromwell believed that Baptism must be checked before political and religious moderates were estranged from the protectorate. Through Fleetwood's pusillanimity the English government in Ireland had become synonymous with rule by an exclusive and extreme sect. A change of policy would necessarily involve the replacement of the governors in Dublin.[75]

Oliver Cromwell hesitated to accept his son's unsentimental advice and recall Fleetwood. Eventually he adopted an unwise compromise: Henry Cromwell was commissioned as major-general and added to the Irish council, in which

---

meeting of many officers of the army in England, (London, 1659); Firth and Davies, i. 201, 244; ii. 594, 614, 628–31; Capp, *The Fifth Monarchy Men*, pp. 239–40; P. H. Hardacre, 'William Allen, Cromwellian Agitator and "Fanatic" ', *The Baptist Quarterly*, xix (1962).

[73] Ivimey, op. cit. i. 242–3; Capp, op. cit., pp. 99–100, 106–7, 122, 124, 126, 130, 134, 196, 267; Bodl., Rawlinson MS. A.13, ff. 24. 26.

[74] Rogers returned to Ireland in 1659, see below, p. 132. For his career after 1653: Capp, *The Fifth Monarchy Men*, esp. p. 261.

[75] *Thurloe State Papers*, ii. 149–50, 163.

capacities he crossed to Ireland in July 1655. Fleetwood remained lord deputy, but returned to England in September 1655. Thus Henry Cromwell had the odium of supplanting Fleetwood in Dublin, without being invested with the power necessary to meet the Baptist furore. Moreover Fleetwood's continuation as lord deputy gave the Baptists a gullible supporter who retained great influence and patronage in Irish matters. Until the end of 1656 the Baptists tried to secure Fleetwood's return to Ireland.

Henry Cromwell's intention on first coming to Ireland in 1655 was to steer a middle course, conciliating all parties. An equal distribution of favour necessarily meant a reduction of the Baptists' exorbitant influence, and this they would not stomach. As early as September 1655 there were reports from Dublin that 'the Anabaptist partie in Ireland are much offended with the Lord Henry Cromwell coming every Lords day to parochiall and publique congregation, and with his chaplaines for preaching against dipping.'[76]

iv. The Decline of Baptism under Henry Cromwell

Henry Cromwell's wish to favour all parties foundered on the Baptists' intransigence. They saw that his policy entailed more than regulating religious observances. It meant taking power from the military, the Baptists' supporters, and restoring it to civilians, mainly opponents of the Baptists. The implications of Henry Cromwell's rule were aptly, if fortuitously, shown by the fact that his arrival had coincided with the first large-scale disbanding of troops: an operation hastily undertaken which revealed various technical problems.[77]

Henry Cromwell's difficulties were increased by the tactless enthusiasm with which moderates rallied to him, aspersing Fleetwood's government.[78] The opposition of the Baptists forced Henry Cromwell to accept these embarrassing allies. His first year in Dublin was spent withstanding the Baptist campaign. Quickly the question was resolved into whether or not Fleetwood should come back.[79] As the decision would be made in London, by the protector and

76 *The Clarke Papers*, iii, ed. C. H. Firth, Camden Society, N.S. 61 (1899), 52.
77 *Thurloe State Papers*, iv. 24, 73—4, 87.
78 Ibid. iv. 327, 348—9, 422.
79 Ibid. iv. 276.

council of state, many of the leading Baptists travelled there to conduct their case. Henry Cromwell was left isolated in Dublin, a prey to fears and rumours.[80] Contrary to his expectations, the protector rejected the Baptists' complaints. Oliver Cromwell, it was reported, knew his son dispensed 'favour and respect to every person in proportion to the trust hee bore in the commonwealth; and if such dispensations had formerly bin unequall or disproportionable, it must follow that some must have more, others lesse of your lo[rdshi]ps countenance then formerly, and consequently noe marvaile if the persons disappointed were angry'.[81] If Oliver Cromwell understood the situation in Dublin so well, it was surprising that he did not increase his son's powers. Rather he left Henry Cromwell to fend for himself.

The events of 1655 and 1656 encouraged Henry Cromwell's tendency to see Baptism as a political problem. Orderly government and the security of the protectorate in Ireland demanded a firm stand against the Baptists. In December 1655 Henry Cromwell agreed with Secretary Thurloe that it was good to use tenderness towards them: 'I have done it, and still doe it'. But already he was entering a rider: he must 'be carefull to keep them from power whoe, if they hade it in their power, would express little tenderness to those that would not submitt to their way'.[82] When the test of political loyalty was applied to the sect, he concluded: 'I doe not thinke that God has given them a spiritt of government; neither is it safe they should have much power in their handes'.[83]

Finding them implacably opposed to him, Henry Cromwell dropped conciliation and 'openly shewed himself against the Anabaptists'.[84] Gaining support in other quarters, his antipa-

---

[80]These fears were played on by Sankey, posing as a sympathetic intermediary, who retailed news that Henry Cromwell's agents in London had been detained. Brit. Mus., Lansdowne MS. 821, ff. 218, 222, 230; *Thurloe State Papers*, iv. 408; v. 177, 278.

[81]Brit. Mus., Lansdowne MS. 821, f. 246v.

[82]*Thurloe State Papers*, iii. 699.

[83]Ibid. iv. 433. Even English Baptists found their Irish brethren too overbearing: Friends' Library, Tracts 323 (16), untitled tract by Thomas Collier, pp. 3–5.

[84]E. Borlase, *The history of the execrable Irish Rebellion* (London, 1680), p. 315; *Thurloe State Papers*, iii. 699; iv. 408, 433.

thy towards the Baptists hardened. By 1659 he could brusquely dismiss the saints' claim to rule, and ask,[85] 'will not the loins of an imposing Independent or Anabaptist be as heavy as the loins of an imposing prelate or presbyter? And is it a dangerous error, that dominion is founded in grace, when it is held by the Church of Rome, and a sound principle when it is held by the fifth-monarchy? '

Official favour was withdrawn from the Baptists: some of their preachers had their government salaries stopped or reduced; others were moved from populous towns to remoter areas where they could do less damage.[86] At the end of 1656 Baptist fury had subsided. This was not the result of theological reconciliation, for conferences between Independents and Blackwood had failed. It was occasioned by a lull in the political campaign against Henry Cromwell and the protectorate. Having failed to dislodge him, the leading Baptist officers in Ireland — Allen, Axtell, Barrow, and Vernon — resigned their commissions in November 1656. They had not abandoned hopes of overthrowing him, but they transferred their energies to England. The effect of their careful mining was seen in 1659, when an attempt was made to impeach Henry Cromwell's secretary, Petty, and when Henry Cromwell himself fell with the protectorate. However, after their resignations in 1656 the officers stopped using the Baptist churches in Ireland, which consequently lost their adventitious support and became purely religious groups.[87]

Deprived of their military followers, the Baptists in Ireland were eager to prove their loyalty to the protectorate. Their professions were evidently accepted by Henry Cromwell, who allowed the Baptists as a religious sect a tacit toleration, preferring 'not to crush them quite . . . lest others take occasion to become insolent and violent'.[88] The political connections were revived briefly in 1659, when the Baptists again had a chance of political domination. After 1660 they

85 Ibid., vii. 454. Cf. the spurious *Lord Henry Cromwels Speech in the House* (n.p., 1659), p. 6.

86 Blackwood, Draper, and Row lost their salaries; Knight was moved from Limerick to County Kerry and Clarke from Galway to Queen's County. The salaries of both were reduced. R.C.B., Seymour MSS., pp. 207, 211, 219.

87 Brit. Mus., Lansdowne MS. 821, ff. 52, 242; *Thurloe State Papers*, iv. 90; v. 508–9, 670–2, 710, 729; vi. 820; vii. 199.

88 Ibid. v. 710; vi. 820; vii. 199; Nickolls, *Original Letters and Papers*, p. 148.

once more declined into a small religious sect anxious to show its loyalty to the established government of Charles II.[89] As a religious phenomenon they lingered on in Dublin, where Blackwood still had a congregation after 1660 and where the Baptists Sankey and William Lamb preached in 1674.[90]

v. The Quakers

As the Baptists declined as a political menace, it at first seemed that their place as a focus for discontent would be taken by the Quakers. We must see whether or not that happened.

After his experience with the Baptists, Henry Cromwell was alive to the political implications of the Quakers. Early in 1656 he told Thurloe, 'our most considerable enemy nowe in our view are the Quakers, who begin to growe in some reputation in the county of Corke'.[91] Henry Cromwell explained his distrust of the sect. 'Their principles and practises are not verry consistent with civil government, much lesse with the discipline of an army. Some thinke them to have noe designe, but I am not of that opinion. Their counterfeited simplicitie renders them to me the more dangerous'.[92] He saw them as the Baptists' successors: a threat to political as well as religious order. In time Henry Cromwell found that he had been wrong: he then relaxed his earlier severity.

The Quakers' early successes in the English garrisons suggested similarities with the Baptists. In particular Quakerism threatened to sweep through the English forces in Munster. Conscious of Fleetwood's mistake, Henry Cromwell acted vigorously. The Munster garrisons had become notorious for their unorthodoxy,[93] thanks to the governors of

---

89 T. Grantham, *Christianus Primitivus* (London, 1678), book iii, pp. 7–9; Peter Row, *The Magistrates Power Vindicated* (London, 1661).

90 Bodl., Carte MS. 45, f. 437; T.C.D., MS. A.6.13.

91 *Thurloe State Papers*, iv. 508. Thurloe referred to this as the first letter 'that mentioned any thinge of the Quakers in Ireland'. Ibid. iv. 530.

92 *Thurloe State Papers*, iv. 508.

93 Colonel Henry Bowen was accused of atheism, and there were alleged to be 'some others of that way towards Corke'. Chatsworth, Lismore MS. 29; Cork's diary, 24 Dec. 1652; R. Baxter, *The Certainty of the Worlds of Spirits* (London, 1691), pp. 23–4; E. Bowen, *Bowen's Court* (London, 1942), p. 31; Mayer, *Trans. Historic Soc. of Lancashire and Cheshire*, N.S. i. 210.

Cork (Robert Phaire)[94] and Kinsale (Richard Hodden). At Cork Phaire was said to allow discussions which strike at the roots of all divine truths, asserting that God is nothing, that Heaven is not local, that the Scriptures . . . are not the work of God . . . ' Even Fleetwood had protested at this tolerance.[95] It was the Quakers, not the Baptists, who excited Hodden's and Phaire's enthusiasm. They would accomplish Ireland's long delayed reformation. Phaire indeed declared that 'more is done by the Quakers than all the priests in the country have done [in] a hundred years'; and Hodden wrote, 'we look for a new heaven and a new earth'.[96] Hodden and Phaire used their considerable local authority to protect the Quakers. The dangers of such patronage were shown by an incident at Kinsale. Hodden had compelled the congregation to listen to a Quaker outburst in the church. When they tried to leave, they were forced back by the garrison, acting on Hodden's instructions.[97] Repetition of such incidents would bring to flash-point the smouldering antagonism between soldiers and civilians in Munster.

As with the Baptists, it was military backing which made the Quakers dangerous. Henry Cromwell, therefore, removed it. Hodden was dismissed from the commission of the peace; Phaire threatened with dismissal. A new commander was appointed in Munster, 'where much want is and hath beene of sobriety in your officers', and Quakers in the army were swiftly cashiered.[98]   In this way military discipline was preserved.

    [94] Phaire was the son of an Anglican minister in County Cork and had served in Inchiquin's army. The life in *D.N.B.* can be supplemented by W. H. Welply, 'Colonel Robert Phaire, "Regicide", his ancestry, history and descendants', *Notes and Queries*, 12th Ser. xii (1923), 123–5, 143–6, 164–7, 185–7, 376. He sheltered an adulterous preacher accused of atheism, Thomas Royle. Nat. Lib. Wales, MS. 11,440–D, 133; Friends' Library, Swarthmore MS. v. 13; Dunlop, ii. 295; Hist. MSS. Comm., *Egmont MSS.* i. 523.

    [95] Nat. Lib. Wales, MS. 11,440–D, 131; *Thurloe State Papers*, iii. 567.

    [96] *The Friends' Library*, ix. 406; Brit. Mus., Lansdowne MS. 821, f. 68. Hodden kept a Quaker chaplain and published a Quaker tract, *The One Good Way of God* (London, 1661). Major Peter Wallis, 'and moste of the chief officers' in County Cork, were said to frequent Quaker meetings. W. C. Braithwaite, *The Beginnings of Quakerism* (London, 1912), p. 216; *Thurloe State Papers* iv. 508.

    [97] Ibid., iv. 672–3.

    [98] Ibid., iv. 672; Brit. Mus., Lansdowne 821, ff. 89, 138; 822, f. 220; Joseph Besse, *A Collection of the Sufferings of the People called Quakers* (London,

The progress of the Quakers in Munster was not typical of the rest of Ireland. Elsewhere their military converts were not numerous or particularly influential.[99]   And even within Munster their supporters had been attracted by the Quakers' spiritual appeal rather than any political use to which they might be put. Only one incident suggested that Henry Cromwell was right to see them as a new centre of political opposition. Reports in March 1657 told of the ring-leaders of opposition — Vernon and Allen — attending a Quaker meeting.[100]   If this was true, nothing came of it. The Quakers in Ireland were careful to allay Henry Cromwell's fears that they 'will rebell against ye Govern[n]m[en]t as it hap[pen]ed in London', maintaining they 'are not of a principle of rebellion, but of a principall of patient suffering'.[101]   Gradually, after the first alarms, Henry Cromwell accepted that they had no underhand aim. Quakers who disturbed church services were still punished, but they were no longer treated as political enemies. This milder policy was reflected in the decline in the numbers of Quakers imprisoned. In 1655, the first (incomplete) year of Quaker activity, seventy-seven were imprisoned. In 1656 the total fell to fifteen; in 1657 five; in 1658 three, and in 1659 only one.[102]

The Quakers' appearance in Ireland had two important effects. Religious moderates and conservatives responded to their challenge by taking up and refining the methods first used to contain the Baptists. Coming hard on the Baptists'

1753), ii. 460; *The Friends' Library*, ix. 406. Phaire eventually became a Muggletonian. J. Reeve and L. Muggleton, *A Volume of Spiritual Epistles*, (n.p., 1755), pp. 91, 104.

99The most important were Capt. Robert Wilkinson in Limerick, Col. Nicholas Kempson (Ludlow's brother-in-law), and Capt. William Morris. Brit. Mus., Lansdowne MS. 821, f. 127; Friends' Library, Swarthmore MS. iii. 3; Braithwaite, *Beginnings of Quakerism*, p. 217; *A Journal of the Life ... of ... William Edmundson* (Dublin, 1715), pp. 18, 25, 31; A. Fuller and T. Holms *A Compendious View of Some Sufferings of the People call'd Quakers* (Dublin, 1731), ii. 107.

100Brit. Mus., Lansdowne MS. 821, f. 334; *Thurloe State Papers*, vi. 222–3. Was the 'Captain Alan' with whom Quakers lodged in Dublin Colonel William Allen? *The Friends' Library*, ix. 404.

101Friends' Library, Swarthmore MS. v. 5.

102Fuller and Holms, *A Compendious View*, ii. 123. For the milder treatment: Brit. Mus., Lansdowne MS. 822, f. 17; Friends' Library, Swarthmore MS. iv. 23.

heels, the Quakers influenced the development of Winter's Independent church and of the former Anglican clergy in Munster. Secondly, the Quakers in these years took hold in Ireland: a hold that proved tenacious and permanent. After the initial alarm, the government accepted their presence. The Quakers' modest success owed most to a sympathetic response from the civilian Protestant population. It was in Munster and Ulster, the areas in which a Protestant society of artisans and craftsmen, smallholders and shopkeepers had existed in 1641, that they made most converts. It was those areas which most nearly reproduced the social conditions in which Quakerism was established in England.[103] Established in the Interregnum, the Quakers survived with a distinctive place amongst Protestant groups in Ireland after 1660. In 1683, for example, the Quakers of Cork were said to be the town's greatest traders. Their political reliability was by then well known.[104]

vi. Winter and the Independents

We must now return to the mainstream of religious life, temporarily forsaken to examine the Quakers. The account has to be resumed at the point when Henry Cromwell took over the Irish government from Fleetwood, in September 1655.

Dr. Samuel Winter, the leader of the Dublin Independents and provost of Trinity College, Dublin, saw the change in government as a fine opportunity to inherit the favour hitherto monopolized by the Baptists. He rallied his congregation to Henry Cromwell's support and tapped his contacts with the Independent churches in other Irish towns, inspiring petitions in Henry Cromwell's favour. The intemperance of these petitions only inflamed the contro-

---

103 Details of Irish Quakers occur in the collections of 'sufferings', of which the most substantial is Fuller and Holms, op. cit. For English Quakers: A Cole, 'Social origins of the early Friends', *Jnl. Friends' Hist. Soc.* xlviii. (1957); R. T. Vann, 'Quakerism and the social structure in the Interregnum', *P. and P.* xliii (1969); J. J. Hurwich, 'The Social Origins of the early Quakers', ibid. xlviii (1970); Vann, 'Rejoinder', ibid. xlviii. (1970).
104 Hist. MSS. Comm., *Ormonde MSS.*, N.S. vii. 95, 104, 121; Crawford, 'The rise of the linen industry' in *The formation of the Irish economy*, ed. Cullen, p. 25; *The council book of Youghal*, ed. Caulfield, p. 371.

versy. As the battle shifted to Westminster, Winter followed the Baptists to England.[105]

In retrospect Henry Cromwell believed that Winter had had a deep-rooted design to engross official favour. That interpretation exaggerated Winter's cunning. Yet there was no doubt that Winter had staked much on Henry Cromwell's arrival, working for his appointment, and identifying the Independents' future with a change in the Irish government.[106] Before September 1655 Winter's influence with the administration had hardly been commensurate with his positions as head of the Independent church and of Dublin University. Winter had perhaps suffered from his connection with John Weaver, a parliamentary commissioner from 1650 to 1653. Weaver, his brother-in-law, had no doubt secured Winter's invitation to Dublin.[107] But Weaver's period of office in Ireland had been troubled. The champion of civilian rule and of the Rump, hostility in the army had forced his resignation.[108] Winter was similarly identified with the civilian party, through his relationship with Weaver and through the composition of his Dublin congregation. As we have seen leading aldermen had joined his church. They had particular reason to dislike Fleetwood's tolerance of the Baptists, since the latter wanted to suppress Dublin's charter and bring the capital under complete military government.[109] These members of Winter's church had compelling reasons for supporting Fleetwood's replacement by Henry Cromwell.

A chance to engage Henry Cromwell in the Independents' cause occurred with his visit to Dublin in March 1654. Winter entertained Henry Cromwell at Trinity College, to good effect. Henry Cromwell's report emphasized the importance

[105]R.C.B., Seymour MSS., p. 17; Brit. Mus., Lansdowne MSS. 821, ff. 46, 52, 218; The Clarke Papers, iii, ed. Firth, pp. 60–1; Nickolls Original Letters and Papers, pp. 137–8; Thurloe State Papers, ii. 117–18; iv. 197, 227, 270–1, 286–7, 327, 348–9, 445; The Register of Provost Winter (Trinity College, Dublin), 1650–1660, ed. H. J. Lawlor, Parish Register Soc. of Dublin, iv. (Exeter, 1907), 17.

[106]Thurloe State Papers, vii. 199.

[107]J.W., The Life and Death of ... Dr. Samuel Winter (London, 1671), pp. 7–8.

[108]See above, p. 18.

[109]See above, p. 62.

of conciliating the Independents.[110]   Boldly Winter gambled on his returning to Ireland to put these suggestions into effect. How much he counted on this was shown by the invitation to Henry Cromwell, immediately after his visit, to become Trinity's chancellor: a direct snub for Fleetwood, the more diplomatic choice.[111]   In 1655 Winter's bold throw seemed to have succeeded. To underline the projected alliance Henry Cromwell was quickly installed as chancellor.[112]

In the difficult months of 1655 and 1656 Henry Cromwell, uncertain and inexperienced, accepted Winter's and the Independents' help. By the end of 1656, having survived the Baptists' onslaught, Henry Cromwell reconsidered the alliance into which Winter had hustled him. It was open to two objections. First, by relying on Winter was he not repeating Fleetwood's mistake, and simply substituting an Independent for a Baptist monopoly? Secondly, was an Independent alliance as valuable as Winter made out? Winter saw himself as the leader of the natural Cromwellian party in Ireland. In England Oliver Cromwell kept close to his old allies, the Independents. It seemed natural to Winter that the English alliance between the protectorate and the Independents should be repeated in Ireland.

In England, however, there were growing doubts about the political wisdom of basing the regime on a narrow sect of the godly. In Ireland such a policy appeared even more unwise. Henry Cromwell saw his task as the re-establishment of English and Protestant authority in Ireland. That task was complicated by the fact that the authority was now his father's protectorate. Religious policy, so far as he was concerned, should be subordinated to that work. He had therefore to find an ecclesiastical policy acceptable to the largest number of Irish Protestants; and to find religious agents with influence over the Protestant population, especially over the substantial men who were to be the foundation of the protectorate in Ireland.[113]

110 *Thurloe State Papers*, ii. 149–50, 163.
111 T.C.D., Mun. P/1/378a.
112 *The Clarke Papers*, iii, ed. Firth, p. 50.
113 Henry Cromwell's thinking is examined in Barnard, *P. and P.* lxi.

Henry Cromwell doubted whether Winter's party met these requirements. His zeal in 1655 had hidden his very limited support.[114] The Independents in Ireland, like the Baptists, were an alien sect introduced in the wake of the Cromwellian army. Where Cromwellian rule was firmly established — in the garrisons — congregations of Independents gathered. To imagine that the Independent churches could extend English authority to those areas whose loyalty was still uncertain was to credit the sect with an illusory strength. The Independent churches had not arisen naturally from Irish Protestant society. In the improbable event of a complete transformation of that society — the transformation intended by the new Cromwellian settlement — the Independent churches would take stronger hold. The churches themselves would never accomplish social change.

Henry Cromwell was prepared to co-operate with Winter and the Independents because they had influence in Dublin and some garrisons. But he needed other allies, who could help gain the backing of the Protestant settlers, especially in Munster and Ulster. Unfortunately Winter was as reluctant to share power as the Baptists had been; he was affronted by the theological implications of Henry Cromwell's new alliances. Winter's growing disenchantment with Henry Cromwell was exploited by politicians until in 1658 there was an open breach between them. Once Winter and the Independents became associated with political opposition, the sect was damned in Henry Cromwell's eyes and it could no longer be trusted with any favour. So with nothing now to lose, Winter and the Independents moved into open opposition in 1658, making common cause with the Baptists and with the English and Irish opponents of the protectorate.

Like the Baptists the Independents acquired a political dimension and their organization was used for political purposes. Two men accomplished this transformation: John Weaver and William Steele. Weaver kept in touch with Winter and with an elder of his congregation, Alderman Daniel Hutchinson. Deeply implicated in English opposition to the protectorate, in 1658 Weaver was able to draw the

114Even in Dublin Winter's hold was far from complete: see below, p. 152.

discontented Irish Independents into that movement.[115] Weaver's intrigues surfaced only in 1658. Clearer, and more persistent, was Steele's behaviour. Steele's outlook was close to the Army Independents and indeed to Fleetwood's, setting great store by liberty of conscience.[116] He was much respected in England, so that Henry Cromwell's complaints against him were often disregarded or taken as further proof of Henry Cromwell's own unsatisfactory opinions.

Steele had a long-standing interest in the propagation of the Gospel.[117] Once in Ireland (in 1656) he intervened in religious life, putting himself at the head of the Independents.[118] He also took it upon himself to advise Henry Cromwell, 'as a tutor or guardian to a minor'.[119] His tactless manner ruffled Henry Cromwell, but there was also a fundamental difference of approach. Steele wanted all the godly to be tolerated, and included the Baptists in that category. On the other hand, members of the Churches of England and Ireland could expect no generosity.[120] Henry Cromwell's policy was the opposite: to investigate ways of winning over former Anglicans and a harsh policy towards the Baptists.

Steele and Henry Cromwell were separated by genuine religious differences. Steele used his political position (as lord chancellor and a councillor) to try to frustrate unacceptable religious policies, and reduced the Irish council to virtual paralysis. He worked to stop Henry Cromwell's appointment as lord deputy in 1657; he exploited his extensive English

115 Brit. Mus., Add. MS. 15,635, f. 60ᵛ; Bodl., Rawlinson MS. A.481, ff. 24ᵛ–25; *Diary of Thomas Burton Esq.* iv. 240; Hist. MSS. Comm., *Egmont MSS.* i. 542; A. R. Maddison, *Lincolnshire Pedigrees*, iii, Harleian Soc. lii (London, 1904), 1046–7; *Thurloe State Papers*, iv. 509; vii. 243, 269.

116 Brit. Mus., Lansdowne MS. 1228, f. 9ᵛ. It was Fleetwood who had insisted on Steele's Irish appointment in 1654, although he was fully occupied as a judge in England. *Thurloe State Papers*, ii. 492–3.

117 Steele was president of a corporation to propagate the Gospel in North America. Brit. Mus., Add. MS. 4274, f. 4ᵛ; Bodl., Rawlinson MS. C.934, f. 3; W. Kellaway, *The New England Company, 1649–1776* (London, 1961), pp. 19, 46, 63–4.

118 *Thurloe State Papers*, vii. 198.

119 Ibid., vii. 198–9. The 'three or four sheets in writing of those rules he thought of most importance', which Steele gave to Henry Cromwell, survive in Brit. Mus., Lansdowne MS. 1228, ff. 7–12ᵛ.

120 Ibid., ff. 8–9ᵛ.

connections to undermine Henry Cromwell's position.[121] Although he embittered life in Dublin, he failed to stop Henry Cromwell's changes. In 1658, after this failure, he considered retirement. However the fall of the protectorate in 1659 briefly restored him to influence.[122]

It was in May 1658 that the decisive breach with Winter, Steele, and the Independents happened, as a result of the convention of ministers which had been summoned to Dublin. Thereafter the leadership of the Irish church passed to those who agreed with Henry Cromwell's policies; and the Independents, guilty of political intrigue, lost all power. It is now time to identify the religious groups which Henry Cromwell cultivated in place of the Independents — the former Anglicans of Cork, and the Scottish Presbyterians of Ulster — and then to investigate the climax of that co-operation, the convention of 1658.

vii. Edward Worth and the Cork Association of Ministers

The leader of the Independents was Winter, the chaplain who had accompanied the parliamentary commissioners to Dublin in 1650. It was perhaps surprising that none of Henry Cromwell's chaplains emerged as his chief religious adviser. Three ministers served in his household, Stephen Charnock, Thomas Harrison, and Francis Roberts.[123] Harrison and Roberts had high reputations before coming to Ireland, Roberts as a leading Presbyterian in London.[124] Yet although Harrison was used as an agent by Henry Cromwell and his choice of Roberts indicated his conservative tastes, neither chaplain exercised any strong influence over national ecclesiatical policy in Ireland.[125] Instead Henry Cromwell

---

121 *Thurloe State Papers*, vi. 446, 506, 632; vii. 198–9.

122 Ibid. vii. 269, 498.

123 Suggestions that Winter and Samuel Mather accompanied Henry Cromwell in 1655 are wrong. *Cal. S.P. Dom., 1654*, pp. 369, 457; C. Mather, *Magnalia Christi Americana* (London, 1702), p. 146.

124 E. Calamy, *An abridgement of Mr. Baxter's History* (London, 1702), pp. 467–8; J. B. Marsh, *Memorials of the City Temple* (London, 1877), pp. 127–8; G. F. Nuttall, 'Presbyterians and Independents', *Jnl. Presbyterian Hist. Soc. of England* x (1952), p. 11; V. Pearl, 'London Puritans and Scotch Fifth Columnists ...', in *Studies in London History*, ed. A. E. J. Hollaender and W. Kellaway (London, 1969), p. 328.

125 Brit. Mus., Lansdowne MS. 821, ff. 218, 222; *Thurloe State Papers*, v. 45, 150, 177, 278.

found a leader amongst the former Anglican clergy of Ireland, Dr. Edward Worth, since 1646 dean of Cork. The policy pioneered by Worth in Munster became a national policy by 1658.

In contrast with the Baptists and Independents, Worth's clerical party consisted of members of Protestant settler families and ministers who had been educated in Ireland. Indeed Worth and his two principal collaborators, Thomas Hackett and Joseph Eyres, had been contemporaries at Trinity College, Dublin, shortly before the rebellion.[126] These men had close contacts with the Munster gentry. Worth had married into the Boyle family and kept in close touch with Broghill.[127]

The Munster clergy had followed the Protestant laity's lead in the civil war. In 1648 the Munster gentry were divided by Inchiquin's defection from the parliamentary cause. Inchiquin tried to bind the province's clergy to his side. The ministers agreed that their oaths obliged them to obey Charles I and acknowledged the authority of Inchiquin and Ormonde.[128] But already a minority of the clergy was following Inchiquin's opponents, Broghill and Sir William Fenton.[129] They accepted the argument that to preserve the Protestant interest in Ireland it might be necessary to work with the new English rulers. However the new rulers were

126*Alumni Dublinenses*, pp. 5, 354, 895; T. U. Sadleir and H. M. Watson, 'A record of 17th century Alumni', *Hermathena*, lxxxix (1957), 56, 57. Eyres was the son of a minister in County Cork; Hackett had been beneficed in the county before 1649. Bodl., Carte MSS. 23, f. 205; 221, f. 555; Brit. Mus., Lansdowne MS. 823, f. 91; W. M. Brady, *Clerical Records of Cork, Cloyne and Ross* (London, 1684), ii. 63, 181, 294; J. G. White, *Historical and Topographical Notes, etc. on Buttevant, Castletownroche ...* (Cork, 1913), iii. 16.

127P. Dwyer, *The Diocese of Killaloe from the Reformation to the close of the eighteenth century* (Dublin, 1878), p. 345; W. M. Mason, *The History and Antiquities of the Collegiate and Cathedral Church of St. Patrick* (Dublin, 1820), p. 205, note f; Worth to Broghill, [?] Jan. 1659[60], Harvard Univ. Lib.. MS. Eng. 218. 22.F.

128Bodl., Carte MS. 23, ff. 203–5, printed as *Lord Inchiquins Queries ...* (The Hague, 1649). See also, J. Cook, *Monarchy no Creature of Gods making, etc.* (Waterford, 1651), sig. [f3]ᵛ.

129Worth did not sign the address to Inchiquin and in August 1649 was absent from the meetings of the Cork cathedral chapter. *State Papers ... of Clarendon*, ii. 501; *The Council book of ... Kinsale*, ed. Caulfield, p. 6; Hist. MSS. Comm., *Egmont MSS*. i. 316–17. For Hackett's contacts with Broghill and other settlers: P.R.O., SP. 63/286, 59; Chatsworth, Cork's diary, 19 Feb. 1653[4].

unresponsive. As yet no distinction was made between uncompromising episcopalians and those prepared to collaborate with the new regime. To the parliamentary commissioners and to Fleetwood and his council Worth and his followers were no better than prelatists and their help was not wanted.

Worth liked Fleetwood's regime as little as Winter did. It allowed religious anarchy in Munster; it obstructed Worth when he tried to check that disorder and sheltered his opponents.[130] If Worth had no support from the government, he had solid backing amongst the Munster settlers and was presented to offices in the gift of local corporations.[131] Even so there was little hope of eradicating religious error in existing conditions. Worth believed three changes were essential. First, his clerical supporters must be bound more tightly together to combat the theological errors. But improved clerical organization would not succeed unless there was a second change. Baptists and Quakers were protected by Munster's military governors. The province's government must, therefore, be returned to civilians, many of whom were Worth's supporters. For this reason Worth backed the campaign to restore municipal charters. However any attempt to re-establish civil government in the corporations was foredoomed so long as the Dublin government was headed by Fleetwood and dominated by the military and Baptist party. Thus the third element in his plan was to work for Fleetwood's replacement.[132]

Henry Cromwell's arrival was the alteration Worth's

---

130 R.C.B., Seymour MS., p. 29; Brit. Mus., Additional MS. 4274, f. 176; Lansdowne MS. 821, f. 198; J. Coleman, 'Some early Waterford clerical authors', *Jnl. Waterford and South East of Ireland Archaeological Soc.* vi. (1900), 179; C. Gilbert, *The Libertine School'd* (London, 1658), p. 53; J. Murcot, *Several Works* (London, 1657), pp. 15–22; E. Worth, *Scripture Evidence for the baptizing the children of covenanters* ([Cork], 1653). The councillors Corbet and Thomlinson tried to have Eyres's salary stopped. Chatsworth, Cork's diary, 10 Aug. 1655; J. Eyres, *The Church-Sleeper Awakened* (London, 1659), sig. [A10]–[A10]V. Dr. John Harding, the principal Baptist in Cork, enjoyed Fleetwood's favour and received many official employments. Brit. Mus., Lansdowne MS. 822, f. 15; Nat. Lib. Ire., 11,961, p. 34; T.C.D., MS. F.4.16, f. 53V; Dunlop, ii. 392, 468, 486; Seymour, p. 112.

131 P.R.O., Dublin, 'Repertory of Cromwell's leases, Chancery, 1656–59', pp. 30, 49; C.B., Jennings transcripts, A/8, 26 Sept. 1655.

132 Chatsworth, Lismore MS. 29, Cork's diary, 17 Feb. 1654[5].

strategy needed. Within a year municipal corporations had been restored, permitting a fruitful alliance between civilian magistrates, who enforced religious order, and the clergy who preached obedience to the existing social and political order.[133]   Moreover Worth's assault on the Quakers in Cork met with an immediate and favourable response from Henry Cromwell.[134]   Assured of the secular arm's support, Worth could now perfect his purely religious organization. In 1656 Worth and Eyres, with 'the rest of the classical Presbiterian ministers' of Cork, set up a weekly lecture from which Independents as well as more extreme clergy were excluded.[135]   The next step was the establishment in 1657 of a Cork association of ministers. Its principal function was to ordain ministers, since Worth attributed much of the recent confusion in Munster to unordained preachers' activities.[136]

The device of an association was not unique to Worth and Cork. Its use had been pioneered in England by Richard Baxter; Winter had introduced it into Ireland during his struggle against the Baptists in 1655. However the Cork association's character differed from these earlier models. Baxter's main concern was with the reunion of sects, comprehending them in a properly regulated church. Winter's association had copied Baxter's directly.[137]   Yet Winter's association had been small in membership, lacked a precisely defined territorial base, and lapsed soon after 1655.[138]   In contrast Worth's interest was not in comprehension. The

133Eyres, *The Church-Sleeper Awakened*, sig. A2–A2^v, a5^v; J. E[yres?], epistle to the reader in S. Ladyman, *The Dangerous Rule* (London, 1658), sig. [a4]^v; J. Murcot, *Several Works*, p. 15.

134R.C.B., Seymour MS. p. 29; *A Journal of ... William Edmundson*, p. 17. Worth's wife became a Quaker. T. Wight and J. Rutty, *A History of the rise and progress of the people called Quakers in Ireland* (Dublin, 1751), p. 96.

135*Thurloe State Papers*, v. 353; Chatsworth, Cork's diary, 3 July 1655.

136*The Agreement and Resolution of Several Associated Ministers, in the County Of Corke* (Cork, 1657); *Thurloe State Papers*, v. 353. There is no record of its ordinations, but probably that of Daniel Burston, later dean of Waterford, was one: D. Burston, Ευχγγελιστης ετι ευχγγελιξομενος, *The Evangelist yet evangelizing* (Dublin, 1662), p. 23.

137Dr. Williams' Lib., Baxter letters, iv. 101; *Reliquiae Baxterianae*, i. 169–70. Cf. G. F. Nuttall, *Richard Baxter*, pp. 64–76; W. A. Shaw, *A History of the English Church during the Civil Wars and under the Commonwealth, 1640–1660* (London, 1900), ii. 152–62, 440–56.

138Only four other ministers were members, and none was settled in Dublin. Seymour, p. 160.

Cork association would help re-establish and enforce fundamental Gospel ordinances. It was intended as a local start to Worth's ultimate aim: the erection of a national church to which adherence would be demanded. Uniformity, not toleration, was his overriding concern. This different emphasis was underlined by the Cork association's English contacts, which were with the London Presbyterian *classes*. Eyres had been a member of a London *classis* earlier in the decade and in 1658 returned to it as an agent from the Cork association.[139] Worth himself discussed religious policy with the London Presbyterians in 1658.[140]

These English connections were important, especially as by 1658 eirenic schemes had failed in England and Presbyterians and Independents were again gravitating towards opposed political, as well as religious, positions.[141] The same polarization happened in Ireland in 1658: Winter aligned with John Owen and Hugh Peter, now hostile to the protectorate; Worth was associated with the English Presbyterians.

In Ireland Worth's influence with Henry Cromwell had steadily increased since 1655. At first Henry Cromwell had seen Worth's value as local; with his influence in Munster he could persuade the recalcitrant clergy there to stop praying for Charles II.[142] Worth's strong local connections could also be helpful in winning over the Protestant settlers of Munster to Henry Cromwell's regime. Increasingly Henry Cromwell relied on Worth, allowing him in 1658 to inaugurate a policy which would apply nationally what the Cork association had already succeeded in doing in Munster. Before looking at

139 Sion College, London, MS. Arc. L.40.2/E.17, 'Minute book of the London Provincial Assembly 1647–1660', ff. 241ᵛ, 242; Brit. Mus., Add. MS. 10,114, f. 30ᵛ; *The Register-Booke of the Fourth Classis in the Province of London 1646–59*, ed. C. E. Surnam, Harleian Soc., 82 and 83 (London, 1953), pp. 48, 127, 141.

140 Brit. Mus., Lansdowne MS. 823, f. 57.

141 G. R. Abernathy, Jr., 'Richard Baxter and the Cromwellian Church', *Huntington Library Quarterly*, xxiv (1961), 229; R. H. C. Catterall, 'The failure of the Humble Petition and Advice', *American Historical Review*, ix (1903), 36–64; A. H. Woolrych, 'The Good Old Cause and the fall of the Protectorate'. *Cambridge Historical Journal*, xiii (1957), 147.

142 Chatsworth, Lismore MS. 29, Cork's diary, 20 Nov. 1655 and 31 Jan. 1655[6]; Brit. Mus., Lansdowne MS. 821, f. 198. In 1656, for the first time, Worth received a government salary. R.C.B., Seymour MS., p. 153, 208.

Worth's emergence as Henry Cromwell's religious leader in 1658, we must trace another ecclesiastical alliance that had become apparent by 1658: with the Scottish Presbyterians of Ulster.

viii.   The Scottish Presbyterians and Ulster

Collaboration with the Scottish Presbyterians in Ulster was inspired by the same motives as the co-operation with Worth: Henry Cromwell's awareness of the Presbyterian ministers' influence over the Protestant population. But because Ulster's Protestant society was more complex than Munster's, the policy was less successful.

Scottish Presbyterianism had come to Ulster with the Scots settlers in the early seventeenth century.[143] Oppressed by Strafford and Bramhall in the 1630s, Presbyterian fortunes revived after 1642 when a Scottish army was sent to Ireland. Under Major-General Robert Monro's patronage a presbytery was established at Carrickfergus in close touch with the Scottish General Assembly.[144] Divisions occurred amongst Presbyterian laity and clergy in 1649, first when the leading Presbyterian, Viscount Montgomery of the Ards, abandoned the Solemn League and Covenant.[145] Political events in England then divided the Kirk. In Scotland the Presbyterians split into two factions. One, the Remonstrants, was so hostile to the Stuarts that it was prepared to collaborate with the Cromwellians; the second, the Resolutioners, pinned its hopes on Charles II as a covenanted king and so opposed the institution of the English commonwealth.[146] Quickly these same divisions spread to Ulster. At

143 On the early history of Presbyterianism in Ulster: Adair, *A True Narrative*, and Reid, *History of the Presbyterian Church in Ireland*; also A. F. Scott Pearson, 'Alumni of St. Andrews and the settlement of Ulster', *Ulster Journal of Archaeology*, 3rd Ser. xiv (1951), 1–13.

144 Adair, *A True Narrative*, pp. 92–4; *The records of the Commissioners of the General Assemblies of the Church of Scotland ... 1648 and 1649*, ed. A. F. Mitchell and J. Christie, Scottish History Soc. xxv (1896), 187, 310.

145 Adair, *A True Narrative*, pp. 153–81; *The records of the Commissioners*, pp. 179, 239, 311–12; *The Complaint of the Boutefeu scorched in his owne kindlings* (London, 1649); *A Declaration by the Presbytery at Bangor* (n.p., 1649); *News from Ireland* (London, 1650).

146 These parties are described by H. R. Trevor-Roper, in 'Scotland and the Puritan Revolution', reprinted in *Religion, the Reformation and social change* (London, 1967), pp. 422–3.

first the intransigent Resolutioners shaped policy, denouncing the new regime in violent language.[147] Faced with apparently implacable hostility from the majority of Ulster Presbyterians, the new administration saw little point in conciliation and instead adopted a policy scarcely less Draconian than that towards the native Irish. In 1653 it was proposed that the Scottish interest in Ulster should be broken by transplanting the obdurate, with their ministers, to Tipperary, Waterford, and Kilkenny. There at least they would have less chance of direct communication with their disaffected brethren in Scotland.[148]

This plan was never implemented, perhaps because of successful objections from the province's landowners whose prosperity would be jeopardized by such an upheaval.[149] Gradually a more conciliatory approach developed, accepting the province's established population, rather than aiming at its replacement. The problem was how to create a party favourable to the protectorate in Ulster. One way was to exploit the divisions there. Presbyterian landowners who had quarrelled with the Kirk, notably Montgomery of the Ards and Lord Clandeboy, were shown exceptional favour and allowed to retrieve their estates. The clerical outcasts from the Ulster presbyteries, the Remonstrants, were conciliated and used as official preachers.[150] In an attempt to balance the Presbyterians, a tolerant policy towards the surviving episcopalians was adopted.[151] Then in 1654 there were hopes that the breach in the presbyteries would be healed. In Scotland the lord president, Broghill, tried to reconcile moderates from both factions to create a new party favourable to the protectorate. One calculation behind Broghill's efforts was to moderate the Ulster Presbyterians' hostility

---

[147]*A Necessary Representation of the Present Evills* (n.p., 1649).

[148]For this scheme: Dunlop, i. cxxxv-cxxxvi; ii. 329–32, 333–4, 337–9, 340, 346–50, 351–4, 360; Steele, ii, no. 516 (Ireland). Contacts with Scotland were curtailed. Dunlop, i. 135; ii. 325–6, 331.

[149]Dunlop, i. cxxxvi. For the activities of two prominent Ulster settlers at Westminster which may have led to the scheme's abandonment: Brit. Mus., Lansdowne MS. 821, ff. 44, 105; *Cal. S.P., Dom., 1654*, p. 64; ibid., *1655*, p. 265; ibid., *1655–6*, pp. 141, 182; Hist. MSS. Comm., *Egmont MSS.* i. 542; *Thurloe State Papers*, iv. 773.

[150]William Montgomery, *The Montgomery Manuscripts*, pp. 202, 210–11, P.R.O., Northern Ireland, D.562/1; Seymour, pp. 97–8.

[151]See below, p. 131.

towards the government.[152]   The breach was not healed and no new party emerged, so once more the authorities were thrown back into dependence on the comparatively moderate Remonstrants. The chances of conciliation working were helped by a shift in the balance of parties in Ulster: the majority of ministers sent to Ireland in the Interregnum were Remonstrants willing to co-operate with the regime.[153]

Overtures towards the Presbyterian ministers to accept government salaries started in 1654, before Henry Cromwell's arrival. However they were not brought to a successful conclusion until November 1655, with Sir John Clotworthy acting as intermediary between the ministers and government, and it was Henry Cromwell who made the policy the lynch-pin of his dealings with Ulster.[154]   In working with the Presbyterians he defied instructions from Westminster, where a far less conciliatory attitude prevailed.[155]   With much justice he was accused of being 'too gentle to ye Scotch and revolting English of Ireland'.[156]   The change in approach had been spectacular. One minister, John Greg, regarded in 1657 as a dangerous influence, was approached by Henry Cromwell to preach on his estate at Portumna, County Galway. In 1658 another of these ministers, John Hart, was empowered to report scandalous ministers in the Derry precinct.[157]

The most startling aspect of Henry Cromwell's favour was not his conciliation of the Ulster Presbyterians (which was based on a realistic assessment of their undoubted hold in the province), but his eagerness to introduce Presbyterianism into other parts of Ireland. His choice of Francis Roberts as a chaplain indicated his sympathy towards Presbyterianism. In 1656 he invited a prominent Presbyterian, John Livingstone,

---

[152]Adair, *A True Narrative*, pp. 205—13; *Diary of Sir Archibald Johnston of Wariston, 111, 1655—1660*, ed. J. D. Oglivie, Scottish History Soc., 3rd Ser. xxxiv (1940), 39; *Thurloe State Papers*, iv. 557.

[153]*Register of the consultations of the Ministers of Edinburgh*, ii. 1657—60, ed. W. Stephens, Scottish History Soc., 3rd Ser. xvi (1930), 154.

[154]Adair, *A True Narrative*, pp. 217—18, 223; Seymour, pp. 98—101.

[155]Dunlop, ii. 580—1.

[156]Brit. Mus., Lansdowne MS. 822, f. 51; *Thurloe State Papers*, vi. 349, 563.

[157]The disloyal spirit in Carrickfergus had been attributed to 'Mr. Grigg's formerly beinge their minister'. Brit. Mus., Lansdowne MSS. 821, f. 101; 823, f. 57; Adair, *A True Narrative*, p. 224; Hew Scott, *Fasti Ecclesiae Scoticanae*, new ed. (Edinburgh, 1928), iii. 262; *Thurloe State Papers*, vi. 349.

to become incumbent of St. Katherine's church in Dublin. Livingstone declined the offer.[158] Perhaps Henry Cromwell had hoped that the establishment of Scottish Presbyterianism in the capital would counteract the episcopalians, Independents, and Baptists already there.

The benefits of his policy in Ulster were apparent peace and security, and a better provision of the Gospel than in any other part of Ireland.[159] The peace, however, was fragile. The Presbyterian clergy were reluctant to admit that accepting government salaries created any obligation to support the regime, and refused to use their influence to discourage royalist activity.[160] Furthermore their influence, even when they chose to wield it, was limited: it did not extend to the unyielding Resolutioners still in Ulster. Finally, the alliance with Henry Cromwell's regime was a matter of convenience and not of principle. The Presbyterians, like Worth and Henry Cromwell, wanted to check religious unorthodoxy, to propagate the Gospel, and to restore the clergy to their legal rights, including tithes.[161] On these issues fruitful co-operation was possible. But the Presbyterians' ultimate object was to impose their theocratic system of church government throughout Ireland, and that Henry Cromwell could not accept. Since no national church was re-erected during the Interregnum, that fundamental difference did not come to the fore. Even so Henry Cromwell felt less confident about the Presbyterians' loyalty than about the Munster Protestants'.

So far as the Ulster Presbyterians were concerned, Henry Cromwell's benevolence brought them unprecedented advantages. They took firmer hold and extended to areas hitherto untouched.[162] Greatly strengthened during the Interregnum,

158 R.C.B., Seymour MSS., p. 204; *A Brief historical relation of the life of Mr. John Livingston* (n.p., 1727), pp. 42–3; Seymour, p. 136; Scott, *Fasti Ecclesiae Scoticanae*, ii. 99–100; T. Witherow, *Historical and literary memorials of Presbyterianism in Ireland* (London and Belfast, 1879), pp. 17–21. Samuel Coxe, the minister settled at St. Katherine's, was 'reputed the soundest Presbyterian in Dublin'. Adair, *A True Narrative*, pp. 231, 233.

159 R.C.B., Seymour MSS., pp. 211–16.

160 Adair, *A True Narrative*, pp. 220–1, 225–6; R.C.B., Seymour MSS., p. 96; J. Kirkpatrick, *An Historical essay upon the loyalty of Presbyterians* (n.p., 1713), p. 301; *Thurloe State Papers*, vi. 563.

161 Kirkpatrick, *An historical essay*, p. 301.

162 Adair, *A True Narrative*, pp. 214–15, 228.

it was the Presbyterians who posed the main threat of Protestant dissent from the re-established Church of Ireland after 1660. Since the Scots in Ulster numbered perhaps 80,000 this was not surprising.[163] By driving them into nonconformity the restored Stuarts created a major political problem for themselves, and demonstrated the merits of the Cromwellians' more comprehensive approach.[164]

ix.   The Dublin Convention of Ministers in 1658, and its effects

The extent to which Henry Cromwell depended on Worth and the Presbyterians, and the way in which that dependence had shaped his religious policy, became most clear during and after the Dublin Convention, which first met on 23 April 1658. Twenty ministers had been summoned from all four provinces of Ireland 'to consult about setling of tyths and [the] parishes affaire'.[165]   Its most important decisions related to tithes, and will be considered with that subject below.[166]   The meeting was intended to be short, simply endorsing decisions already made by the council. However a decision had been reached there only with great difficulty, owing to Lord Chancellor Steele's protracted opposition. The Convention offered a new opportunity of continuing the debate, and was long and acrimonious.[167]

The participants (who apparently included no Baptists) agreed on the need for firm discipline and the enforcement of Gospel ordinances, like infant baptism. It was the restoration of tithes that divided them. Opposition to a restoration was led by Winter, encouraged by Steele and John Weaver. At the

163 P.R.O., SP. 63/305, 113, Memorandum by Col. John Gorges on the 'North of Ireland'. Clotworthy, ennobled in 1660 as Viscount Massareene, persistently attacked the Stuarts' harshness. Nat. Lib. Ire., MSS. 8643(2), E. Nicholas to G. Lane, 23 Sept. 1662; 13,223(2), Massareene to Orrery, 9 Feb. 1660[1]; 13,223(7), same to same, 5 Feb. 1660[1]; Bodl., Carte MS. 45, f. 462ᵛ.

164 At least twenty-four Presbyterian ministers employed by the Cromwellians were rounded up by the Irish government in the summer of 1663; Bodl., Carte MS. 32, f. 655; Nat. Lib. Ire., MS. 8643(4).

165 Sheffield Univ. Lib., Hartlib MS. xv, R. Wood to S. Hartlib, Dublin, 5 May 1658; P.R.O., SP, 63/287, 170ᵛ, 176; *Thurloe State Papers*, vii. 21, 101, 129, 161.

166 At pp. 153–168.

167 Sheffield Univ. Lib., Hartlib MS. xv, (iv), R. Wood to Hartlib, 26 May 1658 and undated but late May/June 1658; P.R.O., SP. 63/287, 176, 177ᵛ.

end of the Convention Winter found himself isolated, with only one supporter.[168]   Victory had gone to the conservatives, the members of Worth's Cork association and of the Ulster presbyteries, both of which groups were well represented.[169]   The changes authorized by the meeting were a triumph for the policies of Worth and the Ulster Presbyterians, and Worth's reputation was enhanced. Immediately after the Convention Worth was sent to England by Henry Cromwell, recommending him to his father as 'of the judgment of the associated ministers in England and practiseth accordingly'. Henry Cromwell stressed Worth's difference from the uncompromising episcopalians rather than from Winter and the Independents. He also failed to make clear to the protector that Worth's schemes for a national church resembled those of the English Presbyterians, and not the Independents'.[170]

During his English visit Worth discussed events in Ireland and schemes for a national church with the London Presbyterians and with divines at Oxford and Cambridge. Worth's experience had relevance to English needs. In County Cork religious peace had been restored through the alliance of clergy and laity. Thanks to Henry Cromwell's support his wider programme — the maintenance of Gospel ordinances, regular ordination, a parochial and tithe-supported ministry in place of itinerant preachers and voluntaryism — was being applied nationally. Little wonder that the English Presbyterians approved Worth's policies, saying that 'they could freely close with the congregationall brethren . . . on the termes . . . presented . . . by the Dublin Convention'.[171] This ignored the fact that in Ireland the terms had been rejected by the leaders of the Independents, and that the policy had been applied only after ignoring the Independents'

[168]Brit. Mus., Lansdowne MS. 1228, f. 13. This address is printed, not altogether accurately, in Reid, *History of the Presbyterian Church*, ii. 560–2. Winter's ally was Edward Wale from Waterford, for whom see below, pp. 136, 140, 141.

[169]Known members of the Cork association, apart from Worth, were Eyres and Ladyman. Three Scottish Presbyterians and an English Presbyterian patronized by Clotworthy came from Ulster. P.R.O , Northern Ireland, MS. D. 1759 1A/1, pp. 218, 219; Chatsworth, Lismore MS. 29, Cork's diary, 2 May 1658; Adair, *A True Narrative*, p. 224.

[170]*Thurloe State Papers*, vii. 162; *Cal. S.P. Dom., 1658–9*, pp. 135, 451.

[171]Brit. Mus., Lansdowne MS. 823, f. 79.

susceptibilities. If unacceptable to English Independents, Worth's policy was unlikely to gain the protector's approval. It soon became clear that the English Independents were far from happy with the results of the Dublin Convention. Steele used his English contacts to asperse Henry Cromwell; Winter came to England in the summer of 1658 to undermine Worth and stir up English Independents; Worth was vilified as an 'Old Protestant' still at heart attached to episcopacy.[172] Hugh Peter raised his voice against Henry Cromwell's Irish policy, reminding him that 'your father dyed as he lived an Independent'.[173] This opposition, recalling the Baptist campaign of 1655 to 1656, made Henry Cromwell more obstinate. In Ireland he pressed ahead with Worth's and the Presbyterians' policies. Denied all influence, both Steele and Winter considered retirement from Ireland.[174] Although the Independent cause was so depressed in Ireland, it began to revive in England and this put fresh heart into Winter.

In September 1658 the English Independents had conferred at the Savoy in London, ostensibly about reuniting Presbyterians and Independents.[175] The *Declaration* issued after this assembly rejected compromise with the Presbyterians and clearly restated Independent principles, insisting on the importance of religious toleration. The London Independents would not be overborne as Winter had been. [176] This firm stand and the expectation of political changes after Oliver Cromwell's death encouraged Winter to return to the fray in Ireland. Inspired directly by the Independents' *Declaration* Winter revived his earlier clerical association, giving it a more formal identity. To reverse the policies formulated by the Munster Protestants and Ulster Presbyterians, Winter organized the clergy of Dublin and

172 Brit. Mus., Lansdowne MS. 823, ff. 186, 130; Bodl., Rawlinson MS. A.54, p. 5; *The Register of Provost Winter*, ed. Lawlor, p. 20.

173 Brit. Mus., Lansdowne MS. 823, f. 130.

174 Ibid., Lansdowne MS 823, f. 87.

175 Henry Cromwell regarded the Savoy conference as another ploy by which the opposition to the protectorate and his Irish government would strengthen itself. *Thurloe State Papers*, vii. 454, 500.

176 *A Declaration of the Faith and Order owned and practiced in the Congregational Churches in England: Agreed upon ... at the Savoy, Octob. 12. 1658* (London, 1659). Thomason's copy is dated 16 Feb. 1658[9]. Evidently the more favourable climate after Cromwell's death led them to set forth their views.

Leinster.[177]   This new association of ministers was committed to the care of the elect, confining itself to the English towns and ignoring the native Irish. Whilst attacking schemes of moderated episcopacy, to which some of Worth's ideas could be traced, it failed to condemn the Baptists. Winter and the Independents were prepared to work with their former enemies against the new enemy, Henry Cromwell, Worth, and the Presbyterians.[178]   Winter's new activity embittered religious life in Ireland, without deflecting Henry Cromwell from his policies.

Henry Cromwell had not wanted to disavow the Independents, rather he had tried to join other religious agents with them. Important theological differences separated Winter from the parties in Munster and Ulster. In fact Henry Cromwell had had no intention of imposing unacceptable practices on the Independents.[179]   Some at least of Winter's opposition had been factious, reluctant to share power so newly won. Also his resistance had been encouraged by Steele and Weaver for political reasons. It was his involvement in opposition that forced Henry Cromwell to rely almost exclusively on the Munster and Ulster groups for leadership of the church. This dependence ran counter to his original policy, and we may question its wisdom. As we have seen there were serious limitations in the value to the government of the Presbyterian clergy in Ulster. Contemporaries argued that reliance on Worth was equally misguided; that Worth was playing a waiting game, feigning compliance whilst remaining a devoted episcopalian, ever watchful for a chance to restore king and bishops. This picture of Worth duping Henry Cromwell is even more convincing (it is alleged) when Worth's behaviour in 1660 is considered. He used his influence to bring the Cork clergy back into the Church of Ireland and was himself rewarded with the junior bishopric of Killaloe.[180]

[177]*The Agreement and Resolution of the Ministers of Christ Associated within the City of Dublin, and Province of Leinster* (Dublin, 1659).

[178]John Brereton, government schoolmaster at Wexford, attributed this to fear of the Baptists in 1659. MS. note on the copy of *The Agreement* in Nat. Lib. Ire., pressmark, I 6551 Dubl.

[179]See below, p. 160.

[180]Only two Protestant nonconformist ministers were expected in Cork. Bodl., Clarendon state papers, 74, f. 52v. Worth's consecration was opposed, because of his past behaviour. Ibid., Carte MS. 221, f. 93.

To see Worth as eager to overthrow the protectorate in Ireland is wrong, since it misunderstands his preoccupations. Worth was the ecclesiastical counterpart of the Protestant gentry of Ireland who supported the new English regime as the best hope for preserving and extending the Protestant interest in Ireland. Forms of government, whether ecclesiastical or civil, were of less importance than survival. Worth explained this in 1660: 'ecclesiastical constitutions are alterable and changeable, and not to be accompted equall with the word of God, in the virtue of which principle when publicq necessity inforced it, wee all omitted many things legally established . . . ; attending the flock though the fold were broken downe rather than exposing the sheep to wolves till the fold should be refixed'.[181]   Worth was prepared to seek an alternative to episcopacy, appropriate to the Interregnum; he opposed those who by holding fast to episcopacy split the Protestant interest;[182]   in 1660 he took part in the London discussions to accommodate the Presbyterians.[183] Henry Cromwell gave him power — more than he had after 1660 — and supported his schemes; in return Worth put all his influence behind the regime which Henry Cromwell represented.

The alliance with Worth was the most productive part of Henry Cromwell's increasingly conservative policy. The tenor of his policy can also be gauged from his other acts of patronage, like his choice of Francis Roberts and the invitation to Livingstone. To undo the damage of ignorant 'mechanic' preachers he patronized 'young Schollers . . . sent from Oxford and Cambridge',[184]   and invited to Ireland

181 Chetham Lib., Manchester, 'MSS. collections relating to Ireland' p. 339, printed in Seymour, pp. 227–9.
182 P.R.O., SP. 63/287, 177ᵛ.
183 *Reliquiae Baxterianae*, i. 232–3; W. Kennet, *A Register and Chronicle Ecclesiastical and Civil* (London, 1728), pp. 187, 195. His collaborator, Hackett, who was briefly dean of Cork in 1660, also took part. Bodl., Carte MSS. 45, f. 192; 215, f. 219; C. A. Webster, *The Diocese of Cork* (Cork, 1920), pp. 274–5.
184 E. C[ooke], *Here is something of concernment in Ireland* (n.p., n.d.), p. 2. Two such young scholars were Jacob Rouse and Edward Baines. For Rouse: R.C.B., Seymour MSS., p. 73; J. B. Leslie, 'Calendar of Leases and Deeds of St. Patrick's Cathedral, Dublin, 1660–1689', *JRSAI*, 7th Ser. iv (1934), 195; J. Rouse, *The Spirits touchstone* (London, 1657). For Baines: Genealogical Office, Dublin, MS. 87, p. 111; Brit. Mus., Lansdowne MS. 822, f. 170; Dr. Williams'

ministers known for their conservative opinions.[185] He took special care of the ministry in Dublin, previously dominated by Baptists and Independents. Two vigorous conservatives were asked to move to the capital;[186] and a Presbyterian was settled there.[187] The surviving Church of Ireland bishops in Ulster were treated with conspicuous leniency, but this was influenced by the province's special needs.[188] A clearer indication of Henry Cromwell's preferences was his offer to another bishop, Griffith Williams, of a government salary after he had preached in Dublin.[189] Williams had been a trenchant supporter of Charles I, joining his court at Oxford and denouncing the parliamentarians so violently that the latter said 'for the three books he wrote in Oxford against the Parliament he deserved . . . to have his head cut off . . . '[190] His stress on regular ordination and opposition to soldiers and tradesmen preaching would be acceptable to Henry Cromwell.[191] A former chaplain to Charles I also preached before him.[192] This readiness to listen to ministers whose

Lib., Baxter letters, iii, f. 158; vi, f. 148; Sion College, MS. Arc. L.40.2/E.17, f. 241v; Seymour, p. 207; *Thurloe State Papers*, vi. 367, 552; Venn, *Alumni Cantabrigenses*, pt. i, i. 113.

185For example, Faithful Teate, a former minister of the Church of Ireland. S. C. Roberts, 'The Quest for Faithful Teate', *Times Literary Supplement*, 19 Apr. 1941; *The council book of Drogheda*, ed. Gogarty, i. 40; F. Teate, *Nathanael*, sig. [A7]v; and *The Uncharitable Informer charitably informed*; *Thurloe State Papers*, vi. 552; vii. 144.

186Ladyman was invited from Clonmel, but does not seem to have come. Brit. Mus., Lansdowne MS. 823, f. 177; Francis Armitage to Broghill, 31 Jan. 1659[60], Harvard, MS. Eng. 218. 22. F; J. D. White, 'Extracts from original wills . . . ', *Jnl Kilkenny and S.E. of Ireland Archaeological Soc.*, N.S. ii (1858–9), 317; Ladyman, *The Dangerous Rule*. Gilbert, the scourge of Baptists and Quakers in Limerick, does not seem to have moved. Brit. Mus., Lansdowne MS. 823, f. 51; R.C.B., Seymour MSS., p. 209.

187Samuel Coxe at St. Katherine's. Coxe was a tenant on Henry Cromwell's Irish lands. Huntingdon Rec. Office, 731 dd Bush no. 32.

188Ibid., no. 146; Brit. Mus., Add. MS. 19,833, f. 27, and Lansdowne MS. 823, f. 57; Nat. Lib. Ire., MS. 11,961, p. 196; H. Leslie, *A Discourse with praying with the spirit* (London, 1660); C. J. Stranks, *The Life and Writings of Jeremy Taylor* (London, 1952), p. 189.

189G. Williams, *The Persecution and Oppression . . . of John Bale . . . and of Gruffith Williams* (London, 1664), p. 13; 'A Sermon Preached at Cork-House before Henry Cromwell' in G. Williams, *Four Treatises* (London, 1667).

190*Cal. S.P. Ire., 1669–70*, p. 372.

191G. Williams, *Four Treatises*, p. 20.

192This was Charles Croke, former rector of Amersham. Zeal for the Stuart cause was said to be the reason for his coming to Ireland about 1650. The wish to

past allegiance and present opinions were unacceptable to English Independents increased suspicion of his Irish policies and built up opposition to his government. The extent to which Henry Cromwell's tastes were shared by the Protestant settlers of Ireland was revealed in 1659–60, when Henry Cromwell's removal forced them to look to their own interests. In so far as those months throw light on the relationship between the English rulers and Irish Protestants, I shall consider them.

x. The Aftermath

In June 1659 Ireland's government was entrusted to political and religious radicals, who threatened to revive the anarchy of Fleetwood's regime. Conservatives were replaced in the commission of the peace by Quakers and Baptists;[193] ministers out of favour under Henry Cromwell had their salaries restored or increased;[194] to undermine the conservative hold over Dublin it was proposed to halve the number of ministers there;[195] John Rogers, now a Fifth-monarchist, returned;[196] Jeremy Taylor was called to Dublin to answer allegations against his beliefs; proceedings were started against the Presbyterian, Lord Montgomery.[197] Winter and the Independents had hoped to share in this turn of fortune. However they found their new allies, the Baptists, as insistent on monopolizing all power as they had been before 1655. The Baptists were said to have boasted 'that before Mayday, there should not be a man in the land should be imployed in

---

settle lands he had acquired through the adventure was a more probable cause. Bottigheimer, *English Money and Irish Land*, pp. 179, 201; *Cal. S.P. Ire., 1647–60*, p. 510; ibid., *Dom., 1655*, p. 63; A. Croke, *The Genealogical History of the Croke Family* (Oxford, 1823), ii. 506–10; *Diaries and Letters of Philip Henry*, ed. M. H. Lee, (London, 1882), p. 48; G. Lipscomb, *The History . . . of Buckingham* (London, 1847–51), iii. 179; J. Ward, *The Lives of the Professors of Gresham College* (London, 1760), p. 308.

193 Hist. MSS. Comm., *Leyborne-Popham MSS.*, p. 141.
194 R.C.B., Seymour MSS., pp. 207, 211.
195 'Mather Papers' *Collections of the Massachusetts Hist. Soc.*, 4th Ser. viii (1868), 550–1.
196 *Cal. S.P. Dom., 1659–60*, pp. 23, 35, 328, 576; *A Sober Vindication of Lt. Gen. Ludlow* (London, 1660), p. 3.
197 Stranks, *Jeremy Taylor*, p. 198; *The Montgomery Manuscripts*, pp. 218–19.

any places of trust but such as walked in their way, meaning as Anabaptists'.[198]

Henry Cromwell's carefully built alliance with conservative clergy and settlers had been overthrown. The new English policy had little support in Ireland. In Dublin porters and watermen threatened to stone unpopular Baptist and Independent ministers; at Trim leading Baptists were ejected from the corporation.[199] Most important the leading settlers acted to end these unacceptable policies, seizing Dublin Castle on 13 December 1659 and imprisoning the parliamentary commissioners. In February 1660 the settlers prepared to govern themselves, whilst the confusion in England lasted, through a Convention, representing all Protestant Ireland. This body was dominated by Henry Cromwell's former allies, the substantial settlers.[200] It continued his policies. In February 1660 there was talk of a proclamation to banish all Baptists, Quakers, 'and sectaries out of this kingdome'.[201] The Convention completed Winter's and the Independents' eclipse, depriving Winter of the provostship of Trinity College, his last source of influence. It continued the task of settling ministers on tithes and other legal dues, and of re-establishing parochial organization. It took special care of Dublin's needs, undoing the damage of 1659.[202] It agreed on the need to re-establish a national church, and still looked to Worth for a solution.[203]

The Convention was far from rushing into the restoration of episcopacy. Its actions, its choice of chaplains and ministers to advise on religious matters,[204] its reliance on Worth,

198George Pressick, *A breife relation of some of the most remarkable passages of the Anabaptists in High and Low Germany in the year, 1521. etc.* ([London], 1660), p. 9; *A Sober Vindication*, p. 11.

199C.B., Jennings transcripts, A/16, 23 Nov. 1659; Nat. Lib. Ire., MS. 2992, f. 6; *A Sober Vindication*, pp. 3, 11.

200Constituencies were as for the Dublin parliament: counties had two members, boroughs only one. *An Account of the chief occurrences ... 12 March—19 March* [1660], pp. 37–8.

201*A letter sent from a merchant in Dublin ...* (London, 1659[60]). No copy of such a proclamation survives, and it was probably never issued.

202*An Account ... 12 March—19 March*, pp. 33, 35, 39; *Cal. S.P. Ire., 1660–2*, pp. 41–2; *Thurloe State Papers*, vii. 909.

203*An Account ... 12 March—19 March*, p. 39; S. Coxe, *Two Sermons* (Dublin, 1660), pp. 27–8.

204The chaplains were Charnock (Henry Cromwell's chaplain); the Scottish Presbyterian, Adair; Edward Baines (for whom see above, p. 130, n. 184); and

and the inclinations of its leading members (especially Broghill and Coote),[205] all showed that the Convention was exploring a different solution: an Erastian Presbyterian system seems to have been favoured. But the Convention was overtaken by Charles II's restoration before it could impose political or religious conditions. Bishops were swiftly restored in Ireland.[206] Nevertheless many Irish Protestants hoped for a modification of the Church of Ireland to comprehend Presbyterians. However there were no changes and few protests. Once again defence of the Protestant interest came first, particularly as the Catholics were mounting a new offensive to regain lost privileges. The Church of Ireland now enshrined the Protestant cause and had to be supported. Yet there were those, including Broghill (since 1660 earl of Orrery), who regretted that the experiements of the Interregnum and of the Convention had failed, and hoped that the established church might still be reformed from within to reconcile the Presbyterians.[207] To express open nostalgia for the Interregnum was impossible after 1660. Yet in some ways the co-operation between Henry Cromwell and the clergy in Munster and Ulster had been a more hopeful period than that after 1660. Great things might have been achieved, had Henry Cromwell not fallen so soon.

Coxe (see above, p. 125, n. 158). S. Coxe, *Two Sermons*, p. [62]; *A Declaration of the General Convention of Ireland, with the late proceedings there, newly brought over by a Gentleman* (London, 1660), pp. 9, 10, 11, 12, 15 (the B.M. Copy lacks pp. 8–16 and I have used the copy in volume x of the Irish tracts, Forster collection, Victoria and Albert Museum); Hist. MSS. Comm., *Ormonde MSS.*, N.S. iii. 386. For its eight advisers, summoned from Ireland's four provinces: *An Account of the chief occurrences*, p. 36.

---

205 For contemporary comments on their lack of enthusiasm: Bodl., Carte MSS. 30, ff. 572, 573; 48, f. 4; Adair, *A True Narrative*, pp. 242, 268. Broghill confessed to Clarendon that he had been 'halfe a Presbiter', Bodl., Clarendon state papers, 73, f. 310. In March 1660 he was in close touch with Presbyterian ministers in Edinburgh. Nat. Lib. Ire., MSS. 32, f. 14; 13,233 (3), letter 7; R. Wodrow, *The History of the sufferings of the Church of Scotland from the Restauration to the Revolution* (Edinburgh, 1721), i. xiv. For Coote's earlier sympathy towards Scottish Presbyterianism, *The Records of the Commissioners . . . 1648 and 1649*, ed. Mitchell and Christie, p. 188.

206 Bodl., Carte MS. 30, ff. 685, 689; R. S. Bosher, *The making of the Restoration Settlement* (London, 1951), p. 157.

207 In 1673 Broghill asked Baxter to formulate proposals that 'would satisfie the non-conformists so far as to unite us all against Popery': Nuttall, *Richard Baxter*, pp. 78, 79, 80, 86, 107; F. J. Powicke, *The Reverend Richard Baxter under the cross (1662–1691)* (London, 1927), p. 170.

VI

ECCLESIASTICAL REFORM

i. The Ministers of the Gospel

The previous chapter showed the effects of religious controversy and suggested that it distracted attention from the
vigorous evangelization of Ireland promised between 1641
and 1649. It also suggested that these contending sects
differed in their interest in preaching to the Irish, the Baptists
and Independents having vitually none. In this chapter I shall
assess the ecclesiastical provisions and reforms during the
Interregnum. Attitudes towards organization and reform
divided the various sects, and we shall find important differences between what happened from 1649 to 1655 (under
Fleetwood) and from 1655 to 1659 (under Henry Cromwell).
It will also be seen that aims and methods in the Interregnum
were shared by reformers in the Church of Ireland, both
before 1641 and after 1660. The reforms during the Interregnum marked less of a break with the past than was
suggested at the time. There were five main aspects to
reform. First, there was a need to improve both the quality
and quantity of the ministers. During the Interregnum cri-
teria as to what made a good minister obviously differed
from earlier ideas. Tests were needed of the minister's fitness
to serve. Improvements in both quality and quantity were
linked with money. If ministers adequate in numbers and in
abilities were to be settled in Ireland their salaries must be
improved. Thus reform of the ministry depended on a second
reform — of their maintenance. A third reform might enable
better stipends to be paid: a reorganization of the church,
especially its parishes, so that more efficient use could be
made of its resources. A fourth reform was to repair the
church's fabric. Finally there was the goal to which all these
improvements were directed: propagating the Gospel
amongst the Catholics. Did the Cromwellians achieve more in
this vital sphere than their allegedly negligent predecessors?

Let us start with the clergy, and try to discover what sort of ministers were employed as government preachers during the Interregnum. Any complete prosopographical study of impossible, owing to lack of evidence. Instead I shall concentrate on an untypical group of ministers, about whom more is known, because they were the leaders of the Cromwellian church in Ireland. This group is formed from those whom the government paid the highest salaries, £200 or more p.a., and numbers twenty-one.[1] These men were the Cromwellian equivalents of the Anglican bishops in Ireland. They were paid high salaries because they were exceptional, in their qualifications or past experience, in their reputations or their commitment to Cromwellian religious policy. One of the reasons why the Protestant Gospel took only an insecure hold was because the majority of government preachers were men of much lower calibre, and less enthusiastic about the innovations of the Interregnum. Repeating the caution that they are not typical, what sort of men led the English church in Ireland?

Twelve of these ministers worked in Dublin. Winter was chaplain to the parliamentary commissioners in 1650; Partridge was Fleetwood's, and Roberts, Charnock, and Harrison were Henry Cromwell's, chaplains; Wootton was chaplain to the King's Inns, the Dublin Inn of Court.[2] Three other of these ministers were invited to Dublin. The other members of this élite were settled in key towns: Carrickfergus (Timothy Taylor), Clonmel (Ladyman), Drogheda (Briscoe and later Teate), Galway (Easthorp), Limerick (Gilbert), and Waterford (Wale).

1 Seymour printed (pp. 206—24) the names of all government-paid ministers in Ireland during the Interregnum. Their salaries, not reproduced by Seymour, were recorded in the civil list. A transcript of the civil list for 1655 is Brit. Mus., Add. MS. 19,833, ff. 12—14; and for 1658—9 in R.C.B., Seymour MSS., pp. 206—14. Information about clerical incomes, unless otherwise stated, comes from these sources. In 1655 ten ministers were paid over £200 p.a.: Roberts (£250); Thomas Harrison (£300); Winter, Brewster, Briscoe, Charnock, Gilbert, Partridge, Taylor, and Wootton. In 1659 another ten ministers were in the category: Baines, Robert Chambers, Coxe, Easthorp, Enoch Grey, John Livingstone (who never accepted the salary), Ladyman, Samuel Mather, the elder Faithful Teate, and Wale. Between 1650 and 1653 Rogers had been paid £200.

2 B. T. Duhigg, *History of the King's Inns, Dublin* (Dublin, 1805), pp. 183, 185; *The Registers of the Church of St. Michan*, ed. Berry, pp. 13, 31, 58; Chatsworth, Lismore MS. 29, Cork's diary, 15 Oct. 1654.

Only three of the twenty-one had connections with Ireland before 1649. Briscoe, Chambers, and Teate were Dublin graduates;[3] and Chambers and Teate had been beneficed in the Church of Ireland. Teate was one of the few recorded ministers in Ireland to show an inclination towards nonconformity in the 1640s.[4] The proportion of university graduates was extremely high. Nathanael Partridge, the former army chaplain and Fleetwood's preacher, was not a graduate.[5] Of the other twenty: eleven came from Cambridge;[6] three were Oxford graduates;[7] three from Trinity College, Dublin; two from Harvard;[8] and one was an alumnus of Glasgow.[9] Clearly the proportion of graduates was much higher than amongst the lower-paid clergy. On the other hand, the proportion of Dublin and Scottish graduates amongst the other clergy was higher. Dublin graduates tended to have been beneficed in the Church of Ireland, and former Anglicans were rarely given the highest salaries. The same was true of the Presbyterians in Ulster, many of whom had been educated at the Scottish universities. Another reason why those who had ministered before 1649 in Ireland usually received smaller salaries was that they were more likely to have other sources of income, tithes retained clandestinely or voluntary contributions.[10]

The preponderance of Cambridge graduates is clear. The zeal of its graduates is taking the Gospel to dark corners is well known, so is their puritanism. Both would be qualifications for Irish service in the 1650s. These Cambridge graduates came to Ireland after ministering in a dark corner

---

[3] *Alumni Dublinenses*, pp. 98, 145, 803. Teate had been vice-provost of the college: J. B. Leslie, *Armagh Clergy and Parishes* (Dundalk, 1911), p. 238.

[4] Bodl., Carte MS. 221, f. 555; F. Teate, *Nathanael*, sig. A2—A2ᵛ.

[5] R.C.B., Seymour MSS., pp. 9, 36, 42, 107; Brit. Mus., Lansdowne MS. 821, f. 226; *Analecta Hibernica*, xv. 263; Matthews, *Calamy Revised*, pp. 382—3.

[6] Baines, Charnock, Coxe, Easthorp, Gilbert, Grey, Harrison, Wale, Winter, Wootton, and John Rogers. Wootton and Charnock were intruded into Oxford fellowships by the parliamentary visitors.

[7] Ladyman, Roberts, and Taylor.

[8] Mather and Brewster. J. L. Sibley, *Biographical Sketches of Graduates of Harvard University* (Cambridge, Mass., 1873), i. 68—73, 78—87.

[9] John Livingstone.

[10] For Scottish graduates: A. F. Scott Pearson, *Ulster Journal of Archaeology*, 3rd Ser. xiv. 1—13; H. Scott, *Fasti Ecclesiae Scoticanae*, ii. 99—100, 331, 350, 386; iii. 120, 157, 164, 192, 211, 381, 398; vii. 527, 528.

(Coxe and Easthorp in County Durham)[11] or in notoriously puritan East Anglia.[12] Experience in America was also regarded as especially relevant to Irish needs, and strenuous efforts were made to attract ministers from North America. Apart from the two Harvard graduates, Dr. Thomas Harrison had ministered there. Other ministers who had been to North America (outside our élite of twenty-one) included the Baptist Patient, Hope Sherard (previously a chaplain of the Providence Island Company), and Thomas Jenner.[13]

High salaries were often an inducement to persuade celebrated preachers to leave England for Ireland. Sometimes they were not high enough.[14] Winter, for example, was supposed to have made a great financial sacrifice in coming to Ireland. On the other hand, Brewster's salary in Norfolk had been only £50 p.a.[15] Some of those who came were already well known in England: Harrison and Roberts were prominent in London; Samuel Mather had been employed by the council of state; Brewster was known to the protector and praised as 'a very holy able man'.[16] Probably the lure of a

11 *C.J.* v. 475, 509; *L.J.* ix. 37, 62; x. 162; Howell, *Newcastle*, p. 231; Shaw, *A History of the English Church*, ii. 330, 368, 369.

12 Brewster, Grey, Rogers, Wale, and Wootton had ministered there. For Brewster: Brit. Mus., Add. MS. 4278, ff. 106–14; Nickolls, *Original Letters and Papers*, pp. 125, 127, 147, 158; F. Peck, *Desiderata Curiosa* (London, 1779), part ii, p. 504; *Thurloe State Papers*, iii. 503, 559, 572, 660; iv. 90, 348, 373, 472–3, 581–2; v. 219, 508–9; Bodl., Rawlinson MS. A.27, f. 489; *C.S.P. Dom.*, *1655–6*, p. 274. For Grey: E. Grey, *Vox Coeli* (London 1649); J. Nickolls, op. cit., pp. 127–8; Shaw, op. cit. ii. 390; J. Stalham, *The Summe of a Conference* (London, 1644), pp. 1, 34. For Rogers: Capp, *The Fifth Monarchy Men*, p. 261; For Wale: Nicholls, op. cit., p. 127; G. F. Nuttall, *Visible Saints* (Oxford 1957), p. 22, n. 1; Peck, op. cit., pt. ii, p. 497. For Wootton: *The Diary and Autobiography of Edmund Bohun, Esq.*, ed. S. W. Rix (Beccles, 1853), p. 28, note d; Henry Wootton, *An Essay on the education of children* (London, 1753).

13 Brit. Mus., Egerton MS. 2646, ff. 58, 76; Lansdowne MS. 821, ff. 200, 206; P.R.O., Dublin, Prerogative will-book, 1664–84, f. 131ᵛ; Chatsworth, Lismore MS. 29, Cork's diary, 22 June 1656; Dunlop, ii. 450–1; 'Mather Papers', *Collections of the Massachusetts Hist. Soc.*, 4th Ser. viii. 4; ibid., 4th Ser. vii (1865), 355–62; Newton, *Colonizing Activities of the English Puritans*, pp. 119, 257, 306–7; Nickolls, *Original Letters and Papers* pp. 44–5; Nuttall, *Visible Saints*, p. 31; Seymour, p. 104.

14 *Thurloe State Papers*, vi. 20.

15 Winter's salary was said to have fallen from £400 to £100. However he was paid £300 in Ireland, £200 as a preacher and £100 as Provost. J.W., *Life and Death of Dr. Samuel Winter*, p. 8; J. Browne, *History of Congregationalism and Memorials of the Churches of Norfolk and Suffolk* (London, 1877), p. 299.

16 Matthews, *Calamy Revised*, p. 344; *Thurloe State Papers*, iii. 572.

high salary was less tempting than a wish to contribute to
Ireland's regeneration. Several of these leading ministers had
made clear their enthusiasm for religious change. Easthorp
claimed to have been the first minister sequestered for his
opposition to Laud's innovations, and Winter had been
arraigned for departing from the Common Prayer Book and
not wearing a surplice.[17] Henry Cromwell's respect for
scholars from the universities was shown in the appointments
of Charnock, Fellow of New College, Oxford; Ladyman,
formerly Fellow of Corpus Christi, Oxford; and Edward
Baines.[18]

The methods by which these ministers had been persuaded
to settle in Ireland varied, but it was rarely the result of an
official invitation. More fruitful were personal contacts and
approaches, especially as members of the army and civil
administration were empowered to procure ministers.
Winter's appointment was clearly linked with his brother-in-
law, Weaver, the parliamentary commissioner. Gilbert grate-
fully acknowledged the part played by his uncle, Colonel
Henry Markham and by Sir Hardress Waller in bringing him
to Limerick.[19] Baines's decision to cross to Ireland was
probably influenced by his uncle, Major Daniel Redman;
Ladyman may well have been persuaded to settle at Clonmel
by his friend and contemporary at Corpus, Joseph Eyres.[20]
Thomas Harrison meeting Brewster on the ship returning
from America persuaded him to consider a ministry in
Ireland.[21] Utilizing the networks of family and professional
connections in England could produce good results. A notable example was that of the Wirral parish of West Kirby.
Samuel Eaton, the parish's most famous incumbent, was

[17]Brit. Mus., Lansdowne MS. 821, f. 261; R. A. Marchant, *The Puritans and the
Church Courts in the Diocese of York, 1560–1642* (London, 1960), pp. 293,
301–2.

[18]Bodl., Rawlinson MS. A.30, f. 529; Rawlinson leters, 52, f. 234; M. Burrows,
The Register of the Visitors of the University of Oxford, 1647–1658, Camden
Society, N.S. xix (1881), pp. 64, 170, 172, 392, 495, 532; Foster, *Alumni
Oxonienses*, early series, iii. 889; and above, pp. 130–1.

[19]C. Gilbert, *The Blessed-Peace-Maker and Christian Reconciler* (London,
1658), sig. [A2]ᵛ; and *A Pleasant Walk to Heaven* (London, 1658), sig. [A2].

[20]Brit. Mus., Lansdowne MS. 822, f. 170ᵛ; J.E., epistle in Ladyman, *The
Dangerous Rule*; Chatsworth, Cork's diary, 3 June 1655; Foster, *Alumni
Oxonienses*, early series, ii. 478; iii. 869.

[21]Brit. Mus., Lansdowne MS. 821, ff. 200, 206.

invited to Ireland but never came. However his assistant, Timothy Taylor, did; so too did the three sons of Eaton's successor, Ralph Marsden: Gamaliel, Jeremiah, and Josiah. Furthermore two of Ralph Marsden's sons-in-law, John Murcot and Edward Wale, were prominent preachers in Ireland.[22] The fact that the Wirral was close to one of the main routes to Ireland probably had an influence on these decisions.[23]

The exact religious persuasions of these ministers when in Ireland are difficult to establish. In 1655 there seem to have been a majority of Independents associated with Winter and opposed to the Baptists.[24] Of the ministers who were paid £200 p.a. for the first time between 1655 and 1659 (during Henry Cromwell's administration) there were a number of known conservatives. Ladyman was described as a Presbyterian and excoriated those who elevated liberty of conscience above all else;[25] Coxe too was called a Presbyterian; Faithful Teate had published defences of uniformity and praised Henry Cromwell; Baines was sent as an agent to the London Presbyterians.[26] Two others offered high salaries for the first time under Henry Cromwell were Dr. Francis Roberts and Livingstone (although he refused the salary), both well-known Presbyterians. Henry Cromwell's shift in religious allegiance was discernible amongst those chosen as church leaders and paid appropriate salaries. However the Cork ministers, including Worth, and the Ulster

22 P.R.O., Dublin, Prerogative will-book, 1664—84, f. 131ᵛ; R.C.B., Seymour MSS., p. 72; S. Eaton, and T. Taylor, *A Iust Apologie for the Church at Duckenfield* (London, 1647); and *A defence of sundry positions and scriptures alleged to justifye the congregationall-way* (London, 1645); *The Life of Adam Martindale*, ed. R. Parkinson, Chetham Soc., old series, iv. 63—4, 66—7, 74; *The Reverend Oliver Heywood, B.A., 1630—1702: His autobiography, diaries, anecdote and event books*, ed. J. H. Turner (Bingley, 1885), iv. 10; Nuttall, *Visible Saints*, pp. 30, 32. Even the Marsden's sister preached in Dublin after the Restoration: Bodl., Rawlinson MS. D.1347, f. 30.

23 Thomas Harrison was ministering there before coming to Ireland; Worth's forbears came from the area. Marsh, *Memorials of the City Temple*, pp. 127—8; Mason, *St. Patrick's Cathedral*, p. 205.

24 Particularly close to Winter in 1655 were Wootton, Taylor, and Gilbert.

25 Ladyman, *The Dangerous Rule*; Wood, *Fasti Oxonienses*, ii, col. 121.

26 For Teate see sources cited above, p. 131; for Baines: Brit. Mus., Lansdowne MS. 822, f. 170; Dr. Williams' Lib., Baxter letters, iii, f. 158; vi, f. 158; Sion College, MS. Arc. L.40.2/E.17, f. 241ᵛ.

Presbyterians were not included among the highest-paid clergymen.

The careers of these twenty-one ministers after 1660 were also untypical in that a majority showed sufficient enthusiasm for the changes of the Interregnum to dissent from the re-established church. Only four of the group are known to have conformed after 1660. Two of them, Roberts and Wootton, had powerful lay patrons in England.[27] Two found preferment in the Church of Ireland, Gilbert as vicar of Belfast and Ladyman, the closest associate of Worth in this group, received special consideration from Ormonde, eventually conformed, and became archdeacon of Limerick.[28] Amongst the known dissenters some, like Winter, Grey, Partridge, Briscoe, and Brewster, severed all ties with Ireland.[29] Others who had come for the first time to Ireland during the Interregnum stayed on after 1660. For example, Edward Wale at Waterford had been quick to declare his allegiance to the restored king, but found the Church of Ireland more difficult to accept. Accordingly he approached the bishop of Waterford 'for admittance to his Diocess, promising a fair complyance, only . . . he would be excused in one thing, the prayers of the Church could not down with him'. The bishop rejected Wale's conditional conformity. However Wale continued to live near Waterford until his death.[30] Of the other ministers who retained Irish connec-

---

[27] Roberts's patron was the earl of Essex, with whom he returned to Dublin in 1672 as chaplain; Wootton's was Francis Brewster, M.P., *The Diary of Edmund Bohun*, ed. Rix, pp. 28–9; Wood, *Athenae Oxonienses*, iii, cols. 1054–5.

[28] *D.N.B.*, R. Baxter, *The Certainty of the Worlds of Spirits*, pp. 215, 247–9; C. Gilbert, *A Preservative against the change of Religion* (London, 1683); Leslie, *Armagh Clergy and Parishes*, p. 65; Nat. Lib. Ire., MS. 2326, p. 105; *Cal. S.P. Ire., 1667–9*, p. 677; Cotton, *Fasti*, i. 134, 347; White, *JRSAI*, N.S. ii. 317.

[29] Matthews, *Calamy Revised*, pp. 76, 382–3; Brit. Mus., Add. MS. 4278, ff. 106–14; Sibley, *Biographical Sketches*, i. 72–3; F. Bate, *The Declaration of Indulgence* (London, 1908), pp. xxviii, xlvii. F. Teate died in 1660; Easthorp's career after being removed from his position at Galway in May 1660 is unknown to me. R.C.B., Seymour MSS., p. 126; *Appendix to the 26th. Report of the Deputy Keeper of the Public Records . . . in Ireland* (Dublin, 1895), p. 836.

[30] Waterford Municipal Records, Corporation book, f. 358; P.R.O., Dublin, Prerogative will book, 1664–84, ff. 130^v, 133^v; D. Burston, *Christs Last Call to his glorified saints* (Dublin, 1666), pp. 29–30. A contemporary manuscript note on the copy in Cambridge Univ. Lib. (pressmark: Hib. 7.665.2) identified Wale as the 'dissenting brother'.

tions some engaged in a purely religious dissent, others dabbled in political opposition.

To the first category belonged those who ensured that Protestant dissent continued in Dublin. Dr. Harrison, Henry Cromwell's chaplain, had gone after his master's recall in 1659 to Chester. In 1670 he renewed contact with Dublin and returned to act as minister of the Independent congregation there until his death in 1682. Harrison was at pains not to antagonize the civil authorities, and praised their 'justice and clemency'.[31] Mather, after a brief spell in England, returned to a congregation in Smithfields, Dublin, in 1662. He too upheld the restored monarchy and new government.[32] Timothy Taylor, another of the leading Cromwellian ministers, became Mather's assistant at Smithfields in 1662 and took over the congregation after Mather's death in 1671.[33] Samuel Coxe, whilst protesting his devotion to Charles II, was removed from his parish in 1660, but continued in Dublin as a nonconformist.[34] These ministers had been forced into dissent by the failure to broaden the established church in 1660. Except at moments of political crisis, they found the Dublin government indulgent towards their activities, more so than the English authorities.[35]

At least three of these ministers were implicated in political opposition as well as religious dissent. Baines,

31 Bodl., Carte MS. 221, f. 174[V]; Marsh's Lib., Dublin, MS. Z.4.5.16, p. 265; *Appendix to the Twenty-Sixth Report of the Deputy Keeper of the Public Records ... of Ireland*, p. 392; Matthews, *Calamy Revised*, pp. 250–1; *The Autobiography of Henry Newcome*, ii, ed. R. Parkinson, Chetham Soc. xxvii (Manchester, 1852), 189–90, 192; epistle by Harrison and D. Rolles, 'Philo-Carolus, P.J.', *Lemmata Meditationum* (Dublin, 1672), sig. [b3][V]–[b4].

32 Bodl., Carte MS. 45, f. 437; Rawlinson MS. D.1347, ff. 25–7; Matthews, *Calamy Revised*, p. 344.

33 Bodl., Carte MS. 45, ff. 437, 465; Rawlinson D.1347, f. 28[V]; T. Jenner, *Quakerism Anatomiz'd and Confuted* (n.p., 1670), sig. [a6][V]; Nuttall, *Visible Saints* p. 30.

34 R.C.B., Libr. MS. 14, 'Vestry books of St. Katherine's and St. James's, Dublin, from 1657', f. 25; ibid., Seymour MSS., p. 117; Baxter, *The Certainty of the Worlds of Spirits*, p. 219.

35 Cambridge Univ. Lib., Baumgartner papers, Strype correspondence, i, f. 1; iv, f. 42; *Collections of the Massachusetts Hist. Soc.*, 4th Ser. viii. 57. Two former official preachers in the 1650s (Zephaniah Smith and Edward Hutchinson) were arraigned before Clonmel assizes in 1664, and seem afterwards to have returned to England: Nat. Lib. Ire., MS. 4908, ff. 13[V], 29[V]; Bate, *The Declaration of Indulgence*, pp. xxiii, xxxix.

Charnock, and Chambers (none of them religious radicals in
the 1650s) were involved in the plot of 1663.[36] Although
they thus tainted Irish conconformists with disloyalty, no
permanent damage was done. Baines continued to minister to
a congregation at Wine-Tavern Street in Dublin; and
Chambers also returned to Dublin about 1673.[37] As can be
seen several of these Cromwellian religious leaders were
responsible for the survival of Protestant dissent after 1660,
especially in Dublin.

This examination shows that the Cromwellians had to
import religious leaders from England to carry out their
policy. Even after 1655, when Henry Cromwell made use of
ministers whose earlier careers had been in Ireland, the
highest salaries still went to those from England. The rank
and file clergy included more who had been beneficed in the
Church of Ireland and educated at Dublin University; a
smaller proportion of graduates and of enthusiasts for religious innovation; and a larger proportion of conformists
after 1660. Of the Cork clergy, for example, Worth and
Hackett became bishops in Ireland; Burston was made dean
of Waterford and Stowell archdeacon of Kinsale.[38] Numerous other official preachers in the Interregnum received high
preferment in the Church of Ireland.[39] The qualifications

36 Use was made of Henry Cromwell's name—both Charnock and Baines had
been close to him. *Cal. S.P. Ire. 1663–5*, p. 79.

37 Brit. Mus., Stowe MS. 202, f. 255; *Cal. S.P. Ire. 1663–5*, pp. 99, 112; ibid.,
1669–70, pp. 26, 57; J. Armstrong, 'An appendix containing some account of the
Presbyterian Congregations in Dublin', in *Sermon; a discourse on Presbyterian
Ordination*, (Dublin, 1829), p. 90; *The Diary and Letters of Philip Henry*, ed. Lee,
p. 252; Matthews, *Calamy Revised*, p. 108. For Baines: Bodl., Carte MS. 45, f.
437; *The Horrid Conspiracie* (London, 1663), p. 14; C. H. Irwin, *A History of
Presbyterianism in Dublin* ... (London, 1890), p. 321; *The Autobiography of
Henry Newcome*, ed. Parkinson, i. 171; ii. 170, 173, 185. Charnock left Ireland
permanently and was licensed as a Presbyterian in England. *Cal. S.P. Ire. 1663–5*,
pp. 99, 111, 112, 120, 124, 125, 126, 133; Hist. MSS. Comm., *Ormonde MSS.* ii.
251; Matthews, *Calamy Revised*, pp. 111–12; *The Tanner Letters*, ed. McNeill, p.
402.

38 Cotton, *Fasti*, i. 251; W. H. Rennison, *Succession lists of the bishops,
cathedral and parochial clergy of the dioceses of Waterford and Lismore*
([Lismore, 1920]), pp. 37, 81, 96, 106, 108, 109, 124, 126; G. D. Stawell, *A
Quantock Family* (Taunton, 1910), pp. 177, 189–93, 359, and appendix xvi, no.
12; Webster, *The Diocese of Cork*, p. 40. Eyres's career after 1660, when he
welcomed the king's return, is unknown. There is no trace of his receiving
preferment in Ireland. Chatsworth, Cork's diary, 14 May 1660.

39 For example: Paul Amiraut, Thomas Bladen, Thomas Coffey, Ambrose Jones
(later bishop of Kildare), Thomas Vesey, Ezekiel Webbe, John Wilkinson.

and publications of the leading Cromwellian ministers made nonsense of contemporary allegations of ignorance. A more serious disadvantage was their lack of previous contact with Ireland. Like the English soldiers and civil governors they tended to bring with them assumptions formed in England and not always appropriate to Irish circumstances. Their backgrounds reinforced the tendency of official policy to concentrate on the spiritual welfare of the Protestant new-comers, neglecting the Protestants who had settled there before 1649 and the Catholic population.

ii. The Approval and Control of the Clergy

The 1650 ordinance for propagating the Gospel in Ireland did nothing to provide ministers, and so set up no machinery for examining the fitness of candidates, or for removing the scandalous. Some of these deficiencies were supplied later in 1650 by the instructions to the parliamentary commissioners, who were authorized to enforce the English ordinances against malignant, pluralist, and scandalous ministers.[40] The parliamentary commissioners received no specific instructions how to remove ministers; or, more important, how they were to be replaced. Throughout the Interregnum methods of selection and control remained informal and improvised, although abuses led to tighter measures. Two areas did, however, have special attention: Munster and Ulster, where religious disaffection was most serious and had a political dimension. The general policy will be described, and then the exceptional measures for Munster and Ulster.

Scarcity of ministers discouraged exacting tests immedi-ately after 1649. Responsibility for procuring ministers was often left to army officers or members of the civil adminis-tration. As we have seen this helped Baptism to take root.[41] A particular minister's fitness for official employment was often decided by the revenue commissioners of the precinct, themselves usually English officers and administrators.[42] In 1652, following the discovery of an official preacher at Cork

40 Dunlop, i. 2, 4–5.
41 See above, pp. 102–5.
42 B.M., Egerton 1762, f. 189v; Dunlop, ii. 294; Murcot, *Several Works*, p. 16; Seymour, pp. 18–19; Webster, *The Diocese of Cork*, pp. 255–6.

with atheistical opinions, Fleetwood and the Dublin government ordered changes. The revenue commissioners were told:[43]

> that such as shall be employed in the work of the ministry should produce ample testimony of their fitness for that service from some congregations in England, who have had experience of their deportment and conversation, and whose duty most properly it is to send out gospel ministers; or else from others our friends in England, or Ireland, who are reputed religious and zealous promoters of godliness, before we can signify our approbation of them.

Thereafter greater care was taken. Individuals in England approached to find ministers for Ireland were generally grave and orthodox: Richard Baxter and his neighbour Colonel John Bridges; John Owen, who was to scour Essex; Thomas Goodwin, who was to search among the fellows of his Oxford college; Philip Nye and John Arrowsmith.[44] Another measure was a meeting arranged in London in 1652 by Oliver Cromwell, Fleetwood, and Hewson with leading divines, including Owen, Thomas Goodwin, Hugh Peter, and Jenkin Lloyd, to devise ways of supplying Ireland. The Irish government itself sent out standardized invitations to preachers, in New England and Norfolk for example.[45] Although testimonials had now to be produced, they could be supplied by laymen, including Baptists. Moreover they were sometimes a mere formality: any minister who could be persuaded to settle on Lord Herbert's Kerry estates was promised approval and a salary of £100 p.a.[46] Ministers came to Ireland, recommended by the English committee for the approbation of ministers at Whitehall, the South Wales commission for propagating the Gospel, and the Scottish presbyteries.[47]

---

[43] Dunlop, ii. 295.

[44] R.C.B., Seymour MSS., pp. 71, 74; Dr. Williams' Lib., Baxter letters, 3, f. 234; Brit. Mus., Lansdowne MSS. 821, f. 113; 823, f. 35; *Cal. S.P. Dom. 1654*, p. 369; Dunlop, ii. 527–8.

[45] *Cal. S.P. Dom., 1651–2*, p. 351; ibid., *1655*, p. 199; Bodl., Firth MS. C.5, ff. 110ᵛ, 111, 118ᵛ, 119; R.C.B., Seymour MSS., p. 90; Seymour, pp. 62–3, 103. Peter wanted 'a labouriouse, constant, sober ministery' established in Ireland. Brit. Mus., Lansdowne MSS. 821, f. 121; 823, f. 364.

[46] R.C.B., Seymour MSS., pp. 1, 2, 3, 4, 5, 6, 8; *The Herbert Correspondence*, ed. Smith, pp. 146–7; Mayer, *Trans. Historic Soc. of Lancashire and Cheshire*, N.S. i. 184, 213.

[47] R.C.B., Seymour MSS., pp. 31, 61; C.B., Jennings transcripts, A/20, 5 Jan. 1657[8]; J. Healy, *History of the Diocese of Meath* (Dublin, 1908), i. 295–6; W. C. Stubbs, 'Finglas, County Dublin, Vestry Books', *JRSAI* xlvi (1917), 28–9.

Henry Cromwell's preference for conservatives was reflected in his greater use of the Scottish presbyteries, the English universities, the county associations of clergy in England, and the London Presbyterian *classes* for recruiting ministers.[48]

After 1652 the testimonials of ministers seeking a government salary were frequently (although not invariably) vetted in Dublin by ministers and laymen nominated by the administration. This was not a formally constituted committee, such as had been set up in England in March 1654 to approve and eject ministers, and those chosen to do this work varied with the vagaries of government policy. The Baptists Patient, Lawrence, and Hewson were amongst these adjudicators.[49] In April 1656 reforms were instituted, intended to produce greater formality. A committee of eleven (four of whom were ministers) was to consult with two members of the council for drawing up rules for the approbation of ministers and schoolmasters, for the removal of the scandalous and disaffected, and to prevent the intrusion of disallowed ministers. This committee was to use as its basis the English ordinance of 1654, and was to meet daily until rules were perfected.[50] On 24 April the committee's report was referred back because no rules had been included.[51] It seems that this committee took over the work of approving ministers.[52] If it produced formal rules, they do not survive. Complaints by the Independent Lord Chancellor Steele suggested that it produced none. Steele believed that its lack of fixed rules turned it into an instrument of Henry Cromwell's clerical reaction and that it inquired more closely into ministers' opinions than the English committee. Steele wanted to promote an act of parliament which would introduce the English ordinance of 1654 into Ireland, so that preachers there could be admitted to salary 'without enquiry made into

---

[48] R.C.B., Seymour MSS., pp. 96, 99, 104; Brit. Mus., Lansdowne MS. 822, f. 244; Sion College, MS. Arc. L.40.2/E.17, f. 241ᵛ; *Reliquiae Baxterianae*, i. 171–2.

[49] R.C.B., Seymour MSS., pp. 22, 23; Seymour, p. 88.

[50] C.B., Jennings transcripts, A/10, 4 Apr. 1656; calendared, incompletely, in Dunlop, ii. 588.

[51] C.B., Jennings transcripts, A/10, 24 Apr. 1656.

[52] Dunlop, ii. 648; R.C.B., Seymour MSS., p. 51. Another minister, Thomas Wilkinson, was added in December 1656. Its composition probably changed between 1656 and 1659: ibid., pp. 46–55, 59.

their principles, as to latitude in the distribution of the healing ordinance; or their being of either judgm[en]t as to discipline; this practice being unwarranted by the usage in England, by the last clause of the ordinance for approbacon of minist[er]s ... and alsoe by the late establisht govern-m[en]t esteeeming such persons fitt, notwithstanding their difference'.[53] Yet the composition of the committee in 1656 suggested it would be sympathetic to Steele's brand of Independency. Only three Baptist officers were included (at this time Henry Cromwell was still trying to work with them); moreover Worth was the only known conservative.[54] Possibly the committee's membership changed after 1656.

The greater care for vetting ministers was accompanied by more determined efforts to root out unauthorized ministers. The most comprehensive effort was two proclamations issued by the Irish council in January 1658. The first stipulated that no minister arriving in Ireland should be given a salary unless he were approved by the Dublin committee or produced a testimonial from two other godly ministers. The second was meant to prevent ministers ejected in England and Scotland coming to Ireland, lest they corrupt the Irish population in its 'judgments and conversations' and make it politically disaffected. The justices of the peace were to compare the names of those preaching with the names in the civil list, and to report discrepancies to Dublin. The justices of the peace were also to encourage the godly and remove the scandalous and insufficient.[55] To help this work in October 1658 Philip Nye, preacher to the council of state in London, was asked to send to Dublin a list of those ejected in England so that they could be stopped from settling in Ireland.[56] After the Dublin

[53] Brit. Mus., Lansdowne MS. 1228, ff. 9–10.

[54] The Baptists were Hewson, Lawrence, and Sankey. Wootton and Alderman Hooke were particularly close to Winter, and Sir Hardress Waller seems to have been an Independent. Sir Robert King had invited Winter's close associate, Murcot, to Dublin. The other members were Sir John Temple, Dr. Harrison, Worth, and Thomas Wilkinson, a minister who dissented from the Church of Ireland after 1660. J. Murcot, *Saving Faith and Pride of Life Inconsistent* (London, 1656); Murcot, *Several Works*, p. 12; *Thurloe State Papers*, vi. 774; T.C.D., MS. N.2.3., 24 July 1661, 28 July 1661, and 6 Sept. 1661.

[55] Steele, ii, nos. 593, 595 (Ireland). No copy of the first is known, but its contents can be recovered from *Mercurius politicus*, no. 404 (18–25 Feb. 1658), p. [366].

[56] R.C.B., Seymour MSS., p. 73.

Convention of ministers in May 1658 its participants were
urged to report suspect ministers in their localities. The
greater care produced an increase in the number of ministers
suspended from their duties. Allegations against them were
generally of two sorts: of moral weakness (drunkenness or
adultery); or of political and theological error.[57]

Although control from Dublin tightened after 1656, execution of the government's policy rested with the justices of
the peace. After 1656, as will be suggested below, the
commission of the peace was remodelled to include Henry
Cromwell's new allies, the substantial settlers.[58] Nevertheless
the great champion of the Independents and opponent of
Henry Cromwell's religious policy, Steele, as lord chancellor
had considerable control over the nomination of justices.[59]
Lethargy, rather than lack of enthusiasm for government
policy, was probably the greatest obstacle to painstaking
inquiries into the clergy.[60]

Greater care was taken of ministers officiating in Ulster
and Munster, which in Munster included a formal committee
of approbation. In Ulster a first step in weeding out recalcitrant ministers had been the imposition of the Engagement in
August 1652. Once the policy of co-operation with the
province's Presbyterians developed, much power was given to
the presbyteries to decide a minister's fitness.[61]

Munster differed from the rest of Ireland in having a
formal commission for the approbation of ministers, established by Oliver Cromwell in 1650 to act 'in like manner as
the honorable committee at Westminster [does] proceed
against scandalous delinquents, or insufficient ministers'.[62]
The need to break the royalist interest amongst the obdurate
episcopalians of the province was the reason for its creation.

---

57 R.C.B., Seymour MSS., p. 93; Brit. Mus., Lansdowne MS. 823, f. 57;
Analecta Hibernica, xv. 277–8; Seymour, pp. 168–9.

58 At pp. 290–1.

59 Chatsworth, Lismore MS. 29, Cork's diary, 10 Feb. 1657[8]; 9 Mar.
1657[8]; Hist. MSS. Comm., *Leyborne-Popham MSS.*, p. 141.

60 J. Eyres, *The Church-Sleeper Awakened*, sig. [a4]ᵛ; Brit. Mus., Lansdowne
MS. 823, f. 91.

61 R.C.B., Seymour MSS., pp. 49, 72; P.R.O., Northern Ireland, MS.
D.1759/1A/1, pp. 123–4; Brit. Mus., Lansdowne MS. 823, f. 57.

62 Cook, *Monarchy no creature of Gods making*, sig. f4.

It sequestered episcopalians.[63] In membership it was balanced between established settlers, like Sir William Fenton, Vincent Gookin, and John Hodder, who had rallied to the Cromwellians;[64] and newcomers, John Baker, John Cook (a religious and political Independent), Colonel Phaire (whose tolerance we have already noticed), and Dr. John Harding (formerly beneficed in the Church of Ireland, but who now became the leading Baptist preacher in Cork).[65] How long this committee functioned we do not know. Possibly its authority derived from Ireton as lord president of Munster, in which case his death in 1651 would have removed its statutory foundation. At all events a new committee was nominated on 24 April 1655.[66]

The 1655 committee had nine members, the majority of whom were opposed to the Baptists and Quakers,[67] and included Dr. Edward Worth. The committee proceeded against those who still clung to the Anglican prayer book, showing how determined Worth was to distinguish his position from that of the implacable episcopalians. The committee's main work, both in 1650 and 1655, was to remove scandalous and delinquent ministers, rather than to vet and settle new ones.[68]

Notwithstanding the existence of this special body, in Munster as elsewhere in Ireland the execution of official religious policy depended on the co-operation of the justices of the peace. One of Worth's followers, Eyres, wanted to add clerical assessors to the bench in ecclesiastical cases; he also feared that the justices were being too lenient with malefactors, and wanted them to have power to examine on oath.[69]

[63]Seymour, pp. 18–19; Webster, *The Diocese of Cork*, pp. 255–6.
[64]Fenton was brother-in-law of Broghill and Lord Cork. Gookin later complained of the religious novelties in Munster. Hodder had been active in the Protestant cause and was later mayor of Cork. Gookin, *The Great Case of Transplantation*, p. 4; *The Council book of Cork*, ed. Caulfield, pp. 1155, and note, 1160, 1174.
[65]Captain Baker's opinions are not known.
[66]Seymour, pp. 90–1.
[67]Abraham Savage was sympathetic to the Cork association. Claudius Gilbert, Worth, and Gookin were known conservatives. Edward Waller and 'Mr' Wetherell probably came from local settler families. Only Major Peter Wallis was said to be favourable towards the Quakers. Brit. Mus., Lansdowne MS. 823, f. 91; *Thurloe State Papers*, iv. 508.
[68]Wood, *Athenae Oxonienses*, iii, cols. 941–2.
[69]Brit. Mus., Lansdowne MS. 823, f. 91.

It may be that the justices were reluctant to proceed against
episcopalians, as Eyres suggested; but in general he found the
magistrates in Cork sympathetic to his aims and the composition of the commission of the peace in Waterford in 1658
suggested that it would support Worth's policy.[70]

The need to quell religious contentions led to more careful
examination of ministers' credentials and opinions, especially
after Henry Cromwell's arrival. However it was easier to vet
newly arrived ministers than to silence those already in
Ireland. Although determined attempts were made to remove
episcopalian clergy, these were far from successful, as I shall
now show.

iii. Unauthorized Ministers

The main reason for a minister to seek official approval was
the wish to be paid a government salary. If an alternative
source of income could be found, then the incentive disappeared and the minister might evade government control.
Three alternative sources of payment existed in the 1650s:
presentation to a living by a lay patron; livings and other
offices in the gift of corporate bodies; and voluntary contributions.

Lay patronage was revived during the Interregnum. If a
patron was not guilty of delinquency then his right of
presentation might be restored. Its revival occurred in 1655
when Sir John Clotworthy was allowed to present in
Antrim;[71] at the same time Lord Cork was more hopeful of
exercising the right.[72] Permission to the earl of Meath to
present in 1657 was seen as the prelude to a general
resumption. However the right was not uncontrolled: the
minister to be presented had to have the committee of
approbation's approval.[73] This was a conciliatory measure,
designed to please the lay patrons (especially in Munster and

---

70 Eyres, *The Church-Sleeper Awakened*, sig. [A2]–[A2]ᵛ; [a5]ᵛ; Ladyman,
The Dangerous Rule, sig. [a4]ᵛ; and below, pp. 290–1.
71 B.M., Egerton 1762, f. 168ᵛ. This seems to have been in response to a request
from Down and Antrim in April 1655. Seymour, pp. 99–100. For Clotworthy
exercising his rights: R.C.B., MS. Libr. 26, Antrim Inquisition, pp. 24, 29, 45, 46,
54, 61; P.R.O., Northern Ireland, MS. D.1756/1A/1, p. 120.
72 Chatsworth, Lismore MS. 29, Cork's diary, 20 May 1655.
73 Ibid., 14 July 1657, 17 Feb. 1658[9], 11 Mar. 1658[9]; Seymour p. 122.

Ulster),[74] enabling them to identify more closely with the official church in Ireland, whilst not allowing them to undermine that church.

If patrons could not present unacceptable ministers to livings in their gift, they could patronize them in other ways. In Ulster the Rawdons installed the uncompromising episcopalian, Jeremy Taylor, as their chaplain; and the Hills were praised by Taylor as 'a family, in which the publick liturgy of the church is greatly valued, and diligently us'd', and sheltered the bishop of Down and Connor, Henry Leslie, throughout the Interregnum.[75] In Munster Lord Cork kept two successive chaplains, one of whom was presented to a living in the family's gift in 1659.[76] Neither of these chaplains was an officially approved minister. Were they, then, unflinching episcopalians whom Cork sheltered? Certainly both conformed to the re-established church after 1660. For the form of worship in Cork's homes during the 1650s we have a positive statement from Dr. Worth, who was questioned by the Irish council as to whether the Common Prayer Book was used. Worth said it was not.[77] Yet Lord Cork heard a large number of preachers in his houses or the local church, some of whom were uncompromising episcopalians and from whom he received communion.[78] It is probable that a discreet flexibility marked Cork's religious observances. His diary also showed that numerous unauthorized ministers had survived and indeed officiated in County Cork.

The patronage of corporations could similarly help those refused government payment. Before 1656 Worth had depended on two livings and the mastership of St. Stephen's

[74] For the Presbyterian, Lord Clandeboye, exercising his right: Bodl., Clarendon state papers, 47, f. 391; William Hamilton, *The Hamilton Manuscripts*, ed. T. K. Lowry (Belfast, n.d.), p. 85.

[75] Stranks, *Jeremy Taylor*, p. 189; J. Taylor, epistle in Leslie, *A Discourse of Praying*, sig. a2.

[76] This was William Smith, who may have come from Virginia. Chatsworth, Cork's diary, 22 June 1656, 20 Feb. 1656[7], 13 Nov. 1659; Brady, *Clerical Records of Cork, Cloyne and Ross*, i. 154; ii. 371. The other was Dr. Peter du Moulin the younger.

[77] Chatsworth, Cork's diary, 31 Jan. 1655[6].

[78] Among these ministers were his cousin Robert Naylor, dean of Limerick, and Edward Synge, dean of Elphin. In 1654 Christmas was celebrated, notwithstanding the orders against superstitious holidays. Ibid., 25 Dec. 1654.

hospital, Cork, to which he had been presented by the Cork and Kinsale corporations.[79] In Dublin the powerful merchant guild appointed episcopalians, whom the government was anxious to silence, as its chaplains in 1649 and 1656. The carpenters' guild of St. Audeon's also sheltered an episcopalian.[80]

Voluntary contributions from their congregations enabled other unauthorized ministers to survive. In Dublin, owing to the absence of predial tithes, payment by parishioners was known before 1649. During the Interregnum even official preachers had their stipends supplemented in this way.[81] No doubt it was this method that allowed episcopalians to officiate at St. Audeon's, St. Michael's, St. Michan's, and St. Nicholas's churches in the capital until 1658. New stringency in 1658 flushed them out, but the fact that they had survived so long is a forceful indication either of government indifference or of the powerful support they enjoyed within Dublin.[82]

In remoter areas it was comparatively easy for unofficial preachers to escape detection. The inquiries of 1657 unearthed several. At Naas an episcopalian was allowed the use of the parish church, although he was not a government preacher, so that he might resist Baptism there.[83] Where ministers were unable to find alternative payment, they took

79 P.R.O., Dublin, Repertory of Cromwell's leases, chancery, 1656–9, pp. 30, 49.

80 Pearse St. Lib., Gilbert MS. 78, pp. 124, 126, 130, 141; Berry, *JRSAI*, 5th Ser. x (1901), 68; R. Ir. Ac., MS. 12.0.13, ff. 6, 6ᵛ, Genealogical Office, funeral entries, 14, p. 13; Seymour, p. 3.

81 R.C.B., Seymour MSS., p. 101; and MS. Libr. 14, Vestry books of St. Katherine's and St. James's, Dublin, from 1657, p. 7; *The Registers of St. John the Evangelist, Dublin*, ed. Mills, pp. 276–7; Wilkins, *Concilia Britanniáe et Hiberniae*, iv. 555.

82 Most surprising is the fact that St. Nicholas's was the church where Winter's congregation met. *The Registers of the Church of St. Michan*, ed. Berry, pp. 8, 10, 13, 34, 35, 41, 42, 43, 44, 61; Mason, *St. Patrick's Cathedral*, p. 197; Seymour, pp. 167–8.

83 This minister, Underwood, became dean of Kilkenny in 1660. Nat. Lib. Ire., Ms. 11,961, pp. 221–2, 311–12; R.C.B., MS. Libr. 26, Kildare inquisition, p. 21; Seymour MSS., p. 59; Bodl., Carte MS. 43, f. 50; Seymour, pp. 178–9; Wilkins, *Concilia Britanniae et Hiberniae*, iv. 555.

to new professions, practising as doctors or keeping schools, and some traded.[84]

It is clear that unauthorized ministers survived and ministered throughout the Interregnum. Again it was unfortunate that time had to be devoted to tracking down and silencing ministers who professed a form of the Protestant Gospel. The need to secure observance of new ceremonies weakened the Protestant offensive against the Catholics. The survival of these ministers was a powerful factor in Henry Cromwell's initial use of Worth and the Ulster Presbyterians, hoping their influence would win the laity away from forbidden forms of worship. That hope was not altogether realized.

iv. The Maintenance of the Ministry

Casual reference has already been made to the fact that officially approved ministers were paid by the state in Ireland during the Interregnum. Closer attention must now be given to that change; first because it was praised as an excellent reform, avoiding the traditional, contentious system of tithes and ensuring an adequate salary for the clergy, and secondly because it was this issue which divided Henry Cromwell and his supporters from Fleetwood, Steele, and their cronies. In Ireland, as in England, the debate on tithes and their replacement mirrored wider divisions over a political settlement.[85] The reform of tithes was like law reform in that both had long been advocated in England and were achieved in Ireland after 1649, serving as possible models for English reforms. Both these reforms were treated by Henry Cromwell as improvisations appropriate to the aftermath of war, but in need of replacement by more traditional methods after 1655. His policy was attacked as retrogressive by the protectorate's opponents.

Before 1649 the clergy of the Church of Ireland were, in theory, supported by rectorial and vicarial tithes and by the glebe. In Ireland, as in England, there had been much lay impropriation of tithes, particularly of the more valuable rector's tithes. If the incumbent was legally entitled to the

---

[84] Brit. Mus., Add. MSS. 15,635, f. 28ᵛ; 19,843, ff. 168ᵛ, 185ᵛ; *The Council book of Youghal*, ed. Caulfield, p. 285; *A 'Census'*, ed. Pender, p. 200.

[85] C. Hill, *God's Englishman* (London, 1970), p. 187.

tithes, it was difficult to extract them from parishioners, particularly when they were Catholic. Where lay patrons paid the incumbent's salary, it was usually a pittance. The other source of support — the glebe — was generally exiguous, if not non-existent.[86] Strafford and Bramhall had tried to resume impropriations and increase glebes, but had only limited success which hardly compensated for the offence given to the powerful impropriators.[87] Only in Ulster, thanks to the recent confiscations and plantation, was the church better supported. Glebes were larger; lay patrons, although numerous, were more careful of their duty to maintain the clergy; and the Ulster tithing table imposed a more equitable tithe.[88] The poverty of the Church of Ireland made it ineffective. Pluralism was a necessity to gain a subsistence, and that entailed non-residence. Some ministers were even obliged to keep ale-houses to survive.[89] Conditions were not propitious for a learned, diligent, and resident clergy, necessary if the counter-reformation was to be combatted.

The Cromwellians accepted the need for better salaries if the Irish ministry was to be improved. As conquerors, using summary methods, it was easier to cut through the obstacles that had defeated Bramhall and Strafford. Tithes were regarded as an unsuitable form of maintenance for several reasons. They made ministers dangerously dependent on and deferential towards the parishioners, patrons, or lay impropriators who paid their salaries. The ministers had to be freed from reliance on the laity, who were often hostile to the religious innovations after 1649, and instead be made dependent on the government which had introduced these

[86] Although concerned with England, Christopher Hill, *The Economic Problems of the Church* (Oxford, 1956), pp. 77–131, is relevant.

[87] Kearney, *Strafford in Ireland*, pp. 119–29; Ranger, 'The Career of Richard Boyle, 1st earl of Cork', chapters 9 and 10.

[88] Hill, *An historical account of the plantation in Ulster*, pp. 91 ff.; R. Mant, *History of the Church of Ireland* (London, 1840), i. 364–5, 396–407. Attempts were made to extend the tithing table to the rest of Ireland. T.C.D., MS. N.2.3., 6 July 1661; Bodl., Additional MS. C.306, f. 170; *Cal. S.P. Ire. 1660–2*, p. 264; *C.J. Ire.* i. 644, 653; *L.J. Ire.* ii. 253, 272, 277, 279, 280, 282.

[89] *The Humble Petition of the Protestant Inhabitants of … Antrim*, p. 4; *Letters and dispatches of Strafforde*, ed. Knowler, i. 187; *Thurloe State Papers*, ii. 733.

changes.[90] Tithes were also disliked because of their small or doubtful yield. Social reformers wanted them replaced because they were a burden on the poor parishioners. Finally, there were objections on theological grounds that tithes lacked Biblical authority and should therefore be replaced by voluntary contributions.

It seemed at first that the changes in Ireland after 1649 had removed this socially oppressive and scripturally unsound device, at the same time giving ministers an adequate and certain income. Let us first see how ministers in Ireland were paid throughout the Interregnum and then see why controversy arose.

One of the weaknesses of the Irish changes was that they were improvisations and lacked an adequate legal basis. The revenue and endowments of the Church of Ireland were confiscated after 1649, but without an ordinance to authorize this.[91] The regime acted less boldly over church property in lay hands. Where a lay proprietor was found guilty of delinquency then tithes were confiscated along with the rest of his property; if innocent, tithes were retained. The value of tithes which passed to the state varied with the incidence of rebellion. In Munster and Ulster where many proprietors retained their estates lay impropriation continued on a large scale. There were, of course, political benefits from upholding this form of property, but the chance to recover the church's alienated wealth and use it to endow the Cromwellian church was lost.[92]

The tithes which were forfeit to the state were treated like other confiscated property and farmed. Thus tithes were not abolished, and it is likely that the burden on the poor

---

[90] Hugh Peter argued this most forcefully in *Good Work for a Good Magistrate* (London, 1651), p. 11. In Ireland this view was repeated by Fleetwood and John Rogers. *Thurloe State Papers*, ii. 733; Rogers, *Ohel or Beth-shemesh*, p. 28; see also Adair, *A True Narrative*, pp. 217–18.

[91] In March 1650 episcopal lands in Ireland were treated as forfeit. Firth and Rait, ii. 355–7; see also, Steele, ii, no. 477 (Ireland).

[92] In 1658 tithes in the state's possession were valued thus: Counties Antrim, Armagh, Down, and Monaghan £51; Derry, Donegal, Fermanagh, Cavan, and Tyrone £116; Cork, Clare, Kerry and Limerick £399; Waterford, Wexford, and Tipperary £1,253; Leitrim, Longford, Mayo, Roscommon, Sligo, and Westmeath £2,242: Nat. Lib. Ire., MS. 2701, pp. 62–3; P.R.O, SP. 63/287, 170ᵛ.

increased, since the farmers of tithes were often the state's
dishonest and ruthless revenue collectors.[93]

It was the Rump which first established the principle of
government payment for ministers in Ireland, specifying that
the six ministers which it had nominated for service in Dublin
in March 1650 should be paid quarterly from the public
revenue, their salaries being charged against the income from
episcopal and capitular lands.[94] In May 1651 a proclamation
of the Irish parliamentary commissioners assigned half the
receipts from church lands to the maintenance of ministers
and schoolmasters.[95] This system of state payment was
universal in Ireland until 1658.

There was no attempt to separate ecclesiastical revenue
from the government's other income, or to ensure that the
revenue covered the cost of the ministers' salaries. However
in 1657 the Irish financial administration was reformed, and
a distinct treasury of tithes established so that the exact yield
of church revenues could be ascertained.[96] This reform
showed that ministers' salaries had to be subsidized from
other sources of revenue. In 1658 preachers' salaries cost
almost £25,000 p.a., whereas church lands brought in only
£2,846, and tithes and glebes £9,173 p.a. Over £12,000 p.a.
had to be diverted to make good the deficit.[97]

This revelation, coming at a time of grave financial stringency, influenced Henry Cromwell's decision to alter the
method of maintenance. Whether the economic motives
weighed more than the theological arguments for change
advanced by Worth and the Ulster Presbyterians we do not
know. At all events Henry Cromwell decided to restore some
of the clergy to direct support by tithes instead of state
payment. This decision was regarded by some as retrograde.
And so it seems, at odds with the Cromwellian desire to
improve the Protestant ministry in Ireland. In the past tithes
had produced a meagre income. How much lower it would

93An apparently unique copy of a printed form for setting tithes to local
farmers in County Meath is in Brit. Mus., pressmark: 806 i.14 (9).
94*C.J.* vi. 379.
95Steele, ii, no. 477 (Ireland).
96Dunlop, ii. 654; *Thurloe State Papers*, vii. 129.
97Huntingdon Rec. Office, 731 dd Bush, no. 18, printed in *Thurloe State
Papers*, vi. 763, where the value of episcopal lands is given as £2,891; ibid. vii.
129.

now be, after the devastations of war. In Counties Armagh, Down, and Louth tithes were worth a quarter to a third less than they had been in 1641; in County Kildare the fall since 1641 had been about 60 per cent.[98] By forcing the clergy back on to tithes, Henry Cromwell would reduce them to a new depth of poverty. Aware of this danger, he included a safeguard in the changes of 1658: ministers returning to tithes would be guaranteed a minimum annual stipend of £80.[99] This provision took much of the force out of the criticisms of the change. Nevertheless there were still problems. How could livings worth less than £80 in 1641 be increased in value? Two solutions were contemplated by the administration. First, the change was to be accompanied by a thorough reorganization, uniting and dividing parishes so that, wherever possible, the new parishes would be worth at least £80 p.a. That intention could not always be achieved, as we shall see in the next section. A second method of achieving the minimum was for the government to make good the deficiency. This destroyed the economical intention behind the change. Not only was the state to lose the revenue from tithes; unless the ministers could increase the yield, government money would still have to subsidize the ministry.

This decision, to return to tithes, was taken first in the Irish council and then endorsed by the Dublin Convention of ministers in May 1658. By the end of 1658 eighty government ministers had been restored to direct maintenance by tithes. By September 1659 the cost of ministers' salaries to the treasury had fallen from £25,000 to £16,000 p.a.[100] Even so the cost still exceeded resources. In 1658 and 1659 the government was falling into arrear with its payments to ministers. After Henry Cromwell's recall in 1659 the return to tithe payment was stopped, producing an acute financial crisis and a general falling into arrears with paying the ministers.[101] The most rapid resumption of support by

[98]These figures are derived from the inquisitions of 1657 and 1658, copies of which are in R.C.B., MS. Libr. 26 and 27. That for Louth is printed in *Journal of the Co. Louth Archaeological Soc.* vii (1929), 19–27.

[99]R.C.B., MS. Libr. 26, Armagh Inquisition, p. 36.

[100]Seymour, pp. 158–9.

[101]Brit. Mus., Lansdowne MS. 823, ff. 140, 158; R.C.B., Seymour MSS., pp. 22, 66; 'Mather papers', *Collections of the Massachusetts Hist. Soc.*, 4th Ser. viii. 50.

tithes occurred in Ulster. Of the eighty ministers paid in this way in 1658 forty-eight worked in the Belfast precinct and eleven in the Derry precinct. One reason for this was the Ulster Presbyterians' enthusiasm for the principle of tithes.[102]   Another was practical. Before 1641 tithes had been most valuable in Ulster. Although reduced in value by the war, the province offered the best hope of tithes producing an adequate income for ministers. The new policy rested on the decision of Henry Cromwell and the Irish council. Efforts were, however, made to give it a more secure legal foundation. In the parliament of 1656—7 a bill was promoted; so too in the 1659 parliament a bill 'for settlement of ye ministry of Ireland upon legall titles and increase of mayntenance wher their tithes and gleabs are defective' was introduced.[103]   Neither measure was passed.

The changes of 1658 were resisted, first in the council by Lord Chancellor Steele and then in the Dublin Convention by Winter and other Independents. Why did the issue generate such bitterness? Before 1649 radicals in the army and religious sects agreed, for various reasons, that tithes should be replaced. In power after 1649 the difficulty of finding an alternative to tithes was quickly discovered, and for want of a substitute tithes continued in England. An attempt by religious zealots in the Barebone's Parliament of 1653 to sweep away tithes before a replacement had been decided alarmed many (including Oliver Cromwell) who had hitherto supported tithes' abolition. Although radicals continued to press for reform, tithes were upheld by the English government throughout the Interregnum.[104]

For radicals in England Ireland offered an example of successful reform. John Rogers, after his return to England, praised the way he had been paid in Ireland as 'orderly and gospel-like', as regular and generous, and as freeing him from dependence on parishioners. He thought Irish practice worthy of emulation in England.[105]   Fleetwood was also a

[102] Kirkpatrick, *An essay upon the loyalty of Presbyterians*, p. 301; Seymour, p. 158.

[103] Brit. Mus., Lansdowne MSS. 821, f. 308; 823, f. 297v.

[104] Generally on this issue: M. James, 'The political importance of the tithe controversy in the Puritan Revolution', *History*, N.S. xxvi (1941), 1—8.

[105] Rogers, *Ohel or Beth-shemesh*, p. 28.

champion of the Irish system which (he believed) offered a middle way between the extremes 'of no allowance to a preaching minister, and that of having tythes at its hight, which hath been such a bone of contention 'twixt minister and people, and so burthensom to many good and tender consciences'. In 1656 Fleetwood asked Henry Cromwell, who was exploring alternatives, 'not to suffer y[ou]r way of tyths to goe out of its present channell but continue your way of maintenance as of late yeares it hath bene done. His highness and councill would be glade it wer so heare. Ther hath bin some late thoughts of making yt worke more easy heare'.[106]

Such enthusiasm ignored drawbacks of the Irish system. Salaries were not always paid regularly; ministers in remote areas had the inconvenience of travelling to their precinct's headquarters to collect their pay. Moreover the loosening of the preacher's connection with a particular parish (commended by Rogers) was seen by conservatives like Worth as a cause of Baptism and Quakerism taking hold, although unacceptable to a majority of Irish Protestants.[107] Above all supporters of the reform often misrepresented it, suggesting that tithes had been abolished in Ireland.[108] This was not so.

When radicals accused Henry Cromwell in 1658 of reintroducing tithes, he exposed (with typical tactlessness) their mistake. The system of payment between 1649 and 1658 was no better than 'a mongrel way between salaryes and tythes'. He suggested that ministers who were content 'that the state be their stewards to set, let and gather the profits, and themselves receive the very specificall money, which ariseth out [of] tythes, instead of tythes in specie, which all of them have done ever since that revenue hath been put into a distinct treasury...' were hypocritical.[109] Much of the opposition in 1658 was based on this mistaken idea that tithes had been abolished between 1649 and 1658. The change was also disliked because it represented a victory for Worth and the Ulster Presbyterians, who wanted a tithe-supported and parochial ministry. Furthermore it brought

---

[106]Brit. Mus., Lansdowne MS. 821, f. 70ᵛ; *Thurloe State Papers*, ii. 445.
[107]R.C.B., Seymour MSS., p. 23; Worth, *The Servant doing*, pp. 30–1.
[108]J. Rogers, *Sagrir, or Doomes-day drawing nigh* (London, 1653), sig. b3.
[109]*Thurloe State Papers*, vii. 129.

the clergy closer to the laity, who were generally hostile to the Baptists and unenthusiastic about the Independents.

Thus there were two elements in the unsuccessful opposition. One disliked Henry Cromwell's alliance with political and religious conservatives in Ireland, of which the policy was a product. The other believed that the return to tithes would damage the church in Ireland, offending those who conscientiously scrupled to receive tithes and impoverishing the ministers. Yet Henry Cromwell had no intention of forcing those with theological objections to tithes to accept them.[110]   As we have seen the changes included safeguards against poverty. Little of the criticism was justified. Indeed it seems that the protracted controversy over the issue arose because it was treated as a symbol of Henry Cromwell's increasing conservatism and deference to the Old Protestants of Ireland, rather than because of its purely theological implications.

The reforms in Ireland after 1649 differed little from those projected or executed in England and Wales. Only the fact that Ireland could more easily be treated as *tabula rasa* allowed a more complete change and so focused the attention of English radicals on Ireland. The Irish system closely resembled that devised by Hugh Peter for Wales and executed in 1649. In Wales tithes were pooled; confiscated church land was used to augment clerical stipends; an itinerant rather than a parochial ministry was preferred. In both England and Wales a minimum stipend of £100 p.a. was introduced.[111] Radical enthusiasm for the Irish reforms was exaggerated; so too were the attacks on the changes in 1658. Both changes paralleled those in England and Wales. This is not, however, to discount the real anger felt in 1658 when it was said (wrongly) that Henry Cromwell was undoing an important reform and restoring tithes.

v.   The Inquisitions of 1657 and the Church's Reorganization

A condition of the return to tithes in 1658 was the reorganiz-

110 Ibid.
111 Claire Cross, 'The Church in England 1646–1660', in *The Interregnum*, ed. Aylmer, p. 104; Hill, 'Propagating the Gospel', in *Historical Essays*, ed. Bell and Ollard, pp. 40–3, 51–2; Firth and Rait, ii. 1000–6; Shaw, *A History of the English Church*, ii. 232–6, 254–9.

ation of parishes to provide ministers with an adequate living. Before the decision of 1658 could be executed information about the necessary parochial changes was essential. The need for such a reorganization was accepted before 1641 and had been admitted in the Long Parliament's projected settlement of Ireland. However it was not until 1656 that the Irish government was empowered to start this work. Again these changes appear to have been linked with Henry Cromwell's arrival and his different idea of Ireland's needs. By February 1657 the restoration of a parochial clergy supported by tithes was under active consideration by his administration.[112] Later in the same year, on 30 July, commissions of inquiry under the Great Seal of Ireland into parochial resources and organization were issued. Taken county by county, returns were to be made by 25 November 1657. In themselves these inquisitions were a large administrative undertaking, requiring the co-operation of the established settlers who acted as commissioners and of local juries which supplied the information.[113] The commissioners were to return the number and value of ecclesiastical livings in each county; the names of lay patrons, impropriators, and incumbents; the value of tithes in 1640 and 1657; the location of churches and their state of repair. However the commissioners had another function, to recommend changes so that the new livings would be worth at least £80 p.a., and so that parishioners should be within three miles of a church.[114] The reports of five of these commissions survive, and the results of a sixth can be recovered.[115] They offer valuable information about

[112]Chatsworth, Lismore MS. 29, Cork's diary, 18 Aug. 1656; Dunlop ii. 583–4, 654–5.

[113]Chatsworth, Lismore MS. 29, Cork's diary, 30 Sept. 1657; R.C.B., MS. T.11, ff. 26ᵛ 60; P.R.O., SP. 63/287, 85 (*Cal. S.P. Ire. 1647–60*, p. 645).

[114]The commission is included in the return for County Armagh, R.C.B., MS. Libr. 27, pp. 34–8.

[115]For Antrim, Armagh, Down, Kildare, and Louth. Copies of the first four in R.C.B., MSS. Libr. 26 and 27; that for Louth is printed by J. B. Leslie, 'Inquisition concerning the parishes of County Louth, 1658', *Jnl. Co. Louth Archaeological Soc.* vii (1929). Details of the Meath inquiries are included in a notebook of Dr. Henry Jones, later bishop of Meath, under the heading 'Unions of Meath livings made by a jury of the County'. R.C.B., MS. T.11, ff. 26ᵛ, 60. Lord Cork mentioned inquisitions in Cork, but the results do not survive. Chatsworth, Cork's diary, 21, 22, and 30 Sept. and 1 Oct. 1657. The Louth inquisition apparently took place a year later than the others. Possibly the return to tithes was at first to be restricted to Munster and Ulster.

the state of the church in 1657, the immensity of the task confronting the Cromwellians, and some insight into their proposed reforms. Let us consider what the inquisitions reveal about the value of livings, the extent of lay patronage and impropriation, the condition of the church buildings, and the supply of ministers.

The value of livings varied greatly from county to county, and was largest in Armagh where few livings were impropriated and most possessed glebes. Although their value had declined since 1640, nine of Armagh's eleven complete parishes were worth over £80 p.a.[116] In County Down the church was less well endowed. Its parishes in 1640 had been worth about £40 p.a. on average; by 1657 the average value had fallen to £32 p.a. Impropriation was extensive, either to the cathedral clergy of Down and Dromore, or to Lords Clandeboye (later earl of Clanbrassil) and Montgomery of the Ards.[117] Conditions in County Antrim were similar to those in Down. The average value of livings in 1640 had been about £40 and had fallen by 1657 to slightly more than £30 p.a. Most of the livings were impropriate to the Connor cathedral chapter or Sir Arthur Chichester, Clotworthy, and Lord Conway.[118]

Unsatisfactory as conditions were in Ulster, apart from Armagh, they were worse in Meath, Kildare, and Louth. The average value of livings in 1640 had been £34 p.a. in Louth, £30 p.a. in Meath, and £23 p.a. in Kildare. By 1657 the figures had dropped to £22 in Louth, £16 in Meath, and a mere £9 in County Kildare. In all three counties there was extensive lay impropriation. In Meath and Louth, however, the largest impropriators had been Catholics, and their rights would be forfeit in 1657.[119]

The inquisitions uncovered unauthorized ministers officiating or still in possession of their livings. The minister at Charlemont, County Armagh, was said to have been 'there a

---

116 R.C.B., MS. Libr. 27, Armagh inquisition. This figure omits the parishes partly in Armagh whose total value is unknown.

117 Ibid., MS. Libr. 26, Down inquisition.

118 Ibid., MS. Libr. 26, Antrim inquisition.

119 R.C.B., Libr. MS. 27, Kildare Inquisition; Leslie, *Jnl. Co. Louth Archaeological Soc.* vii; *The Civil Survey*, v, ed. Simington, appendix A, pp. 378–401; R.C.B., MS. T.11, ff. 60–3.

long time and is yet, who hath no substance but what proceedeth from the benevolence of the people'.[120]   In County Antrim an unauthorized incumbent was Dr. Alexander Colvill, himself one of the commissioners, and formerly a minister in the Church of Ireland.[121]   In Kildare eleven unauthorized ministers were uncovered, including one who had been suspended from duty in 1655 for drunkenness.[122]   Of fifteen ministers recorded in County Meath in 1657 only eight were government-approved ministers.[123]   No doubt the state of affairs revealed by the commissioners prompted the increased efforts in January 1658 to remove these unauthorized ministers.

Having provided information, the commissioners had also to recommend changes. In all counties, except Armagh, dramatic reductions in the number of parishes were proposed. Antrim's sixty-five parishes would be reduced to thirty-two; Kildare's ninety-one to twenty-five; Louth's forty-nine to ten; and in Meath one hundred and five parishes would become twenty-seven.[124]   The need for such sweeping changes had been recognized before 1641. Ussher in his visitation of Meath in 1622 commented, 'if the smallness of the meanes w[hi]ch cometh to the incumbents be regarded then many of the livings ... are fitt to be united to make upp a competent meanes for the minister'.[125]   In 1634 and 1640 bills for the union and division of parishes had been introduced into the Irish parliament. They had not passed, partly owing to fears amongst the lay impropriators that their rights would be curtailed.[126]   The Cromwellians deserve credit for grasping the nettle and going ahead with unions.

120R.C.B., MS. Libr. 27, Armagh Inquisition, p. 12.
121Ibid., MS. Libr. 26, Antrim Inquisition, pp. 1, 58: P.R.O., SP. 63/287, ff. 45, 131; P.R.O., Northern Ireland, D.562/1 and 2; Montgomery, *The Montgomery Manuscripts*, p. 205, and note 38; Scott, *Fasti Ecclesiae Scoticanae*, vii. 528.
122This was Theobald Brenn: R.C.B., MS. Libr. 27, Kildare Inquisition, pp. 26, 27, 31; Seymour, p. 208.
123R.C.B., MS. T.11.
124Ibid., MS. Libr. 26, Antrim Inquisition, pp. 71–88; MS. Libr. 27, Kildare Inquisition, pp. 38–9; Leslie, *Jnl. Co. Louth Archaeological Soc.*, vii, pp. 19–37; R.C.B., MS. T.11, ff. 60–3.
125*The Whole Works of ... Ussher*, ed. C. R. Elrington (Dublin, 1847–64), i. cxxv. Cf. *The Statutes at large ... Ireland* (Dublin, 1786), ii. 494.
126*C.J. Ire.* i. 97, 98, 99, 100, 101, 161; *L.J. Ire.* i. 130, 132.

Unfortunately the unions had to achieve two not always compatible objects: a minimum competence of £80 p.a. and a parish in which all would be within three miles of the church. The commissioners in County Antrim frankly admitted the problem: the parishes in their county were 'not suitable either for sufficiency of maintenance to the ministers or conveniency for resort of the parishioners unto what is held forth in the instructions'. In Armagh there was apparently less difficulty. In Kildare the commissioners seem to have overcome the problem by grossly overestimating the yield of the new parishes, all of which would be worth over £80 p.a. In Meath, where the values of the unions actually accomplished were set down, thirteen of the twenty-five new parishes were worth less than the minimum £80, so that ministers had to hold more than one of the new parishes.[127]

This rationalization was long overdue. Many of the parishes united in 1657 had had no church or incumbent in 1641, and often no Protestant families. Even so the changes led to a charge that the Cromwellians had tried 'to make fewer parishes and fewer ministers' in Ireland.[128] This was unfair. The reforms were intended as the prelude to a more vigorous evangelization and designed to attract more ministers by offering better livings.[129] Expectations in this direction were disappointed. There were not enough ministers to fill these newly created unions. Henry Cromwell himself admitted in 1658 that 'little more than a third part' of Ireland was properly supplied with clergy. Outside the main English settlements there were large tracts of country destitute of ministers. In County Meath more than a third of the parishes created in 1657 remained without incumbents.[130]

The main result of the Cromwellian religious reforms was in fact to raise ministers' salaries, whilst reducing the number

127 R.C.B., MSS. Libr. 26, Antrim Inquisition, pp. 71, 88—9; Libr. 27, Armagh Inquisition, p. 33; Libr. 27, Kildare Inquisition, pp. 29—43; R.C.B., MS. T.11, ff. 60—3.

128 Pressick, *A breife relation*, p. 10.

129 Worth, *The Servant doing*, pp. 30—1; *The Agreement . . . of severall associated ministers in the County of Corke*, p. 18.

130 *Thurloe State Papers*, vii. 129; Brit. Mus., Lansdowne MS. 823, f. 57; Additional MS. 19,845, f. 43; R.C.B., Seymour MSS., p. 48; *Archivium Hibernicum*, vii. 30; Healy, *History of the diocese of Meath*, i. 297; R.C.B., MS. T.11, ff. 60—3.

of clergy in Ireland. With severely strained resources this was inevitable. More ministers, had they come, could not have been paid so generously. These conclusions can be illustrated by comparing Cromwellian provision of ministers with that of the Church of Ireland, although direct comparison is complicated because the unit of ecclesiastical administration changed in 1649 from the diocese to the county.

The diocese of Dromore had had twenty clergy in 1634; the same area had five official preachers in the 1650s. In the west of Ireland, where the transplanted Catholics were to go, the drop in numbers was greater. In 1622 the diocese of Killaloe had forty-seven ministers (many of them non-resident); there were only four official preachers there in the Interregnum.[131] The diocese of Limerick had eleven preaching and twenty-five reading ministers in 1615; the same area had five government ministers in the Interregnum two of whom were settled in the town of Limerick.[132] In 1615 the dioceses of Cork, Cloyne, and Ross had at least eighty-one clergymen. The same area had eighteen official preachers in 1658. In 1669 the Church of Ireland had forty-six ministers in the area.[133] Finally we can compare the number of clergy of the Church of Ireland in Dublin with the Cromwellian provision. In 1630 the Dublin diocese had fifty ministers, of whom eight had livings in the capital.[134] In 1656 there were twenty-six official preachers in the Dublin precinct, of whom ten were assigned to the city of Dublin.[135] At first sight it seemed that Dublin was better supplied with Protestant ministers during the Interregnum This was not so, because the total for 1630 omitted the cathedral chapters of St. Patrick and Christ Church and the fellows of Trinity College,

131E. D. Atkinson, *Dromore: An Ulster Diocese* (Dundalk, 1925), pp. 44–5; Dwyer, *The Diocese of Killaloe*, pp. 145, 298; Brit. Mus., Additional MS. 19,833, f. 13.

132J. Begley, *The Diocese of Limerick in the sixteenth and seventeenth centuries* (Dublin, 1927), pp. 395–6; Brit. Mus., Additional MS. 19,833, f. 13.

133'The Royal Visitation of Cork, Cloyne and Ross, and the College of Youghal', ed. M. A. Murphy, *Archivium Hibernicum*, ii (1913), 175–211; Brady, *Clerical Records of Cork, Cloyne and Ross*, iii. 296, 300; *Analecta Hibernica*, xv. 275; R.C.B., Seymour MSS., pp. 208–9.

134*Archivium Hibernicum*, viii. 56–98.

135*Analecta Hibernica*, xv. 245; R.C.B., Seymour MSS., pp. 203–4.

with whom the Cromwellian ministers in Dublin should more appropriately be compared.

The conclusion from these local comparisons is confirmed by the national totals. In 1655 there were 110 official preachers in Ireland; by 1658 there were about 250.[136] At the end of the 1660s there were estimated to be 500 Church of Ireland clergy. It is likely that the pre-1641 total was higher.[137] Although exact numbers are uncertain, it is clear that the Cromwellians had no more than half the number of ministers deployed by the Church of Ireland.

The major success of the Interregnum was raising clerical salaries. In the 1650s they ranged from £300 to a mere £20 p.a. The average, however, was about £90 p.a. Again we cannot be exact about clerical incomes before 1641. The visitations of Cork and Limerick in 1615, Killaloe and Meath in 1622, and Dublin in 1630, all suggested that the average living was worth less than £20 p.a.[138] The situation in Antrim, Armagh, and Down had apparently been rather better on the eve of war.[139] Even so Anglican ministers could only have an adequate income if they were pluralists, and pluralism entailed non-residence and neglect. Few, except bishops and cathedral clergy, could expect a stipend as generous as that given by the state in the 1650s.[140]

Tacit recognition of the Cromwellian achievement in tackling the reorganization of parishes occurred after 1660. In 1661 the lower house of the Irish convocation asked for a minimum income for ministers to be secured by parochial unions. Until unions could be effected, they suggested that 'the present unions be continued without any change ... ' The bishop of Meath, Dr. Henry Jones (who had been deeply involved with the Cromwellians), used the 1657 unions as the

[136]Brit. Mus., Additional MS. 19,833, ff. 12–14. R.C.B., Seymour MSS., pp. 203–14.

[137]Cal. S.P. Ire. 1666–69, p. 261. In 1692 it was suggested that there had never been more than 400 beneficed clergy in Ireland. Cambridge Univ. Lib., Baumgartner papers, Strype correspondence, i, f. 89.

[138]For these visitations: Archivium Hibernicum, ii and viii; Begley, The Diocese of Limerick; Dwyer, The Diocese of Limerick; The Whole Works of Ussher, i.

[139]See above, p. 154.

[140]Diocesan revenues in 1639 are listed in Kearney, Strafford in Ireland, p. 125. Another list of c. 1680 is in Bodl., Clarendon state papers, 75, ff. 280ᵛ–281.

basis for his reorganization of the diocese after 1660.[141] However the authorities could not acknowledge the merits of Cromwellian reform and they started to do the same work over again, in 1662 passing an act for the union and division of parishes, which adopted the aims of 1657: a minimum salary of £80 and a church serving a radius of three miles.[142] This act seems to have remained a dead-letter, partly because of its cumbersome machinery and also because of the opposition of lay patrons and impropriators.[143] In 1695 another bill for unions was promoted. Its failure led the bishops of Derry and Waterford to expostulate that it 'was of so great moment, and absolutely necessary for the reformation of the church, in point of non-residence, pluralism and unequal distribution of ecclesiastical preferments . . .'[144]

The restored Church of Ireland, although aware of the need for reforms such as had been effected in the Interregnum, achieved little. Zealous bishops, including Edward Worth of Killaloe, tried to recover the church's alienated wealth but were unable to defeat the lay proprietors. Efforts to secure an equitable tithe and to endow all livings with glebes similarly failed. The state church relapsed into the poverty from which it had been briefly lifted in the 1650s.[145] An English visitor to County Kilkenny in 1665 inquired for the church, 'but was answered that their minister lived twelve miles off, and that they had no sermon amongst them, except when he came to receive the tithes, which was but once a year. And the woman . . . told me . . . that they

---

[141]T.C.D., MS. N.2.3, 6 July 1661; *Cal. S.P. Ire. 1660–2*, p. 264; Hist. MSS. Comm., *Hastings MSS.* iv. 100; *i he Works of Bramhall*, ed. Vesey, sig. [o2]–[p1]; R.C.B., MS. T.11, ff. 60–3.

[142]*Statutes at large . . . Ireland*, ii. 495–6.

[143]Brit. Mus., Stowe MS. 202, f. 318. In Meath by 1682 the Irish council had achieved some unions, perhaps those originally effected in 1657. 'Bishop Dopping's Visitation Book, 1682–1685', *Riocht na Midhe*, records of the Meath Archaeological and Hist. Soc. iv, no. 5 (1971), 37, 39.

[144]*L.J. Ire.* i. 567. Cf. 'Remedies proposed for the Church of Ireland (1697),' ed. J. Brady, *Archivium Hibernicum*, xxii (1959), 169.

[145]R.C.B., MS. J.7; Bodl., Additional MS. C.306, f. 170v; Carte MSS. 45, ff. 100–1; 215, f. 185; St. J. D. Seymour, 'Family papers belonging to the Purcells of Loughmore, Co. Tipperary', *Jnl. of the North Munster Archaeological Society*, iii (1913), 203. G. Williams, *The Sad Condition of the Church and Clergy in the Diocess of Ossory* (London, 1665), pp. 26, 31.

had plenty enough of every thing necessary, except the word of God'.[146]

The Cromwellians set on foot changes long projected in Ireland. Their success in raising salaries was offset by a decline in the number of Protestant clergy. In comparison with the Church of Ireland's efforts, they introduced a new vigour. However these changes were not confined to Ireland, but again resembled reforms in England and Wales. In 1646 the Long Parliament had appointed a committee to consider the union and division of parishes. In 1649 there was a survey, county by county, of church wealth: an obvious precedent for the Irish inquisitions in 1657. In 1653 Barebone's Parliament asked for parochial unions 'so that none be above three miles from a publick meeting-place'. Oliver Cromwell authorized unions in September 1654 on the basis of evidence already collected. In Wales too changes were regarded as essential to the better propagation of the Gospel, and were effected.[147]   Thus Ireland followed where the other two countries led.

vi.   The Fabric of the Church

The provision of places of Protestant worship was less important than securing adequate ministers, but nevertheless necessary if Protestantism was to have an impact on the native population.[148]   In the Interregnum the excesses of the sects were linked with their denial of the need for churches and irregular preaching in court-houses and barns. Religious conservatives saw churches as a prerequisite of order and decency in worship.[149]

In Ireland during the Interregnum there were three problems. Church building had been neglected before 1641. Episcopal visitations revealed the parlous condition, owing to rebellion and neglect. The diocese of Meath's 245 parishes

---

146*An Account of the Revd. John Flamsteed*, ed. F. Baily (London, 1835), p. 15.

147*C.J.* iv. 502; vii. 361; Firth and Rait, ii. 1000—6; Shaw, ii. 249—50, 251—2, 603—6; T. Richards, *Religious developments in Wales, (1654—1662)* (London, 1923), pp. 116—33.

148Cf. 'Remedies proposed', *Archivium Hibernicum*, xxii. 171.

149Nat. Lib. Ire., MS. 11,961, pp. 221—2, 311—12; Brit. Mus., Lansdowne MS. 821, f. 334; cf. K. Thomas, *Religion and the decline of magic* (London, 1971), p. 59.

had only seventy-nine churches in repair in 1600, and only forty-nine in 1622.[150] During the 1641 rebellion churches were a natural target and many were destroyed during the war. The inquiries of 1657 revealed the damage and how little had been done to repair it. County Antrim had eighteen churches fit for worship and forty-four in need of renovation or rebuilding. In only six of County Kildare's ninety-one parishes were there churches fit for use; in County Louth four churches were in decent condition, thirty-four were not.[151]

The authorities tried to repair the most obvious damage, concentrating on churches in the main towns. Local levies to finance rebuilding were authorized.[152] In special cases the government itself gave money. £500 was contributed to the renovation of the 'great meeting place' in Waterford: there was also to be a local levy of £200.[153] Corporations and congregations also assumed responsibility. At Kilkenny the common council invited contributions to prevent the total ruin of St. Canice's cathedral. Christ Church, Cork, was renovated before a new minister settled there.[154] In Dublin there were frequent disbursements for work on St. Katherine's, St. Audeon's, and St. John's churches.[155]

After 1660 there was a tendency to blame the decayed condition of churches on the Cromwellians. This was unjust as most of the damage had occurred between 1641 and 1649, and the Cromwellians encouraged repairs. Allegations of vandalism were also generally unfounded.[156] It is true that

150Archivium Hibernicum, viii. 242—3; Healy, History of the diocese of Meath, i. 205, 242—5.

151R.C.B., MSS. Libr. 26 (Antrim Inquisition) and 27 (Kildare Inquisition); The Civil Survey, viii, ed. Simington, pp. 6—216; Journal of the Co. Louth Archaeological Soc. vii. 20—37.

152Nat. Lib. Ire., MS. 11,961, pp. 64, 387; R.C.B., Seymour MSS., p. 20; Analecta Hibernica, xv. 232—3, 235, 240, 241, 242, 250, 255—6, 268; Hore, Wexford (London, 1906), pp. 318, 319.

153Brit. Mus., Egerton MS. 1762, f. 178v; R.C.B., Seymour MSS., pp. 25, 26.

154Kilkenny Municipal Archives, White book, ff. 15—16; J. Graves, and J. G. A. Prim, The History . . . of the Cathedral Church of St. Canice (Dublin, 1857), pp. 43—4; The Council book of Kinsale, ed. Caulfield, pp. 29, 42; Murcot, Several Works, p. 22.

155R.C.B., MS. Libr. 14, Vestry book of St. Katherine and St. James, pp. 1, 15, 22; MS. H.21, Vestry book of St. John the Evangelist, Dublin, 1595—1668, pp. 97, 98, 100, 104, 106; R. Ir. Ac., MS. 12.0.13, f. 6v.

156Cal. S.P. Ire. 1660—2, p. 606; ibid., 1666—9, p. 261.

at Belfast the church was used as a citadel and that at Derry huts were erected inside the church, and occasional churches had been converted into dwelling houses or stables. The Baptist governor of Kilkenny, Axtell, acquired a reputation for vandalism which may have been justified. But in general the Dublin administration acted to prevent profanation and to restore buildings to their proper use.[157] In any case profanation was not introduced into Ireland by the Cromwellians. During the 1630s ale-houses and tobacco shops were erected in the vaults of Christ Church cathedral, Dublin.[158]

Ireland's rulers in the 1650s were confronted not only with their predecessors' neglect and the damage of war but with their own ambitious schemes of reorganization. In order to achieve the object of a church serving a three-mile radius extensive building was needed. Each of the projected new parishes in County Kildare would need a new church: twenty-five in all. The rearrangement in Antrim required eleven new churches. Money was too scarce to allow anything to be done towards implementing this programme. Churches remained in disrepair or unbuilt.

Although the Cromwellian record was decried after 1660, the Church of Ireland had no greater success either in rebuilding or providing new churches in united parishes.[159] In forty-two parishes of the diocese of Meath in 1682 only four had churches fit for worship. In one parish services were held in the church porch; in another in the minister's house.[160] Dismal as the picture was, both in the 1650s and after 1660, the situation was slightly less gloomy than the figures suggested. Many of the parishes without churches had no Protestant inhabitants and were ripe for union. Both the

157Brit. Mus., Egerton 1762, f. 138V; Nat. Lib. Ire., MS. 11,961, pp. 155, 160; R.C.B., MS. Libr. 27, Kildare Inquisition, pp. 12, 31; Bodl., Carte MS. 45, f. 438; Williams, *Four Treatises*, pp. 3—4; and *The Persecution and Oppression . . . of John Bale*, p. 40; *The Bishopric of Derry and the Irish Society of London*, i, ed. Moody and Simms, p. 346.

158*Letters and dispatches of Strafforde*, ed. Knowler, i. 173.

159*Cal. S.P. Ire. 1660—2*, p. 556; Chetham Lib., Manchester, 'MSS. collections relating to Ireland,' p. 342; Bodl., Carte MSS. 45, f. 164V; 221, f. 78. Brit. Mus., Stowe MS. 212, f. 318; Nat. Lib. Ire., MS. 8643 (6), Sir T. Jones to G. Lane, 9 July 1664; T.C.D., Mun. P/I/469 (28).

160'Bishop Dopping's Visitation Book', *Riocht na Midhe*, iv, no. 5, pp. 28—39; *Archivium Hibernicum*, xxii. 163—4; Power, *A Bishop of the penal times*, p. 28.

Cromwellians and the Church of Ireland concentrated their meagre resources where they were most needed, the towns with Protestant communities.

vii. The Conversion of the Irish

The Protestant church in Ireland had to be reformed to make it more effective in its principal task, converting the Irish Catholics. After 1641 there was agreement that the Church of Ireland had been negligent; after 1649 there was an expectation that Ireland's new rulers would be diligent.[161] Unfortunately religious reformers in Ireland after 1649 were distracted by doctrinal and formal controversies, which had been carried over from England and few of which were relevant to Irish conditions. After 1649 there was a tendency to concentrate on reforms which would benefit only the elect or at best those who were already Protestants. This inward-looking tendency in religious policy began to be corrected after 1655, but it was never really overcome. Even after 1660 the Protestant interest was more deeply and permanently divided than it had been in 1641. In this section I shall try to establish what was done towards converting the Irish, and whether or not Ireland's new rulers lived up to their promises of ending the previous neglect.

Verdicts on the Cromwellian performance have varied. A contemporary alleged that having exiled the Irish to Connaught the authorities 'never attempted the sending of the gospel unto them in their own language, or the setting up of any English schooles amongst them . . . to translate them from darkness to light'. A review of Protestant evangelization of the Irish written in 1712 suggested that the 1641 massacre produced such repugnance that thoughts of conversion were abandoned and not resumed until about 1680.[162] Yet a well-known Irish historian praised this aspect of Cromwellian policy in 1937, contending that 'for the first time, the language difficulty was approached in a way which promised results.' Writing again in 1957 the same writer found no cause

---

161 See above, pp. 90–1.
162 *Two Biographies of William Bedell*, ed. Shuckburgh, p. 168; J. Richardson, *A short history of the attempts that have been made to convert the popish natives of Ireland* (London, 1712), p. 26.

for enthusiasm.[163] I shall argue that Cromwellian policy continued to be weakened by the ambiguity which had marked attempts at conversion since the sixteenth century; and that, although some attempts at evangelization were made, they were totally inadequate and compared unfavourably with the efforts of the Church of Ireland.

Catholic worship was forbidden throughout the Interregnum, which should have left the field clear for Protestant missionaries. In 1649, although Oliver Cromwell had distinguished between the authors of the rebellion and their tenants, who had been dupes, the promise of milder policies was not redeemed. Toleration could not include the Catholics' religion.[164] This quickly became clear. The parliamentary commissioners were instructed in 1650 to enforce the laws against papists, and in 1654 the Elizabethan and Jacobean laws against Catholic priests were revived.[165] Ordinances of the English parliament had debarred Catholics from political life; at a local level by-laws excluded them from the government of the towns; all Catholics guilty of rebellion were to be transplanted to Connaught. In 1657 the English parliament imposed a new burden, an oath of abjuration, renouncing the pope's temporal and spiritual power, together with specific doctrines. The penalty for not taking it was transplantation to Connaught.[166] In practice the bulk of the landless Irish Catholics escaped removal. Rather more successful was the government's drive against priests, who at first were executed and then, as peace returned, were imprisoned and exiled. Ireland was not completely cleared of Catholic priests, but their numbers were greatly reduced and their leaders removed.[167] Clearly the Cromwellians had adopted a punitive policy which intended

163 R. D. Edwards, 'The Cromwellian persecution and the Catholic Church in Ireland', in *Blessed Oliver Plunket: Historical Studies* (Dublin, [1937]), p. 73; and 'The Irish Catholics and the Puritan Revolution', in *Father Luke Wadding commemorative volume* (Dublin, 1957), pp. 93–118. The first study contains no references.

164 Abbott, *Cromwell*, ii. 146, 202. The important *Declaration* of 21 Mar. 1650 betrays Ireton's influence. See also Barnard, *P. and P.* lxi. 44.

165 Dunlop, i. 1; Firth and Rait, ii. 834–5; Steele, ii, no. 508 (Ireland).

166 Firth and Rait, ii. 1170–80; Steele, ii, no. 580 (Ireland).

167 B. Millett, *The Irish Franciscans 1650–1665*, Analecta Gregoriana, 129 (Rome, 1964), 241–418; and Millett, 'Survival and Reorganization 1650–95' in *A History of Irish Catholicism*, iii, fascicle 7 (Dublin, 1968), 1–12.

to force the Irish Catholics to renounce their religion under threats. Gentler methods of persuasion were also introduced. The problem was which of these two policies to pursue. The attempt to combine both lessened their effectiveness. How ever this dual approach was well established before 1649, and needs now to be investigated as the background to Cromwellian efforts.

The harsh policy was embodied in Henry VIII's legislation of 1537 which tried to destroy the Irish language by banning its use.[168] The more conciliatory approach had also received royal sanction, first in 1571 when Queen Elizabeth had given a fount of Irish type and then in 1591 with the foundation of Trinity College, the main function of which was to train Protestant missionaries for Ireland, equipping them for the work by teaching them Irish.[169] The use of Irish became the main issue dividing the supporters and opponents of compro-mise with the Irish Catholics. Persuasion was endorsed by James I in 1621, when he ordered Trinity College to look to its task of teaching Irish; and in 1634 when the Church of Ireland adopted canons which permitted parts of divine service to be performed in Irish.[170] These concessions were championed by Bishop Bedell and opposed by Bramhall 'from politicks and maxims of state, and especially from an Act of Parliament, passed . . . in the reign of King Henry VIII for obliging the natives to learn the English tongue'. The same slur of illegality was cast on the efforts after 1660 of Robert Boyle, Archbishop William King, and John Richardson.[171] During the Interregnum official hostility to the Irish language continued. Dr. Henry Jones, who was well placed to know, wrote that it had been 'almost a principle of their politics to suppress that language [Irish] utterly'.[172]

168 28 Henry VIII, c.15, Ireland.
169 B. Dickens, 'The Irish Broadside of 1571 and Queen Elizabeth's types', *Transactions of the Cambridge Bibliographical Soc.* i (1949). For Trinity College, see below, pp. 174, 198.
170 T. Corcoran, *State policy in Irish education* (Dublin, 1916), pp. 16, 65–6; *Constitutions and Canons Ecclesiasticall* (Dublin, 1635), canons viii, lxxxvi, and xciv.
171 *The Works of Robert Boyle*, i. 116, 119; 'Remedies proposed', *Archivium Hibernicum*, xxii. 168; Corcoran, *State policy in Irish education*, pp. 16–17; Richardson, *A short history of the attempts*, pp. 54, 94; *Two Biographies of William Bedell*, ed. Shuckburgh, p. 41.
172 *The Works of Robert Boyle*, i. 109.

Such a view is confirmed by a proclamation of 1657, in which those who wanted to benefit from taking the oath of abjuration and escape transplantation had to bring up their children to speak only English: those between the ages of eleven and twenty had to learn English within a year.[173]   In 1657 the Dublin corporation complained about the non-observance of the Henrician law against Irish and asked for its strict enforcement.[174]   But that complaint indicated negligence, and indeed the second, milder course was also followed during the Interregnum. Efforts to preach the Protestant Gospel in Irish were made. To be successful the policy required a sufficient supply of ministers, not only acceptable to the authorities, but also skilled in Irish, and aids to worship in Irish. Neither of these requirements was met, and so this policy was generally ineffective.

There were two sources of Irish-speaking ministers. For Protestants the main one was Trinity College, Dublin. Its care for teaching Irish fluctuated. While Bedell was provost (from 1627 to 1629) he put great emphasis on this work. His departure led to neglect, and in 1641 the Irish parliament accused the Laudian provost of denying natives their statutory scholarships and of having suppressed the Irish lecture.[175]   Despite its erratic care the college had supplied the Church of Ireland with Irish-speaking clergy. However this, the main source of supply, dried up between 1641 and 1660, first because the college's work was interrupted by the war and then because under Winter Irish studies were neglected, if not suppressed. Winter himself cannot have been totally uninterested in Irish, since he possessed an Irish catechism.[176]   Possibly he did try to learn Irish, but any personal interest was not reflected in policy at Trinity or indeed amongst the Independents in Ireland. Toward the end of the decade there are signs of awareness that more had to be done. In 1657 Henry Cromwell had £500 p.a. set aside for

[173]Steele, ii, no. 580 (Ireland). Unfortunately the only known copy is defective. After the provisions described above, it begins 'no Irish to be spoken . . .', and then breaks off.

[174]Cal. Anc. Recs. Dublin, ed. Gilbert, iv. 117.

[175]Two Biographies of William Bedell, ed. Shuckburgh, pp. 41–2, 295; W. Urwick, The early history of Trinity College, Dublin (London and Dublin, 1892), pp. 44–5.

[176]T.C.D., MS. F.6.3., f. 42^{v}.

'the education of Irish boys at schools, yt such of ym as prove capable, may be p[re]pared for ye universitie, in order to ye propagating civilitie as well as religion among the Irish hereafter, who tis hoped will harken to their owne country men w[i]th less p[re]judice than the English against whom they have something of a national antipathy'. Then in 1659 it was proposed to increase the value of the natives' scholarships at Trinity, as well as endowing another thirty at the projected second college.[177] But until a new supply was produced by the college, the government was dependent on ministers trained there before 1641, who had usually been beneficed in the Church of Ireland and were often lukewarm about the religious innovations of the Interregnum.

A second possible source was converts from Catholicism. The Catholic church, reorganizing itself to meet the Protestant challenge and especially that of Trinity College, quickly realized the importance of instruction in the vernacular. It had an advantage in drawing its priests from the Irish, although not all the seminarists were fluent in Irish. This deficiency was made good by their continental training. In 1650 knowledge of Irish was made an essential qualification for priests coming to Ireland, except to the province of Leinster.[178] Conversions from the Catholic priesthood to Protestantism were few. Yet at least three of the Protestant ministers preaching in Irish in the 1650s were converts.[179] The fact that most preachers in Irish were either former Anglicans or Catholics was a further, strong reason for discrediting the conciliatory policy amongst zealous Protestants, especially those from England who were ignorant of Irish needs.

Such provision as there was in the 1650s was inadequate. In 1651 Robert Chambers (a Dublin graduate and former Church of Ireland incumbent) instructed Irish converts in his

177 Sheffield Univ. Lib., Hartlib MS. xxxiii, R. Wood to Hartlib, 8 Apr. 1657; Urwick, *The early history of Trinity College, Dublin*, p. 67.

178 H. Hammerstein, 'Aspects of the continental education of Irish students in the reign of Queen Elizabeth', in *Historical Studies: VIII*, ed. T. D. Williams (Dublin, 1971), pp. 147, 151; T. J. Walsh, 'Compulsory Irish in France', *JCHAS* lviii (1953), 2.

179 Edmund Burke, 'a late friar'; James Carey; and Hugh Graffan: C.B., Jennings transcripts, A/20, 3 June 1657 and 5 Jan. 1657[8]; Seymour, pp. 105–8, 114–15, 159–60, 176, 208, 212.

Dublin house. In August 1652 £52 p.a. was set aside for those who would preach in Irish in the capital. The need for a more comprehensive campaign was recognized when a committee of six ministers was instructed in 1652 to find ministers fit to be sent into Irish quarters. In Dublin there seems to have been regular preaching in Irish, at St. Bride's church; elsewhere provision was meagre.[180]   In April 1656 the Dublin government again admitted the inadequacy of existing arrangements and set up a committee to consider how the Irish might be brought to public worship and have their children catechized. This committee was also to report what provision for the Protestant Gospel had been made in those areas to which the Irish were to be transplanted.[181]   In theory almost all Catholics were to be corralled in Connaught. Yet provision of the Protestant Gospel there was woeful. Only one preacher, a former minister of the Church of Ireland, was sent by the government to preach in Irish there, and he remained only a few months.[182]

These efforts compared unfavourably with the Church of Ireland's policy before 1641. Bedell had been a conspicuous advocate of preaching in Irish; Ussher also preferred Irish-speakers 'in a country where the greatest part of the people were Irish, that understood no English'.[183]   In 1622 the bishop of Killaloe had wanted recusants' fines to be used for the encouragement of Irish-speaking clergy who will attract 'many of ye natives, who hitherto will not heare us'. The same bishop recorded seven incumbents in 1622 in his diocese able to read the service book in Irish.[184]   Few in the Church of Ireland regarded this situation as satisfactory, and the policy itself came under attack. In the Interregnum attempts to convert the Irish were hampered by an even

180 C.B., Jennings transcripts, A/23, 29 June 1657; Dunlop, ii. 304; *Several proceedings in Parliament* (26 June–3 July 1651), p. 1412; Seymour, pp. 105–8.

181 C.B., Jennings transcripts, A/10, 1 Apr. 1656.

182 This was Philemon Fitzsimons, for whom see: Bodl., Carte MS. 23, f. 203; Seymour, pp. 159–60, 211; Webster, *The Diocese of Cork*, pp. 256, 275.

183 *Two Biographies of William Bedell*, ed. Shuckburgh, pp. 41–2; Parr, *The Life of Ussher*, p. 90.

184 Dwyer, *The Diocese of Killaloe*, pp. 106, 112, 115, 119, 125, 126, 127, 130. The diocese of Meath in 1622 had twenty 'native' incumbents, but how many knew Irish is not recorded. *The Whole Works of Ussher*, i. lxiii–cxviii. Only one Irish speaker was recorded in the Limerick diocese in 1622: Begley, *The Diocese of Limerick*, p. 395.

stronger current of opposition to any concession, and by technical obstacles, most notably the lack of specially trained ministers. After 1655 the administration was urged to make better provision, to send itinerant preachers into Connaught.[185] Worth's Cork association, whose members with their Irish backgrounds were more likely to know the language, paid more attention to converting the Irish. Henry Cromwell also seems to have inspired measures to improve the supply of properly prepared clergy.[186] But at the same time harsh measures admitting of no compromise, notably the oath of abjuration, were imposed from England.

The same weaknesses and confusion appeared in the other policy needed to convert the Irish: the translation and publication of religious books. The Church of Ireland had been stimulated first by Queen Elizabeth's gift of type and then by the 1634 Canons which allowed Irish translations of the Bible and Book of Common Prayer 'so soon as they may be had'.[187] Between 1571 and 1641 basic religious texts in Irish had been printed: a catechism in 1571; the New Testament in 1602; the Book of Common Prayer in 1608; and a manual by Bedell in 1631.[188] The outstanding need was a translation of the Old Testament. In the 1630s Bedell set about supplying it. Unfortunately his use of former Catholics as translators laid him open to attack, and Bramhall had the principal translator arraigned before the court of high commission at Dublin.[189] When the rebellion and Bedell's death halted the work it was incomplete.

The Catholic church had been stimulated by Protestant activity to publish devotional works in Irish, which helped to foster a national consciousness. Their first fount of Irish type

---

185R. Lawrence, *England's Great Interest in the Well Planting of Ireland . . . Discussed* (Dublin, 1656), p. 15.
186*The Agreement and Resolution of Severall Associated Ministers in the County of Corke*, p. 14; Eyres, *The Church-Sleeper Awakened*, sig. [a5]ᵛ–[a8]ᵛ.
187*Canons and Constitutions Ecclesiasticall*, canon xciv.
188On the early history of printing in Irish: Dickens, *Transactions of the Cambridge Bibliographical Soc.* i; E. W. Lynam, 'The Irish character in print, 1571–1923', *The Library*, iv (1924), 286–325; T. B. Reed and A. F. Johnson, *A history of the old English letter foundries* (London, 1952), pp. 175–6.
189Sheffield Univ. Lib., Hartlib MS. v (26), Bedell to J. Dury, 9 Aug. 1641; *Two Biographies of William Bedell*, ed. Shuckburgh, pp. 55, 56, 131–2, 134–6, 141–4, 296, 342, 344–7, 349, 352.

was established at Antwerp in 1611, and a second at Louvain in 1641.[190] Debarred from translating the Bible or missal, they produced what Protestants sneeringly called 'fabulous lives of saints and the rhodomontados of history'.[191] Whilst the Catholics kept worship and the Gospels locked up in a foreign tongue, the Protestants had an advantage, which they squandered by using English and not Irish.[192]

In 1650 Oliver Cromwell accused the Catholic clergy of keeping the word of God from the Irish.[193] In 1660 the same charge could have been levelled against the Cromwellian clergy. Only one work in Irish was published at Dublin during the Interregnum, a translation of William Perkins' *The Christian Doctrine* by a former Church of Ireland minister, Godfrey Daniel.[194] Although the book was popular, Daniel received little official encouragment and only a small salary.[195] It was strange that nothing was done towards completing the Irish Old Testament or translating and publishing the Directory of Worship in Irish. The completed portions of the Old Testament had passed on Bedell's death to Dr. Henry Jones, dean of Bedell's cathedral, and throughout the Interregnum vice-chancellor of Trinity College and close to the Dublin administration. Although 'a confused heap, pitifully defaced and broken', the manuscript served as the basis for the first Irish Old Testament eventually pub-

---

190A third press was established in Rome in 1676. B. Egan, 'Notes on the Propaganda Fide Printing-Press . . .', *Collectanea Hibernica*, ii (1959), 115–24; Reed and Johnson, *Old English Letter foundries*, pp. 68–9; MacCurtain, *Tudor and Stuart Ireland*, pp. 141–2.

191E. R. McC. Dix and S na Casaide, *List of Books . . . printed wholly or partly in Irish* (Dublin, 1905); C. McNeill, *Publications of Irish interest published . . . on the Continent of Europe*, Publications of Bibliographical Soc. of Ireland, iv, pt. i (Dublin, 1930); *The Works of Robert Boyle*, v. 603, 619.

192Richardson, *A short history of the attempts*, p. 45.

193Abbott, *Cromwell*, ii. 201.

194Daniel was a Dublin graduate and probably related to William Daniel, archbishop of Tuam, who had been responsible for the translations of the New Testament and prayer book. Daniel preached in Dublin until 1656; his salary fluctuated between £20 and £40 p.a. C.B., Jennings transcripts, A/23, 29 June 1657; R.C.B., Seymour MSS., pp. 78, 94, 193, 204; *Alumni Dublinenses*, p. 209; Seymour, p. 155.

195For copies of this work in Ireland: R.C.B., MS. T.11, f. 100; 'Bishop Wadding's notebook', *Archivium Hibernicum*, xxix (1970), 72; White, *Jnl. Kilkenny and S.E. Ireland Archaeological Soc.*, N.S. ii. 318.

lished in 1685 through Robert Boyle's generosity.[196] What is
surprising is that nothing was done to forward the work
during the Interregnum. Henry Jones' explanation was the
official hostility towards the Irish language.[197] As we have
seen that hostility was not total. Indeed in 1657 the Dublin
government authorized the purchase of eighty Irish New
Testaments in London, whither the stock had been sent.[198]

An even more serious omission was translating the Directory into Irish. By contrast, in Wales a translation had been
set on foot in 1644; there were also three editions of the
Welsh New Testament between 1647 and 1654 and one of
the whole Bible in Welsh.[199] However Welsh could be
tolerated as Irish, the language of a 'blood-guilty' race, could
not. In the absence of an Irish Directory there would be a
strong temptation for those ministering in Irish, mainly
former Anglicans, to revert to proscribed forms of worship,
especially as the Common Prayer Book was available in Irish.

The wavering policy, between using and banning Irish, was
one reason for this serious omission. Another was perhaps
technical. There was only one fount of Irish type in Ireland
in 1649. It was used in 1652, for Daniel's translation of
Perkins, and then disappeared. Henry Jones said that the
Jesuits had spirited it away to Douai.[200] It is implausible to
think that the Jesuits could remove the type from Dublin
after 1652, when the city was securely in Protestant hands.
But disappear it did, and before any further works could be
published a new fount of Irish type had to be cut.[201]
Obviously the type's disappearance after 1652 put an expensive obstacle in the way of Irish publications, but not an
insuperable one. Had the administration been eager to pub-

196*The Works of Robert Boyle*, i. 109; H. Jones, *A sermon of Antichrist*
(Dublin, 1676), sig. [A2] ᵛ; R. E. W. Maddison, 'Robert Boyle and the Irish Bible',
Bulletin of the John Rylands Library, xli (1958–9), 81–101.

197*The Works of Robert Boyle*, i. 109.

198C.B., Jennings transcripts, A/23, 8 Apr. 1657.

199C. Hill, in *Historical Essays*, ed. Bell and Ollard, pp. 36, 47.

200*The Works of Robert Boyle*, i. 109. In 1648 Miles Symner alleged that the
friars of Athenry had torn the press to pieces for heresy and that the copper
plates were used by tinkers to mend kettles. Brit. Mus., Sloane MS. 427, f. 85.
Some of the type may have migrated to London, since some of its characters were
used to print James Ware's *De Hibernia et Antiquitatibus eius, Disquisitiones*,
(London, 1658). I am grateful to Miss M. Pollard for pointing this out.

201Maddison, *Bulletin of the John Rylands Library*, xli.

lish a translated Directory or Old Testament, they could have had a new fount cast. Simply they were not sufficiently interested in this policy to bother.

Having chronicled these inadequate measures, it is surprising to find that Catholics were converted in apparently large numbers. The evidence of this is not the fact that many Catholics remained in the walled towns and the areas east of Connaught contrary to the government's orders. That was because promiscuous transplantation proved unworkable. Instead the testimony comes from Catholic priests active after 1660. In Counties Dublin and Wicklow they converted 4,000 Catholics who had lapsed during the Interregnum in three years.[202] These conversions owed little to Protestant proselytization and much to the punitive policy of the Interregnum. We may doubt the depth or sincerity of these changes, which rarely amounted to more than an occasional conformity. The authorities were also doubtful and appointed committees to investigate the genuineness of such conversions.[203]

This success suggests that had the Cromwellians followed their harsh measures, which had driven so many priests from Ireland, by vigorous evangelization in Irish the hold of Catholicism might have been loosened. In the remoter parts of Ireland there was widespread ignorance of the principles of any Christian religion, either Catholic or Protestant.[204] It was this ignorance that Oliver Cromwell had promised to end, but which he and his agents in Ireland failed to do. As time passed, the chance receded. Persecution slackened and priests were able to resume their work. The reaction to the oath of abjuration in 1657 showed that many Catholics would not willingly forswear their beliefs. In October 1659 when the Catholic archbishop of Armagh, Edmund O'Reilly, came to

---

[202]*Archivium Hibernicum,* vi. 184–5; vii. 37; Millett, *The Irish Franciscans,* p. 342, and note 146; Power, *A bishop of the penal times,* pp. 23, 33; C.B., Jennings transcripts, A/2, p.B.

[203]Hore, *The Town of Wexford,* p. 311; Seymour, p. 106; Steele, ii, no. 556 (Ireland).

[204]A traveller in 1644 commented, 'the native Irish are very good catholics, though knowing little of their religion': *The Tour of the French traveller M. de la Boullaye le Gouz in Ireland, A.D. 1644,* ed. T. C. Croker (London, 1837), pp. 38–9; John Bossy, 'The counter-reformation and the people of Catholic Ireland, 1596–1641', in *Historical Studies: VIII,* ed. Williams.

Ireland he found a situation which he thought lamentable but which compared quite favourably with Cromwellian efforts. He estimated that there were about 240 priests in the provinces of Dublin and Ulster, which was only a third of the necessary number. However the Cromwellians had hardly more Protestant preachers for the whole country.[205]

It does seem that the rigorous policy immediately after 1649 was relaxed, allowing priests to return and Catholic books to circulate. The question is how far was this a deliberate change in official policy. The easier conditions were partly caused by the political confusion and apparent breakdown of government authority outside Dublin after Henry Cromwell's recall in June 1659. However Archbishop O'Reilly spoke of a new moderation in December 1658.[206] Was this the beginning of a new conciliatory policy? There are signs that Henry Cromwell favoured persuasion; he had vehemently opposed the oath of abjuration.[207] Was it possible that he intended to play upon the divisions amongst the Irish Catholics between secular and regular clergy; between Old English and Gaelic; and between the intransigent ultramontanes and those willing to compromise with Ireland's Protestant rulers — as he tried to exploit the factions amongst the Protestants — even anticipating Ormonde's policy after 1661?[208] We cannot say. Certainly moderation was identified with Henry Cromwell and was ended by his immediate successors in 1659:[209] more than that is conjecture.

A unique opportunity was offered by the reconquest to launch a new and vigorous campaign of evangelization. The need was acknowledged: 'without the care for religion, and

[205]Thomas O Fiaich, 'Edmund O'Reilly, Archbishop of Armagh, 1657–1669', in *Father Luke Wadding commemorative volume*, pp. 192–3; Millett, *The Irish Franciscans*, p. 321.

[206]O Fiaich, op. cit., p. 191. For evidence of greater Catholic activity after 1655 and Catholic literature entering the country: C.B., Jennings transcripts, A/10, 11 July 1656; 6 Feb. 1656[7]; A/23, 26 May 1658; A/30, 27 Apr. 1659; Dunlop, ii. 559–60, 695.

[207]*Thurloe State Papers*, vi. 527.

[208]H. Kearney, 'Ecclesiastical politics and the counter-reformation in Ireland, 1618–48', *Journal of Ecclesiastical History*, xi (1960); J. Brennan, 'A Gallican interlude in Ireland', *Irish Theological Quarterly*, xxiv (1957); Millett, *The Irish Franciscans*, pp. 418–63.

[209]Brit. Mus., Stowe MS. 185, f. 137.

encouraging of a gospel ministry here, this land is likely in the next age . . . to degenerate into meere brutishnesse and barbarism'.[210] Yet the response was disappointing. Above all the Cromwellians failed to establish the English and Protestant religion any more securely than their predecessors. Distractions over theological and political controversy were one reason; the inability to decide between compulsion or persuasion another. The small number of ministers, and the very much smaller number competent to convert the native Irish, were a major disadvantage. Much more research on the clergy and efforts of the Church of Ireland will be needed before we can explain why 'Ireland is the only country in Europe where the counter-reformation succeeded against the will of the head of the state'.[211] However, I believe part of the answer lies in the weaknesses apparent from this study of policy during the Interregnum and common, by and large, to the Church of Ireland in the seventeenth century.

210 Brit. Mus., Lansdowne MS. 823, f. 134.
211 Hammerstein, *Historical Studies: VIII*, ed. Williams, p. 153.

VII

EDUCATION

Education in Cromwellian Ireland was closely connected with propagating the Gospel and had the same objects: the introduction and spread of English habits, language, and religion; and, through these, the securing of English rule. Conceived in almost exclusively political and religious terms, education was largely a government reponsibility during the Interregnum, as it had been in Ireland since the Reformation.

In this and the next chapter I shall examine two separate activities: education, mainly an official concern; and the advancement of learning, usually by private efforts. The first topic — education — requires a review of policy before 1649, and then an examination of official measures between 1649 and 1660. I shall also describe the schools and their masters in the 1650s, and Trinity College, Dublin. Finally I shall review the major educational innovation of the Interregnum: the foundation of a second college in Dublin, and its endowment with Archbishop Ussher's library.

i. Education before 1649

Protestant education in Ireland before 1649 rested on three official acts. The first was a law of 1537, which showed clearly the connection between politics and education. It established parochial schools in which incumbents were to teach their parishioners' children English.[1] The law's weakness was that it assumed an effective and educated clergy, loyal to England, throughout Ireland. It was not a success.[2]

A second act, of 1571, supplemented the earlier law by authorizing diocesan schools, staffed by English masters, throughout Ireland. These schools were to teach Latin and

[1] 28 Henry VIII, c.15 clause ix (Ireland).
[2] Poverty prevented the clergy appointing deputies to keep the schools. 'Remedies proposed . . .', *Archivium Hibernicum*, xxii. 167.

Greek, 'and other grammar learning', preparing youths for the university. In this way, it was hoped, the standard of the Church of Ireland's clergy would be raised.[3] The third measure, which will be considered in greater detail below, was the establishment of Trinity College, Dublin, in 1591.

The seventeenth century saw no additions to these acts. They provided an excellent framework for education: efforts centred on seeing that they were implemented. Sir John Davies, for example, with his usual faith in the law as a panacea, wanted those who disobeyed the statutes relating to education prosecuted. In 1634 the Church of Ireland repeated the incumbents' obligation to keep schools in its new Canons.[4] Observance of the laws seems to have varied widely. Diocesan schools were maintained in the dioceses of Limerick, Cork, Waterford, and Dublin, for example, but not in the small diocese of Ardagh.[5] Episcopal visitations recorded occasional incumbents who kept schools, suggesting that the majority did not. Unfortunately there is no way of telling how many ministers gave informal instruction, and there is a danger of underestimating the amount of Protestant education.[6] Contemporary complaints suggested that there were not enough schools, so that many youths were driven overseas or into the Catholic schools in Ireland.[7] Here, indeed, we come to the major defect of educational policy before 1649: its inability to beat off the challenge of Catholic schools. After the Council of Trent greater attention was paid to the education of Irish Catholics, and from 1592

3 12 Elizabeth I, c.1 (Ireland).

4 Sir John Davies, *A Discoverie of the true causes why Ireland was never entirely subdued* (London, 1612), p. 272; *Constitutions and Canons Ecclesiasticall*, canon xcix; Edward Synge, *A brief account of the laws now in force in the kingdom of Ireland, for encouraging the residence of parochial-clergy, and erecting of English schools* (Dublin, 1723).

5 *Archivium Hibernicum*, ii. 175; viii. 58; Corcoran, *State policy in Irish education*, p. 55; 'Visitation of Waterford and Lismore, 1615', *Journal of the Waterford and S.E. of Ireland Archaeological Soc.* i (1895), 145; 'Visitatio Regalis, 1615, Ardagh', *Journal of the Ardagh and Clonmacnoise Antiquarian Soc.* ii (1940), 28; M. Quane. 'The diocesan schools, 1570–1870', *JCHAS* lxvi (1961), and 'Limerick diocesan school', ibid. lxvii (1962).

6 'The Royal Visitation, 1615. Dioceses of Ardfert and Aghadoe', *Archivium Hibernicum*, iv (1915), 183, 185; Dwyer, *The Diocese of Killaloe*, pp. 170–7.

7 *Cal. S.P. Ire. 1647–60*, p. 316; *Letters and dispatches of Strafforde*, ed. Knowler, i. 188; *Jnl. Waterford and S.E. of Ireland Archaeological Soc.* i. 145.

onwards numerous colleges were founded on the continent to train Irish priests. Within Ireland itself schools were kept by priests which attracted many pupils and taught 'not only the tongues, but likewise the liberal arts and sciences'.[8]

The Protestant response to these new Catholic efforts was ineffectual. Some slight improvements within the existing framework occurred in the early seventeenth century. The confiscations and new plantation of Ulster included specific provision for a school in each county. In 1629 the charters of two new boroughs, Carysfort and Banagher, reserved lands to endow free schools in the towns. However there were delays in building them, and not all had been erected by 1649.[9] Official measures were supplemented by municipal or private care. Except in Ulster such generosity seems to have been meagre, owing to the small number of Protestant corporations or wealthy Protestant settlers. In Dublin the corporation maintained a schoolmaster before 1649. Lord Cork endowed schools at Youghal, Lismore, and Bandonbridge. Such provision was rare.[10] In Ulster there seems to have been more interest in education among the laity. The school at Derry, for example, owed its actual foundation to a merchant, although it had been an object of royal favour; another merchant left money to establish a school at Lifford. Lord Clandeboye, a prominent Presbyterian landowner, maintained a school at Bangor, and considered patronizing the educational reformer, Comenius.[11] The scanty evidence

[8] J. Brady, 'The Irish Colleges in Europe and the Counter-Reformation', *Proceedings of the Irish Catholic Historical Soc.* (1957); P. J. Corish, 'The reorganization of the Irish Church, 1603–41', ibid. (1957); *The Humble petition of the protestant inhabitants of the Counties of Antrim, Downe, Tyrone, etc.*, p. 6.

[9] Corcoran, *State policy in Irish education*, pp. 63–4; *Essex papers*, i, *1672–1679*, ed. O. Airy, Camden Soc., N.S. xlvii (1890), 113–17; Hill, *An historical account of the plantation in Ulster*, p. 216; Moody, *The Londonderry plantation*, pp. 35, 172, 186, 188, 189, 205, 219; M. Quane, 'Carysfort Royal School, Co. Wicklow', *JRSAI* xci (1961); Quane, 'Cavan Royal School', ibid. c (1970); W. A. Reynell, 'The estate of the diocess of Derry', *Ulster Journal of Archaeology*, N.S. ii (1896), 255.

[10] *The council book of Youghal*, ed. Caulfield, pp. 58, 83, 87, 106, 371; D. Townshend, *The life and letters of the great earl of Cork* (London, 1904), pp. 40, 458, 491–2. The school at Bandonbridge had not been built by 1642.

[11] R.C.B., MS. Libr. 26, Down Inquisition, pp. 56, 63; Sheffield Univ. Lib., Hartlib MS. ix (12); G.E.C., *The Complete Peerage*, ii. 222–3; G. H. Turnbull, *Hartlib, Dury and Comenius* (London, 1947), p. 346; Moody, *The Londonderry plantation*, p. 172; Reynell, *Ulster Journal of Archaeology*, ii. 255.

suggests that Ulster was better supplied with schools than
other parts of the country, partly through these private
bequests.

Mention must be made of another educational institution
maintained by the Irish government, although again its
effects were small. Special provision was made for the
education of wards, paying for their maintenance at Trinity
College, Dublin, and establishing a school in Dublin for them.
Here too the motive was political: to convert the wards to
English ways and Protestantism.[12]

ii.   The Government and education, 1649–1660

The earlier distinction between three sorts of education – in
the parish, the diocesan grammar schools, and at Dublin
University – was preserved during the Interregnum. On 8
March 1650 an ordinance was passed in England 'for the
encouragement and encrease of learning, and the true knowledge and Worship of God, and the advancement of the
protestant gospel in Ireland'.[13] This grandiloquent title
showed that the close connection between education and the
state religion was to continue, but the ordinance did little for
Irish education beyond endowing a school in Dublin, increasing Trinity College's endowments, and providing for a second
college in Dublin. A second ordinance, of 26 September
1653, attended to the grammar schools outside Dublin,
previously maintained by the Church of Ireland. Using the
unit of the county, the 1653 ordinance authorized the
reservation of confiscated lands for the support of free
schools, to a maximum value of £1,000 in each county. This
measure's effectiveness depended on there being a surplus of
land once the adventurers' and soldiers' claims were met; it
also had to wait until those lands had been assigned.[14]

A third measure dealt with education in the parishes. The
incumbents who had previously been supposed to keep
schools had been replaced by government-appointed ministers. Their educational function was taken over by govern-

12 Victor Treadwell, 'The Irish Court of Wards under James I', *Irish Hist.
Studies*, xii (1960), 8, 12, 13, 14.
13 Firth and Rait, ii. 355–7.
14 Ibid. ii. 730.

ment-appointed schoolmasters, paid by the state from the profits of confiscated church lands. The Cromwellian schoolmasters were a distinct, but subordinate element in the ecclesiastical establishment.[15]

The Cromwellians criticized the Church of Ireland's earlier efforts as roundly as their provision of the Gospel, and urged better care if the English interest was to be secured. The native Irish had to be taught 'civility and pious behaviour'; the Protestants 'learned languages, Hebrew, Greek, and Latin, and all liberal sciences'.[16] Successive governors of Ireland between 1650 and 1659 were instructed to advance Protestant education. Yet little had been achieved by January 1656, when the Irish council sought guidance from the English council of state as to how Irish children were to be given a Christian education. The need for more comprehensive measures became even more urgent when the oath of abjuration was imposed in 1657. Its requirement that children should learn English within a year could hardly be enforced unless facilities for instruction were available.[17]

The Dublin government intended to improve education by seeing that money formerly given for that purpose was properly used. In 1656 the government was authorized to inquire into schools previously erected in Ireland, their endowments, and how much they had been worth in 1640. Where these revenues were less than £100 in any county, they were to be supplemented by the state. This information was collected together with details of parochial organization and wealth by commissioners in 1657.[18] These returns offer vivid glimpses into the state of official education in a few counties.

In comparison with the clergy, schoolmasters were not generously paid, usually between £20 and £40 p.a. There were a few official schoolmistresses, who were paid only £5 or £10 p.a. Nevertheless the schoolmasters' salaries were as high as those paid in schools endowed in the early eighteenth

15 Steele, ii, no. 477 (Ireland).

16 *A Discourse concerning the affaires of Ireland*, p. 8; J. V. Belcamp, *Consilium et Votum Pro Ordinando ac Stabilienda Hibernia* (London, 1651), pp. 22, 27, 37.

17 Dunlop, i. 2; ii. 561; Brit. Mus., Additional MS. 5014; Stowe MS. 185, f. 138; T.C.D., MS. F.2.1, f. 160; Bodl., Carte MS. 67, f. 160; Steele, ii, no. 580 (Ireland).

18 Dunlop, ii. 583–4.

century.[19] If it was hard to procure enough ministers for Ireland, it was much more difficult to obtain masters and in 1659 there were only thirty-five throughout the whole country. Like the ministers they were concentrated in the English garrisons, making a mockery of their supposed role in converting the Irish.[20] In 1658 the commissioners for County Louth reported that no free school was known to have existed in the county, and recommended Atherdee as a suitable site, together with five other places as fit to have elementary schools. In County Kildare there were two schools in 1657, only one of which had a government-paid master. There were also three Protestant schoolmistresses in the county 'fit to teach children', but without salaries. Despite this recommendation, they never received them. The Antrim commissioners asked for four schoolhouses to be built and masters appointed.[21] In County Down there had been schools at Bangor and Down before the war. The Cromwellians maintained the Down school, but had reduced the master's salary from £30 p.a. to £20 p.a.[22] In County Armagh there was one official schoolmaster, but four others teaching without state payment. A fifth, 'lately come out of England', was recommended for a salary. The Armagh commissioners asked for eight new schools to be erected and maintained, alongside the existing one in Armagh.[23] This suggests a hunger for education in Ulster, which is confirmed by William King (later archbishop of Dublin) who received his education in County Tyrone at this time. After the dislocation of the war, children flocked to the schools when they were re-established, and in 1658 'seventy or eighty

[19] M. Quane, 'Preston Endowed School, Navan', *Riocht na Midhe*, iv, no. 2 (1968), 54; Quane, 'The Ranelagh Endowed School, Athlone', *Journal of the Old Athlone Soc.* i (1969), 24–5; Quane, 'Athlone Classical School ...', ibid. i (1970–1), 91.

[20] Brit. Mus., Additional MS. 19,833, ff. 22^v–24^v; R.C.B., Seymour MSS., pp. 122–3.

[21] Leslie, *Journal of Co. Louth Archaeological Soc.* vii. 38; Seymour, p. 225; R.C.B., MS. Libr. 27, Kildare Inquisition, p. 37; MS. Libr. 26, Antrim Inquisition, p. 89.

[22] Ibid., MS. Libr. 26, Down Inquisition, p. 63. Lord Clandeboye in his will of 1659 acknowledged an obligation to support the Bangor school and three others. Hamilton, *The Hamilton Manuscripts*, p. 85.

[23] R.C.B., MS. Libr. 27, Armagh Inquisitions, pp. 9, 11, 13, 16, 23, 25, 27, 30, 32; Seymour, p. 226.

pupils of both sexes congregated to the woman who was schoolmistress'.[24]   It seems that Ulster, probably best-provided with education before 1649, showed greatest eagerness for a better provision in the 1650s. Contacts with the Scottish universities helped some of the gaps in the state's provision to be filled.

It is difficult to describe what sort of men were official schoolmasters during the Interregnum, owing to lack of evidence. But they appear to have been a motley collection, including graduates of English universities attracted to Ireland for the first time, former soldiers, and ministers ejected from their benefices in England.[25]   Some of the masters had been incumbents of the Church of Ireland before 1649: too little trusted to be employed as preachers, they made acceptable masters.[26]   Apart from the Dublin schoolmaster, William Hill, who will be considered below, we know nothing of the masters' intellectual accomplishments, except that some claimed to be skilled in Greek and Latin.[27]   As in the period before 1649 there is a danger of accepting this inadequate provision as the sum of Protestant education. Clearly this was not so. Official preachers, some of whom had been schoolmasters, catechized and taught children.[28]   Also there were unauthorized masters, some of whom were revealed by the 1657 inquisitions and others whose pupils entered Trinity College, Dublin, during the decade. Such unofficial masters were found mainly in Ulster and Munster (at Baltimore, Bandon, Cork, Kinsale, and Mallow). Often they were episcopalian clergy eking out a livelihood.[29]

[24] C. S. King, *A great Archbishop of Dublin* (London, 1906), p. 3.

[25] Robert Pierce, master at Coleraine, had been a Fellow of King's, Cambridge; Robert Whitehall, master at Limerick, had been ejected from his Studentship at Christ Church, Oxford; Maurice Owen, at Cashel, had been a captain. C.B., Jennings transcripts, A/58, 1653; Foster, *Alumni Oxonienses*, early series, iv. 1619; Venn, *Alumni Cantabrigenses*, i. iii. 329.

[26] Seymour, pp. 225—6.

[27] C.B., Jennings transcripts, A/20, 12 Dec. 1656, 13 July 1657, and 12 Feb. 1657[8].

[28] Brit. Mus., Lansdowne MS. 823, f. 134.

[29] T.C.D., MS. N.1.4.20a, pp. 20—33; *The Register of Derry Cathedral (S. Columb's) ... 1642—1703*, ed. R. Hayes, Parish Register Soc. of Dublin, vii (Exeter and Dublin, 1910), 112.

iii. Private efforts

As before 1649, so in the Interregnum the official educational system was supplemented by private efforts. Corporations continued and extended their care. Dublin appointed
and paid a master to teach writing and arithmetic. The
borough of Waterford asked for a grant of land to maintain a
free school: a request that was rejected. In Kilkenny part of
the profits of justice was reserved for educating youths after
the English fashion.[30]
    The redistribution of lands offered chances to endow
schools. Edward Roberts, the Baptist auditor-general,
strengthened his claim to certain lands by promising to found
and maintain a school at Strabane. In Ulster there was private
interest in education: Rawdon was prepared to use the tithes
of Lisburn to support a free school there; Sir Arthur
Chichester petitioned the government for a salary for the
master of the Dungannon free school; in 1656 Sir John
Clotworthy proposed the establishment of a college at
Antrim, which he hoped to staff with a prominent Scottish
Presbyterian.[31]
    More generally it was hoped that the adventurers would
use some of their newly acquired lands to endow schools, as
indeed they were encouraged to by the 1653 act of settlement. Samuel Hartlib and his circle, in particular, looked to
the adventurers, but in vain.[32]
    The most important official scheme, actually im-
plemented, was Erasmus Smith's. His benefaction, common
enough in England, was unique in Ireland at the time. Smith
was a prominent London merchant and alderman who was
involved in the adventure for Irish lands and its subsequent

    [30] *Cal. Anc. Recs. Dublin,* ed. Gilbert, iv. 65–6; Brit. Mus., Egerton MS. 1762,
f. 178[v]; Kilkenny Municipal Archives, White book, f. 14[v]; *The town book of
Belfast,* ed. Young, p. 57.
    [31] Roberts received his lands, but we do not know if the school was built. Brit.
Mus., Additional MS. 19,845, ff. 24[v], 35; Harleian MS. 4784, ff. 27[v]–35; P.R.O.,
SP.63/287, 51, 175[v]; Nat. Lib. Ire., MS. 11,961, p. 420; *The Letters and Journals
of Robert Baillie,* ed. D. Laing (Edinburgh, 1841), iii. 312.
    [32] *The Works of Robert Boyle,* v. 282; *The Diary and Correspondence of Dr.
John Worthington,* ed. J. Crossley, Chetham soc. xiii (1847), i. 166.

settlement.[33] Smith was also zealous in his concern for propagating the Gospel and improving Protestant education, proving a generous benefactor of Christ's Hospital and later acting as a governor of Robert Boyle's corporation for propagating the Gospel in North America.[34] Smith decided to use his Irish lands to advance the Protestant interest there. He attributed the rebellion and sins of Ireland to the lack 'of bringing up the youth ... either in publique or private schooles, whereby thro' good discipline they might be principled in literature and good manners'. He wanted the children of his Irish tenants to be brought up 'in the fear of God and good literature, and to speak the English tongue'.

To accomplish this pious intention Smith vested some of his Irish lands in trustees, who were to use the revenue to found and maintain schools.[35] Since the scheme had the same aims as official policy it was given government help.[36] In December 1657 eighteen trustees were appointed, who were to establish five schools: one at Sligo, another on Smith's Galway lands, two more on his Tipperary and Antrim estates, and a fifth wherever the remainder of his land was allocated. Each master was to be paid £40 p.a. The curriculum was to include the teaching of grammar and 'original tongues', reading, writing, and the casting of accounts. Initially the pupils were to be drawn from the poor on Smith's own estates. The most promising were to be sent to Trinity College, Dublin, with scholarships of £10 p.a. for four years.

This was a generous scheme and a hopeful precedent to other owners of Irish lands. However its implementation depended on the estates' profitable settlement and the passage of an act of parliament, neither of which had been

[33] *Cal. S.P. Ire. 1647–60*, p. 502; ibid., *Adventurers, 1642–59*, pp. 9, 57–8, 62, 229–30, 307–8, 392, 396; *D.N.B.*; Bottigheimer, *English Money and Irish Land*, p. 210.

[34] *The Works of Robert Boyle*, i. 96.

[35] The indenture is in Lodge's transcripts from Cromwell's chancery rolls, P.R.O., Dublin, MS. 1.a.53.56, p. 425. An incomplete version, omitting the names of most of the trustees, is printed in Corcoran, *State policy in Irish education*, pp. 80–2. On the whole venture see: M. V. Ronan, *Erasmus Smith endowment* (Dublin, 1937); M. Quane, 'The Abbey School, Tipperary', *JCHAS* lxv (1960); and Quane, 'Drogheda Grammar School', *County Louth Archaeological Journal*, xv (1963), 210–16.

[36] Brit. Mus., Additional MS. 19,845, f. 25; Lansdowne MS. 822, ff. 116, 134.

achieved by 1660. The scheme was too useful to be laid aside and eventually Charles II confirmed the lands and the trust in 1669.[37]   Thirty-two governors were now nominated, of whom only six had been amongst the original trustees in 1657; the number of schools had fallen from five to three, at Drogheda and Galway and in Tipperary.[38]   Other changes were made to reduce the original project's puritan tone, making it more acceptable to the Church of Ireland. Even so the schools were exempted from episcopal visitation during Smith's lifetime; and two of the schools had as their first masters former official preachers of the Interregnum who had failed to conform to the re-established church.[39]

The original trustees in 1657, apparently chosen by Smith, showed the religious character of the benefaction.[40]   Apart from trustees chosen for their official positions, there were six clergymen and four Cromwellian aldermen of Dublin. Of the clergymen four were prominent Dublin Independents; the other two were Henry Cromwell's chaplain, Harrison, and the vice-chancellor of Trinity, Dr. Henry Jones. The four aldermen were members of Winter's Independent church in the 1650s and retained covert nonconformist sympathies after 1660. Two of these aldermen acted as successive treasurers of the schools.[41]   Evidently Smith preferred to entrust his scheme to godly divines and aldermen, rather than to those interested in the advancement of learning, believing that Ireland wanted education, not educational reform.

[37]Guildhall Lib., London, Christ's Hospital muniments (uncatalogued), 'Erasmus Smith Esqr. His booke relateing to his charityes in Ireland', f. 27ᵛ; and box labelled 'Erasmus Smith', brief of letters patent, 26 March 1669; *An Act for explaining of some doubts* . . . (Dublin, 1665), pp. 48, 63–4; Hist. MSS. Comm., *Ormonde MSS.*, N.S. iii. 17.

[38]The six were: Dr. Henry Jones, John Bisse, Hierome Sankey, Edward Roberts, Daniel Hutchinson, John Preston.

[39]They were Joseph Scott, former Fellow of T.C.D. (for whom see below p. 203), and James Wood, Independent minister at Youghal in the 1650s. He was replaced in 1679 by John Shaw, probably the preacher on Aran Island in 1657 (when it had been assigned to Smith). Guildhall Lib., 'Erasmus Smith His Booke', ff. 25, 57ᵛ; box 'Erasmus Smith', E. Smith to D. Hutchinson, 11 Apr. 1671; Seymour, p. 220.

[40]Smith went to Ireland in 1657. Guildhall, Lib., MS. 11,588/4, p. 401.

[41]The Independent ministers were Winter, Samuel Mather, Wootton and Robert Chambers; the aldermen were Hutchinson, Hooke, Preston, and Tighe. Hooke had died by 1669 and was replaced by Ald. Ridgley Hatfield, who had a similar background. Tighe and Hutchinson were the treasurers.

Smith's benefaction did benefit Ireland, but not until 1669. After 1660, with the Protestant interest better established, more private benefactions occurred. Amongst those who had been influential during the Interregnum Lord Orrery, Bishop Worth, Sir Maurice Eustace, and Alderman John Preston (one of Smith's trustees) all founded Protestant schools.[42] It is noteworthy that a number of these schools had masters who were Protestant nonconformists.[43] Events of the Interregnum perhaps encouraged greater awareness of the need for more Protestant schools, but little was achieved between 1649 and 1660. However, when the Church of Ireland resumed the main responsibility for education after 1660, although helped by these more numerous benefactions, the number of schools remained too low to combat Catholicism. It was in converting the Irish that the deficiencies of Protestant education, both in the Interregnum and after 1660, showed most clearly.[44] In the 1650s there is no record of masters being appointed to teach the Irish. The best the government could do was adopt occasional palliatives. A few Irish orphans were to be sent to Cheshire as apprentices in exchange for English youths.[45] As we have seen, Henry Cromwell inspired a grant of £500 p.a. for educating Irish boys and preparing them for the university, but whether this scheme was ever put into effect is doubtful.[46] Another expedient was to continue an unofficial form of wardship (as in England the Court of Wards had not been legally abolished). The custody of minors — often

---

[42] P.R.O., Dublin, M.2449, p. 57; F. W. X. Fincham, 'Letters concerning Sir Maurice Eustace ...', *Eng. Hist. Rev.* xxxv (1920), 257–8; W. Sheridan, *A Sermon preach'd at the funeral ... of Sir Maurice Eustace* (Dublin, 1665); M. Quane, 'Charleville Endowed School', *JRSAI* lxxxviii (1958); Quane, *Riocht na Midhe*, iv, no. 2, pp. 52–5; *The Whole Works of Sir James Ware* (Dublin, 1739), i. 597.

[43] Quane, *JRSAI* lxxxviii. 33–4.

[44] After 1660: Guildhall Lib., 'Erasmus Smith His Booke', f. 43ᵛ; *Cal. S.P. Ire. 1663–5*, p. 496; 'Remedies proposed', *Archivium Hibernicum*, xxii. 163, 168; W. Mercer, *The Moderate Cavalier* ([Cork], 1675), p. 20; P. Power, *A bishop of the penal times*, pp. 23, 33; *Economic Writings of Petty*, ed. Hull, i. 72; M. Quane, 'Castledermot Charter School', *Journal Co. Kildare Archaeological Soc.* xiii (1961–3), 463–4; J. Swift, *Irish Tracts, 1720–23*, ed. H. Davis (Oxford, 1948), p. 202; Synge, *A brief account*, p. 7.

[45] Dunlop, ii. 563, 592.

[46] See above, pp. 174–5.

orphans and Catholics — was granted to individuals in return for guarantees that the youths would be educated in 'piety and good literature'.[47] None of these devices was likely to produce many converts.

The failure was all the more serious because, the government ban of 1654 notwithstanding, papists were keeping schools.[48] As with the treatment of priests, the reign of terror during and immediately after the war gradually gave way to greater laxity. Typical of the complaints about papist masters was one from the Protestant master in County Leitrim in 1660. Having officiated for eighteen months, he was greatly discouraged by 'the multitude of Popish schoolmasters near and about the same place'.[49]

It is clear that the government gave less attention to Protestant education than to the Gospel, and so the masters received only a small share of the attenuated resources. Efforts to recover traditional income, although promising better provision, had not succeeded by 1660. Official masters were too few and not appropriately qualified for the work of conversion. This review leads one to endorse the harsh judgement of Lady Ranelagh, who was deeply interested in education and by no means hostile to the Cromwellians. She wrote in 1659:

'if in the beginning of our professions to a reformation in these last 18 years, we had fallen to this practice, and paid as many schoolmasters as we have done military officers, listing regiments of children under them to be by them train'd up in the nurture and admonition of the Lord . . . we had by this time reaped better fruits of our labours and expences then disappointment, division, poverty, shame and confusion.' [50]

iv. Schools in Dublin

The only educational success of the Interregnum was in Dublin. As with the propagation of the Gospel the

47 Hist. MSS. Comm., *Egmont MSS.* i. 564; Nat. Lib. Ire., MS. 11,959, pp. 136—8; P.R.O., Dublin, MS. 2.3.25, f. 127; and Ferguson MS. xiii, p. 61; King's Inns, Dublin, Prendergast MS. i, pp. 37—8; *Analecta Hibernica*, xv. 252—3; *The Civil Survey, VI*, ed. Simington, p. xvii.

48 Brit. Mus., Additional MS. 5014; Steele, ii, no. 528 (Ireland).

49 R.C.B., Seymour MSS., p. 153; C.B., Jennings transcripts, A/5, 15 May 1655; A/9, 3 Dec. 1655; King's Inns, Dublin, Prendergast MS. ii, p. 309; *Archivium Hibernicum*, vi. 188, 189, 192; vii. 49; Corcoran, *State policy in Irish education*, p. 24.

50 *The Diary and Correspondence of Dr. John Worthington*, ed. Crossley, i. 166.

Cromwellians concentrated their greatest educational efforts on the capital. This emphasis had first become clear in the ordinance of 8 March 1650, which promised the endowment of a free school in Dublin to educate scholars for the university.[51] However that scheme languished until 1658 when a committee was appointed to put it into effect. In Febrary 1659 the committee proposed that £330 p.a. be settled on the school: £100 p.a. for its master, and forty scholarships of £5 p.a. for poor boys.[52] A bill was drafted in 1659 to put this design into practice. The school was to be named 'The Lord Protector's School'; governors were to administer its endowments; its masters were to teach 'good literature', Latin, Greek, and Hebrew, and to instil knowledge and fear of God.[53] The political upheavals of 1659 prevented this scheme being accomplished.

Thus the Cromwellians' most ambitious project perished. Nevertheless schools functioned in Dublin during the Interregnum, which were the successors of earlier institutions. Before 1649 the two principal Dublin schools were those maintained by the dean and chapter of St. Patrick's and the 'free' school supported by the corporation.[54] Since the confiscated lands of St. Patrick's were to be one of the supports of 'The Lord Protector's School', the latter institution was obviously intended to replace St. Patrick's School, which was suspect because of its connection with the Church of Ireland. Not only was the new school not erected, St. Patrick's School continued throughout the 1650s. Its master, John Golborne (a former Church of Ireland minister and Fellow of Trinity College), was not paid by the government. Yet he sent pupils to Trinity College in the 1650s.[55]

A school was maintained by the government in Dublin, which was probably a successor to the corporation's free

51 Firth and Rait, ii. 355—7.

52 Huntingdon Record Office, DD 731, no. 17; Sheffield Univ. Lib., Hartlib MS. xxxiii, R. Wood to Hartlib, 9 Feb. 1658[9]; Urwick, *The early history of Trinity College, Dublin*, p. 68.

53 T.C.D., Mun. P/1/376.

54 In 1639 the free school's fees were 3s. a quarter. *Archivium Hibernicum*, viii. 58; *Cal. Anc. Recs. Dublin*, ed. Gilbert, iii. 354, 364, 400, 442.

55 T.C.D., MS. N.1.4.20a, pp. 20—34; *Alumni Dublinenses*, p. 330; Cotton, *Fasti*, ii. 240, 253, 259; J. Golborne, *A friendly apology in the behalf of the womans excellency* (London, 1674); Seymour, pp. 142, 212.

school. Until 1656 its work was weakened by unsatisfactory masters, one of whom was dismissed for neglect and drunkenness, and the other remained there less than a year.[56] Matters improved with the arrival of William Hill in 1656. A contemporary in Dublin commented 'by w[ha]t I know of yt Mr. Hill, I cannot but conclude here will be a very flourishing grammar schoole ere long'.[57] What were Hill's special qualities that excited such expectations?

Hill, born in Warwickshire, entered Merton College, Oxford, in 1634 and by 1639 was a probationary Fellow. Shortly afterwards he became schoolmaster at Sutton Coldfield in his native Warwickshire, which school (according to Anthony Wood) 'he brought into great credit during his abode there'. Hill moved to London, where he developed a second career, as a doctor, and in 1649 took medical degrees at Oxford. Another sign of his scientific interests was his epitomizing the works of Lazarius Riverius (a scientist in whom there was a contemporary interest).[59] In Dublin after 1656 Hill may have resumed his medical practice.[60] By 1656 Hill had had a varied career and enjoyed the character 'of a man of good learning, and of great knowledge in the Greek tongue'. We do not know why Hill came to Dublin, but his profuse praise and the date of his arrival suggest a connection with Henry Cromwell.[61] Hill's reputation as a classical scholar was consolidated when, in 1658, he published an edition of Dionysius' *Periegesis* which proved a popular textbook.[62] Hill's claim that he produced pupils 'well grounded in Greek and Latin' seems justified. He also

[56]Bodl., Carte MSS. 173, f. 16; 221, f. 557ᵛ; R.C.B., Seymour MSS., p. 170; *Alumni Dublinenses*, p. 352; Cotton, *Fasti*, i. 51; *The Registers of the Church of St. Michan*, ed. Berry, pp. 173, 180; Seymour, p. 221.

[57]Sheffield Univ. Lib., Hartlib MS. xxxiii, R. Wood to Hartlib, 8 Apr. 1657; R.C.B., Seymour MS., p. 175.

[58]The earlier masters had been paid £40 and £60 p.a. Brit. Mus., Additional MS. 19,833, f. 22ᵛ.

[59]Foster, *Alumni Oxonienses*, E.S. ii. 714; A. Boate, *Observationes Medicae de Affectibus Omissis* (London, 1649) sig. A5ᵛ; A. Wood, *Athenae Oxonienses*, iii, ool. 800.

[60]Brit. Mus., Additional MS. 19,843, f. 171ᵛ.

[61]W. Hill, Διονυσιου Οικουμενης Περικγκσις, *Dionysii orbis descriptio* (London, 1658), sig. *2, **4ᵛ; Wood, *Athenae Oxonienses*, iii, col. 800.

[62]Bodl., Rawlinson MS. D. 1433; *The Whole Works of Sir James Ware*, ii. 347; Wood, *Athenae Oxonienses*, iii, col. 800.

maintained that his Dublin pupils were well versed in the principles of the Protestant religion.[63]   Anthony Wood's complaint that Hill was 'a man of those times and a sider with factious people' suggested that he accepted the religious changes of the Interregnum. This view is also supported by complaints in 1660 about the lack of schools in Dublin 'where the young church . . . may be trained up in the good old lessons of tithes and parochial discipline'.[64] Yet Hill's religious principles were sufficiently flexible for him to accept preferment in the Church of Ireland after 1660. Schemes for maintaining the school at public expense after 1660 foundered and responsibility was resumed by the Dublin corporation, which retained Hill as master with the much reduced salary of £15 p.a. After 1662, however, Hill retired to his living at Finglas, where he still took pupils.[65]

Hill's was the most important Dublin school. Of thirty-eight undergraduates of Trinity College known to have been educated in Dublin during the 1650s eighteen had been taught by Hill. However twelve of the thirty-eight came from Golborne at St. Patrick's School. The fact that Golborne had no official salary raises the possibility that he was not well affected to the regime, although in 1659 he was appointed reader at Christ Church, Dublin.[66]

One other official act connected with the Dublin schools deserves mention. In March 1656 a committee was appointed to visit the free and grammar schools in Dublin and elsewhere. Its main purpose was to see that religious orthodoxy prevailed. Nevertheless it had educational objectives as well, of which the most interesting was to inquire whether the methods in the schools were 'agreable to the rules and discipline used in the free-schooles of literature in England and Holland, known to any of the said committee'.[67] Two of the committee — Petty and Worsley — had lived in Holland

[63] R.C.B., Seymour MSS., p. 175.

[64] *An Account of the chief occurrences . . . 12—19 March* [1660], p. 33.

[65] Hist. MSS. Comm., *Hastings MSS.* iv. 119; *Cal. Anc. Recs. Dublin*, ed. Gilbert, iv. 119, 283—4, 326; Stubbs, *JRSAI* xlvi. 31; T.C.D., Mun. P/1/469, Lord Kingston to Provost Seele, 30 May 1663; D. Loftus, *Liber psalmorum Davidis . . .* (Dublin, 1661); J. Stearne, *De electione et reprobatione dissertatio* (Dublin, 1662), sig. [c4]ᵛ.

[66] T.C.D., MS. N.1.4.20a, pp. 20—33; Seymour, p. 212.

[67] Corcoran, *State policy in Irish education*, p. 76.

and were interested in educational reform. Possibly their inquiries led to Hill's appointment; but no far-reaching reforms can be traced back to the committee.

v. Trinity College, Dublin

Trinity College, Dublin, was at the centre of Cromwellian educational policy in Ireland, as it had been the hub of state schemes between 1591 and 1641. Founded in 1591, the college was intended as a Protestant seminary, training ministers for the Church of Ireland and educating those who would otherwise be sent to Catholic and continental colleges. The college failed to stop continental education, but it did produce ministers for the Protestant church.[68] Although not untouched by intellectual currents, the college reflected fashions in religion rather than in ideas.[69] The Cromwellians envisaged no alteration of the college's function. However it had to be harnessed to a new ecclesiastical policy, so that it would produce ministers for the state church who were opposed to episcopacy and the Common Prayer Book. To fulfil this function the college had to be remodelled, removing the Provost and Fellows.

The college's important place in Cromwellian religious and educational schemes was shown by the ordinance of 8 March 1650 to propagate the Gospel in Ireland. The college's endowments were increased; and fifteen trustees were appointed to regulate the college, empowered to displace the existing Fellows, to administer its funds, and to make statutes.[70] These trustees were a heterogenous group, most of whom were chosen because of their links with Oliver Cromwell (who had pressed the Rump to pass the measure) or with Bulstrode Whitelocke (who had steered the ordinance through parliament).[71] They included John Owen and Jenkin Lloyd, divines who had been in Ireland with Cromwell

[68] Hist. MSS. Comm., *Salisbury MSS.* xiii. 500; Corcoran, *State policy in Irish education*, pp. 49, 62; J. Morrin, *Calendar of the Close and Patent Rolls, Ireland, Elizabeth* (Dublin, 1862), ii. 227.

[69] H. Kearney, *Scholars and Gentlemen* (London, 1970), pp. 66–70, 95–6.

[70] New statutes had to be approved by the English parliament: Firth and Rait, ii. 355–7.

[71] Whitelocke's son James, recently made a Fellow of All Souls, Oxford, was a trustee. Robert Stapleton, in Ireland with Cromwell, was connected with Whitelocke. *The Clarke Papers*, ed. Firth, ii. 72; Abbott, *Cromwell*, i. 653; ii. 21,

and connected with the ordinance; officers serving in Ireland and recently appointed members of the civil administration there.[72] Several of the trustees held positions in the English universities.[73] Only three of them had close connections with Ireland before 1649: Dr. John Harding, a minister long resident in Ireland who had suffered for his enthusiasm for the parliamentary cause; Sir Robert King, a prominent settler who was also interested in educational schemes; and Dr. Henry Jones, vice-chancellor of Trinity since 1646 or 1647.[74]

This method of government by trustees quickly proved inconvenient because absence in England, service in the field, and deaths made it increasingly difficult to produce a quorum. By 1654 the ordinance seems to have been amended, and in 1659 it was proposed to replace it, 'being deficient', with new arrangements.[75] Yet in theory it was the 1650 ordinance that governed the college's management throughout the decade.

In 1650 the trustees had two tasks. The ultimate object of remodelling the college to accord with Cromwellian schemes had initially to take second place to the more pressing need of reviving the college which was close to dissolution. Until 1655 recovery remained the principal task. The war had gravely diminished the college's customary revenues, nor were the additional endowments promised in 1650 immediately forthcoming. The college's needs had to be supplied from the Dublin treasury.[76] One of Winter's main achievements as Provost was his vigour in ordering and visiting the

27, 29, 61, 349; Whitelocke, *Memorials of the English Affairs*, iii. 345–6; H. E. Chetwynd-Stapylton, 'The Stapiltons of Wighill and Myton', in *Chronicles of the Yorkshire Family of Stapleton* (London, 1884), p. 34; cf. Brit. Mus., Lansdowne MS. 822, f. 23.

[72]Officers included Ireton, Henry Cromwell, Venables, Sankey, and Whitelocke. Basill was attorney-general and John Cook chief justice of Munster.
[73]Ralph Cudworth, Sankey and Whitelocke (both Fellows of All Souls), Lloyd (Fellow of Jesus, Oxford), Owen (Dean of Christ Church, Oxford) and Goddard, Cromwell's physician in Ireland, soon to be Warden of Merton, Oxford.
[74]T.C.D., Mun. P/1/371. For King and Harding, see pp. 119 n, 147 n, 149.
[75]Yale Univ. Lib., Osborn collection, W. Petty to Hartlib, 1 Mar. 1653[4]; Brit. Mus., Stowe Ms. 185, f. 137; T.C.D. Mun. P/1/376.
[76]Nat. Lib. Ire., MS. 11,959, p. 23; T.C.D., General Registry from 1626, p. 78; *Analecta Hibernica*, xv. 266, 317.

college's estates, recovering its income. Even so in 1658 the
revenues were said to be 'in some particulars very slender and
meane', and the need for additional revenue was acknowledged.[77]

Trinity's good government and its filling the role projected
for it depended on three things: the statutes, the Provost, and
the new Fellows. As we have seen, the trustees were empowered in 1650 to make new statutes. Changes were
considered. In 1651 the parliamentary commissioners (not
the trustees) approached John Owen, now vice-chancellor of
Oxford, and Thomas Goodwin, President of Magdalen
College, Oxford, to advise 'what laws, rules, orders, and
constitutions are fit to be established in the . . . College'.
Nothing had been done by 1657 when Owen was again
consulted. Asked to send a copy of Oxford's statutes to
Dublin, Owen doubted whether the regulations of either
Oxford of Cambridge were suitable 'for ye promotion of ye
good ends of godlinesse and solide literature which are in
your ayme'. Instead he suggested that a group in England be
asked to frame ordinances specifically for Trinity College.[78]
If this advice was taken, which seems unlikely, no changes
resulted.

The failure to produce new statutes meant that the college
was governed throughout the Interregnum by those of 1637,
imposed by Laud as chancellor of the university. The
Laudian association might have made them unacceptable in
the 1650s, but in fact they had introduced few changes and
generally maintained the curriculum established by Bedell's
statutes between 1627 and 1629.[79] There appear to have
been no radical changes in the 1650s, but only minor
adjustments: for example, demanding certificates of competence in Greek and Hebrew from candidates for bachelors'
degrees.[80]

[77] *The Register of Provost Winter*, ed. Lawlor, p. 3; Huntingdon Rec. Office,
DD 731, no. 17; T.C.D., Mun. P/1/376; Urwick, *The early history of Trinity
College, Dublin*, p. 63.

[78] Dunlop, i. 10—11; Brit. Mus., Lansdowne MS. 822, f. 178.

[79] Laud's statutes are printed by R. Bolton, *A Translation of the Charter and
Statutes of Trinity College, Dublin* (Dublin, 1760), pp. 24—118. Bedell's,
modelled on those of Cambridge, are printed in J. P. Mahaffy, *An epoch in Irish
history* (London, 1903), pp. 327—75.

[80] T.C.D., General Registry from 1626, pp. 87—8, 89, 91. Cf. W. A. L. Vincent,
The state and school education, 1640—60 (London, 1950), pp. 17—19.

In the absence of changes in the statutes, the temper of the Provost and Fellows was of even greater importance. Winter, the Cromwellian Provost, shared the conception of the college as a Protestant seminary, producing ministers of his own Independent persuasion.[81] Oliver Cromwell, as lord lieutenant, approved Winter's appointment on 3 June 1652: Winter was already occupying the office the previous year.[82] His deep involvement with a particular party damaged the college in so far as his conduct as Provost was drawn into more general religious and political controversy, much as the Laudian Provost Chappell had been criticized. In 1655 Winter's hold increased when his chief critic among the Fellows was removed and a number of new Independent Fellows were elected. For those of a different religious outlook or with a wider conception of education, Winter's regimen at Trinity was unsatisfactory. About 1658 there were attacks on the exclusive care for religion in the college: 'we have a long time been ruled by those who went for good men, now let them be good scholars too, that our university may be as famous for learning as hitherto it hath been thought for piety'.[83] Winter was subjected to a number of attacks, but even when he lost official favour in 1658 he remained secure in Trinity, and it was not until March 1660 that the General Convention dismissed him.[84]

The college, like the English universities, had to be purged to accord with the new political and religious systems. However it was not until 1655 that the remodelling of Trinity College was successful. Between 1650 and 1655 there were evidently too few suitable candidates to impose exacting tests, and indeed several of the Fellows appointed in these early years were unsympathetic to Winter's and the new government's policies. The scarcity of candidates was also shown in the fact that five of the seven known Fellows appointed between 1650 and 1655 were Dublin graduates.

[81] J.W., *The Life and Death of Dr. Samuel Winter*, sig.[BI]ᵛ; pp. 10–11; Dunlop, i. 10–11.

[82] T.C.D., General Registry from 1626, p. 74; Nat. Lib. Ire., MS. 11,959, pp. 11–12, 23, 24.

[83] Marsh's Lib., Dublin, MS. Z.3.1.1., item 72.

[84] T.C.D., General Registry, from 1626, p. 92; *An Account of the chief occurrences . . . 12–19 March* [1660], p. 36; T. C. Barnard, 'Trinity at Charles II's restoration in 1660', *Hermathena*, cix (1969), 48.

The leader of the Fellows opposed to Winter seems to have been Joseph Travers, a former Fellow of the college in 1624 and archdeacon of Kildare. Early in 1655 there were serious contentions in the college and defiance of Winter's authority. Travers was accused and removed from his Fellowship. He took his revenge in the spring of 1660 when he led the successful attack on Winter.[85] None of the other Fellows was as outspoken as Travers, but several seem to have shared his sympathies. John Stearne returned as a Fellow in 1651, and accumulated offices throughout the Interregnum. Even in the Interregnum he allowed two of his books to be prefaced by three Anglican bishops and by Jeremy Taylor. He had been accused of disaffection with Travers in 1655, but was able to survive. However in 1660 he again joined Travers to attack Winter.[86] Caesar Williamson had previously been a Fellow of Trinity College, Cambridge, and an Anglican incumbent in England until he lost his livings through his royalism. Made a Fellow of Trinity College, Dublin, in 1644 he was able to recover that post in 1654. Williamson conformed to the Church of Ireland after 1660, and although 'in a crazed condition' eventually became dean of Cashel.[87] Another Fellow, Joshua Cowley, showed clear episcopalian sympathies in the 1650s, joined in the attack on Winter in 1660, and then conformed to the Church of Ireland.[88] The other Fellows may have been more cautious in their behaviour, but only one of those appointed between 1650 and 1655 can be accounted a firm supporter of Winter and the changes. This

[85] Brit. Mus., Egerton MSS. 212, f. 36. 1762, ff. 142v–143; T.C.D., General Registry, from 1626, p. 81; Barnard, *Hermathena*, cix. 46; H. Barrow, *The relief of the poore* (Dublin, 1656), p. 7; Urwick, *The early history of Trinity College, Dublin*, p. 61.

[86] Brit. Mus., Egerton MS. 1762, ff. 142v–143; Bodl., Carte MS. 59, f. 223; Barnard, *Hermathena*, cix. 46–7; J. Stearne, *Seu. De Morte Dissertatio* (Dublin, 1649), sig. a7; Stearne, *Animi Medela* (Dublin, 1658), sig. [b4]–c[1]v.

[87] T.C.D., General Registry from 1626, p. 92; General Registry from 1640, p. 50; Marsh's Lib., Dublin, MS. Z.4.5.16, ff. 32, 107, 109, 112; Bodl. Carte MS. 173, f. 9v; Cotton, *Fasti*, i. 109; ii. 62, 171; Foster, *Alumni Oxonienses*, E.S. iv. 1647; J. B. Leslie, *Derry Clergy and Parishes* (Enniskillen, 1937), p. 95; A. G. Matthews, *Walker Revised* (Oxford, 1948), p. 287; Wood, *Fasti Oxonienses*, ii, col. 34.

[88] *Alumni Dublinenses*, p. 184; 'Original letter of Bishop Jeremy Taylor on theological studies', *Irish Ecclesiastical Journal*, no. 102, v (Dublin, 1 Jan. 1849), 199; Barnard, *Hermathena*, cix. 48–9; H. B. Swanzy, *Succession lists of the diocese of Dromore*, ed. J. B. Leslie (Belfast, 1933), p. 68.

was Nathanael Hoyle, a Fellow of Trinity in 1631, who had
been involved in the attacks on Provost Chappell in the
1630s. His opinions were acceptable to the visitors at Oxford
who appointed him to a Fellowship at Brasenose College in
1648. During the Interregnum Hoyle, as well as returning to
Trinity, acted as an official preacher in Ireland; he failed to
conform after 1660.[89]
The chance to bring the college into line with Winter's and
the government's aims occurred in 1655. Travers was removed. Then in March 1655 delegates from the Independent
churches in Ireland complained of the want of godly Fellows
in the college, and proposed eight candidates of their own.[90]
Winter's own position in the Independent church makes it
probable that he had inspired this petition. The suitability of
these candidates was referred to Winter and two of his closest
associates. It was, therefore, hardly surprising that five of
them were elected Fellows.[91] The names of a further four
Fellows appointed after 1655 are known.[92] Most of these
men were much closer in outlook to Winter: two were his
sons; another, Francis Saunders, belonged to his Dublin
congregation;[93] others had been educated at Trinity since
Winter became Provost;[94] five had been nominated by the
Independent churches; at least five became nonconformists
after 1660. William Leckey was executed for his part in the
1663 plot; Joseph Scott became master of the Erasmus Smith
school at Drogheda, but had to be dismissed for his 'total
noncomformity'.[95] In 1660 it was alleged against Winter that

89 *Alumni Dublinenses*, p. 413; *Register of the Visitors of the University of Oxford*, ed. Burrows, p. 174; *The Reverend Oliver Heywood*, ed. Turner, iv. 322; Mahaffy, *An epoch in Irish history*, pp. 240–2; Turner, *A history of Presbyterianism in Dublin*, p. 8; Seymour, pp. 29, 32, 214; Urwick, *The early history of Trinity College, Dublin*, pp. 60, 73.

90 Brit. Mus., Egerton MS. 1762, f. 150ᵛ; Seymour, pp. 104–5.

91 Gamaliel Marsden, John Price, Joseph Scott, Edward Veel, and the younger Samuel Winter.

92 Josias Winter, Francis Saunders, Robert Norbury, and William Leckey.

93 Saunders came from Cottingham, Yorkshire, where Winter had been minister before coming to Ireland. T.C.D., General Registry, from 1626, p. 82; Nickolls, *Original Letters and Papers*, p. 138; Venn, *Alumni Cantabrigenses*, i. iv. 13.

94 Samuel and Josias Winter, Gamaliel Marden, Francis Saunders, John Price.

95 Adair, *A True Narrative*, p. 280; *Cal. S.P. Ire. 1669–70*, p. 454; *The Horrid Conspiracie of such impenitent traytors*, p. 14; T.C.D., MS. 1.4.20a, pp. 49, 51, 53, 54, 62, 69; Guildhall Lib., 'Erasmus Smith His Booke', f. 43ᵛ; Ronan, *Erasmus Smith Endowment*. For the nonconformity of Veel, Marsden, and

he had intruded his nominees into Fellowships; certainly this was true of those elected after 1655. However he was unable to dislodge those appointed before 1655 (apart from Travers), and their survival meant that his hold was never complete. About 1658 he was attacked; in 1659 some of the Fellows had episcopalian sympathies.[96] Nevertheless there had been an important addition of Fellows who shared Winter's religious outlook, who preached the Gospel and taught others to do so.

Godly Fellows were of no use without undergraduates to teach. We have finally to consider how far the college recovered in numbers from the devastations of the war. Recovery was slow. It was not until May 1654 that we have a record of degrees conferred: fourteen B.A.s and five M.A.s.[97] The number of matriculations gradually rose. In the three years, 1657 to 1659, eighty-three undergraduates matriculated, an annual average of twenty-seven. Between 1661 and 1669 the average was 33·3.[98] During the Interregnum undergraduate numbers did not reach the 1641 or the 1661 totals. Nevertheless there was a steady improvement, so that the foundations of Trinity's expansion after 1660 were laid during the Interregnum.

An analysis of the places of birth and education of Trinity's recorded undergraduates during the 1650s showed that the college was not monopolized by those born or settled in Ireland. The necessary information survives for 120 entrants. Of these sixty-four (53·3 per cent) had been born in Ireland; forty-seven (39 per cent) in England; five in Wales; two on the Isle of Man and two in America. In the period from 1661 to 1681 Petty calculated that only about 22 per cent of Trinity's entrants had been born in England.[99]

Norbury: Matthews, *Calamy Revised*, pp. 339, 367, 501; Bodl., Rawlinson MS. D.1347, ff. 25–30; *The Rev. Oliver Heywood*, ed. Turner, iv. 36–7; T. Simmons, *The Conqueror Crown'd* (London, 1708).

96 *Irish Ecclesiastical Journal*, no. 102, v. 199.

97 In 1655 there were again 14 B.A.s. Between 1619 and 1625 the average number of B.A.s was fifteen; in 1661–81 it was twenty. T.C.D., General Registry from 1626, pp. 75–82; K. T. Hoppen, *The common scientist in the seventeenth century* (London, 1970), p. 66.

98 T.C.D., MS. 1.4.20a, pp. 26–32; Hoppen, *The common scientist*, p. 67.

99 Petty's calculations, preserved at Bowood, are quoted in Hoppen, *The common scientist*, p. 66.

Contemporary circumstances go some way towards explaining the much higher proportion in the Interregnum. The
recent influx of soldiers, civil administrators, and new settlers
meant that such men's sons, if sent to Trinity, would have
been born and often educated in England. This explanation is
not altogether convincing because the majority of entrants
did not come from such families. There is strong evidence
that Trinity College, at least in this period, served the
north-west as its university. Thirty-two of the forty-seven
English-born undergraduates came from Lancashire, Cheshire,
Shropshire, and Yorkshire. There were hopes that Trinity
might also serve as a university for Wales.[100]

Lack of information makes it impossible to classify the
undergraduates' social backgrounds. The Irish-born ones
tended to come from Dublin and Munster, reasonable enough
since these were areas of Protestant plantation. The small
number from Ulster is perhaps accounted for by the
Presbyterians' preference for the Scottish universities. During
the Interregnum few sons of the prominent Munster settlers
or Dublin merchants were sent to the college, perhaps owing
to its Independent tone.[101]   Amongst prominent newcomers
only Thomas Herbert, clerk to the Irish council, and Colonel
John Bridges entrusted their sons to Winter.[102]   The most
sizeable group were the sons of the clergy, both those
beneficed before 1649 and those employed in the 1650s.

Although Winter secured godly Fellows, skilled in teaching, they made no deep impression on their charges, few of
whom held fast to Independency after 1660.[103]   But perhaps
the nonconformist minister, John Hickes, acquired the beliefs
that brought him to the scaffold for complicity in

---

[100]Brit. Mus., Sloane MS. 4062, f. 145.

[101]Exceptions were the sons of the Munster settlers, Sir Valentine Browne and
Henry Becher. T.C.D., MS. 1.4.20a, pp. 27, 31.

[102]Both youths had been educated by Hill in Dublin: ibid., p. 31. Cf. 'Sir
Thomas Herbert of Tintern: a parliamentary royalist', *Bulletin of the Institute of
Historical Research*, xxix (1956).

[103]One graduate, William Burton, became a dissenting minister in Ireland, apart
from the Fellows mentioned above. *Analecta Hibernica*, xv. 273; *The Registers of
S. Catherine, Dublin*, ed. Wood, p. 94; Seymour, p. 208.

Monmouth's rebellion in 1685 from his education at Trinity.[104]

vi.   The second college at Dublin

The idea of a second university college had had a long history before 1650. In the sixteenth century there had been proposals for universities at Armagh, Clonfert, and Limerick.[105] Trinity College itself was to be the first college of the projected University of Dublin.[106] It was to the English parliament's credit that in 1650 they embodied one such scheme in the ordinance for propagating the Gospel in Ireland: a second college was to be erected alongside Trinity College, Dublin.[107] Nothing was done towards realizing this benefaction until 1656: in November of that year Henry Cromwell was said to be 'about a very noble designe, of making another colledge in this city, and putting things unto a better way for the advancement of ingenious learning'. Progress was still slow; in June 1657 the scheme was 'ever and anon talked of'.[108]   One reason for these delays was the distraction caused by Samuel Hartlib's more ambitious schemes for the advancement of learning, which will be described in the next chapter. Only when Hartlib's main plan had been abandoned was the second college again taken up. In December 1658 a committee was appointed by the Irish council to make detailed proposals, which it did in February 1659.[109]

The second college was to have exactly the same establishment as Trinity College: provost, vice-provost, seven senior and nine junior fellows, and seventy scholars of whom thirty

104 *Alumni Dublinenses*, p. 395; *The Last Speech of* ... *Mr. John Hicks* ([London], 1685); J. Hickes, *A True and Faithful Narrative* (n.p., 1671); Hickes, *A Discourse of the Excellency of the Heavenly Substance* (London, 1673); Matthews, *Calamy Revised*, p. 260.

105 Corcoran, *State policy in Irish education*, pp. 49, 50.

106 Mahaffy, *An epoch in Irish history*, pp. 63–5.

107 Firth and Rait, ii. 355–7. In August 1650 Robert Child wrote of a new academy to be erected at Kilkenny. Had he been misled by the Irish administration being temporarily at Kilkenny into thinking it was to be the second college's site? 'Winthrop Papers', *Collections of the Massachusetts Historical Soc.*, 5th Ser. i (1871), 162.

108 Sheffield Univ. Lib., Hartlib xxxiii, Wood to Hartlib, 23 Nov. 1656, 3 Mar. 1656[7], 24 June 1656 *recte* 1657.

109 Ibid., Wood to Hartlib, 8 Dec. 1658 and 9 Feb. 1658[9].

were to be natives.[110]   The annual cost of each college would be £1,649 p.a. The revenues which the ordinance of 1650 had assigned for these purposes were inadequate, and it was proposed to supplement them by an assessment throughout Ireland. One of the committee which had made these recommendations, Sir Maurice Eustace, then drafted a bill to effect the design. The new college was to be named after Oliver Cromwell; it was to be administered by governors who would nominate the first fellows and make its statutes, and who would retain power to visit the college and censure or suspend its members.[111]   Unfortunately the political confusion of 1659 prevented this bill's enactment and the project was not executed. Yet its fulfilment was intended: Ussher's library was bought for the college; Henry Cromwell purchased Cork House in Dublin and bestowed it on the college.[112]   Generally Henry Cromwell's interest seems to have breathed new life into the design. But what was the college's function to be?

There were two possibilities. Either the college would simply supplement Trinity as another Protestant seminary; or it would have a different curriculum perhaps embodying the aspirations of the champions of the new science who were to be found in Henry Cromwell's administration. There is no evidence that the second college was to be founded specifically to advance the new learning. In 1654 Petty, speaking of the 1650 ordinance, wrote that 'there is no course that I know taken to advance any kind of learning by that large donation'. However in 1656 Wood linked the second college with designs for 'the advancement of ingenious learning', but so ambiguously that we cannot tell whether these were separate or a single scheme.[113]   Possibly Hartlib's friends and supporters hoped to capture the new establishment much as

110The schedule of recommendations is in Huntingdon Rec. Office, DD 731, no. 17, which is printed in Urwick, *The early history of Trinity College, Dublin*, pp. 68–72.

111A draft of the bill is T.C.D., Mun P/1/376.

112Chatsworth, Lismore MS., Cork's diary, 23 Apr. 1657 and 24 Oct. 1657; Huntingdon Rec. Office, 731 DD, nos. 11, 31, 32.

113Yale Univ. Lib., Osborn collection, Petty to Hartlib, 1 Mar. 1653[4]; Sheffield Univ. Lib., Hartlib MS. xxxiii, Wood to Hartlib, 23 Nov. 1656.

they did the contemporary college at Durham.[114] The detailed provisions of 1659 offered little scope for intellectual innovation. Indeed the only serious possibility lay in two of the five professorships which were to be shared by Trinity and the new college. There were to be chairs of physic, including natural philosophy, and mathematics: both these subjects were already taught at Trinity.

Although there was a chance that the new college might be receptive to the new science, it was not founded for that reason. The fragmentary evidence suggests that it was intended principally as a Protestant seminary. Throughout the Interregnum various schemes circulated for training ministers for Irish service. In general, however, the English universities did little for Ireland's needs, and it became increasingly clear that better provision of ministers would be secured only by expanding institutions in Dublin.[115] The second college's missionary purpose, and the absence of innovation in its curriculum, is strongly suggested by the character of the committee which planned it. An examination of the committee's membership also reveals the conservatism of Henry Cromwell's nominees, especially when they are compared with the trustees of Trinity College appointed in 1650.

The committee included office-holders serving in their official capacities.[116] Most of the other members were either Old Protestants, almost uniformly conservative; and clergymen, also of conservative outlook. The Old Protestant settlers included the earl of Thomond, an obscure man who subsequently acquired a reputation as a drunkard and a nonconformist. Politically he was a conservative and was arrested later in 1659 for his suspected disaffection.[117] More con-

114G. H. Turnbull, 'Oliver Cromwell's College at Durham', *Research Review*, research publication of the Institute of Education, Univ. of Durham, iii (1952), 1–10.

115Brit. Mus., Sloane MS. 4062, f. 145; *Reliquiae Baxterianae*, i. 171–2; M. Poole, *A model for the maintaining of students of choice abilities at the university* (London, 1658), sig. [A3], p. 11.

116To this category belonged Basill, the attorney-general, also a trustee a Trinity; Roberts, auditor-general; Capt. James Stopford, experienced in the treasury; Robert Gorges, clerk to the council; and Capt. John Bridges, a trustee of almshouses and hospitals in Ireland.

117G.E.C., *The Complete Peerage*, xii, pt. i, p. 709; Calamy, *An abridgement of Mr. Baxter's history*, p. 468; *Calendar of the Clarendon State Papers, 111*, ed. W. D. Macray (Oxford, 1876), p. 381; ibid. *IV*, ed. F. J. Routledge (Oxford, 1932), p. 106.

spicuous for his political attitudes was Arthur Annesely, who had been secluded from the Long Parliament at Pride's Purge and who was said to be in touch with the royalists in 1658. Annesley was sympathetic towards the Presbyterians, owned a celebrated library, and became a founder Fellow of the Royal Society. He was also very friendly with Henry Cromwell.[118] Sir Paul Davies had been clerk to the Irish privy council in 1630 and was active in the Protestant interest during the war. He was typical of the conservatives favoured by Henry Cromwell and who melted away to the royalists in 1659.[119] Perhaps the most surprising member of the committee was Sir Maurice Eustace, another office-holder in Ireland before 1641, and who had been imprisoned by the Long Parliament for seven years and who was suspected of disaffection in Dublin in 1656. Despite his past Eustace was commended by Henry Cromwell and probably included in the committee for his legal expertise.[120] Two of the Old Protestant members, Dr. Dudley Loftus and Sir James Ware, had scholarly interests. Loftus served the usurpers as a judge and was professor of civil law at Trinity College in 1655. His intellectual interests were catholic and he too owned a celebrated library, but his greatest fame was as an Orientalist. Loftus was resolutely on the side of the ancients in the contemporary intellectual struggle, translating an Armenian commentary on Aristotle and later ridiculing the Dublin Philosophical Society.[121] Ware, if less violent than Dr. Loftus, was hardly more likely to support innovation. He had been an office-holder in Ireland and was imprisoned by the

---

[118] G.E.C., *The Complete Peerage*, i. 1344; *The Nicholas Papers, IV*, ed. G. F. Warner, Camden soc., 3rd Ser. xxxi (1920), 205; *Thurloe State Papers*, vi. 777; Turnbull, *Hartlib, Dury and Comenius*, pp. 10, 28, 30, 381 n. 7; *Bibliotheca Anglesiana* ([London] 1686).

[119] *Thurloe State Papers*, vi. 71; vii. 624–5.

[120] C.B., Jennings transcripts, A/10, 20 Oct. 1656 and 16 Jan. 1656[7]; Brit. Mus., Lansdowne MS. 821, f. 3ᵛ; *Calendar of the Clarendon State Papers, III*, ed. Macray, p. 81; F. E. Ball, *The judges in Ireland* (New York, 1926), i. 262–4, 344–6; Dunlop, ii. 629, n. 2; *Thurloe State Papers*, vii. 635; Chester City Record Office, ML/3/336.

[121] *D.N.B.*; G. T. Stokes, *Some worthies of the Irish church* (London, 1900); *The Clarke Papers*, iii, ed. Firth, 50; C. Galanus, *Logica, seu introductio in totam Aristotelis philosophiam* (Dublin, 1657); Hoppen, *The common scientist*, pp. 159–66; *Thurloe State Papers*, vii. 606; Marsh's Library, Dublin, MS. Z.4.15; 'Sir Thomas Molyneux', *Dublin University Review*, xviii (1841), 315.

Long Parliament after 1647. His great contribution to Irish scholarship was as a historian and antiquarian.[122]

Against these political and intellectual conservatives can be set only one member of the committee with a known interest in the new learning: Dr. Robert Gorges, clerk to the Irish council, who had been a member of the experimental science club in Oxford earlier in the decade.[123]

In religious outlook the majority of the committee was conservative. The exceptions were three Baptists: Edward Roberts (included in his official capacity as auditor-general), Dr. John Harding, and Hierome Sankey (both of whom were trustees of Trinity College). The committee's clerical members were conservatives. Apart from Dr. Harding, they were Dr. Henry Jones, Trinity's vice-chancellor, Dr. Edward Worth, and Dr. Francis Roberts, Henry Cromwell's Presbyterian chaplain.

Had Henry Cromwell wanted to make the new college a centre of the new learning, he would surely have included in the committee some of the supporters of experimental science in Dublin at this time — like Petty, Anthony Morgan, Robert Wood, Miles Symner, or Benjamin Worsley. Their omission shows this was not his intention. Other omissions may also tell something of the new college's purpose. It was strange that Winter, the Provost of Trinity and leader of the Independents, was not a member. This was a measure of his fall from favour in 1658. Indeed there was scarcely a religious Independent on the committee.[124]   Again we must ask whether or not this was deliberate. The membership of the committee raises the possibility that it was intended to found a college that would balance Winter's Independent seminary at Trinity, reflecting the religious tastes of Worth and Roberts, and of the Old Protestant settlers, most of whom refrained from sending their sons to Winter's Trinity. This is, of course, conjecture, but the conservative temper of the committee is clear.

122 *D.N.B.*

123 M. Purver, *The Royal Society: concept and creation* (London, 1967), p. 125; cf R. Gorges, *The Story of a family ... being a history of the family of Gorges* (Boston, Mass., 1944).

124 The only member closely associated with Winter was Col. John Bridges.

The scheme, frustrated by the political changes of 1659, was taken up by the General Convention in March 1660 and was still circulating after Charles II's restoration. In 1662 the lord lieutenant and Irish privy council were authorized to reserve £2,000 p.a. from the king's Irish revenues to establish a second college, 'The King's College', as part of Dublin University.[125]   Lord Essex (lord lieutenant from 1672 to 1677) showed interest in this project, but it never came to fruition and Ireland had to wait until the nineteenth century for its second college.[126]

If Dublin never saw Oliver the Lord Protector's College, these efforts had one lasting result, the return of Ussher's celebrated library to Dublin. On Ussher's death in 1656 there was a danger that the library would be sold to a foreign purchaser. The English council of state intervened to prevent that. English institutions were interested in acquiring the library, but the army in Ireland was persuaded to buy it (for £2,500) and give it to the projected second college. Henry Cromwell appears to have been important in inspiring this generosity, as well as Ussher's nephews Dr. Henry Jones and Sir Theophilus Jones. The books arrived in Dublin after July 1657. Although Henry Cromwell had given Cork House to accommodate them, they had to be stored in Dublin Castle where they remained until 1660. Once hopes of a second college faded, the problem arose of what to do with the library. Charles II solved it by giving it to Trinity College, thus diverting to himself much of the credit of securing an appropriate home for the collection.[127]   During the Interregnum there were other demonstrations of care for learning. Dr. Henry Jones, as well as keeping fresh the memory of the 1641 massacre, secured the Book of Kells for Trinity College;[128]   Miles Symner also presented the college with

125 *An Account of the chief occurrences . . . 12—19 March [1660]*, p. 35; *An Act for the better execution . . .* (Dublin, 1662), p. 122.

126 Essex's chaplain was Francis Roberts, a member of the earlier committee. Brit. Mus., Stowe MS. 212, f. 320. In 1692 William King wanted a seminary established at Derry to combat the Scottish Presbyterians. Cambridge Univ. Lib., Baumgartner papers, Strype correspondence, i, f. 100v.

127 A fuller account is Barnard, *Long Room*, iv. 9—14.

128 A. Gwynn, 'Some notes on the Book of Kells', *Irish Hist. Studies*, ix (1954), 132—61; *The Tanner Letters*, ed. McNeill, p. 440; W. O'Sullivan, 'The donor of the Book of Kells', *Irish Hist. Studies*, xi (1958—9), 5—7.

manuscripts previously owned by monasteries.[129]   These successful efforts of preservation conflict with the stereotype of the Cromwellians as vandals and despoilers. On occasion, obviously, barbarism occurred. However there is no doubt that official policy favoured education and the university, although mainly for political and religious reasons. Lack of money and suitable schoolmasters prevented any great success; given more time a second college would have been created and more masters appointed. In general educational policy in the Interregnum resembled Protestant policy before 1641 and after 1660. The departures can be traced to Oliver Cromwell, in inspiring the ordinance of 1650 and (with his council) stopping a foreign sale and preferring an Irish destination for Ussher's library; and to Henry Cromwell, perhaps for attracting William Hill to Dublin, and certainly for bringing the second college close to existence and inspiring the purchase of Ussher's library.

---

[129] i.e. T.C.D., MSS. B.2.3. and D.4.8.

VIII

THE ADVANCEMENT OF LEARNING

i. The background

Education in Cromwellian Ireland continued to have a political and religious purpose. The schools and the university remained impervious to the new learning, which stressed experiment and utility. As in England educational and intellectual innovation had to take place outside the existing institutions. This chapter will trace the reception and spread of the new scientific spirit, and will argue that although there was some interest in the advancement of learning in Ireland before 1649 the Interregnum saw a great increase in this interest, largely through the activities of a small circle of Samuel Hartlib's friends and followers who had been attracted to Ireland. Much of this chapter will be devoted to an examination of this group's outlook, projects, and achievements. Furthermore, I shall argue that their presence whilst producing few concrete results significantly altered intellectual attitudes making possible the foundation of the Dublin Philosophical Society in 1683.

As yet new intellectual currents amongst Irish Catholics in the seventeenth century have been little investigated. The close contacts with continental universities and the introduction of foreign books into Ireland indicate that new ideas must have touched Ireland.[1] On the other hand Catholic education, no less than that of the Irish Protestants, was usually designed to equip religious missionaries and discouraged bolder speculation. Amongst Irish Protestants it was Archbishop Ussher who ensured that Ireland did not become totally isolated from the European intellectual world. Two acts of patronage, in particular, illustrate his interests. First, he lured Nathanael Carpenter, a determined opponent of scholasticism, to Ireland, as his chaplain and then as master

---

[1] Hammerstein, *Historical Studies: VIII*, ed. Williams, pp. 143–4.

of the school for royal wards in Dublin. Unfortunately nothing is known of Carpenter's career in Ireland.[2]

Secondly, Ussher was a patron of Arnold Boate, a Dutchman who had studied medicine at Leyden and who arrived in Dublin in 1636. Arnold Boate practised as a doctor (his patients included Ussher and Strafford) and on the outbreak of war became physician-general to the army in Leinster.[3] In 1641 Boate and his brother Gerard Boate published, at Dublin, an attack on the peripatetic philosophy still dominant.[4] Arnold Boate left Ireland in 1644, but his brother now developed an interest in Ireland. Like his brother, Gerard Boate had studied medicine at Leyden and was keenly interested in medical reform.[5] In 1647 Gerard Boate was appointed physician to the army in Ireland, but did not arrive there until 1649, when he was also made doctor at the military hospital in Dublin. He had little time to apply his ideas before his death in January 1650.[6]

The Boates were important because they occupied a pivotal position, linking the earlier stirrings of interest in science in the 1630s with the later activities of the Interregnum. Gerard Boate influenced the early thinking of Robert Boyle; he seems also to have been connected with Benjamin Worsley.[7] Moreover it was the Boates who first involved Samuel Hartlib in an Irish venture. In 1645 Gerard Boate started to compile a natural history of Ireland, which would

---

[2]N. Carpenter, *Chorazin and Bethsaida's Woe* (London, 1633); Carpenter, *Achitophel, or, the picture of a wicked politician* (n.p., 1629), sig. A3; C. Hill, *Intellectual Origins of the Civil War* (Oxford, 1965), p. 305; Wood, *Athenae Oxonienses*, ii. col. 421.

[3]A. Boate, *Observationes Medicae de Affectibus Omissis*, sig. [B4]ᵛ; G. Boate, *Irelands Naturall History*, p. 180; H. J. Lawlor, 'Primate Ussher's Library before 1641', *Proceedings of the Royal Irish Academy*, 3rd Ser. vi (1901), 240; *Two Biographies of William Bedell*, ed. Shuckburgh, p. 118; Brit. Mus., Sloane MS. 4771, f. 50; *A Remonstrance of divers remarkable passages and proceedings of our army in the kingdome of Ireland* (London, 1642).

[4]*Philosophia naturalis reformata* (Dublin, 1641).

[5]*Nieuw Nederlandsch Biografisch Woordenboek* (Leyden, 1918), iv, cols. 211–12; Sir George Clark, *A history of the Royal College of Physicians of London* (Oxford, 1964), i. 262; C. Webster, 'English medical reformers of the Puritan Revolution: a background to the "Society of Chymical Physitians" ' *Ambix* (1967), p. 20, n. 19.

[6]*C.J.* v. 247; *Cal. S.P. Dom. 1649–50*, pp. 66, 588.

[7]C. Webster, 'New light on the Invisible College', *Trans. Royal Hist. Soc.*, 5th Ser. xxiv.

apply new standards of exact observation to the description of the country. The compilation also had utilitarian and propagandist purposes: to encourage a new Protestant plantation by giving accurate information and by hinting at the potential riches for the adventurers (of whom Boate was one);[8] and to vindicate English rule by showing that the English were the 'introducers of all good things in Ireland'.[9] When Gerard Boate died in 1650 only the first part of the book had been completed. Hartlib intervened and saw it through the press, and then cast about for successors who might finish the *Naturall History*, constantly pressing his correspondents in Ireland into the work.

There were other signs of interest in educational reform and innovation in Ireland before 1649, apart from Carpenter's and the Boates' work. Benjamin Worsley, an important figure in the Interregnum, came to Ireland first in some unspecified capacity in Strafford's household, and in 1641 became surgeon-general to the Irish army.[10] Sir Richard and Sir William Parsons helped Boate in the compilation of his *Naturall History*; Bishop Bedell interested himself in Johnson's universal character, a project that was taken up by Hartlib's friends in the 1650s; Lord Clandeboye wanted to patronize Comenius; Ussher, Bedell, and Bishop John Richardson of Ardagh corresponded with Dury and Hartlib in the 1630s.[11] The King family of Abbey Boyle seem to have been sympathetic to the new currents: Edward King was Milton's friend; Miles Symner (professor of mathematics at Trinity College in the 1650s) was presented to livings in the family's gift in the 1630s; Sir Robert King became Dury's brother-in-law and showed interest in the improvement of education.[12] In London in the 1640s there was a group of Protestant settlers from Ireland in close touch with Hartlib,

[8] Bottigheimer, *English Money and Irish Land*, pp. 177, 199.

[9] Boate, *Irelands Naturall History*, p. 114.

[10] Bodl., Clarendon state papers, 75, f. 300; *Alumni Dublinenses*, p. 895; Hist. MSS. Comm., *Ormonde MSS.* N.S. ii. 256–7, 284–5.

[11] Boate, *Irelands Naturall History*, sig. [A7]–[A7]^v; Barnard, 'Miles Symner and the new learning in seventeenth-century Ireland', *JRSAI* cii (1972), 137; Sheffield Univ. Lib., Hartlib MSS. v (12) and (16); *The Effect of Master Dury's Negotiation* (n.p., n.d.), p. 2.

[12] R.C.B., MS. Libr. 41, p. 128; *C.J.* viii. 287; Firth and Rait, ii. 355–7; Turnbull, *Hartlib, Dury and Comenius*, p. 247.

which has led Mr. Charles Webster to argue that this Anglo-Irish circle formed the nucleus of the 'Invisible College'. Members of this group included Worsley, Gerard Boate, Robert Boyle, and his sister, Lady Ranelagh. On its fringes were Clotworthy, Lord Broghill, and Arthur Annesley.[13] The evidence, although slight, is sufficient to show that the rapacity of the Protestant planters was combined with sympathy for the projects and reforms of the Hartlib circle. Indeed there were special reasons why Irish Protestants should support schemes that offered to strengthen the Protestant interest, improve the plantation of Ireland, and facilitate the exploitation of Ireland's hidden wealth. These earlier stirrings of interest were renewed and strengthened in the Interregnum as the result of the presence in Ireland of the new science's supporters, William Petty, Benjamin Worsley, Robert Child, Miles Symner, Robert Wood, and Anthony Morgan. Before considering the ways in which learning and experimental science were advanced, I shall sketch the careers and interests of these men.

ii. The Hartlib circle in Ireland

Hartlib acted as the link between these men, supplying them with books, news, and ideas from England and the continent, prodding them into action, and introducing them to like-minded spirits. Common to all was an impatience with the universities as preserves of sterile scholasticism; a veneration of Bacon and adherence to his principles (sometimes in a vulgarized form); and the wish that all knowledge should have a useful application. Most of these men were brought to Ireland by the Cromwellian reconquest and employed there in the technical work of resettlement. Ireland, indeed, offered unique opportunities to prove the usefulness of their knowledge.

   Of the group William Petty is the most celebrated: his was the most brilliant and successful career. Born in 1623, he was educated abroad, first at the Jesuit college at Caen where Descartes had been taught, and then at Leyden where he studied medicine. Not only did Petty familiarize himself with

13 Webster, *Trans. Royal Hist. Soc.* xxiv (1974). I am grateful to Mr. Webster for showing me a draft of this article before publication.

the latest theories and discoveries, he met leading scientists, including the mathematician John Pell, Hobbes, and Mersenne.[14] Petty returned to England, going to Oxford where he was rapidly drawn into the scientific club. At Oxford promotion was rapid: a Fellow of Brasenose about 1650 and shortly afterwards reader in anatomy. Even before going to Oxford Petty's talents had caught Hartlib's eye and he was praised as a 'most rare and exact anatomist, and excelling in all mathematical and mechanical learning'. Through Hartlib he was introduced to Worsley and Robert Boyle, and helped to a professorship at Gresham's College in London. Petty's impatience with traditional learning was already clear. In 1648 he published a scheme for the advancement of learning which showed the similarity between his outlook and Hartlib's.[15] He attacked those 'that doe not know the things they talk and dispute so much about', and who busied themselves 'spinning the cobwebs out of bare suppositions and out of principles which though [they] may be true, yet are remote, abstracted and generall'. Petty dismissed the schoolmen for having nothing better to offer than words, 'words meerely chimerical, signifying nothing, a language fitter to be used in another imaginary, phantasticall world, then in this reall one'. Petty measured all knowledge against the yardstick of utility. By this standard even Descartes was found wanting. Indeed Petty wrote,

till Mounsr. des Cartes hath approved himself a philosopher in this sense, I shall prefer Cornelius Drebbel[16] before him, though he understand no Latin, as one yt hath done more though said less. I have wearied myself running through Aristotles, Galens, Campanellas, Helmonts, Paracelsus and des Cartes, their imaginary principles, and

---

14W. Petty, *The Discourse made before the Royal Society the 26 November 1674*, sig. [A8]ᵛ–[A9]; Q. Skinner, 'Thomas Hobbes and his disciples in France and England', *Comparative Studies in Society and History* viii (1966), 154, 160, 165. Generally on Petty: E. Fitzmaurice, *The Life of Sir William Petty, 1623–1687* (London, 1895); E. Strauss, *Sir William Petty: portrait of a genius* (London, 1954); I. Masson and A. J. Youngson, 'Sir William Petty', in *The Royal Society: its origins and founders*, ed. H. Hartley (London, 1960).

15*The Works of Robert Boyle*, v. 256, 257; *The Advice of W.P. to Mr. Samuel Hartlib ...* (London, 1648); Turnbull, *Hartlib, Dury and Comenius*, pp. 46, 49, n. 2, 433; *Winthrop Papers, v. 1645–49*, ed. A. B. Forbes, Massachusetts Historical Soc., (Boston, Mass., 1947), p. 221.

16For Drebbel (1572–1633) see: Rosalie Colie, 'Cornelius Drebbel and Solomon de Caus; two Jacobean models for Solomon's House', *Huntington Library Quarterly*, xviii (1954–5), 245–60.

find much witt and phancy in them all . . . but doe look upon the best of them as nut shells in comparison of the knowledge of slibber sauce[17] experiments I judiciously and selectly made.

Petty concluded this intellectual credo: 'I . . . never knew any man who had once tasted the sweetness of experimentall knowledge yt ever afterward lusted after ye vaporous garlick and onions of phantasticall seeming philosophy.'[18]

Petty's reputation before 1652 rested largely on his medical work, and it was this that led to his first employment in Ireland. In 1652 he was persuaded to go as physician to John Lambert, 'a favourer of ingeniose and usefull arts', who had been nominated as Irish lord deputy. Lambert never took up the post, but Petty went to Ireland as physician to the army, arriving there about October 1653. Once in Dublin Petty also established a thriving medical practice which he valued at £1,600 p.a.[19] However he was soon distracted from medicine by the technical problems of Ireland's resettlement; in December 1654 he contracted with the Irish government to measure and survey the forfeited lands. This, the 'Down' survey, was completed by March 1656, but the complicated and controversial work of allocating estates and adjudicating between the rival claims occupied Petty until 1659.[20] Petty's talents had found new scope in the survey; his success brought further public employment, as clerk to the Irish council and secretary to Henry Cromwell. He was also involved in public controversy from which he did not shrink. First there was a long-standing feud, dating back at least to

17 Slibber sauce is defined by O.E.D. as 'a compound or concoction of a messy, repulsive or nauseous character, used especially for medicinal purposes'.
18 'Mr. Pettys letter in answer to Mr. Moore', Sheffield Univ. Lib., Hartlib MS. vii (123), printed in Turnbull, 'Samuel Hartlib's influence on the early history of the Royal Society', Notes and Records of the Royal Society of London, x (1953), 120—1; and C. Webster, 'Henry More and Descartes: some new sources', The British Journal for the History of Science, iv (1969), 367—8.
19 Petty, Reflections on some persons and things, pp. 3, 17; W. Burdet, A Wonder of Wonders (London, 1650); H. M. Sinclair and A. H. T. Robb-Smith, History of the teaching of anatomy in Oxford (Oxford, 1950), pp. 12—13, 71. As physician to the army Petty was paid £14 per month: Bodl., Rawlinson MS. A.208, pp. 387, 418, 434, 440, 449.
20 The history of the . . . Down Survey by Doctor W. Petty, ed. T. A. Larcom, Irish Archaeological Soc. (Dublin, 1851), pp. 22—30, 236—49; Oirechtas Lib., Dublin, MS. 3.G.12; Brit. Mus., Additional MSS. 19,845 and 35,102; Dunlop, ii. 680—1; Proposals to the Adventurers for lands in Ireland (London, 1658); Thurloe State Papers, vii. 114.

1652, with Worsley; this was inflamed when Petty took over from Worsley the work of surveying in 1654, and rumbled on throughout the decade.[21] It may have been personal in origin, but it rapidly acquired political significance, because Worsley was linked with the Baptist and military opposition to Henry Cromwell and the protectorate, while Petty, by temperament a *politique*, was firmly identified with Henry Cromwell and his policies. These tensions came to a head in 1659 when Hierome Sankey, aided by Worsley, tried to impeach Petty and thus strike at Henry Cromwell's administration.[22]

Petty summed up the importance of his Irish experience in the 1650s as 'by attempting new difficulties' to stretch his 'own capacity and intellect, the which not only is formed and fashioned, but much expanded by such employments'.[23] As well as helping Petty's intellectual development, service in Ireland brought him influence, fame, and fortune.

Closest to Petty in his contemporary reputation and influence was Benjamin Worsley. Worsley differed from Petty in that when he returned to Ireland in 1652 he had already played an important part in public affairs. Worsley was born in 1617 or 1618, and first came to Ireland to serve in Strafford's household, remaining after Strafford's departure as surgeon-general of the army. Lacking formal education, Worsley decided to enter Trinity College, Dublin, but the times were unpropitious for study and he resolved to travel to Flanders. On his way he was detained in England, and became a close associate of Hartlib and Robert Boyle, probably joining the latter in the 'Invisible College'.[24] In 1647 the Long Parliament reappointed him surgeon to the army in Ireland, but instead of taking up the post he went to Holland. There he engaged in studies similar to Petty's,

21 Yale Univ. Lib., Osborn collection, Petty to Hartlib, 23 Oct. 1652; and 17 Oct. 1655; Petty, *Reflections*, pp. 12–15.
22 *A brief of proceedings between S[i]r Hierom Sankey and Dr. William Petty* (London, 1659); Petty, *Reflections*, pp. 37–8; *Thurloe State Papers*, vii. 651.
23 Petty, *Reflections*, p. 15.
24 General accounts of Worsley are in L. F. Brown, *The first earl of Shaftesbury* (New York, 1933), pp. 129–31, 140–7; and J. B. Whitmore, *Notes and Queries*, clxxxv. (1943). See also: Bodl., Clarendon state papers, 75, f. 300; *L.J.*, vii. 401; Turnbull, *Hartlib, Dury and Comenius*, pp. 260, 262; Webster, *Trans. Royal Hist. Soc.* xxiv.

showing special interest in commercial questions. He became involved in a project to bring royalist Virginia under the Long Parliament's control, and as a result came to know several leading members of the Rump (notably Henry Vane and Strickland) as well as prominent London merchants.[25] No doubt it was these contacts which secured Worsley appointment as secretary to the newly established council of trade in 1650. This was a position of influence which Worsley evidently used, for, if we are to believe him, he was the 'first sollicitour' for the Navigation Act of 1651. At this time Worsley published two pamphlets on colonial policy which drew on his knowledge of Holland and urged a system of free ports so that England could create a flourishing re-export trade.[26]

In 1652 Worsley's work with the council of trade ended and he was appointed (perhaps through Vane's advocacy) secretary to the parliamentary commissioners in Dublin.[27] Worsley was not eager to serve in Ireland and quickly returned to England in 1653 when there was a chance of accompanying Lord Lisle on his embassy to Sweden. When Whitelocke and not Lisle was sent to Sweden, Worsley crossed to Ireland again. The secretaryship had been filled by another, but he was made surveyor-general.[28] Worsley's methods of surveying were criticized by Petty as 'absurd and insignificant', and in 1654 he was supplanted in the main work of surveying, although he remained surveyor-general until 1658, when he was replaced by Petty's friend Vincent Gookin.[29] Indeed, while Petty's career in Ireland advanced,

25 Bodl., Clarendon state papers, 75, f. 300; Sheffield Univ. Lib., Hartlib MS. xxxiii (2); *Cal. S.P. Colonial, 1574–1660*, pp. 331, 332, 339.

26 Bodl., Clarendon state papers, 75, f. 300, [Worsley], *The Advocate* (London, 1651); B. W[orsley], *Free Ports* (London, 1652) (both books are reprinted in R. W. K. Hinton, *The Eastland trade and the commonweal* [Cambridge, 1959]); Cooper, 'Social and economic policy' in *The Interregnum*, ed. Aylmer, pp. 133–6; J. E. Farnell, 'The Navigation Act of 1651', *Econ. Hist. Rev.* xvi (1964), 441; Firth and Rait, ii. 406; Petty attacked *The Advocate* and also the idea of free ports: *Some reflections*, p. 89; *A treatise of taxes and contributions* (London, 1662), pp. 41–2.

27 Yale Univ. Lib., Osborn collection, Petty to Hartlib, 23 Oct. 1652; O'Hart, *Irish landed gentry*, p. 244.

28 *Cal. S.P. Dom. 1652–3*, pp. 272, 395; Mackenzie, *Bulletin of the Institute of Historical Research*, xxix. 80

29 Petty, *Reflections*, pp. 13–15; Barnard, *Eng. Hist. Rev.* lxxxviii. 357.

Worsley's languished. The reason was his political and religious opinions.

Worsley had had close ties with the Rump Parliament, and regretted its ejection, the more so when the protectorate was inaugurated. Through visits to England he kept in touch with old associates, including Henry Vane. In April 1659 he complained of the rottenness and corruption of the government 'of Lordly and wicked men'; by joining in the attempted impeachment of Petty he tried to overthrow it.[30] The Rump's return briefly restored him to favour.[31] Worsley's religious beliefs were complex. Although associated with a party that included many Baptists, there is strong evidence that Worsley was a Socinian. Certainly he owned an unusual number of very rare Socinian books and corresponded about the doctrine.[32] While in Ireland his taste for religious speculation grew. Worsley spoke of himself as contemptible, mere dirt in God's eyes, and asked 'what is dyrt he should thinke himselfe so goode, and so great, as to take upon him to iudge what designes were fitt to be promoted in the world . . . ? '[33] There were, then, good grounds for suspecting Worsley's affection to the protectorate. Henry Cromwell, probably encouraged by Petty, reduced Worsley's influence until in 1658 his only public employment was as a justice of the peace in Queen's County.[34] The treatment of Worsley showed the limitations of Henry Cromwell's alliance

[30] Sheffield Univ. Lib., Hartlib MS. xxxiii, 20 Apr. 1659; Hist. MSS. Comm., *De L'Isle and Dudley MSS.* vi. 496–8; *The Parish Registers of St. Mary Aldermary, London . . . 1558–1754*, ed. J. L. Chester, Harleian Soc., Registers, vol. v (London, 1880), p. 26; Brit. Mus., Lansdowne MS. 821, f. 352; *The Works of Robert Boyle*, v. 267.

[31] Chatsworth, Lismore MS. 31, no. 50; *A breife of the pleadings before a committee of the Councel of State . . . March the 13 1659[60]* (n.p., n.d.); *Cal. S.P. Dom. 1659*, p. 13; Bridges, *A Perfect narrative of the grounds*, p. 4; *The Works of Robert Boyle*, v. 291; *Diary of Sir Archibald Johnston of Wariston, iii, 1655–60*, pp. 161, 166, 168.

[32] Sheffield Univ. Lib., Hartlib MS. lxii (21), W. Rand to Worsley, 11 Aug. 1651; *Catalogus librorum . . . Benjaminis Worsley, tum duorum aliorum* (London, 1678); H. J. MacLachlan, *Socinianism in seventeenth century England* (Oxford, 1951), pp. 112, 115, 134.

[33] Sheffield Univ. Lib., Hartlib MSS. xxxix (4), letter of 7 Apr. 1658; xlii (1), letters of 31 Oct. 1654, 29 Nov. 1654, 14 Feb. 1655[6]; *The Works of Robert Boyle*, v. 282–3.

[34] Clarendon state papers, 75, f. 300v; Dunlop, ii. 692. For Worsley as a J.P. for Dublin: T.C.D., MS. F.3.18, f. 139v; Whitmore, *Notes and Queries*, clxxxv. 124.

with conservatives, denying the Irish administration the advice of a talented man, particularly expert in matters of trade. There is no evidence that Worsley was called upon to advise on commercial policy. Indeed, although he acquired lands in Ireland, service there was an unimportant episode in his life and after 1659 he severed links with the country, finding that his abilities were again in demand in England.[35] The animosity between Petty and Worsley was also unfortunate in that it divided the adherents of the new learning in Ireland, and contributed to the failure of Hartlib's most ambitious schemes.

Worsley's intellectual attitudes had been formed before his return to Ireland in 1652. In 1648 he informed Hartlib that he had 'abdicated much reading of bookes, vulgare received traditions, and common schoole opinions . . . ', and would henceforth believe 'only that w[hi]ch is immediately deduced from, or built up on, reall, or certayne, experiments'.[36] As an example he used the determining of a plant's properties. 'Certaine experiments' were 'a farr more pleasant, convincing and delightfull demonstration' than the mere repetition of 'a botanique lecture'. Like Petty Worsley insisted that all knowledge must be useful.[37] In 1657, from Ireland, Worsley attacked the schoolmen entrenched in the universities and their master, Aristotle. He predicted 'there is a time coming which they little think off wherein most of their present learning will have a very little repute or authority left to them.'[38]

Of the other members of the Harlib circle in Ireland, Robert Child was born in Kent, educated at Cambridge, and then studied medicine at Leyden and Padua. In 1641 he migrated to New England where he became entangled in the colony's religious contentions. Returning to England, Child renewed his acquaintance with Hartlib. In 1651 he accepted Colonel Arthur Hill's invitation to go to the latter's estate at

35 P.R.O., Dublin, l.a.53.56, pp. 445–6, 463; Petty, *Reflections*, pp. 31–2.
36 Sheffield Univ. Lib., Hartlib MS. xlii (1), Worsley to Hartlib, Amsterdam, 27 July 1648. One of the few philosophers whom Worsley praised was Paracelsus, 'a clear and rationall man'. Yet even he was 'intoxicated now and then . . . with the sight of his own knowledge'. Ibid. xlii (1), Worsley to Hartlib, Dublin, 14 Feb. 1655[6].
37 Ibid. xxxvi (7), letter of 16 Feb. 1646[7].
38 Ibid. xxxiii (2), letter of 20 Oct. 1657.

Lisburn in County Antrim, where Child remained until his death early in 1654. Child shared Hartlib's wide-ranging interests, but in Ireland his main concern was with husbandry and its improvement.[39]

Anthony Morgan's interest in science was that of an amateur, albeit a gifted one. Born in 1621 or 1622, Morgan fought for the king in the civil war, but changed sides in 1645.[40] He came to Ireland with the army in 1649. Henry Cromwell, after his arrival in 1655, entrusted Morgan with confidential missions, regarding his as a loyal supporter.[41] Morgan may have had scientific leanings before coming to Ireland; in 1648 he was made a doctor of medicine at Oxford. Once in Ireland he was accounted a member of the Hartlib circle: in 1653 Petty called him the only man in Dublin 'curious in matters of art and learning', and regarded him as his 'chiefest friend'.[42] Morgan's main work in Ireland was political and administrative: his legal skills were particularly esteemed.[43]

Robert Wood did not come to Ireland until 1656. Born about 1622, Wood had been a contemporary of Robert Boyle at Eton College. His education was continued at Oxford and then, less conventionally, at Albury in Surrey with the famous mathematician, William Oughtred. Oughtred acknowledged Wood's help in writing *Clavis Mathematica*, the publication of which Wood supervised. Wood himself acquired a high reputation as a mathematician.[44] In 1649 he

[39]There are accounts of Child in G. L. Kittredge, *Robert Child, the Remonstrant* (Cambridge, 1919), reprinted from *Publications of the Colonial Soc. of Massachusetts*, xxi; and Turnbull, 'Robert Child', ibid. xxxvii (1947–51), 21–44.

[40]There is a life of Morgan in *D.N.B.* See also: *Diary of Thomas Burton*, ed. Rutt, iii. 248; Firth and Davies, i. 117–18, 124–5, 127.

[41]Nat. Lib. Ire., MS. 11,959, pp. 122, 138, 240–1; Brit. Mus., Lansdowne MS. 822, ff. 45, 84; *Thurloe State Papers*, v. 349; vi. 730; *Diary of Thomas Burton*, iv. 405.

[42]Sheffield Univ. Lib., Hartlib MSS. viii (h), Morgan to Sir Edward Foard, Chester, 22 Feb. 1653[4]; xxxiii, Wood to Hartlib, 2 Mar. 1658[9]; Yale Univ. Lib., Osborn collection, Petty to Hartlib, 1 Mar. 1653[4]; *The Works of Robert Boyle*, v. 259, 297; *The history of the Down Survey*, p. 263. Wood, *Fasti Oxonienses*, ii, col. 106.

[43]King's Inns, Black book, f. 130; *C.J., Ire.* i. 382.

[44]There is a life of Wood in *D.N.B.* See also Sheffield Univ. Lib., Hartlib MS. xxxiii, Wood to Hartlib, 1 July 1657 and 31 Aug. 1659; Bodl., MS. Aubrey, 6, f. 40; J. Aubrey, *Brief lives*, ed. A. Clark (Oxford, 1898), i. 120; William Oughtred,

was made a Fellow of Lincolń College, Oxford, by the parliamentary visitors. In Oxford he joined the experimental science club. In March 1656 he came to Hartlib's notice when he sent the latter a scheme for decimal coinage entitled 'Ten to One'. Quickly he became a regular and valued correspondent of Hartlib.[45]

A major break in Wood's career occurred in 1656 when he took up an unspecified post in Henry Cromwell's Dublin household. Possibly it was Wood's interest in currency that led to the appointment: fiscal reforms were under consideration in Ireland, and in October 1658 Wood seems to have been appointed receiver-general of revenue.[46] In Ireland he accompanied Henry Cromwell on tours of duty, and was also used on delicate missions to Scotland and England.[47] Wood was nominated professor of mathematics in the new college at Durham, but the project lapsed in 1660 before he had taken up the post.[48]

Wood praised the new learning, and applied his own knowledge of mathematics in several utilitarian schemes. However he did not jettison all traditional learning. For example, he praised his education at Oxford since it enabled him to methodize 'what others of excellent parts have invented'. Nor would he abandon the philosophical side of mathematics for the practical, arguing that without 'their speculative root in their owners head to sustaine them, I looke upon them but as cropt flowers in a pot, compared w[i]th those growing in the garden'.[49]

The last member of the group to be considered, Miles Symner, differs from the others because all his recorded career had been spent in Ireland. Although stimulated by the

Clavis Mathematica (Oxford, 1652), sig. [A6]; Oughtred, *The Key of the Mathematicks* (London, 1647), sig. [B6][v]; *Mr. William Oughtreds Key of the Mathematicks* (London, 1694), sig. [A1].

45 Sheffield Univ. Lib., Hartlib MS. xxvii (20); Purver, *The Royal Society: concept and creation*, p. 125, n. 109; *Diary and Correspondence of Dr. John Worthington*, ed. Crossley, ii. 72; C. Webster, 'Decimalization under Cromwell', *Nature*, ccxxix (12 Feb. 1971), 463.

46 C.B., Jennings transcripts, A/23, 13 Oct. 1658.

47 Sheffield Univ. Lib., Hartlib MS. vii (116), Wood to Hartlib, 13 Oct. 1658, Brit. Mus., Lansdowne MS. 823, f. 106; Hist. MSS. Comm., *Portland MSS.* i. 690.

48 Turnbull, *Research Review*, iii. 4—5.

49 Sheffield Univ. Lib., Hartlib MS. xxxiii, Wood to Hartlib, 28 Aug. 1657, 25 May 1659.

arrival of Hartlib's friends, his enthusiasm for experimental science had been acquired earlier. Symner was educated at Trinity College, Dublin, being a scholar there in 1626, and was apparently beneficed in the Church of Ireland in the 1630s.[50] By 1648 he was serving in the army in Ireland, becoming a major and chief engineer. In 1652 he was made professor of mathematics at Trinity College, Dublin. He was much concerned with the land survey and, after 1656, with setting out soldiers' estates. Symner evidently disliked the controversial side of this work and according to Petty was unable to attend to 'the clamorouse part'.[51]

In 1648 Symner set out his intellectual beliefs, declaring 'my scope is for reall and experimental learning. I abhor all those ventosities, froth and idle speculations of ye schooles.' He went on to criticize the futility of the scholastic curriculum at the universities, concluding 'if I have profitted but little more then they, the fault lyes in the sterility of my understanding, not the goodnes of my method'.[52] It remains mysterious where Symner had acquired his experimental method. One possibility was through Ussher's library and correspondents; another possible contact with Arnold Boate; a third was Symner's known Welsh connections; Sir Robert King may also have introduced Symner to the Hartlib circle in London.[53] At all events Symner fell eagerly on the group's schemes in Ireland during the 1650s.

This review of the careers of the Hartlib circle's members shows that all were given public employment in Ireland. As yet there has been no study of the role of Irish government service in the careers of Englishmen in the seventeenth century, so it would be unwise to argue that there were unique opportunities for advancement in Ireland of the Interregnum. However the scale of the land survey and redistribution was new, and clearly required unusual talents, such as Petty, Worsley, and Symner possessed. It is also clear that Petty, Wood, and Morgan were particularly close to Henry

[50]Symner's career and the problems connected with it are discussed in Barnard, 'Miles Symner and the new learning in seventeenth century Ireland', *JRSAI* cii.

[51]*The history of the Down Survey*, p. 208.

[52]Brit. Mus., Sloane MS. 427, f. 85, Symner to Sir Robert King (?), Dublin, 24 Oct. 1648. A copy of this letter in the Hartlib MSS. is endorsed 'To Sir Robert King'.

[53]Barnard, *JRSAI* cii.

Cromwell. This raises the possibility that Henry Cromwell's favour amounted to an official endorsement of the intellectual programme with which they were identified. I shall consider that question in more detail below. What is evident is that Ireland offered work appropriate to the group's technical skills. It was moreover a country especially attractive to pioneers and innovators. With existing institutions swept away, intellectual radicals (no less than religious or legal reformers) would be unencumbered by tradition and could test new notions and institutions. Estates awaited occupation and improvement; rich deposits of minerals were reputed to exist in Ireland. But it was not only material treasure that would be uncovered; there was a heady belief that 'the intellectual cabinets of nature', in Ireland as elsewhere, were about to yield up their secrets.[54]

Having sketched these careers, it is time to consider in more detail the activities of the Hartlib circle, first in public service, then in projects inspired directly by Hartlib in England, and finally in their private undertakings. I shall also examine activity outside the Hartlib circle. In conclusion I shall relate these projects and achievements to intellectual life after 1660, and particularly to the foundation of the Dublin Philosophical Society.

iii. The Land Surveys

The survey and redistribution of confiscated land was the major administrative and technical achievement of the Interregnum; its accomplishment owed much to Petty and the effeciency of his 'Down' survey between 1654 and 1656. Knowledge of the Down survey comes largely from Petty's own accounts, which perhaps overstress his originality. As yet there has been no modern assessment on the survey's general influence on the diffusion and improvement of technical and scientific skills in Ireland.[55]

54G. Boate, *Irelands naturall history*, sig. [A6]. Robert Child wrote that 'The great secrets that have a long time bin hid will shortly be manifested.' Sheffield Univ. Lib. xv, Child to Hartlib, 11 Mar. 1651[2].

55*The history of the Down Survey*; Lord E. Fitzmaurice, *The life of Sir William Petty*; Strauss, *Sir William Petty: portrait of a genius*. Cf. C. C. Gillespie, 'Physick and philosophy: a study of the influence of the College of Physicians of London upon the foundation of the Royal Society', *Journal of Modern History*, xix (1947), 222–3; Hoppen, *The common scientist*, p. 13.

The earlier plantations in Ireland had required the surveying and mapping of lands, although smaller in area, and so
stimulated improvements.[56] Petty was able to draw on the
skill of experienced men already in Ireland, like Symner and
Captain William Webb.[57] Furthermore Petty may have exaggerated the shortcomings of Worsley's work in 1653 and
1654. The novelty of the Down survey was its daunting scale
and the standards of accuracy to which it aspired. Many of
the problems were logistical, training and equipping sufficient
men, and organizing the limited resources to best advantage.
It appeared that Petty triumphantly overcame these difficulties for the survey was completed in March 1656. In all,
Petty alleged, 1,000 people were involved in the work. For
many of the routine tasks soldiers were used. To avoid the
delay and expense of relying on England for a supply of
equipment, Petty tried to foster instrument making in Dublin
and himself experimented with measuring dials.[58] However
mathematical instruments had already been bought in
England in 1653.[59] Moreover any improvement in technical
expertise among Irish instrument makers was short-lived:
after 1660 Irish scientists were still dependent on supplies
from England.[60]

Two official acts were intended to help the survey. In
1652 the parliamentary commissioners (not the trustees of
Trinity) appointed Symner professor of mathematics at
Trinity College. The motive was not any disinterested desire
to advance science, but 'forasmuch as there is a great

[56] W. Petty, *Hiberniae Delineatio*, ed. J. H. Andrews (Shannon, 1969), pp. 2–3.

[57] C. Molyneux, *An Account of the family and descendants of Sir Thomas Molyneux, Kt.* (Evesham, 1820), pp. 20, 23–4; S. Molyneux, 'Practical problems concerning the doctrin of projects', without title-page; W. P. Pakenham-Walsh, 'Captain Thomas Rotherham, Knt., and Nicholas Pinnar, directors of fortifications in Ireland, 1617–1644', *The Royal Engineers' Journal*, x (1909), 124–34. There was a watchmaker named William Webb in Dublin in 1649; for this and Capt. Webb's earlier activities: *Cal. S.P. Ire. 1633–47*, pp. 4–5, 86; G. Fennell, *A list of Irish watch and clock makers* (Dublin, 1963), p. 39.

[58] Yale Univ. Lib., Osborn collection, Petty to Hartlib, 22 Jan. 1653[4], 19 Feb. 1653[4]. There were enough professional surveyors in Ireland to protest at the use of soldiers: *The history of the Down Survey*, pp. 18, 20–1.

[59] Bodl., Rawlinson MS. A.208, pp. 456–457.

[60] *The Works of Robert Boyle*, v. 241–2; Southampton Corporation Rec. Office, DM 1/1, ff. 2, 6, 95–95ᵛ; Hist. MSS. Comm., *Eleventh report*, appendix, part iii, p. 3; E. G. R. Taylor, *Mathematical practitioners in Tudor and Stuart England* (Cambridge, 1954), p. 256.

occasion for surveying of lands in the country, and that there are divers ingenious persons, soldiers and others who are desirous to be instructed . . .'[61] Symner's lectures were not confined to members of the university, but how many future surveyors heard them is unknown. Also Symner was frequently absent from Dublin and we may therefore doubt the regularity of these lectures.

The second measure was the publication at Dublin in 1654 of a short manual for surveyors by Henry Osborne.[62] Since the only press at Dublin was monopolized by official publications, Osborne's book must have had government approval and was clearly intended to remedy the want of formal instruction among the surveyors.[63]

Obviously the survey encouraged the wider diffusion of technical skills in Ireland, but those skills did not have to be supported by any advanced or sophisticated intellectual substructure. For those already interested in new ideas it offered a chance of testing them, of public employment, and of personal profit.[64] Neither Petty nor Worsley was attracted to Ireland specifically to work on the survey, but some surveyors were. An example was Henry Osborne, author of the manual already mentioned. Osborne, a chandler from London, worked on the survey and settled in Ireland, where he amassed a considerable fortune.[65] Osborne developed wider scientific interests, particularly in astronomy, corre-

---

[61] T.C.D., General Registry from 1626, p. 95; Yale Univ. Lib., Osborn collection, Petty to Hartlib, 1 Mar. 1653[4].

[62] *A more exact way to delineate the plot of any spacious parcel of land* (Dublin, 1654).

[63] Petty wrote 'wee have no printing but of orders and declarations': Yale Univ. Lib., Osborn collection, 1 Mar. 1653[4].

[64] Worsley was paid £200 p.a. as surveyor-general, and received £200 in lands which were confirmed by Charles II. Brit. Mus., Additional MS. 19,833, f. 4; *An Act for the better execution*, p. 52. Petty said he arrived in Ireland with £480 and made £9,000 from the survey. He acquired lands in Kerry and Limerick. M. F. Cusack, *A history of the kingdom of Kerry* (London, 1871), pp. 284, 287; H. W. E. P. Fitzmaurice, marquess of Lansdowne, *Glanerought and the Petty-Fitzmaurices* (London, 1937), pp. 7–9; Petty, *Reflections*, p. 17; H. Wood, 'Sir William Petty and his Kerry estate', *JRSAI* 7th Ser. iv (1934), 22–44.

[65] In 1685 Osborne was said to have spent £4,000 on a purchase in England. Southampton Record Office, DM 1/1, f. 96; P.R.O., Dublin, Ferguson MS. xiii, p. 131; Brit. Mus., Egerton 1762, f. 158; T.C.D., MS. N.I.4a, pp. 488, 511, 513, 527, 541, 561; Hardinge, *Trans. Royal Irish Academy*, Antiquities, xxiv. 77–83; *A 'Census'*, ed. Pender, p. 482; Taylor, *Mathematical Practitioners*, p. 240.

sponding with Jeremy Shakerley and Robert Hooke, having his observations used by Halley and his work praised by William Molyneux.[66] Osborne was no doubt untypical, but in his case we do see the survey influencing the career of a man who went on to contribute to Ireland's intellectual life. In England, it has been argued, men with practical and technological preoccupations were important in bringing about the seventeenth-century scientific revolution. Almost all the champions of the new science in mid-seventeenth-century Ireland were men of this sort, deeply involved in utilitarian schemes, like the survey.[67] Other practical schemes in which they were involved were those suggested by Hartlib, which I shall now describe.

iv. Hartlib's Irish Projects

Three schemes made Hartlib pay close attention to what happened in Ireland during the Interregnum. He hoped to obtain a grant of Irish lands, the income of which would be used to finance a clearing-house for scientific and experimental work, there were also hopes of an additional grant of Irish land which would provide Hartlib himself with a secure income; and, finally, Hartlib was anxious to have Boate's *Naturall History* completed.

Hartlib had a vision of a reformed society, a utopia which he called 'macaria', and throughout his life he lobbied for its creation. In the perfect macaria there would be generous provision for the advancement of learning. Until macaria itself was realized, Hartlib worked for the establishment of its various parts. In particular he pinned his hopes on an office of address, or foreign correspondency, which would put on a more formal basis the work already done by Hartlib, acting as a central repository of information about current discoveries and inquiries. Only institute and execute the right research, collect and codify the results, and (it was thought) the

[66]Southampton Record Office, DM 1/1, ff. 88, 96, 98, 100, 116, 124, 131, 133; W. Molyneux, *Dioptricks*, (Dublin, 1692); Molyneux, *Sciothericum telescopicum* (Dublin, 1686), p. 6; R. T. Gunther, *Early science in Oxford*, vii (Oxford, 1930), 631; ibid. xii (Oxford, 1939), 151; *Philosophical transactions*, xiv (1684), 749.

[67]C. Webster, 'The authorship and significance of *Macaria*', *P. and P.* lvi (1972).

mysteries of the world would be revealed and all controversies determined. Such a correspondency, requiring foreign agents and codifiers of material, would be costly: it was to Ireland that Hartlib turned hopefully as a source of money. The scheme offered no particular benefit to Ireland itself. However the efforts to procure such a grant throw interesting light on the attitudes not only of Hartlib's followers but of the Irish administration.

In 1656 a definite plan was circulating and presented to the council of state. The intention was to purchase soldiers' debentures (redeemable against Irish land) to a maximum value of £10,000. The debentures would be satisfied with land either in Counties Carlow or Kilkenny, or in the towns reserved for the state. The income from this property would then be used to endow the foreign correspondency.[68] On 25 December 1656 the council of state referred the request to a committee, to be drawn from Scobell, Jessop, Gabriel Beck, Rushworth, Hartlib himself, and Richard Sydenham. Although nominated, Hartlib did not serve. The committee reported favourably on the scheme in August 1657, and Oliver Cromwell and the council of state authorized Henry Cromwell and the Irish council to contract with the petitioners.[69]

The proposals had been made in the names of Richard Eccleston, formerly a merchant in Hull,[70] and James Rand, a prominent apothecary employed at the hospitals of Ely and Savoy Houses in London.[71] They were not, however, the authors: the scheme's conception belonged to Hartlib, and he had been encouraged to turn to Ireland as a source of revenue by Worsley. Thus Worsley was concerned in the matter, and

68 There are accounts of the design in J. J. O'Brien, 'Commonwealth schemes for the advancement of learning', British Journal of Educational Studies, xvi (1968), 30—42; Turnbull, Hartlib, Dury and Comenius, pp. 54—6; C. Webster, ed., Samuel Hartlib and the advancement of learning (Cambridge, 1970), pp. 61—2. In general I have relied on the Hartlib MSS. and the sources cited below.

69 Sheffield Univ. Lib., Hartlib MS. xlvii (1, d). The maximum value of debentures to be bought was raised to £12,000.

70 Ibid. xlviii (1, f); Cal. S.P. Dom. 1653—4, p. 379; ibid., 1654, p. 136; ibid., 1660—1, p. 323; Hist. MSS. Comm., Fifth report, appendix, pp. 20, 22, 24; Hinton, The Eastland trade, pp. 123, 130.

71 Cal. S.P. Dom., 1652—3, pp. 333, 341, 445; ibid., 1653—4, pp. 44, 66; Webster, Ambix, xiv. 24, 36.

through him Robert Boyle and John Dury. Worsley was himself in London while the proposal was being considered by the committee; his lobbying was successful and the order made by the council of state was in the terms proposed by Worsley.[72]

The progress of the design now depended on its reception in Dublin. It was introduced to the Irish council in January 1658, by Colonel Hierome Sankey.[73] The council seemed favourable, and set up a committee. Again Worsley went to work behind the scenes, declaring 'the more testimonyes are given of it, the better and more repute it will have here'. Hartlib was asked to write to Lord Chancellor Steele; Robert Boyle to Petty; and Broghill was approached to urge it on Henry Cromwell, who was already believed to be friendly towards the scheme.[74] Worsley was optimistic about finding subscribers to buy the debentures, and himself contributed £700 or £800.[75] Then, in the summer of 1658, the design was checked. Worsley identified the cause of this as Petty, who was going to England to find out more about the project. Worsley was fearful lest Petty convert the scheme to his own ends, and accordingly instructed Hartlib and Robert Boyle how they were to answer Petty's questions. In particular Worsley stressed the importance of keeping control over the drafting of the foundation's statutes and over the nomination of the trustees. He wanted Hartlib, Dury, Robert Boyle, and John Sadler as trustees, and was anxious 'not to choose any in whom there shall be a suspicion of want of faithfulnes, religion and piety'.[76] Petty, Worsley suspected, 'had a mind to divert that revenue from both those persons and those upright, honest and sincere aimes, for w[hi]ch it was intended, and under the notion of the state's care to put himselfe into the management of it'. Worsley's experience of the way in which Petty had displaced him from the survey

[72] Sheffield Univ. Lib., Hartlib MS. xxxiii (2), Worsley to Hartlib, 26 May 1658; The Works of Robert Boyle, v. 269.

[73] Sheffield Univ. Lib., Hartlib MS. xlvii (3), letter of 27 Jan. 1657[8].

[74] Sheffield Univ. Lib., Hartlib MS. xlvii (3), letter of 10 Feb. 1657[8]; The Works of Robert Boyle, v. 277.

[75] Sheffield Univ. Lib., Hartlib MS. xxxiii (2), letter of 26 May 1658, which is quoted in The Works of Robert Boyle, v. 278–9. £3,600 worth of debentures were bought.

[76] Sheffield Univ. Lib., Hartlib MS. xxxiii (2), letter of 5 May 1658.

obviously increased his tendency to mistrust Petty. By June 1658 the scheme had been laid aside; Worsley had lost £700 or £800; and both he and Hartlib blamed Petty.[77]

Why was it that Petty undermined a scheme which emanated from the circle of which he had been a member and with whose objects he was still in sympathy? Two reasons can be offered: one personal; the other political. When Petty first heard of the scheme, he claimed that he thought it was the work of Eccleston and Rand, not of Hartlib, and accused them of plagiarizing a paper entrusted to Hartlib nine years earlier. Initially Petty's opposition was based on a misunderstanding, and once it had been removed Petty promised his help.[78] Yet that assistance was not forthcoming. Instead Petty proposed an alternative scheme: the establishment of 'a college or colony, of twenty able learned men, very good Latinists, of several nations . . . ' In conjunction with his long-held idea of a history of trades, Petty saw these schemes 'as the great pillars of the reformation of the world'. Hartlib was not enthusiastic. In December 1658 Petty produced another proposal, based on the adventurers' obligation to endow education in Ireland. It does seem that Petty made these suggestions so that he could regain the initiative and exclude his rival Worsley.[79]

Petty was able to stop the scheme for a foreign correspondency supported by Irish lands through his influence with Henry Cromwell. He was helped by the political affiliations of Worsley and his supporters. Worsley, as we know, was connected with the political opposition in Ireland; so too was Colonel Sankey who had introduced the scheme to the Irish council. Sankey was a Baptist suspected of duplicity by Henry Cromwell.[80] Another sign that this proposal had emanated from Henry Cromwell's opponents was the fact that Fleetwood's help had been sought in the summer of

[77]Sheffield Univ. Lib., Hartlib MS. xlvii (3), letters of 9 and 23 June 1658; *The Works of Robert Boyle*, v. 281.

[78]Ibid. v. 298; cf. O'Brien, *British Journal of Educational Studies*, xvi. 38, n. 1. For Petty's agreement with Hartlib on the need for an office of address: Sheffield Univ. Lib., Hartlib MS. vii (123); *The Advice of W. P. to Mr. Samuel Hartlib*.

[79]*The Works of Robert Boyle*, v. 280–1, 282.

[80]Brit. Mus., Lansdowne MS. 821, ff. 78, 246ᵛ, 271; A. J. Shirren, ' "Colonel Zanchy" and Charles Fleetwood', *Notes and Queries*, cxcviii (1953); *Thurloe State Papers*, iv. 408, 422, 506, 743; v. 303.

1658.[81] A further indication that the design was intended to advance the party was Worsley's insistence that the trustees should be faithful, religious, and pious. Once suspicions were entertained, his insistence could be interpreted as a wish to pack it with men hostile to Henry Cromwell's conservative policies. There was, then, enough evidence to represent this as a covert political design, and so discredit it with the ever-suspicious Henry Cromwell; there is little doubt that these suspicions were unfounded. What rankled with Petty and caused his original hostility was his exclusion from the scheme. It was easy enough in the factious atmosphere of 1658 to draw the project into religious and political controversy. It was, however, unfortunate that the poisoned relations between Worsley and Petty should have introduced these divisions and so defeated a hopeful scheme. Petty's behaviour over the project was an additional reason for the attack by Sankey and Worsley in the 1659 parliament.

One of the attractions of the correspondency was the income of £250 p.a. it gave Hartlib.[82] Hartlib's maintenance was a perennial problem for himself and his admirers. Ireland traditionally was regarded as booty for English conquerors, and in the Interregnum there were frequent grants of Irish land to reward Englishmen. If John Owen and Thomas Goodwin could be supported in this way, why not Hartlib? As early as 1656 Robert Wood was thinking along these lines.[83] With the failure of the ambitious scheme of a correspondency, the more modest plan of a grant of lands for Hartlib was revived. Men of influence in Ireland who had been introduced to Hartlib's work, like Harrison (Henry Cromwell's chaplain) and Dr. Henry Jones, were enlisted in the design.[84] Once again Broghill was asked to use his influence with Henry Cromwell, and a copy of one of Hartlib's works was to be presented to Henry Cromwell.[85]

[81] Sheffield Univ. Lib., Hartlib MS. xlvii (3), letter of 5 May 1658.

[82] *The Works of Robert Boyle*, v. 280

[83] Sheffield Univ. Lib., Hartlib MS. xxxiii, Wood to Hartlib, 13 May 1656; *Thurloe State Papers*, vi. 539, 558, 683, 763, 820. Cf. Firth, *The last years of the Protectorate*, ii. 161.

[84] Sheffield Univ. Lib., Hartlib MSS. xv, Wood to Hartlib, undated; xxxiii, same to same, 9 Feb. 1658[9]. Dr. Jones owned a copy of Hartlib's *Legacy*; R.C.B., MS. T.11. f. 100v.

[85] Sheffield Univ. Lib., Hartlib MS. xxxiii, Wood to Hartlib, 16 Nov. 1658, 4 Jan. 1658[9], 9 Feb. 1658[9], 21 Mar. 1658[9].

Eventually it was proposed that he be granted 371 acres of former church lands in County Limerick. On 29 April 1659 the Irish council authorized a lease of twenty-one years at an annual rent of £5 p.a. As the income from the lands was only £20 p.a., it was no compensation for the income lost with the failure of the correspondency.[86] Even this meagre competence was denied Hartlib. The great seal of Ireland had not been affixed to the order before the political changes halted all legal proceedings. All Hartlib received from Ireland were gifts of money from Miles Symner and Dr. Henry Jones.[87]

Hartlib's third project, the completion of Boate's *Naturall History*, offered some benefits to Ireland itself. The *Naturall History* has been recognized as marking a major change in the scientific description of Ireland.[88] In place of legend and hearsay, Boate relied on exact observation, and produced a sober and well-organized account which introduced new standards of accuracy. Boate's book had a polemical as well as scientific purpose. It was intended to encourage a new plantation of Ireland, as Hartlib announced on the title-page, 'for the common good of Ireland, and more especially for the benefit of the adventurers and planters therein'. The political purpose would have appeared most clearly in the book's fourth section, projected but never written by Boate, which would treat of 'the natives of Ireland, and their old fashions, laws, and customes', showing 'the great paines taken by the English, ever since the conquest, for to civilize them, and to improve the country'.[89]

Boate's *Naturall History* was an admirable example of the useful application of scientific knowledge. Whoever continued it needed to combine exact inquiry with enthusiastic support of the Protestant interest in Ireland. Hartlib wanted the book completed because it would contribute to Ireland's resettlement, and encourage 'not only . . . the calling in of exiled Bohemians and other Protestants also, and

86 Ibid., Hartlib MS. xxxiii, Wood to Hartlib, 20 Apr. 1659, and 11 May 1659.
87 Ibid., Hartlib MS. xxxiii, Wood to Hartlib, 29 June, 31 Aug., and 29 Oct. 1659, 5 Dec. 1660, 19 Jan. 1660[1], 23 Mar. 1660[1].
88 F. V. Emery, 'Irish geography in the seventeenth century', *Irish Geography*, iii (1958), 264–7; Y. M. Goblet, *La Transformation de la géographie politique d'Irlande au xviie siècle dans les cartes et essais anthrogéographiques de Sir William Petty* (Paris, 1930), i. 54.
89 Boate, *Irelands naturall history*, sig. [a6]^v.

happily ... the invitation of some well affected out of the
Low Countries ...'[90] He regarded the collection of accurate
information about Ireland's geography as the prerequisite of
successful husbandry, and thus the basis of trade and prosperity.

The first two men approached by Hartlib to finish the
book were Robert Child and Arnold Boate. Child felt
hampered by his recent arrival in Ireland and because the
country's unsettled condition prevented him travelling beyond Lisburn. Nevertheless he set to work investigating the
flora and geology around Lisburn, and by 1653 could report
that he had 'got some stubble for ye Irish naturall history'.[91]
Child was continuing Boate's political purpose, taking 'notice
of ye customes of the Irish and English and Scots and
[making] some politick observations, concerning the settlement of Ireland'.[92] Child's isolation and lack of books was
mitigated by the arrival of Petty and Worsley. Both were
asked 'to take notice of what so ever worth the observation
occurreth, yt wee may by little and little perfectly understand these parts'.[93] Hartlib gave direction to these inquiries
by drawing up a list of 'interrogatories', alphabetically arranged questions about natural phenomena. These were
printed as an appendix to the 1652 edition of the *Legacy of
Husbandry* and were dispatched to Ireland. Hartlib set great
store by having the interrogatories fully answered.[94]

Another hopeful sign had been Arnold Boate's decision to
return from the continent to Ireland. He had supplied his
brother with much of the material for the *Naturall History*;
he was also an enthusiastic supporter of the Protestant
interest.[95] On his way back to Ireland, late in 1653, Arnold
Boate died. Hartlib was despondent and called upon Child

90 Ibid., sig. A3–A3ᵛ. So eager was Hartlib to attract settlers from Holland that
he proposed the book's translation into Low Dutch: *The Works of Robert Boyle*,
v. 264; *Thurloe State Papers*, ii. 61.

91 Sheffield Univ. Lib., Hartlib MS. xv, Child to Hartlib, 29 Aug. 1652 and 2
Feb. 1652[3].

92 Ibid., Hartlib MS. xv, Child to Hartlib, 29 Aug. 1652.

93 *The Works of Robert Boyle*, v. 259, 261; Sheffield Univ. Lib., Hartlib MS. xv,
Child to Hartlib, 2 Feb. 1652[3].

94 S. Hartlib, *An appendix to the Legacie of Husbandry*, p. [102] ; *The Works of
Robert Boyle*, v. 261, 264; *Thurloe State Papers*, ii. 61.

95 T.C.D., MS. F.2.3., ff. 283, 287–287ᵛ; Bodl., Clarendon state papers, 46, ff.
8, 34, 69, 109, 132ᵛ, 196ᵛ.

and Robert Boyle, temporarily in Ireland, to carry on the
work. But early in 1654 Child died and Boyle returned to
England.[96]   Although Petty had sent Hartlib some im-
pressions of Ireland, he and Worsley were too occupied with
public business to take on the *Naturall History*.[97]

In 1656 Hartlib's hopes recovered with Robert Wood's
arrival in Ireland. Wood was willing to finish Boate's book,
but was hampered (as Child had been) by his unfamiliarity
with the country. Tours of duty with Henry Cromwell
gradually overcame that impediment, until by October 1658
Wood had visited three-quarters of Ireland's counties.[98]
Rather than waiting Wood had sought assistance in 1656, and
received it from Miles Symner, whose work as chief engineer
and surveyor of fortifications had taken him on extensive
travels.[99]   Through Wood and Lady Ranelagh Symner was
drawn into Hartlib's orbit. Hartlib's published schemes for
the practical and profitable application of knowledge came as
a revelation to Symner. He read Boate's *Naturall History* and
Hartlib's interrogatories; eagerly he agreed to correct 'diverse
faults' in the *Naturall History* and to help Wood answer the
interrogatories.[100]   Symner quickly replaced Wood as the
principal worker on the project, but his official duties left
him little time to jot down his observations. Symner sent
four sheets of corrections to the *Naturall History* to Hartlib.
Following the alphabetical format of the interrogatories,
these revealed Symner's knowledge of Ireland and his capacity for direct observation. Although this new material
reached Hartlib, it was not incorporated in a revised edition
of the *Naturall History*.[101]   Of Symner's more ambitious

96 *The Works of Robert Boyle*, v. 259; R. E. W. Maddison, *The life of the
honourable Robert Boyle, F.R.S.* (London, 1969), p. 84.

97 Yale Univ. Lib., Osborn collection, Petty to Hartlib, 22 Oct. 1652, 19 Feb.
1653[4].

98 Sheffield Univ. Lib., Hartlib MSS. vii (116), Wood to Hartlib, 13 Oct. 1658;
xxxiii, same to same, 27 May 1657 and 7 Jan. 1657[8]; xv, same to same, 26 May
1658.

99 Ibid., xxxiii, Wood to Hartlib, 8 Apr. 1657; Barnard, *JRSAI* cii. 135.

100 Sheffield Univ. Lib., Hartlib MS. xxxiii, Wood to Hartlib, 13 May 1656
recte 1657.

101 Ibid., Hartlib xxxiii, Wood to Hartlib, 13 May 1657, 24 June 1656 *recte*
1657, 27 July 1657; xv, Wood to Hartlib, 5 May 1658. The sheets are in Hartlib
MS. lxii (45). The first is missing.

undertaking, to supply the unwritten sections, there is no trace and it is unlikely that he ever started on them.

Hartlib's death in 1662 removed the prime mover in this scheme. However this was not quite the end of the story. There is an uncanny parallel between the work of the Boates, Child, Symner, and Wood, and the collection of material about Ireland's natural history set in train by William Molyneux in 1682.[102] Molyneux, like Hartlib before him, had questions printed for his helpers' guidance. The leading spirit of the Dublin Philosophical Society duplicated, unconsciously, work done by the Hartlib group in the 1650s.[103] It was not the only sphere in which this happened.

Tangible results were few: no foreign correspondency was created; Hartlib received no Irish lands; Boate's *Naturall History* remained incomplete. Yet the indirect effects were considerable: schemes in England involved close interest in Irish events; Hartlib's correspondents in Ireland kept in close touch with him, and as a result received much news of scientific and educational designs; the members of the circle in Ireland were stimulated in their inquiries; and, finally, the Irish administration was made aware of Hartlib's projects. For more concrete evidence of the advancement of learning we must turn to the circle's private activities.

v. Private achievements

The activities of Child, Wood, Symner, Petty, Morgan, and Worsley were multifarious. Intellectual curiosity, Ireland's practical needs, and hope of profit were mixed in these endeavours. They also showed the complexity of the intellectual background.[104] Worsley admired Paracelsus, and was interested in alchemical theories and astrology;[105] Petty spent much time on inventions like his system of double-writing, a double-bottomed ship, and competing with Worsley to invent a dial which would convey the time to all

102Hoppen, *The common scientist*, pp. 21–2, 200–1.

103A copy of Molyneux's queries is in Bodl., Ashmole MS. 1820 a, f. 221, and is reprinted in Hoppen, *The common scientist*, pp. 200–1.

104Cf. P. M. Rattansi, 'The intellectual origins of the Royal Society', *Notes and Records of the Royal Society*, xxiii (1968).

105Sheffield Univ. Lib., Hartlib MS. xlii, (1), letters of 14 Feb. 1655[6]; 14 Oct. 1657.

five senses;[106] Symner, on Robert Boyle's behalf, tried to discover whether or not geese were generated from barnacles (he suspected they were);[107] Robert Wood published a plan for calendar reform.[108] Such interests were inseparable from their lasting achievements.

Public employment tended to lessen private inquiries as the decade progressed.[109] Shortly after arriving in Ireland Petty had joined Robert Boyle in demonstrating the circulation of the blood. Boyle, in Ireland in 1653, dissected animals; Anthony Morgan was allowed the bodies of prisoners after execution for dissection, and experimented with dials with his friend Petty.[110] Worsley renewed his interest in manufacturing saltpetre, needed for gun-powder, which had engaged his attention in the previous decade. In 1654 he contracted with the Irish administration to supply 10,000 lbs. of saltpetre.[111] Symner kept alive interest in publishing Johnson's universal character, a design encouraged by Bishop Bedell and of interest to Hartlib.[112] There were suggestions that an office of address be established at Dublin to collect and disseminate information on Irish trade. Robert Wood advised a friend to undertake this work and was given by Petty a catalogue of particulars relating to Ireland's contemporary trade.[113]

Three areas of activity deserve special attention — husbandry, astronomy and medicine — and will illustrate the real

106 H. W. E. P. Fitzmaurice, marquess of Lansdowne, *The Double-bottom or twin-hulled ship of Sir William Petty* (Oxford, 1931); W. Petty, *A declaration concerning the newly invented art of double writing* (London, 1648); Yale Univ. Lib., Osborn collection, Petty to Hartlib, 22 Sept. 1657.

107 Royal Society of London, Boyle letters, vii, f. 49; Sheffield Univ. Lib., Hartlib MSS. xv, Wood to Hartlib, 9 Feb. 1658[9]; xxxiii, same to same, 2 Mar. 1658[9]; xxxi (14); *The Works of Robert Boyle*, v. 261.

108 R. Wood, *A New Al-moon-ac for ever* (London, 1680), and *Novus Annus Luni-solaris* (London, 1681).

109 Sheffield Univ. Lib., Hartlib MS. xv, Wood to Hartlib, 26 May 1658; Petty, *Reflections*, p. 20.

110 *The Works of Robert Boyle*, v. 242; King's Inns, Dublin, Prendergast MS. i, p. 41; Yale Univ. Lib., Osborn collection, Petty to Hartlib, 22 Jan. 1653[4], 19 Feb. 1653[4], 28 June 1654.

111 Sheffield Univ. Lib., Hartlib MSS. lxvi (15) and lxxi (11c); *Analecta Hibernica*, xv. 249; *The Works of Robert Boyle*, v. 232–3, 259; *L.J.* viii. 573; Petty, *Reflections*, p. 107; Webster, *Trans. Royal Hist. Soc.*, 5th Ser. xxiv.

112 Barnard, *JRSAI* cii.

113 Sheffield Univ. Lib., Hartlib MS. xxxiii, Wood to Hartlib, 7 Jan. 1656[7] and 8 Apr. 1657.

advances made. The publication and completion of Boate's *Naturall History* was intended to improve Irish agriculture. Robert Child, who had written part of Hartlib's *Legacy of Husbandry*, first showed interest in agricultural innovation. From Ulster he reported enthusiasm for schemes of improvement and a thirst for new information. Bogs were being drained; flax, hops, sainfoin, Flanders clover-grass, and woad were all being cultivated; and fruit-trees were planted. The need of reconstruction after the war partly explained this activity; but there was too a genuine interest in new methods.[114] Worsley and Robert Wood continued agricultural experiments: with cultivation of fruit-trees and of madder,[115] better ways of fermentation,[116] rearing silk-worms,[117] and cures for animals' ailments.[118] Worsley and Petty talked of establishing a physic garden at Dublin. Although nothing came of the scheme, Worsley planted over a thousand rose bushes in his own garden.[119]

Astronomy progressed in this period thanks to Symner and Wood. In 1648 Symner was making astronomical observations in Ireland. To help these inquiries Symner constructed a quadrant of six-foot radius, and was considering making a sextant.[120] Contact with Hartlib helped Symner in these studies: he was sent a paper by Robert Boyle on telescopes; in March 1657 he received 'with a very hearty welcome' a copy of Hevelius's *Dissertatio, De Nativa Saturni Facie*, sent by Hartlib. Symner was stimulated to inquire after Hevelius's *Selenographia*, a copy of which the author

114 Sheffield Univ. Lib., Hartlib MS. xv, Child to Hartlib, 13 Nov. 1651, 23 June 1652, 29 Aug. 1652. Cf. Kenneth Dewhurst, 'The genesis of state medicine in Ireland', *The Irish Journal of Medical Science*, 6th Ser. no. 368 (Aug. 1956), pp. 373–4.

115 Sheffield Univ. Lib., Hartlib MSS. vii (116); xxi (8); lxx(7).

116 Ibid., Hartlib MS. xlii, letter of 28 Aug. 1657.

117 Ibid., Hartlib MSS. xxi (8), John Moore to Hartlib, Dublin, 25 Jan. 1654[?5]; lxvi (27); lxi (f).

118 Ibid., Hartlib MS. xxxiii, Wood to Hartlib, 9 Feb. 1658[9] and 11 May 1659.

119 Ibid., Hartlib MS. xv, letter of 28 Oct. 1653; lv (21); lxx (7); cf. E. St. J. Brooks, 'Henry Nicholson: first lecturer in botany and the earliest physic garden', *Hermathena*, lxxxiv (1954).

120 Brit. Mus., Sloane MS. 427, f. 85.

was said to have presented to Trinity College.[121]   Hartlib also
communicated a letter from Huygens in which his recent
observations of Saturn were described. Symner made a copy
of this letter for himself. Similarly Symner copied a paper
from Mercator which Hartlib had sent to him and Wood.[122]
Another indication of Symner's serious interest in astronomy
was the tribute paid by Thomas Salusbury in his translation of
Galileo to 'those two able mathematicians', Symner and
Wood. Towards the end of the century Archbishop William
King referred to 'the observations made by Dr. Sommers,
that fixed the latitude of Dublin at 53°20''. These calculations, made at Trinity College, were presumably by
Symner.[123]   Henry Osborne, the surveyor who had come to
Ireland in the 1650s, also displayed a high proficiency in
astronomy.[124]   Yet when William Molyneux started to interest himself in the subject in 1682 he lamented the lack of
astronomers in Dublin, although he admitted that the city
contained several knowledgeable mathematicians. Molyneux
believed that in 'the promotion of astronomy . . . little has
yet been done'; his judgement was the result of ignorance of
Symner's, Wood's, and Osborne's work.[125]

The history of medicine presents a different aspect. Before
1649 three traditions could be discerned. First, there were
the doctors of the native Irish, who used traditional herbal
remedies. Robert Child dismissed them as 'generally illiter-
ate'.[126]   Secondly, there were Catholic doctors drawn from
the Old English families and practising among them, who
were educated at continental universities. The best-known

121 Sheffield Univ. Lib., Hartlib MS. xxxiii, Wood to Hartlib, 3 Mar. 1657, 2
Mar. 1657[8]. Neither of the copies of *Selenographia* now at T.C.D. has any sign
of being a presentation copy.

122 These are bound into a T.C.D. copy of Hevelius's *Dissertatio* (pressmark:
L.aa.5); Sheffield Univ. Lib., Hartlib MS. xxxiii, Wood to Hartlib, 8 Apr. 1657.
No contact between Huygens and Hartlib is recorded in *Hartlib, Dury and
Comenius*, nor is the letter in *Ouevres complètes de Christiaan Huygens* (The
Hague, 1888–1950).

123 T. Salusbury, *Mathematical Collections and Translations* (London, 1661),
i, sig. *2; *Correspondence of scientific men of the seventeenth century*, ed. S. J.
Rigaud (Oxford, 1841), p. 241.

124 See above, pp. 228–9.

125 Southampton Record Office, DM 1/1, ff. 16^v, 95^v.

126 Francis Shaw, 'Irish medical men and philosophers', in *Seven Centuries of
Irish Learning, 1000–1700*, ed. B. O'Cuiv (Dublin, 1961), pp. 87–101; Sheffield
Univ. Lib., Hartlib MS. xv, Child to Hartlib, 2 Feb. 1652[3].

member of this group was Thomas Arthur, educated at Bordeaux and Rheims, who treated Ussher before 1641. He escaped transplantation in the 1650s and attended Henry Cromwell and other leading members of the administration.[127]

A third group of doctors consisted of Protestants, drawn to Ireland by posts in the army. After 1641 the needs of the Protestant army led to the appointment of a succession of practitioners with high skills and interest in medical reform: Worsley, Arnold and Gerard Boate, and Petty. Another hermetic physician who came to Ireland was Dr. John Unmussig (or Brün), a doctor of medicine of Franecker and widely travelled in Europe. In August 1656 he was appointed physician for the Cork precinct, and rented property in County Cork in 1663.[128] The tradition of employing advanced practitioners continued after 1660 with William Currer's appointment. Warfare in seventeenth-century Ireland gave scope to improved techniques in medicine, as it did in engineering and fortification.

Doctors of high talents served in Ireland, but the principal need was rudimentary medical care and not advanced ideas. The disputes between the adherents of the traditional, Galenic medicine and the new hermetic chemical physicians taking place in England during the Interregnum, were a luxury which Dublin could not afford.[129] Demands for reform in Ireland centred on administrative and institutional changes. Petty, for example, wanted 'an academick hospital in Dublin, for the study and administration of medicine', which would realize his desire for a 'noscomium academicum', or teaching hospital, first expressed in 1648.[130]

---

[127] There are accounts of Arthur in *D.N.B.*; M. Lenihan, 'The fee-book of a physician of the 17th century', *Jnl. Kilkenny and S.E. of Ireland Archaeological Soc.*, N.S. vi (1867); J. D. H. Widdess, *A history of the Royal College of Physicians of Ireland 1654–1963* (Edinburgh and London, 1963). See also: *The Transplantation to Connacht, 1654–58* ed. Simington, pp. xx, 101. A list of Arthur's books shows a preponderance of Galenic and Hippocratic works. He also owned works by Erasmus and by Ramon Lull. Brit. Mus., Additional MS. 31,885, ff. 8–13.

[128] Nat. Lib. Ire., MS. 11,961, p. 127; Bodl., Rawlinson MS. B.508, f. 13; Webster, *Ambix*, xiv. 31, n. 72.

[129] Ibid., pp. 16–41.

[130] Petty, *Reflections*, p. 164; *The Advice of W.P.*, p. 9; cf. H. W. E. P. Fitzmaurice, *The Petty Papers*, ii. 172 ff.

There is no evidence that the military hospital in Dublin in the 1650s reflected Petty's ideas.[131]

The supply of trained doctors in the 1650s was inadequate. Joseph Waterhouse claimed he was the only physician who accompanied the English army in 1649.[132] Although the supply improved slightly, the regime had to use Catholic doctors. Efforts were made to provide doctors for the poor.[133]

New medical methods made little visible headway. The main advance of the decade was institutional and Hartlib's followers had no part in it. In England the college of physicians was being assaulted by reformers as a monopolistic preserve of outmoded and corrupt practices. It was a measure of how far behind London Ireland lagged that progress should consist of the establishment in Dublin of such a college. The Dublin College of Physicians was not formally founded until 1667. However its origins could be traced back directly to 1654, when John Stearne had established a separate medical faculty at Trinity College.[134] Stearne was the driving force behind the College. A great-nephew of Archbishop Ussher, he had been educated partly at Oxford and Cambridge, where he met exponents of the new science (notably Seth Ward). His own work, however, showed no sympathy for their outlook. Stearne was a traditionalist, and there was no question of the College of Physicians being consciously organized as a vehicle for new methods,[135] although some of its first Fellows (Petty and Currer) were innovators.

131 T.C.D., MS. F.2.1., ff. 168, 170; Dunlop, ii. 473; Bodl., Rawlinson MS. A.208, pp. 403, 426, 431, 440, 453; C. H. Firth, *Cromwell's Army*, paperback ed. (London, 1962), p. 261 and n. 2.

132 Brit. Mus., Lansdowne MS. 823, ff. 58, 282, 284, 285.

133 C.B., Jennings transcripts A/1, 7 May 1655, A/5, 22 Jan. 1655[6], A/6, 4 May 1655, A/16, 20 Oct. 1659, 1.E.10.85, 11 Aug. 1654, 8 Jan. 1654[5]; Brit. Mus., Egerton 1762, f. 166; King's Inns, Dublin, Prendergast MS. ii, p. 270; Nat. Lib. Ire., MS. 11,961, p. 127; *The Transplantation to Connacht*, ed. Simington, p. 125.

134 T.C.D., General registry from 1640, p. 65; Webster, *Ambix*, xiv. 16–21; Widdess, *A history of the Royal College of Physicians of Ireland*, pp. 6–10, 14–16.

135 Stearne, *Anima Medela*, sig. [a4]ᵛ–[b2]; *Clarissimi Viri, Adriani Heereboordi, Philosophiae Professoris ordinarii, Disputationum De Concursu Examen, A Johanne Stearne* (Dublin, 1660).

Educational institutions in Cromwellian Ireland were untouched by the new learning. Trinity College's curriculum was firmly based on Aristotle throughout the Interregnum;[136] the second college was not planned by supporters of experimental science and seems to have been conceived in entirely traditional terms. Yet, as we have seen, public employment attracted or kept Hartlib's friends in Ireland. Did this mean that special efforts had been made to patronize them? Wood praised Henry Cromwell as 'a passionat and great lover of learning';[137] his initiative in purchasing Ussher's library, in setting on foot the project of the second college, and in bestowing Cork House have already appeared; so too has the fact that Petty, Wood, and Morgan had close connections with him. Henry Cromwell, chancellor of Dublin University, was a patron of learning, but not of the new learning.

The members of the Harlib circle, like Broghill, Worth, and the Scottish Presbyterians, had a programme. In so far as it made Ireland more secure and prosperous, and strengthened Protestantism, Henry Cromwell might accept it. But there is no evidence that in using Hartlib's friends he was endorsing their schemes of intellectual reform. Men of ability and loyalty were in short supply. The services of Wood, Petty, Morgan, and Symner (but not Worsley) were welcomed. So far as Henry Cromwell was concerned, Petty's scientific principles were important only because they made him a better administrator.

The progress of new ideas depended on the presence in Ireland of Harlib's friends. The Cromwellian resettlement gave them the chance of public employment in Ireland. Otherwise the state did little to help their schemes. There has been a tendency to see the king's restoration in 1660 bringing down a curtain: after 1660 there are different actors in a new play. With scientific activity (as indeed with political and

136The notebook of Henry Dodwell (who entered T.C.D. in 1656) supports the view that the curriculum was unchanged. Bodl., MS. St. Edmund Hall 16 (I am grateful to Dr. K. T. Hoppen for bringing this to my notice); R. Bolton, *A translation of the Charter and Statutes of Trinity College, Dublin.* There is no evidence to support the contrary view expressed in D. A. Webb and R. B. McDowell, 'Courses and teaching in Trinity College, Dublin, during the first 200 years', *Hermathena,* lxix (1947), 15–16.

137Sheffield Univ. Lib., Hartlib MS. xxxiii, Wood to Hartlib, 3 Mar. 1656[7].

religious life) this was not so. In this final section I shall show how the Hartlib circle continued their work in Ireland and helped to make possible the Dublin Philosophical Society.[138]

vi. The Hartlib circle and the Dublin Philosophical Society

The champions of the new science in Ireland lost only one adherent: Benjamin Worsley, who left the country permanently in 1659 to resume his work on commercial and colonial policy in England. He remained friendly with Lady Ranelagh and his Irish lands were confirmed.[139] Sir Anthony Morgan was elected to the Irish parliament of 1661; he too had Irish estates. In 1664 he decided to return to England. In London he had been elected a founder Fellow of the Royal Society, and was much at its meetings. He died in 1668.[140]

Three members of the circle kept close connections with Ireland and helped in the further diffusion of scientific ideas. Symner resumed his career in the church of Ireland, helped by his kinsmen, Dr. Henry Jones and Dr. Ambrose Jones, both bishops. He also retained offices at Trinity College, acting as its auditor, and lecturing in mathematics until 1683. He died in 1686.[141] Immediately after 1660 Wood, who was ejected from his Oxford Fellowship, was helped by Dr. Worth, now bishop of Killaloe, and Lady Ranelagh. He had little difficulty weathering the political changes. As early as 1661 he was appointed to the Irish council of trade, and threw himself enthusiastically into questions of banks and credit.[142] Wood developed his earlier interests in fiscal matters, submitting memoranda on Irish trade and the customs, and becoming comptroller and accountant-general in

138 See the fuller argument in T. C. Barnard, 'The Hartlib Circle and the origins of the Dublin Philosophical Society', *Irish Historical Studies*, xix (1974).

139 *The Works of Robert Boyle*, v. 563; K. H. D. Haley, *The first earl of Shaftesbury* (Oxford, 1968), pp. 255–8, 260, 284, 289–90; E. E. Rich. 'The first earl of Shaftesbury's colonial policy', *Trans. Royal Hist. Soc.* 5th Ser. vii (1957), 53. 61.

140 Brit. Mus., Additional Charter 7055 (Morgan's will); *C.J. Ire.*, i. 382, 660; *Cal. S.P. Ire. 1663–5*, p. 131; Royal Society of London, Journal book, i. 45, 50, 66–7, 87, 88, 104–5, 111, 113, 115, 116, 129, 141, 142, 143, 151–2, 156, 159, 167, 173, 178, 180, 181, 190, 193, 226, 302.

141 Barnard, *JRSAI* cii.

142 Sheffield Univ. Lib., Hartlib MS. xxxiii, 31 Oct. 1661 and 23 Mar. 1661[2]; *Cal. S.P. Ire. 1669–70*, p. 683; ibid. *Dom. 1678*, pp. 552–3, 578.

Ireland.[143]   Wood was also licensed to practise medicine. From Ireland he corresponded with John Wallis, the mathematician, and himself composed mathematical papers.[144] He divided his time between Ireland and England, where he was much in the company of scientists, and in 1681 was elected a Fellow of the Royal Society. In 1680 Wood was appointed mathematical master at Christ's Hospital, recommended as 'a very learned person and perticularly in the mathematics . . . nor does he deserve honors for his universal learning only, but for his general knowledge of men, of government, of ye affairs of ye world, and very extraordinarily of ye revenue'. Wood proved negligent and had to be dismissed, after which he returned to Dublin and his Irish employments, dying there in 1685.[145]

Petty's talents were also sought by the restored royalists in Ireland. But although he participated in public affairs, he never again enjoyed the high favour Henry Cromwell had allowed him. His scientific work was diffused over a wide area, perhaps too wide because he never repeated the solid achievement of the Down survey.[146]   Petty was a Fellow of the Royal Society and often in England. These three men supply a link between the activities of the 1650s and those stimulated by the foundation of the Dublin Philosophical Society in 1683. Such a link was not, however, recognized by the creator of the Philosophical Society, William Molyneux. He bemoaned the fact that he lived in a kingdom 'barren of all things', and founded the Society to overcome that isolation.[147]   This suggested that nothing had changed in the thirty years since Petty and Robert Boyle had complained that Ireland was 'a barbarous country' and an 'obscure

[143] Lascelles, *Liber munerum publicorum Hiberniae*, i, part ii, pp. 132, 136, 137; *The Correspondence of Henry Hyde, earl of Clarendon*, ed. S. W. Singer (London, 1828), i. 245, 567.

[144] Royal Society of London, Boyle letters, vii, no. 25; Boyle papers, xxv, pp. 145−50; Aubrey, *Brief lives*, ii. 147; *Philosophical transactions*, no. 3 (London, 1681), pp. 45−7; Wood, *Fasti Oxonienses*, ii, column 168.

[145] Bodl., Rawlinson MSS. A.178, f. 133; A.183, f. 7; A.194, f. 258ᵛ; E. H. Pearce, *Annals of Christ's Hospital* (London, 1908), pp. 110−12; *The life, journals and correspondence of Samuel Pepys*, ed. J. T. Smith (London, 1841), i. 286−7; *The correspondence of Isaac Newton* ed. J. F. Scott (Cambridge, 1967), iv. 113.

[146] Lansdowne, *The Petty-Southwell correspondence*, p. 61.

[147] Southampton Record Office, DM 1/1, ff. 2, 95ᵛ.

corner', and had informally organized 'the visible church of philosophers' to lighten the darkness.[148] Perhaps neither Petty's nor Molyneux's complaints should be taken at face value. Both men perhaps exaggerated their originality by belittling what had gone before. There had certainly been scientific activity in Ireland before Petty's arrival or the Philosophical Society's foundation. Also to expect their interests to be shared by more than a few kindred spirits was unrealistic. By 1683 Molyneux was able to find sufficient men to constitute a society, and to put their inquiries on a formal basis, with rules and papers read and recorded. It was the institutionalization of activity that was new, not the activity's nature, which was essentially the same. Many of the Philosophical Society's inquiries repeated and even duplicated the activities of the 1650s.[149]

The historian of the Dublin Philosophical Society, following William Molyneux, has tended to play down the earlier activities, suggesting that the Society's foundation initiated something new.[150] I believe that the Society is more convincingly seen as the culmination of an interest in the new science which had been growing steadily in Ireland at least since the 1630s and which received a great fillip in the 1650s. This earlier influence was both direct and indirect. Wood was still in Dublin on the fringes of the Society, known to Molyneux, the friend of George Tollet (another member) and the partner of James Bonnell (a third member).[151] Symner had lectured at Trinity College where Molyneux was an undergraduate; he was succeeded as mathematics lecturer by St. George Ashe (an important figure in the Society); he had collaborated with Adam Molyneux (William's uncle) on surveys and had been a colleague of Samuel Molyneux (William's father) in the army.[152] Above all it was Petty who linked the Hartlib circle with Molyneux and his friends. Petty, 'in whose conversation' Molyneux was 'sometimes

148 *The Works of Robert Boyle*, v. 241, 297; Yale Univ. Lib., Osborn collection, Petty to Hartlib, 22 Oct. 1652, 22 Jan. 1653[4].

149 Barnard, *Irish Historical Studies*, xix.

150 Hoppen, *The common scientist*, pp. 7, 11.

151 Ibid., p. 114; Southampton Record Office, DM 1/1, f. 73ᵛ; Royal Society of London, Boyle papers, xxv. 145; Taylor, *Mathematical practitioners*, p. 270.

152 Barnard, *JRSAI* cii. 140; Barnard, *Irish Historical Studies*, xix.

happy', became first President of the Philosophical Society in 1684, and tried, unsuccessfully, to fashion the Society to reflect his own preoccupations.[153]   This appointment acknowledged, if unconsciously, the debt to the Hartlib circle.

It has been argued that there was another important difference between the work of the 1650s and the 1680s, that the former lacked an 'organic relation to Irish life'.[154] Greater prosperity, the growth of Dublin, and the establishment of a Protestant political ascendancy may all have made possible the Philosophical Society's foundation, creating a class of Protestant gentry interested in experiment. But such interest had not been lacking earlier. The patronage in the 1630s and 1640s has been mentioned. In the Interregnum it was Colonel Arthur Hill who invited Robert Child to Lisburn; two of Hartlib's closest associates were members of the Boyle family, Lady Ranelagh and Robert Boyle; Lord Broghill and Lord Cork did what they could to help Hartlib's designs; Dr. Henry Jones showed interest in the schemes; Miles Symner's education and career had been in Ireland. The Hartlib circle was not without roots in Irish Protestant society. After 1660 we find Irish Protestants, like Lord Anglesey, Lord Massareene (formerly Sir John Clotworthy), and Sir Robert Southwell, among the Fellows of the Royal Society. Obviously they were not scientists, but it denotes some interest, and meant that they met scientists. A further indication of continuing interest in Hartlib's and other schemes was a revival after 1660 of the plan for a foreign correspondency. Charles II apparently authorized the sale of houses to the value of £2,000 'for setting up a correspondence of learning and incouragement to such as improve it, like a Royal Society in Dublin'.[155]   But the Dublin Royal Society never materialized.

The Hartlib circle was not the only group which made possible the Dublin Philosophical Society. After 1660 there were several signs of mounting interest amongst those newly returned to Ireland, like William Currer, the physician, or Richard Heaton, the botanist. There was the realization of

---

[153]Southampton Record Office, DM 1/1, f. 16ᵛ; Hoppen, *The common scientist*, pp. 86, 202–3.

[154]Hoppen, *The common scientist*, p. 11.

[155]The reference is undated. Nat. Lib. Ire., MS. 8643 (2).

Stearne's College of Physicians, which included army doctors
from the Interregnum (Abraham Yarner, Joseph Waterhouse,
and James Fountain) as well as Petty.[156] Physicians formed
an important element in the Dublin Philosophical Society.
The continentally educated Catholic doctors who had treated
Protestants in the Interregnum, but who were now excluded
from the College of Physicians (men like Arthur, Cornelius
Borr, and Gerald Fennell) may have played a part in the
diffusion of interest.[157] Certainly in 1687 there were enough
skilled Catholic doctors for James II to agree to their
incorporation in a college of physicians at Kilkenny.[158]
Then there were shadowy figures, like Richard Carney,
employed by the state in the 1650s and later reputed to be 'a
learned mathematician': probably he was an astrologer, but
astrology had its place in advancing scientific understanding.[159] Our present, uncertain state of knowledge about
Ireland in Charles II's reign makes it impossible to do more
than indicate tentative influences. What is clear is the continuity between activity before 1660, and indeed before 1649,
and the Dublin Philosophical Society. Scientific interest grew
slowly but steadily: even in 1683 it was shared by very few,
who found official institutions no less than the majority of
their fellow countrymen unsympathetic towards their aims.

156 For Yarner: Brit. Mus., Additional MS. 19,843, f. 131; King's Inns, Dublin,
Prendergast MSS. i, p. 137; ii, p. 701; *Captaine Y[arner]s relation of the battaile
of Kilrush* (London, 1642); Dunlop, ii. 694; Widdess, *A history of the College of
Physicians of Ireland*, pp. 11, 19. Waterhouse represented Newry in the General
Convention of 1660: *An account of the chief occurrences ... 12—19 March*
[1660], p. 37. For Fountain: *Cal. Anc. Recs. of Dublin*, ed. Gilbert, iv. 142, 151.

157 Brit. Mus., Additional MS. 19,885, f. 192ᵛ; T.C.D., MS. N.l.4a, p. 487;
King's Inns, Dublin, Prendergast MS. ii, p. 270; *Facsimiles of National
Manuscripts of Ireland*, ed. J. T. Gilbert (London, 1884), part iv, 2, no. lxxi. On
Borr, who was educated at Leyden, see: C. Borr, *Disputationum practicarum de
Historii Aegrorum Decima-Nona. De Caecitate* (Trajectum ad Rhenum, 1650);
Cal. Anc. Recs. Dublin, ed. Gilbert, iii. 556—7. *Letters of denization*, ed. Shaw, p.
328; R. I. Smith, *English speaking students of medicine at Leyden* (Edinburgh,
1932), p. 26. On Fennell: C.B., Jennings transcripts, 1.E.10.15, 8 Jan. 1654[5];
The transplantation to Connacht, ed. Simington, p. 125.

158 *Cal. S.P. Dom., Jan. 1686—May 1687*, p. 214; ibid., *June 1687—Feb. 1689*,
pp. 57—8.

159 *Analecta Hibernica*, xv. 308; 'Extracts from the journal of Thomas Dineley,
esq.', *Journal of the Kilkenny and S.E. of Ireland Archaeological Soc.*, N.S. vi
(1867), 90.

IX

THE ADMINISTRATION AND REFORM OF THE LAW

The enforcement of English law throughout Ireland was regarded as essential to Anglicizing and governing the country. The Cromwellians shared this belief, but their task was complicated not only by the dislocation caused by the war, but also by their desire to reform the law. The purpose of this chapter is to examine the reconstruction of the Irish legal system between 1649 and 1660, and the extent to which it was reformed. The origin of reforms must also be traced, to see whether they were the result of a campaign in Ireland itself before 1649 or whether they were introduced by Ireland's new rulers after 1649. Finally, to assess the courts' efficiency, I shall consider the judges, both in Dublin and the localities.

i. The Irish legal system before 1649

To describe the Irish legal system before 1649 is not easy, since Ireland 'not only still awaits its Reeves or Holdsworth, it even lacks an elementary text-book on Irish legal history'.[1] The thorough application of English law was essential if the English conquest of Ireland was to be made secure. The introduction of English law had begun in Henry II's reign. However, like the other aspects of English authority, its operation was limited to Dublin (where the central courts were erected), and its immediate environs. The Irish retained their own legal code — the Brehon law — administered by a hereditary class of lawyers.[2] Only in James I's reign was the whole of Ireland shired, a development which allowed the establishment of English courts on a county basis, with justices of the peace at the lowest level, and regular circuits

---

[1] F. H. Newark, *Notes on Irish legal history* (Belfast, 1960), originally published in *Northern Ireland Legal Quarterly*, vii (1947), 121.

[2] G. J. Hand, *English law in Ireland, 1290–1324* (Cambridge, 1967), esp. pp. 1–20; D. B. Quinn, *The Elizabethans and the Irish* (Ithaca, N.Y., 1966), pp. 16–17.

of judges on assize, and which stimulated the collection and publication of the Irish statutes. To achieve the complete Anglicization the Brehon law was proscribed: gavelkind was outlawed in 1606 and tanistry in 1608.[3]

Many parts of Ireland had been brought within the orbit of English law less than fifty years before the Cromwellians' arrival, and consequently the law had only a fragile hold which the war loosened. Nevertheless the Irish legal system generally conformed to English practice. This meant that during the Interregnum Ireland's needs were closer to England's than to Scotland's where a native system of law still prevailed.[4] Without the need for thorough Anglicization, Cromwellian reforms of the law in Ireland were less spectacular than the contemporary changes in Scotland.

By the early seventeenth century the Irish legal system consisted of four courts the functions of which paralleled those of the English central courts. The four were: the king's bench, common pleas (also known as the court of chief place), the exchequer, and chancery. The king's bench exercised original civil and criminal jurisdiction, and appellate jurisdiction over the common pleas. Common pleas itself was limited to the hearing of civil suits in which no crown interest was involved. Its business was the smallest of the four courts. The court of exchequer, apart from its financial work and authority in revenue cases, could determine pleas between subject and subject, and also had an equity jurisdiction. Chancery, the fourth court, had been the last to develop, in the sixteenth century. Its extensive powers over equity and common-law cases rapidly made it the busiest court. The civil side of king's bench, for example, declined with competition from chancery, where litigants' cases were tried before a jury. There was some overlapping of jurisdictions which inevitably

3 Sir Richard Bolton, *A Iustice of Peace for Ireland* (Dublin, 1638), sig. *2 Davies, *A Discoverie of the true causes*, pp. 167, 168, 264; *His Maiesties Directions for the ordering and setling of the courts and course of justice within the Kingdome of Ireland* (Dublin, 1622 and 1638), reprinted and edited by G. J. Hand and V. W. Treadwell, in *Analecta Hibernica*, xxvi (1971); G. A. Hayes-McCoy, 'Gaelic Society in Ireland in the late sixteenth century', *Historical Studies: IV*, ed. Hayes-McCoy (London, 1963), pp. 52, 54; *The Statutes of Ireland*, ed. R. Bolton (Dublin, 1621), sig. [a5].

4 Trevor-Roper, 'Scotland and the Puritan Revolution', in *Religion, the Reformation and social change*, pp. 420—1.

created rivalry, especially between the older courts and the popular chancery.[5]

This basic system of four courts was complicated by two presidency courts, in the provinces of Munster and Connaught, and a palatinate court in Tipperary (a tribute to the Butler family's influence there). The Tipperary court was suspended between 1621 and 1662.[6] The courts of Munster and Connaught had first been established in 1569 as aids to the country's conquest. Their powers, at first martial, remained wide throughout the seventeenth century.[7] They were to have a place in Cromwellian plans.

Having outlined the legal system, we must now examine its workings. Chancery's popularity resulted from the other courts' flaws. Atrophied by formality and precedent, their procedure had become slow and cumbersome, so that litigants turned to chancery for speedier relief. However by the seventeenth century chancery itself was being slowed down by accretions.

In England similar shortcomings provoked a crescendo of literary protest. In Ireland pamphlet controversy of this sort was virtually unknown. The absence of printed protests does not necessarily mean that there was no dissatisfaction. In the early seventeenth century the landed classes in Ireland used the law to safeguard and improve their position. Irish Protestant landowners were hardly less litigious than their English counterparts. As a result the law became an increasingly lucrative profession in Ireland. The lawyers, with their own inn of court in Dublin (King's Inns), gained greatly in strength, organization, and influence. However residence at one of the London inns of court remained a necessary qualification for practice in Ireland.[8] Clients began to resent

5 A. G. Donaldson, *Some comparative aspects of Irish law* (Durham, N.C., and London, 1957), pp. 8–9; Newark, *Notes on Irish legal history*, pp. 13–17.

6 *Appendix to the fifteenth report of the Deputy Keeper of the Public Records in Ireland* (Dublin, 1873), pp. 32–7; V. H. T. Delaney, 'The palatine court of the liberty of Tipperary', *American Journal of Legal History*, v (1961), 95–117.

7 Brit. Mus., Harleian MS. 967, ff. 164 ff; 'His Maiesties Directions', *Analecta Hibernica*, xxvi. 198, 200; R. Lascelles, *Liber munerum publicorum Hiberniae*, i, part ii, 186, 189.

8 G. E. Hamilton, *An account of the honourable society of King's Inns, Dublin*, (Dublin, 1915), ch. 1; C. E. Bedwell, 'Irishmen at the Inns of Court', *Law Magazine and Review*, 5th Ser. xxxvii (1911–12), 268–77; W. R. Prest, *The Inns*

the lawyers, by whom (it was believed) they were being fleeced. Protests concentrated on the demand that fees be regulated. The Irish administration did what it could, regulating the fees charged by court officials, but it could do nothing to control the barristers' fees.

Lawyers were important in the Irish parliament's opposition to Strafford. Catholic lawyers, led by Patrick Darcy, argued Ireland's legislative independence and were to the fore in the General Assembly of the Catholic Confederation at Kilkenny. Similar arguments about Ireland's constitutional position were advanced by Protestant lawyers after 1660.[9] The lawyers' association with other Irish members of parliament helped to protect them from attack. The law also was praised for political reasons. Because Strafford used the prerogative courts — castle chamber, and the courts of wards and high commission — to bypass the familiar processes of the four courts, the traditional system gained prestige and was indeed regarded as the embodiment of justice that was not arbitrary but governed by set and known forms. The inflexibility and cumbersomeness of the courts' proceedings, which might otherwise have been criticized, appeared instead as virtues. Sir Richard Bolton, an Irish judge, praised the common law, contending that its excellence was such 'as that there is no humane law, within the circuite of the whole world . . . so apt and profitable, for the honourable, peaceable and prosperous government of the kingdomes of England and Ireland, and so necessarie for all estates, and for all causes concerning life, lands or goods . . . ' In 1641 an Irish member of parliament attacked the innovations in justice introduced by Strafford as 'the gray-haired common lawes funerall'.[10]

---

of Court under Elizabeth I and the early Stuarts (London, 1972), pp. 33, 36; Ranger, 'Strafford in Ireland: a revaluation', in *Crisis in Europe, 1560—1660*, ed. Aston, pp. 279—80.

[9] Barnard, *P. and P.* lxi; Beckett, 'The Confederation of Kilkenny reviewed', *Historical Studies: II*, ed. Roberts, p. 34.

[10] R. Bolton, *A Iustice of Peace for Ireland*, p. 1; *Remarkable propositions by the councell in Ireland humbly recommended to the Parliament in England* (London, 1642); *A speech made by Captaine Audley Mervin to the Upper House of Parliament in Ireland, March 4 1640[1]* (London, 1641), p. 1.

The law itself was not attacked; fees were. But agitation against fees was only incidentally connected with law reform. One could demand a reduction of fees in a court without wanting its constitution changed. Legal fees were no more than one example of an evil rife in all branches of the administration. Before 1641 there were regular, but generally unsuccessful attempts to regulate fees. From 1614 onwards parliamentary and other committees were set up to reform fees. Charles I and Strafford genuflected before the ideal of cheap justice and an end to extortionate fees, but achieved little.[11] Attempts were made by the government to standardize fees, tabulating and displaying them. Wandesford, Strafford's master of the rolls, caused a table of fees to be displayed in chancery 'so that the most ignorant persons need not be imposed on'.[12] The publication of these charges was no guarantee that they were observed. In 1641 the traditional parliamentary committee to regulate fees reappeared, suggesting the problem was as bad as ever. Moreover nothing had been done to control barristers' charges.[13]

Reforms of the law, as distinct from fees, were slight, and initiated by the government in the interests of administrative efficiency. The acts passed removed technicalities in procedure which had added greatly to the dilatoriness and expense of the law and which had been exploited by the wealthy landowners to keep others from justice. Efforts were made to stop cases being brought in Dublin to embarrass and impoverish defendants from remote parts of the country.[14] The law relating to debt, one of the most criticized aspects of legal procedure, was improved to facilitate the recovery of just debts by discouraging obstructions such as the improper use of writs of error or *supersedeas*.[15] Attempts were made

11 Brit. Mus., Harleian MS. 2143, ff. 72–3; *Cal. S.P. Ire. 1625–32*, pp. 339–40; ibid., *1647–60*, p. 191; *C.J. Ire.* i. 25, 27, 37, 100; A. Clarke, *The Graces, 1625–41* (Dundalk, 1968), p. 20; Clarke, *The Old English in Ireland* pp. 48, 57, 245; *Letters and Dispatches of Strafforde*, ed. Knowler, i. 186, 292–3, 304, 319–20.

12 T. Comber, *Memoirs of the life and death of . . . Lord Deputy Wandesforde* (Cambridge, 1778), ii. 90; *State Papers of Clarendon*, i. 95; O'Grady, *Strafford and Ireland*, i. 337. Cf. J. W. Jones, *Politics and the Bench* (London, 1971), p. 111.

13 *C.J. Ire.* i. 162–3, 229–30, 250; *A speech made by Captaine Audley Mervin*, p. 26.

14 10 Car. I, cc. X, XI, XII (Ireland); 10 and 11 Car. I, cc. VIII and X (Ireland).

15 10 Car. I, c. VIII (Ireland).

to safeguard the innocent against the arbitrariness of sheriffs and their deputies: a recurrent grievance throughout the century. Another act tried to stop the manipulation of juries.[16]

Although these measures reached the statute book, it is unlikely that they were rigorously enforced. However this body of legislation shows what Strafford's administration felt to be the most pressing problems. It was to the same matters — the quashing of proceedings on technical errors, delays in executing justice owing to obstructive pleadings, the law of debt, the intimidation of juries, and the malpractices of sheriffs — that the Cromwellians in Ireland gave most attention.

ii. The Campaign for law reform

The Irish legal system before 1641 was imperfect, yet there was no serious pressure for reform. Changes introduced after 1649 were either prompted by administrative convenience (like Strafford's adjustments) or were the result of the English campaign for law reform. Many of the army radicals who ruled Ireland after 1649 had participated in the long and vocal agitation for law reform.

Some of the English complaints were relevant to the Irish situation. The ostentatious wealth of the lawyers and the size of their fees were resented. The power and exclusiveness of legal society, perpetuated by the complexity and obscurity of the law, locked in an archaic tongue, made it another monopoly ripe for attack. In England, as in Ireland, the parliamentary opposition had looked to the common law courts as a defence against the personal rule of Charles I. The tight alliance between parliament and the common lawyers had shielded the law from any fundamental attack. Only when the power of their common enemy, the king, had been broken, did the alliance weaken and the demands for reform become more thoroughgoing.[17]

There were in England two attitudes towards reform: one moderate; the other radical. Moderates were moved by a

16 10 Car. I, c. XIII, XVI, XIX (Ireland).
17 On law reform: C. R. Niehaus, 'The issue of law reform in the Puritan Revolution', Harvard D.Phil. 1960; M. James, *Social problems and policy during*

spirit similar to that which had inspired the Irish legislation of 1634 and 1635. The substance of the law was sound: simplify procedure, and then the old hulk would once more be seaworthy. The more radical approach, which gained ground after 1642, held that existing law was corrupt or unsatisfactory and must be swept away. At the heart of this view was the feeling that the laws of God were the basis of human law, and English law had accordingly to be altered. This view need not produce radical conclusions. It had had supporters since the Reformation. During the civil war army radicals like Oliver Cromwell, Hugh Peter, Fleetwood, and John Cook agreed that the laws of England must be made consonant with God's laws, but without supporting the abolition of the existing laws. The most extreme reformers were the Fifth Monarchists, who wanted the Mosaic code of law introduced into England as a necessary preparation for the Fifth Monarchy. The Fifth Monarchists were not interested in reforming the existing courts, but in the imposition of a harsh code as the corollary of a religious dogma. In the Barebone's Parliament of 1653 they were prepared to abolish existing courts without first planning replacements. These proposals, and in particular the threat to chancery, vital for the confirmation of land transactions,[18] set the defenders of property (including Oliver Cromwell) against the Fifth Monarchists and discredited schemes of fundamental reform.[19] Henceforth law reform was slow and piecemeal.

Pamphlets throughout the civil war and the army's manifestos showed the preoccupation with law reform. When the parliament's army conquered Ireland, the concern was carried there. The officers destined for Irish service in 1649 made the familiar requests: of speedy, cheap, and certain justice, with proceedings in English.[20] But the officers were interested in having the reforms introduced into England rather than

the Puritan Revolution, pp. 326–35; G. B. Nourse, 'Law Reform under the Commonwealth and Protectorate', Law Quarterly Review, lxxv (1959), 512–29; D. Veall, The popular agitation for law reform during the Puritan Revolution, 1640–60 (Oxford, 1970).

18 Menna Prestwich, Cranfield: politics and profits under the early Stuarts (Oxford, 1966), p. 321.

19 Capp, The Fifth Monarchy Men, ch. 7.

20 The humble petition of the officers now engaged for Ireland (London, 1649), p. 4.

Ireland. The army in Ireland never agitated for legal reform as they did for religious changes. This lack of interest is probably explained by the rudimentary nature of the Irish legal system between 1649 and 1655, and by the failure of the majority of soldiers to acquire a settled interest in Ireland and with it the need to use Irish courts.

Such interest as was shown in the progress of law reform in Ireland came from Oliver Cromwell and his nominee as chief justice of Munster, John Cook. Their concern benefited Ireland, but their underlying intention was to test and perfect innovations which could later be applied in England. Cook's work in Munster was the most interesting and important contribution to law reform in Ireland, and will be considered in some detail. It was, however, exceptional. In the main Cromwellian efforts concentrated on supplying justice as part of the reimposition of English authority, and achieved this at first with improvisations but increasingly by re-establishing the old legal machinery. It is to this, the more orthodox response to the problems of 1649, that I turn first.

iii. The legal system, 1649 – 1655

War, and the rival political authorities in Ireland, dislocated the legal network between 1641 and 1649. In 1649 the Catholic clergy told Ormonde that the people 'see no face of justice exercised amongst them', and asked for assizes, quarter sessions, and machinery in each county for the redress of grievances. In at least one instance Ormonde responded by issuing a comprehensive commission to try cases in Ulster.[21] By 1649, however, Ormonde's authority was shrinking weekly, and responsibility for supplying justice increasingly fell to the English invaders. Cromwell improvised machinery which would serve until the whole country was pacified and more usual methods could be used. On 29 December 1649 it was reported in London that Cromwell had 'settled courts of judicature at Dublin, for the present, to proceed by way of the chancery'. At the same time the presidency court was re-established in Munster.[22]

---

21 R. Cox, *Hibernia Anglicana* (London, 1679), part 2, appendix xxv, p. 168; Hist. MSS. Comm., *Ormonde MSS.* N.S. i. 157.

22 Whitelocke, *Memorials of the English Affairs*, iii. 134; cf. P.R.O., Dublin, Lodge MSS. 1.a.53.56, p. 402.

When Cromwell left Ireland in 1650 care for the law there passed to the Long Parliament and its commissioners in Dublin. Gradually justice was reimposed, slowly extending outwards from the centre of English rule at Dublin. By 1651 commissioners for the administration of justice had been appointed for Dublin, and were soon supplemented by commissioners for Leinster. The wide powers of these commissioners showed that they had replaced the judges of the old four courts at Dublin.[23] Only Leinster and Dublin, the area of the English pale, had a permanent provision of judges between 1650 and 1655. Judges were delegated to try cases in other parts of Ireland. Thus in 1651, Thomas Dungan, one of the commissioners for justice in Leinster and Dublin, was sent to Ulster; in 1653 James Donnellan, another of the Leinster commissioners, went to Ulster; also in 1653 John Cook, chief justice of Munster, was dispatched to Connaught.[24] These *ad hoc* commissions seem to have replaced the itineration of judges on circuit. Only in the spring of 1655, on the eve of the four courts' restoration, were there signs of a thorough provision of justice throughout Ireland.[25] Parts of the country were still unprovided for: in 1658 the western county of Kerry had its first *nisi prius* 'since the wars'.[26]

The parliamentary commissioners in Ireland had been instructed in October 1650 to consider the arrangements for the administration of justice, and to recommend improvements. In August 1652 their powers were widened to cope with Ireland's impending settlement so that they could 'erect, allow, alter or continue any court or courts' which they deemed necessary.[27] What operated between 1650 and 1655 was a three-tier system. At the highest level were the commissioners for justice in Dublin and Leinster, and the judges of the Munster presidency court, all of whom were

23 T.C.D., MS. F.3.18, ff. 108ᵛ, 104–5.
24 Dunlop, i. 77–8, ii. 335.
25 King's Inns, Dublin, Prendergast MS. ii, p. 324; Nat. Lib. Ire., MS. 11,961, pp. 7, 38; Dunlop, ii. 485; M. Hickson, *Ireland in the seventeenth century* (London, 1884), ii. 236; *Mercurius politicus* no. 252 (5–12 Apr. 1655), p. 5255. The judges and commissioners for the administration of justice in 1655 are listed in Brit. Mus., Additional MS. 19,833, f.3ᵛ.
26 *The Herbert Correspondence*, ed. Smith, p. 153.
27 Dunlop, i. 2, 263–4.

sent on occasional forays into Ulster and Connaught. The parliamentary commissioners themselves were invested with wide judicial powers, which they may have used on visits to remote areas.[28] At a lower level, authority was divided between revenue commissioners and justices of the peace. The commission of the peace seems to have been revived only slowly. The earliest surviving commission is that of 4 November 1651 for Leinster. The next, for Dublin, is dated 15 September 1653. Not until 1655 is there evidence of a more general use of justices of the peace.[29]

The Cromwellian administration used the revenue commissioners for a wide range of local duties previously discharged by the justices of the peace, and this caused friction as the commission of the peace was gradually revived. Apart from collecting the assessment the revenue commissioners were empowered to enforce the laws against treason, felonies, and adultery, and the recent English ordinances intended to reform manners. They could also imprison those whom they regarded as dangerous, administer oaths, and call for witnesses and records.[30] The revenue commissioners were mostly drawn from those who had arrived in Ireland since 1649, either as soldiers or members of the civil administration. Godliness and political reliability were the essential qualifications, rather than legal skill or probity. Even when honest, the fact that they were interlopers, often of humble origin and radical in religious opinions, gave offence to the established Protestant settlers who had hitherto supplied the commission of the peace. The impression gained ground that 'many who are invested with a military capacity are no great friends to the laws of the land'.[31] Much of the friction arose from the former local rulers of Ireland being supplanted by newcomers. But there was also a clash between two different codes of law: one, represented by the justices of the peace, was the customary civil law; the other was military law

28 Firth and Rait, ii. 494–5.

29 T.C.D., MS. F.3.18, ff. 110, 139^v; *The council book of Drogheda*, ed. T. Gogarty, p. 33; 'Letters, etc., of early Friends', *The Friends' Library*, ix. 406; J. P. Swan, 'The justices of the peace for the County of Wexford', *JRSAI*, 5th Ser. iv (1894) 67; J. M. Taylor, *Roger Ludlow: the colonial lawmaker* (New York and London, 1900), p. 148.

30 Mayer, *Trans. Historic Soc. of Lancashire and Cheshire*, N.S. i. 243.

31 Ladyman, *The Dangerous Rule*, sig. [a4].

imposed by the revenue commissioners. The blurred demarcation between military and civil law allowed some revenue commissioners to encroach on the jurisdiction of others. John Weaver, the parliamentary commissioner, had championed civil justice against military rule, and had had to resign. In 1654 Richard Pepys, a member of the Irish council and a judge, was alarmed by the 'arbitrary governement of the courts'.[32]

The revival of the four courts in 1655, the restoration of municipal charters in 1656, and the greater use of the commission of the peace, amounted to a virtually complete recreation of the legal system as it had been before 1641. These changes accorded with Henry Cromwell's insistence on legalism and his antipathy towards the military party and its practices; they also aided his alliance with the substantial settlers who once more enjoyed local power as justices of the peace. In 1655 the revenue commissioners were shorn of their legal powers; all army officers 'ceased to be any longer civile justiciaries, and dispencers of fines and death at their discretions'.[33]

As well as the three main institutions — the commissioners for the administration of justice, the justices of the peace, and the revenue commissioners — the Cromwellians issued other, more specialized legal commissions. The want of a power to decide testamentary cases and prove wills (owing to the abolition of ecclesiastical jurisdiction) was made good by Dr. Dudley Loftus's appointment as a commissioner for such cases.[34] In December 1652 the members of a high court of justice to try the Irish rebels were nominated.[35]

Through these agencies justice was provided. However they were regarded as only temporary. These were the years when justice 'did not sit in her wonted person'. As early as 1651 the parliamentary commissioners had been asked to recommend what permanent legal arrangements should be made.

32 Brit. Mus., Lansdowne MS. 821, f. 117; Bodl., Carte MS. 63, f. 618; Marsh's Lib., Dublin, MS. Z.3.2.17 (2), f. 16; Gardiner, *History of the Commonwealth and Protectorate, 1649–1660*, iii. 329; V. Gookin, *The Author and Case of Transplanting the Irish Vindicated* (London, 1655), sig. A2ᵛ, pp. 9–10; Hist. MSS. Comm., *Portland MSS.* i. 672.
33 *Thurloe State Papers*, v. 647.
34 T.C.D., MS. F.3.18, f. 107ᵛ.
35 Ibid., f. 136.

A study of the existing machinery led Fleetwood to conclude that the people of Ireland 'are in a very sad and oppressed condition through delays and want of justice'.[36] The delays in making better provision were caused largely by dilatoriness at Westminster.

In 1653 the parliamentary commissioners in Dublin had recommended changes in the legal system, arguing that the absence of 'the ordinary way of justice' made it more difficult to restore English authority or to settle Ireland. In particular the lack of a court of chancery or of a great seal impeded the registering of land conveyances which bulked so large in Ireland's resettlement.[37] Fleetwood specifically asked for chancery's re-establishment. He also proposed economies so that two courts would replace the old four: chancery, and a court of upper bench with cognizance of pleas formerly heard in the court of common pleas.[38] The English government accepted the need to re-erect regular courts in Ireland, yet it was extremely slow to do anything.[39] Not until 1654 was a decision made. This ignored Fleetwood's economical suggestions: all four courts were to be re-established. An act to effect this was introduced into the 1654 parliament, but had not passed when it was dissolved.[40] It was only in July 1655 that the council of state itself authorized the preparation of new seals for the courts of exchequer, upper bench, and common pleas.[41] Judges were appointed to each of these courts. However the transmission of the great seal and the appointment of a lord chancellor were delayed, and chancery when eventually resurrected had to be placed in commission for a year.[42]

The limited and ill-defined powers of the improvised courts between 1649 and 1655 increased pressure to restore the old courts, whose known procedures once more seemed

36 *Discourses political and moral of the conveniency and justice of reserving some lands in Ireland* (n.p., n.d.), p. 3; Dunlop, i. 4; *Thurloe State Papers*, ii. 224.

37 *Thurloe State Papers*, ii. 224; iii. 744; Dunlop, ii. 384, 449, 457; cf. Firth and Rait, i. 1164; Dunlop, ii. 580.

38 *Thurloe State Papers*, ii. 733, iii. 196, 305.

39 Ibid., ii. 633; *C.J.* vii. 162.

40 Ibid., vii. 415.

41 Brit. Mus., Lansdowne MS. 821, f. 3ᵛ; *Cal. S.P. Ire., 1647–60*, pp. 815–16; Lascelles, *Liber munerum publicorum Hiberniae*, i, part ii, p. 16.

42 *Thurloe State Papers*, iii. 697.

attractive to those confronted with the Cromwellians' summary methods. Yet the improvisations had been praised by
English army radicals, who saw them as important first steps
towards law reform. We have now to discover why it was so
easy to dismantle these innovations and replace them with
the old courts in 1655. Reform of the law in Ireland was
dependent on events in England, and in England there was
uncertainty as to what to do. Fleetwood summed up the
difficulty when he wrote, 'if I could tell whether any
regulation were intended in England, I thinke it were best to
stay till that time, before wee doe any thing actually heere'.
Fleetwood's attitude resembled that of the army Independents, anxious to see 'the corruptions and delayes' of the law
removed, but equally anxious to dissociate himself from
those who wanted the law overthrown.[43] The members of
the Irish administration showed no great interest in law
reform, although two of its members (Thomlinson and
Steele) had served on committees for law reform.[44] Steele by
delaying his removal to Ireland after he had been appointed
lord chancellor hampered the cause of an efficient legal
system by forcing chancery to be kept in commission.

Only one man in the Irish administration showed a deep
interest in law reform and protested against the restoration of
the four courts in 1655 as a betrayal of the reforming
programme to which the army was committed. This lone
voice deserves particular attention because it belonged to the
man who had presided over the most highly praised part of
the Irish legal system between 1649 and 1655, John Cook,
the chief justice of Munster. In 1655 Cook was offered office
in one of the restored four courts. In declining he set out his
reasons and attacked the traditional system of justice. 'If I
should now countenance any old oppression I should be the
most egregious dissembler that ever sat upon a bench', he
wrote.[45] It is time to examine Cook and his work in
Munster, and to see why he was so eager for reform.

---

[43] *Thurloe State Papers*, iii. 697.
[44] *C.J.* vii. 74. The statement that John Cook served on this committee is
wrong, and probably resulted from his being confused with George Cock: H. N.
Brailsford, *The Levellers and the English Revolution* (London, 1961), p. 651.
[45] Bodl., Rawlinson MS. A.189, ff. 390–390ᵛ.

iv. *John Cook and the Presidential Court of Munster*

W. C. Abbott dismissed Cook as 'a man of dubious reputation then [in 1649] and still more dubious thereafter'. The reason for this remark is not clear. Very different was the view of an early nineteenth-century historian who extravagantly claimed that Cook's memory was 'still hallowed in the traditions of the peasantry, and his posterity still reap the fruits of his virtues . . . '[46] More important than either of these jejune judgements is the reputation that Cook enjoyed amongst his contemporaries. His part in Charles I's trial damned him with royalists. On the other hand his legal work in Ireland was praised by Oliver Cromwell and Edmund Ludlow.[47] It was to the party of army Independents that Cook belonged; its rise to power was the occasion of his own public employment.

Cook was born about 1609, the son and heir of Isaac Cook of Burbridge in Leicestershire. At the age of fourteen, in 1623, Cook entered Wadham College, Oxford. Later in the same year he was admitted to Gray's Inn, and in 1631 became a barrister of the inn. This conventional training was supplemented by travels on the continent, during which Cook revealed the other interest, religion, which (together with the law) shaped his career. In Rome he engaged in religious debate; at Geneva he lived in the house of Diodati, the celebrated theologian.[48]

Only with the civil war did Cook become prominent as a lawyer. In 1646 he represented John Lilburn at his trial, and then in 1649 he was appointed solicitor for the commonwealth at Charles I's trial. In the absence of the attorney-general, Steele, the brunt of prosecuting the king fell on Cook. His leading part in Charles's condemnation led to Cook's own execution after the restoration. Cook repeated his belief that Charles's execution was necessary until his own

---

46 Abbott, *Cromwell*, i. 729–30; W. C. Taylor, *History of the Civil Wars in Ireland* (Edinburgh, 1831), ii. 65.

47 *The Memoirs of Edmund Ludlow*, ed. Firth, i. 246–7, ii. 127.

48 *D.N.B.*; Foster, *Alumni Oxonienses*, E.S. i. 320; Foster, *Register of the admissions to Gray's Inn, 1521–1889* (London, 1889), p. 171; *The Memoirs of Edmund Ludlow*, ii. 309; 'Papers relating to Thomas Wentworth, first earl of Strafford', ed. C. H. Firth, *Camden Miscellany, ix*, Camden Soc., N.S. liii (1895), 15, 19. A fanciful royalist pamphleteer alleged that Cook became a monk in Italy: *Mercurius elencticus*, no. 56 (6–13 Feb. 1648[9]), sig. N3.

death.[49] Cook was rewarded: first, by being made master of
St. Cross Hospital, near Winchester;[50] and at the beginning
of 1650 with his appointment as chief justice of Munster.
Cook was already in Ireland, having gone thence with
Cromwell in the summer of 1649, and so was able to enter
into the office quickly.[51] Cook, although not Cromwell's
first choice, was well qualified for the post, having not only
legal training and experience, but also an earlier connection
with Ireland. He had gone to Ireland about 1634, remaining
there three years during which time he caught Strafford's
eye. The latter entrusted Cook with a project to revise and
reprint the Irish statutes. This work was never published,
allegedly because Cook misappropriated the funds.[52] However the scheme gave him valuable insight into the difficulties
of codifying and condensing the law.

His stay in Ireland apparently turned Cook into an admirer
of Strafford, finding the latter's interest in expediting and
cheapening the law commendable. Cook went so far as to
suggest that Strafford's work had earned him a deserved
popularity with the poor in Ireland. This praise of Strafford,
coming in 1641, is interesting, because it alleged that
Strafford had achieved real improvements in the Irish legal
system, and also because it provided Cook with a model for
his own work in Munster during the 1650s.[53]

Cook's religious beliefs influenced his desire for legal
reform and his work as chief justice of Munster. His outlook
was that of an Independent, similar to Oliver Cromwell, to
Fleetwood, and to Hugh Peter. Like others who had experienced the rigorous imposition of Anglican uniformity during
the 1630s, Cook venerated liberty of conscience. Belittling
the divisions between sects as a mere multiplication of names,

[49] *The Speeches and Prayers of some of the late King's Judges* (London, 1660),
p. 41.

[50] *C.J.* vi. 246.

[51] Bodl., Rawlinson MS. A.189, f. 397; Abbott, *Cromwell*, ii. 186–7; *A true
relation of Mr Iohn Cook's passage by sea from Wexford to Kinsale* (London,
1650), p. 3; *C.J.* vi. 258.

[52] 'Papers relating to ... Strafford', *Camden Miscellany, ix*, p. 15; *Mercurius
elencticus*, no. 56, sig. N2ᵛ–N3. A John Cook was admitted to the King's Inns in
1634: P.R.O., Dublin, Lodge MSS. 1.a.53.72, unfoliated; cf. J. Cook,
Redintegratio amoris (London, [1647]), p. 78.

[53] *Camden Miscellany, ix*, p. 17. There has been no attempt to study Strafford's
legal reforms in Ireland.

he was prepared to extend toleration to 'all that walk humbly and holily before the Lord'.[54] Cook, like Fleetwood, was perhaps too credulous of professions of godliness; on the other hand, he shied away from schemes of religious discipline, seeing the spectre of Laudian intolerance. Cook, for example, feared the Scottish Presbyterians, believing that if their religion was imposed in England 'it would undoubtedly cost ten times more bloud to remove it, then ever it hath done to abolish episcopacy'. In 1647 Cook turned to the army as the best defence against Scottish Presbyterianism; at the same time seeing it as the best hope of accomplishing reform.[55] Cook's religious outlook coincided with that of Ireland's governors from 1649 until 1655, but thereafter he found himself increasingly out of sympathy with Henry Cromwell's more conservative policies.[56]

Much of Cook's importance and influence lay in his ability to articulate sentiments common amongst the army Independents. Nevertheless his published programme of reforms included novelties. His approach to law reform was distinguished by his legal knowledge which tempered the radicalism born of his concern for the poor. Initially Cook's interest in law reform arose from his defence of the profession against violent and (he believed) ill-informed critics. In his first work on this theme, *The Vindication of the Professors of the law*, published in 1646, Cook insisted that lawyers had no monopoly of faults. Frequently abuses of which clients complained were of the latter's making, having embroiled themselves in protracted litigation against their counsels' advice.[57] However, he appreciated the strength of feeling against the lawyers and realized that it must be appeased if disaster was to be averted. Cook conceded the need for changes, and wanted the profession itself to take the initiative: 'that the reverend judges, learned lawyers, and experienced officers and clarkes of all courts, speedily consult and agree together to propound some proper expedient

---

54 *The Speeches and Prayers of the late King's Judges*, p. 31; J. Cook, *What the Independents would have* (London, 1647), esp. pp. 3, 4, 9, 13, 14.

55 Cook, *Redintegratio amoris*, pp. 43, 63–4; Cook, *The Vindication of the Professors . . . of the law* (London, 1646), p. 82.

56 *Thurloe State Papers*, v. 353.

57 *The Vindication*, p. 9.

to . . . parliament, for cheap and summary justice . . . ' Reforms coming from lawyers would be less extreme than those imposed from outside. At this time Cook's arguments for compromise are stronger than his indignation at the law's defects. Some of his suggestions — better that fees be reduced voluntarily than that they should be abolished completely — were evidently appeals to the self-interest of his colleagues.[58] They failed.

As Cook returned to the law, and its defects, in later books, his enthusiasm for reform increased. The experiences of his own family gave him insight into the problems of those who went to law: Cook's father had been sued for £300 and spent £700 defending the suit; his brother and brother-in-law (not to mention other acquaintances) had had similar troubles.[59] Cook could, then, see the law from both the lawyers' and the suitors' sides. His approach was also coloured by his belief that the law should not conflict with the law of God. In this there was no novelty. It led him to a position similar to Oliver Cromwell's and the moderates', not the Fifth Monarchists'. Cook rejected literal reliance on the code of Moses, since what had suited the Jews, 'by nature a cruell people', was not automatically appropriate to England.[60]

Cook wanted to reconcile the touchstone of divine precept with that of reason. 'No humane law', he insisted, 'ought to live any longer than the reason of it continues (for reason is the soule of all humane laws without exception . . .).[61] The law's function was utilitarian. When it departed from reason it ceased to be useful. The law was society's servant, 'if it be found inconvenient or mischevious in theorie or practise it must be changed'. Cook was contemptuous of unthinking reliance on tradition and deference to precedent common in the legal profession. He ridiculed the defence of laws for no reason other than their antiquity: 'if we stand upon the excellency and the antiquity of our lawes because they came in with the Romans, and were never altered by Danes,

58Cook, *Unum Necessarium* (London, 1647), pp. 66−7.

59Bodl., Rawlinson MS. A.189, ff. 393−395v.

60Cook, *Vindication of the Professors*, sig. A3v, pp. 4, 18; Cook, *Unum necessarium*, pp. 43−4.

61Ibid., p. 65; Cook, *Vindication of the Professors*, p. 18.

Saxons, or Normans, then it is death . . . '[62] To counteract
this conservatism Cook wanted changes in legal education. A
study of history would end 'this over-doting upon old forms',
and would show instead that laws were simply the inventions
of men to meet specific needs. In short, his proposed
education would elevate reason and dethrone formality.[63]

Cook also wanted the law to be accessible to all, and for
this reason he criticized excessive technicality of procedure
which kept the law a mystery to all but the lawyers. Like
most reformers he wanted the statutes translated from
Norman French into English, and an end to the use of Latin
in the courts: 'it is not enough to speake or write that some
may understand . . . , but so that all cannot possibly but
understand'.[64] Trivial errors in forms of pleading or in the
working of writs frequently caused cases to be quashed, thus
adding greatly to the cost and time of securing just rights.
Cook demanded an end to this reliance on technical accuracy, saying he would rather 'dispence with 10000 formalities
and niceties in Law, then neglect the doing of justice; rather
suffer all the courses of the court to be broken and shivered
into attomes, then suffer one poor man to be undone by a
mispleading or error in the proceedings'.[65] To make justice
cheaper he wanted fees reduced and the poor to have justice
'for such fees as they are able to pay' or 'for Gods sake'.[66]
Another way of improving the law was decentralization. For
the poor the strain of constant attendance at Westminster,
sometimes for years, deterred all but the most resolute from
continuing their suits. He wanted greater power given to
judges on assize to settle private suits; to make these local
jurisdictions really effective he suggested that the courts mix

62 Cook, *Monarchy no creature of Gods making*, sig. c3.

63 Cook's scheme was to include three years spent in the study of divinity, and
four in 'the morall and rational part of the common law': *The Vindication of the
Professors*, pp. 55–6, 59–60; *Redintegratio amoris*, p.24; Prest, *The Inns of
Court under Elizabeth I and the early Stuarts*, pp. 170–2.

64Cook, *Monarchy no creature of Gods making*, sig. [d]1; *The Vindication of
the Professors*, sig. a3v–a4; pp. 15, 18, *Unum necessarium*, p. 68; cf. *Leveller
manifestoes of the Puritan Revolution*, ed. D. M. Wolfe (New York, 1944), pp
139, 192, 226, 266, 353.

65Cook, *Redintegratio amoris*, p. 3.

66 Cook, *Monarchy no creature of Gods making*, p. 26; *Redintegratio amoris*, p.
14 *recte* 24; *Unum necessarium*, p. 68; *The Vindication of the Professors*, sig.
A3v, pp. 30, 34.

equity with their common-law jurisdiction. This innovation would help particularly in the recovery of debts.[67]

Cook's emphasis was on improving the existing courts rather than replacing them. He escaped the absurdities of his fellow lawyers who resisted all change, and could even mock those 'high commendations which is [sic] given of our lawes, that if Adam had not sinned in paradise, all the world should have been governed by the common law of England'.[68] Cook might mock, but he too believed that potentially the laws of England were the best in the world. However, to realize that potential they must be constantly reviewed and reformed by parliament.[69] Cook, knowing and valuing the law, avoided the extremes of the Fifth Monarchists. Alternatives had to be devised, preferably by experts, before there could be any changes. Chancery, the court most violently attacked by the Fifth Monarchists, was defended as an institution by Cook, although he admitted its blemishes. His aims could be summed up as, 'that justice be easie and speedie, and mercie showne to the poore . . . '[70] In England, although he wrote extensively, Cook had no chance to put his projects into practice. His appointment as chief justice in Munster gave him the opportunity to show the genuineness of his concern.

Oliver Cromwell himself had conceived the use of the Munster presidency court as an instrument of legal reform. On 31 December 1649 he had invited John Sadler, a master in chancery and Cambridge don, to accept the chief justiceship.[71] Cromwell revealed what he hoped Sadler would do:

we have a great opportunity to set up, until the parliament shall determine otherwise, a way of doing justice amongst the poor people, which, for the uprightness and cheapness of it, may exceedingly gain upon them, who have been accustomed to as much injustice, tyranny and oppression from their landlords, the great men, and those that should have done them right, as, I believe, any people in that which we call Christendom. Sir, if justice were freely and impartially administered here, the foregoing darkness and corruption would make it look so much the more glorious and beautiful . . .

67Cook, *Redintegratio amoris*, p. 15; *The Vindication of the Professors*, sig. A3v, pp. 7, 92.
68Cook, *Monarchy no creature of Gods making*, sig. b3v.
69Cook, *The Vindication of the Professors*, p. 35.
70Cook, *Monarchy no creature*, sig. C2—C4, c[1]v—[c2]; *The Vindication of the Professors*, pp. 28—9, 83.
71Abbott, *Cromwell*, ii. 186—7.

As a further inducement Cromwell offered Sadler 'a standing salary' of £1,000 p.a. This was generous indeed; certainly 'more than hath usually been allowed'. (In 1608 the chief justice's salary was £100 p.a.)[72] It would free Sadler from dependence on the usual allowances 'which have been to others . . . , but a colour to their covetous practices'.

Sadler was not lured over either by the chance to do good or by the salary, remaining instead at Cambridge where he was made Master of Magdalene College. In his place Cook was appointed at an annual salary of £500 p.a.[73] Cook was more than adequate as a replacement for Sadler. His interpretation of his duties in Munster was close to Cromwell's intentions, and indeed won Cromwell's approval who contrasted Cook's efficiency with the dilatoriness of judges at Westminster. Both Cromwell and Cook appreciated the wider implications of what was done in Ireland. Cromwell contended that Ireland after 1649 'was as a clean paper . . . , and capable of being governed by such laws as should be found most agreeable to justice; which may be so impartially administered, as to be a good precedent to England it self . . .'[74]

In Ireland, the work of demolition, the great step from which moderates shrank, had been accomplished by the war. This enabled the Cromwellians to improvise, perfecting simpler, local courts, putting into effect reforms long adumbrated, testing them in Ireland before they were introduced into England. It was Cromwell's intention, and Cook's, that Ireland should serve as a model for England. Cook later wrote,

never was there so fair a morning as we have lately seen. Ireland was like a white paper, apt to receive any good impression, and in regard that ye Lord hath given a supersedeas to the old courts here, it was hoped that . . . such an expedient for speedie and sure justice might have been settled, that though Ireland be but the younger sister, yet England might have been the learner and gainer by her.

To Cook it seemed that the four courts had been removed by divine providence: for this reason their restoration in 1655 was an offence against God, who had 'put a stop to the old

72 Brit. Mus., Harleian MS. 697, f. 167ᵛ.

73 Ibid., Additional MS. 19,833, f. 3ᵛ; cf. *A Perfect diurnall of some passages and procedures of and in relation to the armies in England and Ireland*, no. 15 (18–25 Mar. 1649[50]), p. 137.

74 *The Memoirs of Edmund Ludlow*, i. 246–7.

tyrannical proceedings, and freed the poor protestants in Ireland from the Norman yoake by suspending by force, and seeming to abolish, the old courts and tedious formalities . . . '[75]

As chief justice of Munster Cook introduced reforms which he had long advocated. Justice in the province, he alleged, became both swift and cheap. He claimed to have decided over 600 cases in two or three months; and Oliver Cromwell said that Cook 'determined more causes in a week, then Westminster-Hall in a year'.[76] Having no other employments, Cook devoted all his energies to the Munster court, which speeded procedure. Justice was cheapened by removing superfluous officers and reducing fees: the judges received salaries from the state and took no fees; there were, apparently, no attornies and each man pleaded his own case.[77] It was a decentralized court. Cook promised the inhabitants of Munster 'that they should never be fetcht up to Dublin, to dance attendance, as they did afore the rebellion'. To make the court yet more local the lord president of Munster, Ireton, authorized a change (of which Cook approved) whereby the court operated on a county basis 'in the nature of assizes or sittings'.[78] The other features of the court most pleasing to Cook were the use of subpoena and attachment of goods rather than persons; and the court's combination of common law and equity (the reform which Cook had urged in 1647). He also commended the method of settling debt cases. The money was repaid in instalments, which were decided by a jury of neighbours at equitable rates. This prevented debtors defaulting and being imprisoned whilst their families starved, and the creditor recovered his debt.[79]

---

[75] Bodl., Rawlinson MS. A.189, ff. 390, 397; Cook used the image of a white paper at a gathering of army officers in 1652. It was used by Petty to describe Ireland after 1660. Hist. MSS. Comm., *Egmont MSS.* i. 514; Petty, *A treatise of taxes and contributions*, sig. [A4].

[76] *The Memoirs of Edmund Ludlow*, i. 246.

[77] Bodl., Rawlinson MS. A.189, f. 398; Cook, *Monarchy no creature of Gods making*, sig. e4.

[78] Cook, *Monarchy no creature of Gods making*, sig. e4. For instances of these assizes: Chatsworth, Lismore MS. 29, Cork's diary, 10 July 1652, 27 Nov. 1652, 20 Dec. 1652; *The council book of Youghal*, ed. Caulfield, p. 293; Hist. MSS. Comm., *Egmont MSS.* i. 568.

[79] Cook, *Monarchy no creature*, sig. e4–f[1].

With this praise of the court's excellence it is surprising that it was not imitated. But far from being used as the model for the reorganization of either the Irish or English courts, the Munster presidential court had been dismantled by 1655. Ireland had been a white paper; there had indeed been 'a doore of entrance standing wide open' for legal improvements. Yet all the Cromwellians could do was to revive the four courts unchanged, 'w[i]thout plucking out the teeth and tearing the lyons claws in pieces, nay without so much as pairing the nailes or pruning the exuberant branches of superfluities'.[80] What reason was there for this apparent betrayal of earlier, solemn engagements to reform the law? And why in particular was Cook's much praised work in Munster discontinued?

Cromwell's and Cook's accounts of the Munster court at first suggest that it was a Cromwellian invention of 1649. This was not so. What Oliver Cromwell had done in 1649 was to revive the old presidential court. Obviously he saw that it could be made an instrument for cheap and summary justice. However his decision was also inspired by the 'many petitions from inhabitants of the province of Munster', and (as Cook acknowledged) the court was revived 'as formerly'.[81]

The presidency courts in Munster and Connaught had first been created in 1569. The Munster court's exact powers before 1649 are not known, but were probably very similar to those in the commission issued to Broghill as lord president of Munster by the council of state in 1660. Broghill was empowered to hear 'all civil actions, as well real as personal, and all suits and controversies whatsoever happening betwixt party and party'. Gaol deliveries could be held at the lord president's discretion, having cognizance of 'all treasons, felonies, and other criminal offences whatsoever'. Clearly the court's powers were extensive.[82]

Cook was well satisfied with the traditional powers of the Munster court: 'the forme and method of proceedings hath

80 Bodl., Rawlinson MS. A.189, ff. 390–390ᵛ.

81 Cook, *Monarchy no creature of Gods making*, sig. [e4].

82 Brit. Mus., Egerton MS. 2542, f. 334. Broghill's powers were the same as those granted to Mountrath as lord president of Connaught later in 1660 and printed in Lascelles, *Liber munerum publicorum Hiberniae*, i, part ii, 190. For the earlier commissions of 1608 and 1615 see: Brit. Mus., Harleian MS. 697, ff. 164 ff; J. Lodge, *Desiderata curiosa Hiberniae* (Dublin, 1772), ii. 34–5.

not by me been altered in any point considerable; but indeed the originall constitution of the court seeme [*sic*] to me to be excellent'. The special virtues he singled out were all well-established features: the procedure for debt was 'a most excellent and admirable composition of a court'.[83]   But as well as the benefits of the old constitution, Cook inherited its weaknesses, of which the most serious was the absence of authority to determine cases in which the title to land was involved. Also it could deal with debts worth not more than £40. Similar, if not identical, restrictions had existed earlier.[84]   The only important innovation had been to set up assize courts in each county.

Cook worked with the materials to hand. His praise obscured the nature of those materials. The Munster court was a prerogative body, part of the network which Strafford had used to circumvent the common law and, perhaps, to give justice to the poor. Cook used the Munster court in much the same way as Strafford had employed the council of the north. Cook's known connection with, and admiration for, Strafford may have encouraged him to emulate the latter's methods. It was a debt which could not be acknowledged openly in the Interregnum, so that the embarrassing and indeed anomalous character of the court was glossed over. The court's anachronistic position may well have been the reason for its abolition. Its survival depended ultimately on the revival of full presidential government in the province. Oliver Cromwell had commissioned Ireton as lord president of Munster late in 1649, intending him as a replacement for Charles I's nominee, Portland. Ireton's appointment was confirmed by the English parliament and made possible the creation of a full presidential government, 'consisting of the Lord President, two gownemen, viz. a first and second iustice, and other commissioners'.[85]   But when Ireton died in 1651, no new lord president was appointed.

The failure to nominate a successor made the continuance of the presidential court an anomaly. The future of the

---

83 Cook, *Monarchy no creature of Gods making*, sig. [e4]ᵛ–fl.

84 'His Maiesties Directions', *Analecta Hibernica*, xxvi, 198.

85 Cook, *Monarchy no creature of Gods making*, sig. [e4]. Among those who assisted in the court as commissioners were Sir William Fenton, Thomas Cokely and Walter Carwardine: Brit. Mus., Additional MS. 19,868, ff. 150ᵛ–151.

presidential governments was under discussion in England and Ireland. In 1651 the parliamentary commissioners at Dublin opposed further appointments as 'an unnecesary burthen to the state'.[86] Economy was one reason for abolishing the provincial councils and courts; another was political. The actual lord president of Connaught, Sir Charles Coote, and the likely lord president of Munster, Broghill, were suspected by the army Independents who doubted their loyalty to the commonwealth. To the Independents no successor to Ireton was better than Broghill as lord president.[87] Coote had been made lord president of Connaught in 1645. After 1649 there were efforts to have the post suppressed. Eventually, after much hesitation, his patent was renewed in 1655. It remained a titular honour: no presidential court or council functioned in Connaught during the Interregnum.[88]

Ireland's rulers between 1652 and 1655 were apparently hostile to the presidencies; thanks to them the Munster court was discontinued. In contrast, Henry Cromwell seems to have favoured provincial government, as a way of conciliating the Protestant settlers, especially in Munster. There were signs that he contemplated a revival of the Munster presidency.[89] However it was not until 1660 that the council of state in England made Broghill lord president and nominated a council: dispositions which were confirmed by Charles II.[90]

Although political and economic motives were probably behind the ending of Cook's work in Munster, it is also evident that his work there did not enjoy universal praise. The court's authority was limited. Nor was it always as expeditious as Cook claimed. The widow of a Captain Plunkett tried to recover the money outstanding on a contract between her husband and Broghill. Here, surely, was

---

86 Dunlop, i. 94.

87 Ireton and Col. John Jones doubted their loyalty. Nat. Lib. Wales, MS. 11,440 D, 17; Thomas Morris, 'Memoirs of Orrery', prefixed to *A Collection of the State Letters of Orrery*, with separate pagination, p. 18.

88 Brit. Mus., Egerton MS. 212, f. 27; Lascelles, *Liber munerum publicorum Hiberniae*, i, part ii, 189.

89 Hist. MSS. Comm., *Egmont MSS.* i. 589; *Thurloe State Papers*, vii. 574.

90 Brit. Mus., Egerton MSS. 2542, f. 334; 2551, f. 69; Hist. MSS. Comm., *Egmont MSS.* i. 611; Lascelles, *Liber munerum publicorum Hiberniae*, i, part ii, 185.

a case in which Cook's professions of helping the humble against the powerful might be tested. In 1660 the case was still undecided. Plunkett's widow had not received one penny of the debt and lamented the failure of justice. Extraneous factors hampered speedy decisions: records had been dispersed or destroyed during the war. In cases relating to contracts and land the inconveniences would be great. Nor do we know that the widow's claim in this case was good. Even so the case was too similar to the old, dilatory processes to inspire complete confidence in Cook's extravagant claims.[91]

Cook's success owed much to the summariness of his procedure. He himself admitted that there was criticism of the method as 'an inovation and precipitous iustice'.[92] Cook's sympathy with the poor and humble, and Oliver Cromwell's strictures against the great men of the province, suggested that the court might be used to free the tenantry from the landlords' oppressions. Together with the court's powerlessness to adjudicate land titles or substantial debt cases, this meant that it was more useful to the commonalty than to the leading Protestant settlers. The second earl of Cork's experience showed his dislike of Cook and the court. Lord Cork regarded Cook as his enemy, especially after two cases relating to lands tried before him in 1652. In the first case, between Cork and Valentine Greatrakes, Cook was allegedly so partial to Greatrakes 'that hee in court privately bespoke Carwarden, a councellor, to bee for Greatrakes; and when the cause was to be pleaded hee did argue more for him then any of his councell . . . ' In the second case Cork maintained that Cook 'contrary to all law, justice and proofe so pleaded in the behalfe of Pine, who was allyed to Greatrakes, that the verdict wold have gonne against me if I had [not] non suited myselfe ag[ains]t this verdict . . . This businesse was so shamefull that Mr. Hoare, my lawyer, vowed that cold he otherwise get heard hee wold never more plead in that court'.[93]

Cork's cousin, Dean Michael Boyle, furnished further examples of Cook's partiality. Boyle told Cork that

91 Nat. Lib. Ire., MSS. 13,192, unfoliated; 13,222 (2), item 4.
92 Cook, *Monarchy no creature of Gods making*, sig. [e4] v.
93 Chatsworth, Lismore MS. 29, 20 Dec. 1652, 21 Dec. 1652, 19 Aug. 1656.

after by a jury hee was awarded a debt of 100 li. and 20 li. for interest . . . the cheife justice, contrary to the verdict of the jury, put downe with his owne hand 20s. instead of 20 li. for the interest; he likewise told mee that having before the commissioners of the revenew sued one for a debt and gained execution the cheife justice, upon the oath of the person sued that hee was not worth 5 li., gave him dismisse, refusing to give way that he shold be lyable to the debt thogh he proved perjured and worth more then the debt.[94]

Whether or not Cook was guilty of malpractices, he seems to have leant over to help the small men and so antagonized influential landowners like Cork. Dislike of Cook was increased by his association with religious radicals in Munster, notably Colonel Phaire. In general the objections were against Cook rather than the court. Even the subordinate judges, Carwardine and Halsey, were more popular with the landowners, because more amenable to their wishes.[95] The suppression of the court was not wanted by the Protestants of Munster. Indeed after 1655 they petitioned for its revival, with a different chief justice.[96]

The exact date of the Munster court's demise is unknown. In May 1654 the second justice, Halsey, was still drawing his salary, and in May 1655 Cook participated in an assize at Cork, so the court may have continued until the four courts' restoration in 1655.[97] However changes had started by 1654, when commissioners for the administration of justice were sent into Munster. Moreover Cook was detached from the court in 1654, doing judicial work in Dublin and Athlone.[98] These other duties left him little time to officiate in Munster and also made him discontented. In 1655 he confessed 'I have sat some months at Dublin upon thorns, and with pricks in my conscience'. This unease turned to outright opposition when the decision to restore the four courts was revealed in 1655 and Cook himself was offered a post.[99]

Cook attacked the four courts because they enshrined many of the abuses which he had written against and which he had avoided in Munster: they were slow, inefficient, and

94 Chatsworth, Lismore MS. 29, Cork's diary, 24 Dec. 1652, 26 Jan. 1652[3].
95 Ibid., 21 and 22 Dec. 1652, 12 and 24 Jan. 1652[3], 17 July 1654.
96 Bodl., Carte MS. 44, f. 669; Clarendon state papers, 74, f. 52.
97 *Analecta Hibernica*, xv. 251; Hist. MSS. Comm., *Egmont MSS*. i. 568.
98 Ibid. i. 542; King's Inns, Dublin, Prendergast MSS. i, pp. 229, 441; ii, pp. 225, 324; Taylor, *Roger Ludlow*, p. 148.
99 Bodl., Rawlinson MS. A.189, f. 390[v].

unjust. The guilty escaped and the innocent suffered through technicalities. With the courts reappeared the sinecurists who battened on them. Once more equity and common-law jurisdictions were separated in different courts. As well as attacking details, Cook lamented a lost opportunity. Circumstances in Ireland, virtually *tabula rasa*, made it 'no hard matter to propound an exped[ien]t for speedie and easie justice'. Indirectly Cook was accusing Oliver Cromwell of betraying past promises: Cook appealed to him because there was 'power sufficient in his highnesse the lord protector' for 'the performance and making good of his many solemn promises . . . and ingagements for the good of the nations'.[100] Cook's eloquent appeal went unheeded: no one was now as scrupulous as he in honouring old promises.

Cook's refusal of office in the four courts involved no immediate sacrifice. He continued to sit with the commissioners at Athlone and then moved to Mallow to adjudicate on the claims of the former inhabitants of the Munster sea-ports.[101] By 1657 his official duties in Ireland were ended, and he returned to England where he tried to prevail on Oliver Cromwell to revive the Munster presidency court.[102] In 1659, following a judge's death, Cook was again offered the second justiceship of the upper bench. In 1655 he had refused it; in 1659 he accepted.[103] Why did he perform this volte-face? There are two possible explanations. First, Cook may have needed profitable employment. At various stages of his career his interest in money was stressed.[104] His conscience could be salved by arguing that as a judge he could do more towards moderating the law than by his continuing abstention from office. The other reason may be

[100] Bodl., Rawlinson MS. A.189, ff. 385ᵛ, 396.

[101] Dunlop, ii. 467, 535, 604–5, 613, 618; Prendergast, *The Cromwellian settlement of Ireland*, pp. 231, 232, 233; *Thurloe State Papers*, iv. 554–5, v. 354. Cook was for a time after 1655 recorder of Waterford, where he had acquired property. Pender, *JCHAS*, 2nd Ser. lii. 155, 168; *The Civil Survey*, vi, ed. Simington, pp. 133, 191; Nat. Lib. Ire., MS. 8643 (3).

[102] *Thurloe State Papers*, vi. 666.

[103] Ball, *The judges in Ireland*, i. 343; *Thurloe State Papers*, vii. 594; Dunlop, ii. 691; Chatsworth, Lismore MS. 30, no. 89.

[104] In 1646 Hamey called him 'a needy lawyer, an unknown hierophant and obvious cheat': Royal College of Physicians, B. Hamey to I. Dorislaus, 20 Aug. 1646, quoted in J. Keevil, *The Stranger's Son* (London, 1953), p. 107 (I owe this reference to Dr. W. R. Prest).

that Henry Cromwell was contemplating a revival of the Munster court, although it was no longer in that court that Cook was to work.

Nothing is known of Cook's service as a judge in 1659. In any case legal proceedings came to a halt in Ireland in September 1659. Identified with the party that briefly returned to power in 1659, the political changes of 1660 ended Cook's career.[105] He was taken prisoner, sent back to England, and there tried for his part in Charles I's trial. On 16 October 1660 he was executed.

Celebrated as a pamphleteer, reviled as a prosecutor of the king, Cook's reputation has fluctuated. Amongst his contemporaries he was deservedly commended for his judicial work in Ireland. Cook's concern with reforming the law was sincere: in Ireland his pertinacity in this cause was unique. Yet there were ambiguities in his work in Munster, obscured in his own and his friends' accounts. The court was reinvigorated by Cook's presence. However the court itself was not a new invention but part of the traditional legal system which Cook condemned and which Strafford had been denounced for using. Also Cook's partisanship, in politics and religion, affected his judicial work. It may well have benefited the poor; it undoubtedly antagonized the powerful. For Cook that was no bad thing, but for the Irish government increasingly eager to cultivate the substantial landowners, it was. We know too little of the court's workings to give any firm judgement, except that Cook's was the most determined attempt to improve the law in Ireland during the Interregnum.

v. The administration of the law

After the four courts' revival in 1655 the chance of radical reform receded. Henceforward adjustment had to come from within the restored traditional system. Procuring an adequate number of judges and enforcing the law throughout the whole country were now stressed, rather than reform. The changes that occurred were mostly of an unsensational sort,

---

105C.B., Jennings transcripts, A/16, 2 Dec. 1659; Dunlop, ii. 707; *The Memoirs of Edmund Ludlow*, ii. 104—5; *A Sober Vindication of Lt. Gen. Ludlow*, p. 11.

similar to those of 1634 and 1635. The two most important reforms were to use English as the language of procedure and to pay the judges.

At the assizes at Derry in January 1656 the chairman celebrated 'the law books [being] thrown open before us; and being translated into our mother tongue, we can now, without relying on the subtlety and sophisms of the lawyers, and the weak crutches of human learning, pry into those secrets which were hidden from our forefathers, and speak our minds in plain English ...'[106] This was an obvious benefit to the English and Protestant population. Amongst Irish-speaking Catholic; the value was much less, but there is no evidence that Irish-speakers used the four courts during the Interregnum. The court at Athlone which judged the qualifications of those to be transplanted to Connaught employed interpreters.[107]

The payment by the state of salaries to judges freed them from dependence on fees and allowances. The lord chancellor, Steele, was paid £1,000 p.a. for that office and another £1,000 as a member of the Irish council. The heads of the other courts received £500 p.a.[108] This was generous, but it did not attract new recruits to accept judicial office in Ireland. Attornies' fees could not be controlled. Also the numerous minor officials of the four courts reappeared after 1655. This source of patronage was too useful to be abolished.[109]

Cook had indicated another way in which justice was cheapened in Munster, by not having any attornies in the court. Lord Cork, however, was represented by a lawyer; it seems as if Cook took the part of lawyer for Cork's opponents.[110] This was probably not the result of official policy, but of the dearth of qualified lawyers in Ireland immediately after 1649. Indeed the government was alarmed

106'Extract from the papers of Sir Henry Butler (of the Ormond family) delivered at the Quarter-Sessions held at Londonderry, 21 Jan. 1655[6]', *Anthologia Hibernica*, i (Dublin, 1793), 413. Cf. *Statutes at large: Ireland*, ii. 230.

107*Analecta Hibernica*, xv. 297.

108Brit. Mus., Additional MS. 19,833, f. 3^v; Egerton MS. 212, f. 1^v; *The Clarke Papers*, ed. Firth, iii. 72.

109Brit. Mus., Lansdowne MS. 822, ff. 111, 126; Lascelles, *Liber munerum publicorum Hiberniae*, i, part ii, *passim*.

110Cook, *Monarchy no creature of Gods making*, sig. e4; and above, p. 273.

by this situation which encouraged all and sundry to set up as lawyers and plead their own cases: it was scarcely less dangerous than the freedom of anyone preaching the Gospel. The Irish government took steps to help King's Inns, so that it could train properly qualified lawyers.[111] A historian of the King's Inns suggested that the Cromwellians were more generous towards the institution than the Stuarts.

Three formal measures were intended to improve the supply of justice. In 1653 the parliamentary commissioners issued instructions for the guidance of commissioners for the administration of justice. This contribution belonged to the period of improvisation before the four courts' restoration. These instructions set out forms of procedure and the wording of writs. Delays were to be eliminated by putting limits on the time for adjournments; excessive reliance on technical accuracy — a target of Strafford, Cook, and the army radicals — was ended.[112] The intention was to facilitate summary but not arbitrary justice. In 1655 there were efforts to make the government's local judicial agents apply these practices. Judges on assize were enjoined to a closer surveillance of their subordinates. The scarcity of suitable men for sheriffs or revenue commissioners meant that too often these officers were dishonest. In 1655 there were stricter controls over sheriffs to stop the distraint of innocent men's property and the sale of offices and blank warrants. Sheriffs had also been guilty of imprisoning without trial.[113] But these were endemic ills, and there is no reason to suppose that the Cromwellians cured them.

The improvement in procedure in debt cases was a limited but useful reform. Changes in the treatment of debtors had occurred during the Interregnum in England and Scotland. In Munster Cook had inherited an equitable system of payment. An ordinance of 1653 attempted a more comprehensive

111 King's Inns, Dublin, Black book, ff. 123, 124ᵛ, 131ᵛ, 132, 139; *Cal. Anc. Recs. of Dublin*, ed. Gilbert, iv. 124–5; Duhigg, *History of the King's Inns, Dublin*, p. 177; *The Herbert Correspondence*, ed. Smith, p. 124.

112 *Instructions to be duly observed by the iudges of every respective court of iustice . . .* (Dublin, 1653).

113 Brit. Mus., Lansdowne MS. 1228, f. 8ᵛ; Nat. Lib. Ire., MS. 11,959, pp. 143–4; *A declaration . . . for removing and preventing of some mistakes in government in Ireland* (Dublin, 1655).

reform of debt proceedings in Ireland. The creditor was protected against evasion by the debtor remaining in prison in full enjoyment of his estate. The debtor was offered relief if he exposed his whole estate for settlement.[114]   This provision closely resembled a demand in *The Agreement of the People*,[115] in 1648, and was a rare example of part of the army radicals' programme being realized in Ireland. Whether or not the reform brought real results we do not know.

The third reform was of chancery. In 1659 new orders for the court's regulation were published. The adjustments were not radical, aiming rather at simplifying and expediting procedure, and again avoiding undue reliance on technicalities.[116]   What is odd about these valuable, if unsensational changes, is their late date. They were not the product of the first flush of reforming zeal after 1649; nor were they made when chancery was re-established in 1656. Indeed there can scarcely have been time to implement them before the court's operations were halted in September 1659. These *Rules* were issued by Lord Chancellor Steele's authority. How far he was responsible for their content we can only guess. Steele had served on a law reform committee in England and was asked to hasten to Ireland to help in the reform of the law. Possibly the *Rules* were a belated sign of interest in reform.[117]

The extreme paucity of Irish legal records, and the fact that two of these changes are known through the fortuitous survival of evidence, must make us cautious about belittling law reform in Ireland. But once the Munster court was abolished, it seems that achievements were of the same modest order as in England. Certain judicial appointments suggest an attempt to decentralize chancery, with masters in chancery extraordinary for Ulster and Munster, and in

---

114 A summary of this proclamation, dated 24 Aug. 1653, is printed in Steele, ii, no. 524 (Ireland). The only known copy is in Philadelphia. I have used the photocopy which is P.R.O., Dublin, M.3150.

115 *Leveller manifestoes*, ed. Wolfe.

116 *Rules and Orders to be observed in the proceedings of causes in the High Court of Chancery* (Dublin, 1659). The only known copy is in the Biddle Law Library, University of Pennsylvania. It is being edited for *Analecta Hibernica* by Dr. G. J. Hand, to whom I am most grateful for a photocopy.

117 St. Patrick's College, Maynooth, Renehan MS. ii. 256.

Tipperary (the last appointment raises the possibility that the Tipperary palatine court was to be resurrected in an attenuated form).[118]   A further change was in the law of treason, dictated by the difficulty of convicting the Irish rebels under the existing Irish law.[119]   More generally attempts were made to iron out differences between English and Irish law, and to ensure that it was English law that prevailed there. Judges were asked to advise which English laws needed to be introduced into Ireland and which Irish laws should be repealed.[120]   Behind that question lurked the fundamental issue of the constitutional relationship between England and Ireland. The projected union between the two countries would have completed Ireland's assimilation. However it was never given a legal foundation, and so doubt remained, especially over such contentious issues as the exact status of Poynings' 'law'.[121]

After 1649 the first priority of the government was to supply justice. Reform, although desirable, was less urgently needed than in England; and in Ireland itself there was little pressure for change. Ideas of reform were introduced from England, notably by Cook, but after 1655 the emphasis was even more strongly on making the old courts function well, and securing competent judges and enough barristers. Reform was not excluded, but there was no hope of innovation. This policy was acceptable to the majority of Protestant settlers who had no wish to see radical changes. Complaints about the courts under the Cromwellians were few, and arose mainly from the cessation of justice in the autumn of 1659. The four courts, the assizes, and quarter-sessions were what the settlers wanted and had after 1655. In the absence of fundamental reform, the efficiency of the courts rested on their judges, to whom the next section is devoted.

118 Lascelles, *Liber munerum publicorum Hiberniae*, i, part ii, p. 97; Brit. Mus., Egerton 212, f. 11; C.B., Jennings transcripts, A/26. In England a similar decentralization was proposed: Firth and Rait, ii. 951.

119 *Thurloe State Papers*, ii. 89, 94, 148; Dunlop, ii. 406—7; Firth and Rait, ii; 831.

120 T.C.D., MS. F.3.18, f. 104; Brit. Mus., Additional MS. 5014, article 5; Stowe MS. 185, f. 136; Bodl., Carte MS. 67, f. 307ᵛ; Dunlop, ii. 451; Hist. MSS. Comm., *Egmont MSS*. i. 579—80.

121 Brit. Mus., Stowe MS. 185, f. 139. Cf. A. Clarke, 'The history of Poynings' Law, 1615—41', *Irish Historical Studies*, xviii (1972).

vi.   The judges

Probably the greatest defect of the Irish legal system in the Interregnum was the lack of judges. Few suitably qualified men could be persuaded to leave England, and the administration was reluctant to entrust lawyers in Ireland with high office. The normal complement of each of the four courts was three judges. During most of the Interregnum three of the four courts had only one judge; the fourth (common pleas) perhaps had two.[122] The government knew that this situation was unsatisfactory and tried to improve it.

Always it had been difficult to attract competent judges to Ireland. The necessity of having politically reliable judges in the 1650s narrowed the field still further. One reason why Fleetwood had suggested that only two of the four courts be re-established was the near impossibility of finding enough judges. Agents in England sought recruits for Ireland, but with little success.[123] At first the English administration used the judges who survived in Ireland. All four of the commissioners for the administration of justice in Leinster appointed in 1651 — Sir Edward Bolton, James Donnellan, Thomas Dungan, and Sir Gerald Lowther — had held judicial office in Ireland under Charles I.[124] Similarly the candidates proposed by Fleetwood in 1654 included several with Irish experience before 1649.[125] However the English council of state was reluctant to use men with long connections with Ireland because of doubts about their affection to the English regime.

In 1655, with the four courts' revival, five judges were nominated by the English council of state: Lowther, Miles Corbet, Donnellan, Edward Carey, and John Cook.[126] The

[122] T.C.D., MS. F.2.1., f. 161; Bodl., Carte MS. 44, f. 666ᵛ; Brit. Mus., Harleian MS. 4892, f. 88; *Cal. S.P. Ire. 1660–2*, pp. 524–6; *Statutes at large: Ireland*, ii. 230. Briefly, in 1659, upper bench had two judges (Basill and Cook); and John Santhy was appointed a puisne judge in the court of exchequer.

[123] Brit. Mus., Lansdowne MS. 821, ff. 93, 103; Bodl., Firth MS. c.5., f. 114; *Thurloe State Papers*, ii. 733; iii. 196, 744; iv. 433, 509, 545; vi. 858; vii. 593–4.

[124] Lowther was chief justice of common pleas in 1634; Donellan had been chief justice of Connaught and a judge in common pleas; Dungan was third baron of the exchequer; and Edward Bolton succeeded his father, Sir Richard, as chief baron of the exchequer in 1639.

[125] Lowther, Donnellan, Sir James Barry, and John Bisse.

[126] *Cal. S.P. Ire. 1647–60*, p. 815.

previous year Richard Pepys, as well as being appointed to
the Irish council, was made chief justice of upper bench. In
1656 William Steele was nominated lord chancellor.[127] Of
these seven proposed judges, five were newcomers from
England, and only two — Lowther, nominated as chief justice
of common pleas, and Donnellan, to be second justice in the
same court — were Irish settlers. Even the complaisant
Fleetwood complained of the neglect of well-qualified and
experienced candidates already in Ireland and the preference
for younger Englishmen.[128]   Similarly Richard Pepys reported that Dungan and Edward Bolton were 'slyghted and
undervalued . . . and accounted as unworthy': objections dismissed by Pepys as captious. Dungan was ignored because of
his Irish birth and being 'ye only p[ro]testant of his
famely'.[129] Similar objections threatened Donnellan's career.
In 1655 there were attempts to rescind his appointment,
because of his Irish background and notwithstanding his zeal
in the Protestant interest. Henry Cromwell defended
Donnellan, but it is not clear whether Donnellan's appointment as second justice was upheld.[130] This policy kept from
office several talented men at a time when the bench in
Ireland was grossly understaffed.[131] Of the two Anglo-Irish
judges appointed, both were placed in the least important
court, and one perhaps never officiated.

Two of the judges nominated in 1655, Carey and Cook,
refused office. Let us consider the judges who certainly took
office: Lowther, Pepys, Corbet, and Steele. Lowther was a
conspicuous representative of Old Protestant interests. Admitted to King's Inns in 1619, Lowther was the godson and

---

[127] Brit. Mus., Additional MS. 4184, f. 47; Bodl., Carte MS. 63, f. 618. *Cal. S.P. Dom., 1654*, pp. 453, 563, 564, 568.

[128] *Thurloe State Papers*, iii. 559.

[129] Bodl., Carte MS. 63, f. 618. Dungan's lack of office reduced him to a low condition: Duhigg, *History of the King's Inns, Dublin*, p. 187.

[130] The son of an archbishop of Tuam, his appointment in 1637 had been seen as a sop to the native Irish. *Cal. S.P. Ire., 1633–47*, pp. 168, 178; Clarke, *The Old English in Ireland*, p. 119; *Thurloe State Papers*, iii. 744; iv. 40, 376, 509; Brit. Mus., Lansdowne MS. 821, f. 111; King's Inns, Black book, f. 117; Lascelles *Liber munerum publicorum Hiberniae*, i, part ii, 80.

[131] Pepys suggested that Barry, 'an able and honest man', and Bisse, 'a man of learninge and integrity', be made judges: Bodl., Carte MS. 63, f. 618.

heir of a justice of common pleas.[132]   His rise was rapid, and
helped when, in 1634, the earl of Cork paid £1,000 to secure
his appointment as chief justice of common pleas. Lowther,
once appointed, proved a loyal servant of Strafford rather
than of Lord Cork, and was impeached by the Irish parliament in 1641. During the rebellion he showed great zeal in
the Protestant cause and equally great hostility to the
Catholics.[133]   In the Interregnum Lowther championed Old
Protestant interests; and Broghill seems to have played a part
in his reappointment in 1655.[134]

The other three judges, Pepys, Corbet, and Steele, who
presided over the upper bench, the exchequer, and chancery
respectively, were newcomers from England. In the past
efforts had been made to appoint English judges as a way of
Anglicizing Irish justice.[135]   These three men were also
members of the Irish council, and as such involved in political
and religious controversy. As we have seen, Pepys was a
conservative supporter of Henry Cromwell's policies; Steele
put himself at the head of the Independents in Ireland and by
1658 was openly opposed to Henry Cromwell; Corbet had
links with the Baptist opposition and was identified with the
party against Henry Cromwell. Unfortunately their judicial
work was, on occasion, drawn into the disputes. Early in
1655 Corbet took advantage of Pepys's absence from the
council (owing to illness) to recommend that the court of
upper bench be suppressed, a move which Pepys saw as an
attempt to deprive him of employment.[136]   In 1658 Steele
alleged that some Irish judges 'upon occasions give their
opinions in points of law not according to their conscience,
but to please'. Probably Steele was referring to Pepys's
conspicuous support of the decision to restore tithes.[137]

132 E. T. Bewley, 'Some notes on the Lowthers who held judicial office in
Ireland in the seventeenth century', *Transactions of the Cumberland and
Northumberland Antiquarian and Archaeological Soc.* N.S. ii (1902); P.R.O.,
Dublin, Lodge MSS., alphabetical list of members of King's Inns from 1607,
unfoliated.

133 *Cal. S.P. Ire. 1633–47*, pp. 36, 175; *Letters and dispatches of Strafforde*,
ed. Knowler, i. 392; *Lismore papers*, ed. A. B. Grosart (London, 1886–8), 1st
Ser. iii. 280; iv. 25; Hist. MSS. Comm., *Egmont MSS.* i. 238, 314.

134 Hist. MSS. Comm., *Egmont MSS.* i. 541, 543, 547, 565.

135 *Cal. S.P. Ire. 1575*, p. 52; ibid., *1577*, pp. 111, 124.

136 Bodl., Carte MS. 63, f. 620.

137 *Thurloe State Papers*, vii. 198.

The Irish council was scarcely better staffed than the bench. The three judges could ill be spared from the council board. During term time the council's meetings were reduced to three each week, in the afternoons.[138]   Both the courts and the council suffered from this duplication of duties. To relieve part of the burden it seems that commissioners were appointed to assist the judges on circuit and in the four courts.[139]

Pepys was an elderly man when he came to Ireland, attracted (it seems) by the chance of improving his fortune. He was a younger son. Connections with Edward Montagu perhaps helped in his appointment. Educated at the Middle Temple, of which he was treasurer in 1648, his career advanced in the Interregnum: in 1654 he was made a serjeant-at-law and soon afterwards a baron of the English exchequer.[140]   In Ireland he showed himself sympathetic to the Old Protestants and Henry Cromwell. His conservatism won him some telling tributes. Lord Cork noted that Pepys was 'much for the ministrye and the law', in contrast with some of his radical colleagues; Henry Cromwell praised him as 'a good councellor, and a good judge, and indeed a right honest man'; whilst Robert Wood said he was 'much beloved and had a great reputation for integrity'.[141]   His death inspired a eulogy from Robert Maxwell, the bishop of Kilmore, and tributes from Dr. Worth, whose policies Pepys had supported in the council.[142]

Steele had been more prominent than Pepys before coming to Ireland. In the 1640s he had been amongst the radicals in London; in 1649 he became recorder of the city; and in 1654 represented it in parliament. He had taken part in several of

138Nat. Lib. Ire., MS. 2322, f. 267; C.B., Jennings transcripts, A/10, 20 Oct. 1656; Sheffield Univ. Lib., Hartlib MS. xxxiii, Wood to Hartlib, 21 Mar. 1658[9].

139Chatsworth, Cork's diary, 13 July 1657; Ladyman, *The Dangerous Rule*; Devon County Record Office, Courtney MSS., 1508/Irish deeds; Cork's diary, 14 May 1659.

140*D.N.B.*, Bodl., Carte MS. 63, ff. 618, 620, W. C. Pepys, *Genealogy of the Pepys Family, 1273–1887* (London, 1887), pp. 57–62; C. H. Hopwood, *A Calendar of the Middle Temple records* (London, 1903), pp. 77, 159.

141Chatsworth, Cork's diary, 13 July 1657; *Thurloe State Papers*, vii. 590; Sheffield Univ. Lib., Hartlib MS. xxxiii, Wood to Hartlib, 4 Jan. 1658[9].

142R. Maxwell, *In obitum clarissimi integerrumique viri D. Richardi Pepys Armigeri* (Dublin, 1658[9]); Worth, *The servant doing*, pp. 29–31.

the *causes célèbres* of the 1640s, culminating in Charles I's trial, at which he was to officiate as attorney. Illness, however, prevented him participating. His assurances that this was no diplomatic indisposition were evidently accepted, because he received new offices. In 1654 he was made chief baron of the English exchequer.[143] In the same year he was appointed to the Irish council, at Fleetwood's insistence, although it was clear that he could not be spared from England. Fleetwood suggested the unsatisfactory compromise, 'if at present he cannot come, yet let him have ye name and waite w[ha]t providence will order concerning his coming or stay'.[144] Even when appointed lord chancellor in 1656, Steele did not immediately come.

Steele may have been responsible for the chancery *Rules* of 1659; otherwise he showed more interest in religious controversy than in legal reform. Contemporary comments from political opponents indicated that he was an impartial judge. Even Bishop Griffith Williams commended Steele because, 'although he hated my person, he said, though I deserved it not, I should have justice, and so he did me justice presently . . .'[145]

The third judge who was also a councillor was Miles Corbet. His conduct excited condemnation which seems to have had some justification. The second son of a prosperous Norfolk family, whose fortunes were based on the law, Corbet was educated at Cambridge and Lincoln's Inn.[146] Yarmouth was his special sphere of influence: he was its town clerk and recorder, and sat for it in the 1628, Short, and Long Parliaments. In the Long Parliament Corbet aligned

143There are accounts of Steele in *D.N.B.*, and Ball, *The judges in Ireland.* See also; Brit. Mus., Additional MS. 21,247, ff. 172, 174; *Cal. S.P. Dom.* 1649–50, p. 130, ibid., *1651*, pp. 11, 325; ibid., *1653–4*, pp. 79, 88, 98, 100, 105, 356, 373, 419, 425; ibid., *1654*, pp. 1, 6, 46, 70, 82, 88, 146, 169, 233, 243, 323, 362–3. ibid., *1655*, pp. 43, 90, 91, 95, 96, 98, 100, 218, 255, 383; J. Nalson, *The trial of Charles I* (Oxford, n.d.), p. 18; Brenner, *P. and P.* lviii, 98; *Mr. Recorders Speech to the Lord Protector . . . the eighth of Febr. 1653[4]* (London, 1653[4]).

144*Thurloe State Papers*, ii. 492–3. While still in England Steele was nevertheless paid £1,000 p.a. as an Irish councillor: Brit. Mus., Additional MS. 19,833, f. 3.

145P.R.O., SP. 63/287, 52; G. Williams, *The persecution and oppression of John Bale*, p. 29.

146For Corbet's life: *D.N.B.*; A. E. C[orbet], *The family of Corbet* (London, n.d.), pp. 259–61; Keeler, *The Long Parliament*, p. 142.

himself with the radical and war party, and was rewarded with a clerkship in the court of wards and, in 1648, a registrarship in chancery, reputedly worth £700 p.a.[147] Appointed a parliamentary commissioner for Ireland in 1650, Corbet had no special connection with Ireland, other than the common one of being an adventurer.[148] In 1654 there was talk of omitting him from the Irish council because of his connection with the opposition to the protectorate, but he was saved by Fleetwood, and so remained to oppose Henry Cromwell.[149]

Before coming to Ireland Corbet had acquired an ill odour as chairman of the committee of examinations (of royalists). He was accused of acting 'contrary to Magna Carta, the Petition of Right, and all those laws of God and man, which in the kings time were in use . . . ' This criticism, from an unsympathetic source, might be dismissed were it not for similar comments, and especially Pepys's strictures against Corbet's behaviour, in Ireland. As a member of the court to hear the claims of Catholic rebels, Corbet (according to Pepys) was 'p[ro]voakeing and extreme and unjust'. More generally Pepys alleged that the 'arbitrary power he [Corbet] condemned in ye king he would exercise heere and putt ye judges uppon if he could'.[150] On the other hand, Ludlow, a political ally of Corbet, defended him, saying that 'he impaired his own estates for the publick service, whilst he was the greatest husband of the treasure of the common-

147D. Brunton and D. H. Pennington, *Members of the Long Parliament* (London, 1954), p. 80; L. Glow, 'Political affiliations in the House of Commons after Pym's death', *Bulletin of the Institute of Historical Research*, xxxviii (1965), 50 and n. 1; *The mystery of the good old cause briefly unfolded*, p. 8; Underdown, *Pride's Purge*, pp. 151, 371; Clement Walker, not a disinterested writer, alleged that Corbet was £3,000 in debt in 1640, 'more than he was worth'. He was said to receive another £1,000 as chairman for the committee for scandalous ministers: *The Compleat History of Independency* (London, 1661), part i, p. 168.

148J. R. MacCormack, 'The Irish adventurers and the English civil war' *Irish Hist. Studies*, x (1955–6), 46.

149*Thurloe State Papers*, ii. 492; iii. 145.

150Bodl., Carte MS. 63, ff. 618, 620; *Memoirs of Denzil Lord Holles* (London, 1699), p. 130; *The Knyvett Letters, (1620–1644)*, ed. B. Scholefield (London, 1949), pp. 35, 145–8, 150–7, 159, 161; J. Lilburne, *Innocency and truth justified* (London, 1645), pp. 13–15; *Persecutio undecima* (1648), p. 33; Thomas, *Religion and the decline of magic*, p. 372, n. 3; Walker, *The Compleat History of Independency*, part i, p. 55.

wealth'. This defence not only exaggerated Corbet's control, as chief baron of the exchequer, over the Irish adminis-tration's financial affairs, it also ignored his acquisitions of Irish lands.[151]   Corbet had an unsavoury reputation by 1649, which he did nothing to efface in Ireland. Even so detailed charges against him are few: those of Pepys and from the Irish General Convention in 1660, which complained of 'the late exorbitant proceedings . . . in the tyme of the late chief baron Corbet'.[152]   The main charge against him was of determining cases for which there was a remedy at common law, and his proceeding with these cases on English bills was condemned as 'an apparent violacon of the laws of the land, and the rights of the people'.[153]

Otherwise the complaints against the judges were vague or trivial. Irregularities were said to have crept into chancery, and the Munster presidency court through 'its longe dis-continuance and by ye phanatick practices of ye late userpers'.[154]   Most of the shortcomings arose from having only one judge in each court. With the possible exception of Corbet, the Cromwellian judges were able and conscientious men who compared well with their predecessors and suc-cessors in Ireland. In 1662 Petty commented that Ireland 'is seldom enough able to give due encouragment to profound judges and lawyers, which makes judgements very carnal . . . ', and Clarendon declared that 'the law is . . . little understoode' by the Irish judges.[155]   By paying generous salaries to judges, the Cromwellians may well have attracted better men: unfortunately there were not enough.

The problem of judges was comparable to that of ministers of the Gospel. At the apex of the Cromwellian system were men of undoubted ability, who were well paid. But they were too thinly spread in Ireland, and to make the law run throughout the country it was essential to have sufficient able judges to staff the lower courts. We must now consider

---

151 *The Memoirs of Edmund Ludlow*, ii. 332; Bodl., Carte MS. 41, f. 636.
152 Bodl., Carte MS. 44, f. 666ᵛ.
153 This was not a new practice: 'His Maiesties Directions', *Analecta Hibernica*, xxvi. 197; *C.J. Ire.* i, appendix, p. 198.
154 Bodl., Carte MS. 44, f. 666ᵛ; Clarendon state papers, 79, f. 184ᵛ.
155 Petty, *A treatise of taxes and contributions*, p. 28; Nat. Lib. Ire., MS. 13,222 (2), letter 6; Ball, *The judges in Ireland*, i. 276.

these subordinate judges. Some who acted as assistants in the four courts and elsewhere, like John Bisse, John Santhy and William Halsey were highly enough regarded to be appointed Irish judges after 1660.[156]   During the Interregnum there were four masters in chancery, three of them (Thomas Caulfield, Bartholomew Foulke, and Dr. Dudley Loftus) were probably members of Old Protestant families.[157]   The fourth, Dr. Jonathan Edwards, came to Ireland with the Cromwellians in 1649. Edwards was a doctor of medicine and employed as a government preacher in the 1650s.[158] Caulfield and Loftus were reappointed masters in chancery after 1660, while Foulke became chancellor of the Tipperary palatinate court.[159]

Another important, if exceptional, judicial body was the commission to adjudicate claims on forfeited lands. In work of this nature the administration was not prepared to use Anglo-Irish judges. Instead, in 1654, Pepys, Corbet, John Cook, Philip Carteret, William Allen, John Reading, and Roger Ludlow were nominated.[160]   Both Carteret and Allen were closely connected with the Cromwellian army and were Baptists. Allen, although in origin said to be a feltmaker, may have had a legal training; he was admitted to King's Inns in 1654.[161]   Reading had been invited from England in 1653.[162]   The most interesting member of the group was

156 Disloyalty was imputed to Halsey after his promotion to chief justice of Munster in 1660: Bodl., Clarendon State papers, 83, ff. 283—4.

157 A Thomas Caulfield was elected to the General Convention of 1660 for Newtown, Co. Down. *An Account of the chief occurrences ... 12—19 March* [1660], p. 36. Foulke was clerk of common pleas in Co. Louth during the Interregnum, a judge for probate and testamentary cases, and represented Tipperary in the General Convention. Ibid., p. 38; C.B., Jennings transcripts, A/15 and A/26; Brit. Mus., Egerton MS. 212, f. 11.

158 P.R.O., Dublin, Ferguson MS. xiii, p. 94; R.C.B., Seymour MSS., p. 106; Dunlop, ii. 394: *Cal. Anc. Recs. Dublin*, ed. Gilbert, iv. 210; Cotton, *Fasti*, ii. 302, 309, 355; iii. 377; J. B. Leslie, *Ossory Clergy and Parishes* (Enniskillen, 1933), p. 93; Seymour, pp. 140, 183, 211.

159 *Cal. S.P. Ire. 1660—2*, p. 525; Lascelles, *Liber munerum publicorum Hiberniae*, i, part ii, 58.

160 Dunlop, ii. 455—6.

161 Nat. Lib. Wales, Deposit 409 B, p. 28; King's Inns, Dublin, Black book, f. 114. A William Allen, son of William Allen of Cheapside, London, entered Gray's Inn in 1634. He has never been identified with Adjutant-General Allen. Foster, *The Register of admissions to Gray's Inn, 1521—1889*, p. 204.

162 Bodl., Firth MS. c.5, f. 114; King's Inns, Dublin, Prendergast MS., ii, p. 438; I. Roots, 'Cromwell's Ordinances', in *The Interregnum*, ed. Aylmer, p. 149.

Roger Ludlow. He had had a long and distinguished career in New England which gave him unusually appropriate qualifications for judicial office in Ireland. After a conventional education at the Inner Temple, Ludlow went to New England where he undertook administrative duties: first, as an assistant to the Massachusetts Bay Company, and then, in 1635, as a commissioner for the government of Connecticut. In 1638 he became Connecticut's lieutenant governor.[163]   So far as Connecticut's legal institutions were concerned the colony was in the same condition as Ireland after 1649: a white paper. Ludlow largely framed the constitution of 1639 and devised a civil code of laws in 1650. The latter, regulating the activitites of colonial life, treated many of the topics of foremost interest to Ireland's settlers: the possession, acquisition, and retention of land. Biblical authority was used to determine which should be capital offences.[164]   In 1654 Ludlow came to Ireland, encouraged no doubt by his cousin, Edmund Ludlow, and his son-in-law, Nathanael Brewster.[165]

In Ireland no use was made of Ludlow's experience: he was given no chance to innovate, and indeed was employed in relatively humble capacities.[166]   Thus, although English army officers were employed in judicial work, usually these subordinate judges were men with appropriate qualifications or experience. Finally we should consider the lowest echelon of the judiciary, the commission of the peace, because its attitude would be important in the success or failure of Cromwellian policy.

It was not until 1655 that the commission of the peace was widely revived in Ireland. Other local courts were re-established with the restoration of municipal charters in 1656; also in 1656 courts leet, baron, and of piepowder, together with courts of record for trial of personal actions worth less than £200, were authorized in the market towns

---

163 For Roger Ludlow: *D.N.B.*; *The Memoirs of Edmund Ludlow*, ed. Firth, ii. 104, note 2; Taylor, *Roger Ludlow*.

164 *The Code of 1650, being a compilation of the earliest laws and orders of the General Court of Connecticut* (Hartford, n.d.), esp. pp. 21, 28–9, 35.

165 J. H. Perry, *Roger Ludlowe* (Fairfield, 1914), p. 20.

166 King's Inns, Dublin, Prendergast MS. ii, pp. 821, 825, 851, 878; Brit. Mus., Additional MS. 19,833, f. 3ᵛ; Dunlop, ii. 673; Taylor, *Roger Ludlow*, pp. 153, 154–5.

of newly planted areas.[167]   Unfortunately we have few
details of the composition of the commission of the peace.
However the limited evidence suggests a shift back to Old
Protestants after 1655. The earliest commission of the peace
is for Leinster in 1651.[168]   It included three of the commissioners for the administration of justice in the province,
the attorney-general, the recorder of Dublin, and Dr. Dudley
Loftus: all men of wide legal experience. Apart from the
mayor of Dublin and Alderman Daniel Hutchinson, five of
the Leinster justices of the peace were Old Protestant
settlers,[169]   six were military commanders, and three members of the civil administration. In all, twelve of the justices
had been settled in Ireland before 1641; ten were newcomers.
A similar pattern is found in the sixty-three justices of the
peace for Dublin nominated in 1653, except that the newcomers included more members of the civil administration
based in the capital and a larger proportion of the Old
Protestants were Dublin aldermen.[170]

The commission of the peace for Wexford, named in
March 1655, was dominated by newcomers. Four judges were
included to guarantee some degree of legal knowledge.[171]
Only four Old Protestants, one of whom was absent in
England, were named. There were nine Cromwellian officers
and four members of the civil administration.[172]   In areas not
heavily planted with Protestants before 1641 (like Wexford),
the Cromwellians had to rely on new settlers as their local
agents. After Henry Cromwell's arrival there seems to have
been a deliberate effort to appoint Old Protestants wherever
possible. Religious and political extremists were removed

167Dunlop, ii. 580; *The Bishopric of Derry and the Irish Society, i, 1602–70*,
ed. Moody and Simms, p. 291; *Cal. Anc. Recs. of Dublin*, ed. Gilbert, iv. 124–5.
168T.C.D., MS. F.3.18, f. 110.
169Sir Robert King, Sir Theophilus Jones, Sir John Hoy, Sir Edward Bagshaw,
and Sir John Sherlock.
170Two of the Dublin commission had always to be drawn from Lowther,
Donnellan, Dungan, and Bolton, and the mayor of Dublin. T.C.D., MS. F.3.18, f.
139v.
171Pepys, Lowther, John Cook and William Halsey: Swan, *JRSAI*, 5th Ser. iv.
67.
172The Old Protestants were Sir Charles Coote, Annesley (in England), Sir
Walsingham Cooke, and Nicholas Loftus. Brit. Mus., Lansdowne MS. 821, f. 3;
Calendar of the Clarendon State Papers, ed. Macray and Coxe, ii. 198; Bodl.,
Clarendon state papers, 88, f. 261.

from the bench.[173]   From the Conway letters we can detect the prominence of Rawdon, Arthur Hill and Clotworthy in the commissions for Counties Down and Antrim.[174]   In Kildare the five justices of the peace who officiated at the quarter-sessions in September 1658 included at least four established settlers, all civilians.[175]   In March 1658 Lord Cork was added to the commissions of the peace for Counties Waterford and Cork. The majority of his fellow justices were Old Protestants like him.[176]

The sparse evidence shows that the commission of the peace was used by Henry Cromwell to consolidate his alliance with the substantial settlers, using them rather than the officers of the English army to represent the protectorate in the localities. Such a policy was limited by the uneven nature of earlier plantation, and perhaps too by the control exercised by Steele as lord chancellor over the appointment of justices of the peace. Politically it was a wise policy, helping to win Old Protestants to the regime.[177]   It was, however, inimical to reform, allowing the oppressions of great men and landlords which Oliver Cromwell had condemned in 1649. But as with the four courts in Dublin, so with justice in the counties, the emphasis after 1655 was on making the traditional system work well.

In contrast with other areas of policy, it was the period between 1649 and 1655 that saw the major legal reforms. This was the result of Oliver Cromwell's and Ireton's personal

---

173 'Letters etc., of early Friends', *The Friends' Library*, ix, p. 406.

174 P.R.O., SP. 63/287, 6, 27, 39ᵛ, 147, 168, 170, 200.

175 Comerford, *Collections relating to the dioceses of Kildare and Leighlin*, i. 320. The four Old Protestants were Meredith, chancellor of the exchequer, Sir John Hoy, Daniel Hutchinson, and Richard Tighe. The fifth was William Sandes. A William Sandes was in Ireland in 1642; during the Interregnum there was a Baptist William Sondes; after 1660 a William Sondes with nonconformist leanings was created baronet. J. and J. B. Burke, *A genealogical and heraldic history of the extinct . . . baronetcies of England, Scotland and Ireland* (London, 1844), p. 614; Ivimey, *A history of the English Baptists*, i. 245; *C.J. Ire.* i, appendix, p. 39; Nickolls, *Original letters and papers*, p. 145; *The town book of Belfast*, ed. Young, p. 72; *Letters of John Pinney, 1679–99*, ed. G. F. Nuttall (Oxford, 1939), p. 52.

176 Chatsworth, Lismore MS. 29, Cork's diary, 10 Feb. 1657[8], 9 Mar. 1657[8], 13 Apr. 1658.

177 For a similar process in England: Underdown, in *The Interregnum*, ed. Aylmer, p. 177; Underdown, *Pride's Purge*, pp. 342–3.

interest, and in particular the scope that they allowed to
John Cook. In general army Independents were more interested in reforms than the conservatives favoured by Henry
Cromwell after 1655. The improvisations after 1649 were
also made possible by the immediate aftermath of war. The
return of peace was accompanied by a desire to restore
traditional forms of justice. Cook's summary methods in
Munster may also have been disliked because they discriminated against those who had previously manipulated the law
to their own ends. The Cromwellians showed that they were
no more enemies of the law than enemies of learning. Care
was taken in the choice of judges and the training of
barristers; real improvements — the payment of judges, the
use of English, reform of the debt law and of chancery —
were attempted. What was lost was the chance to refashion
the Irish legal system and to test there reforms for England.
This was something that Cook had wanted to do, but there
was little pressure from those already settled in Ireland for
such far-reaching changes.

X

CONCLUSION

There were three important elements in English policy towards Ireland in the Interregnum. Each must now be assessed before coming to a general conclusion about the policies I have described. The three elements are: first, the policy formulated in England; and then the policies decided in Ireland, by Oliver Cromwell, Ireton, and Fleetwood between 1649 and 1655, and thereafter by Henry Cromwell.

Many of the major acts concerning Ireland originated in England: the confiscation of rebels' land, the adventure for lands, the settlement of soldiers' arrears, the transplantation to Connaught, and the oath of abjuration. Also the more general lines of policy, continuing the Anglicization of Ireland by spreading the Protestant Gospel and education, establishing English industries, and enforcing English law, and the tenor of commercial policy, were decided in England. Those reponsible for decisions in England changed during this period. The original form of Ireland's settlement had been laid down by the Long Parliament in 1642: it was then amplified by the Rump (in the act of settlement of 12 August 1652) and by the Barebone's Parliament (through the act of satisfaction of 26 September 1653). Later measures, such as the oath of abjuration, were decided by Oliver Cromwell, as protector, his council of state, and the protectorate parliaments. These shifts in power in England, from the Long Parliament to the army and to Cromwell, produced no fundamental changes in policy for Ireland, but only variations of emphasis. There was agreement over confiscating the rebels' lands and instituting a new plantation. The only important difference was Oliver Cromwell's greater interest in Ireland's welfare than either the Rump or the protectorate parliaments. In the 1640s he had been identified with a forward policy of reconquest; he was concerned with the welfare of the English army in Ireland; he was conscious of his and the army's duty to justify their God-given victories by punishing the guilty Irish and advancing Protestantism. While in Ireland between 1649 and 1650 Oliver Cromwell proceeded vigorously, introducing legal changes in Dublin and Munster, pressing the Rump to pass the act for the propagation of the Gospel in Ireland, and taking steps to advance Protestantism. But once he left the island and when he was protector, Cromwell showed less care for Ireland. Although he was capable of individual acts of generosity, these acts did not amount to a consistent policy, and he did nothing to overcome the council of state's or parliament's neglect of Irish business.

The freedom of the governors in Dublin to initiate policies was limited. It was greatest during Oliver Cromwell's months there as lord lieutenant when he was able to improvise and use summary methods as he reconquered the country. Thereafter acts of parliament, ordinances, and the detailed instructions given to the parliamentary commisssioners and councillors curtailed freedom. But if the general lines of policy were drawn at Westminster, the character of the governors in Dublin could make a significant difference to policy, as was shown by the very different complexions of Fleetwood's and Henry Cromwell's regimes.

As a preliminary to my conclusions, it is worth reviewing the verdicts of earlier historians on these three policies. In contrast with the voluminous treatment of the civil war in Ireland and the history of the Confederate Catholics, the 1650s have received short shrift. The reasons are not hard to find. To Irish historians the 1650s are obviously a less attractive subject than the 1640s, offering no record of incipient nationalism or heroic and successful defiance of England, but only butchery, flight, or monotonous martyrdom. Also, whereas the participants in the struggles of the 1640s wrote to justify their behaviour, most of them left Ireland between 1649 and 1652 and so tell us little of what Cromwellian rule was like. Those Irish Protestants who did remain in Ireland and who co-operated with the new regime were not anxious to broadcast the fact after 1660. This reticence appears, for example, in the various biographies of Lord Broghill which misrepresent or pass hastily over his activities in the Interregnum.[1]

The accounts of English historians writing in the seventeenth century are equally limited. First, there was a general reluctance to speak well of the usurpers; secondly, about their activities in Ireland, especially when the war was over, there was deep ignorance. Such weaknesses are found even in the greatest of these historians, Clarendon. Although Clarendon wrote a history of the Irish rebellion, it ends with the departure of Ormonde's deputy, Clanricarde, in 1652.[2] Clarendon's history of the English rebellion suffers as a result of his being an exile in the 1650s, and his remarks about policy in Ireland are very generalized. Nevertheless Clarendon, as well as exemplifying the prevailing ignorance of the 1650s, illustrates another tradition in the historical treatment of the period: a relatively sympathetic view of Henry Cromwell. Similar characteristics are found in the *History* of Edmund Borlase. Although Borlase was more sympathetic than Clarendon to the usurpers and had had access to the accounts of Dr. Henry Jones, the vice-chancellor of Trinity College during the Interregnum,[3] he passes hurriedly over the 1650s, only sparing some praise for Henry Cromwell.

These early historians give little detail on the 1650s, and are generally unable (or unwilling) to understand the premisses of Cromwellian policy. Later historians, reflecting the growth of nationalism in Ireland, tended to draw the policy of the 1650s into contemporary controversies, using it to illustrate the cruelties and injustices of English domination. As a result those anxious to uphold English authority in Ireland used the past, and even the Interregnum, to support

---

[1] T. Morris, *A sermon preached at the funeral of the right honorable Roger earl of Orrery* (London, 1681); T. Morris, 'Memoirs of Orrery', prefixed to *State letters of Orrery*. The manuscript versions of the latter (Brit. Mus., Sloane MS. 4227 and P.R.O., Dublin, MS. 473) include passages suppressed in the published text. There is another memoir by John Love in P.R.O., Dublin, MS. 2449.

[2] E. Hyde, earl of Clarendon, *The history of the rebellion and civil wars in Ireland* (Dublin, 1719/20).

[3] E. Borlase, *The history of the execrable Irish Rebellion* (London, 1680), p. 19; J. Nalson, *An impartial collection of the great affairs of state* (London, 1682), ii. 534–5; J. Ware, *The history and antiquities of Ireland*, ed. W. Harris (Dublin, 1764), ii. 199. Cf. R. MacGillivray, 'Edmund Borlase, historian of the Irish rebellion', *Studia Hibernica*, ix (1969).

their case. The most extreme example of such an apologist was Froude, writing in the 1880s to defend the policy of coercion, and turning to Oliver Cromwell as the original and most successful exponent of the policy. Froude's contentions run counter to the evidence. In particular he praised the commercial policy of the Interregnum, alleging that 'for the first and last time the sole object of the English government was to further to the utmost possible degree, the advancement and prosperity of Irish industry'; and that Ireland's interests were no longer subordinated to England's.[4] None of this was true. Similarly, although there was an impressive recovery from the devastations of war and efforts were made to foster agriculture and manufactures, Froude's statement that Ireland 'never prospered as she prospered in the years of the Protectorate' is sheer fantasy. His basic defence of Cromwellian policy — that the Irish respect 'a master hand, though it be a hard and cruel one', and that had repression continued the Catholic Irish would have embraced Protestantism — is equally questionable.

Froude's praise of commercial policy was quickly disputed.[5] But it was his second statement that Cromwellian policy would, in time, have loosened Catholicism's hold that has excited most criticism among perceptive twentieth-century historians. Robert Dunlop, for example, anxious not to judge the Cromwellians too hastily, nevertheless believed that ultimately their policy failed because it was not responsible for the conversion of a single Irish Catholic.[6] Sir Charles Firth took a similar line: the change in landownership, substituting Protestants for Catholics, was a matter of indifference to the bulk of the native population: the prohibition of their religion was not, and it kept alive a 'spirit of discontent and revolt'.[7] More recently Professor Beckett has suggested that the permanent result of Cromwellian policy was to unite the hitherto discrete Old English and Gaelic Irish as Catholics threatened by the intolerant and discriminatory policy of a Protestant regime.[8]

[4] J. A. Froude, *The English in Ireland in the eighteenth century* (London, 1887), i. 149–53.

[5] Firth, *The last years of the Protectorate*, ii. 173.

[6] Dunlop, i, pp. clxi–clxii.

[7] Firth, *The last years of the Protectorate*, ii. 145.

[8] Beckett, *The making of modern Ireland*, p. 115.

Thus the inclination of historians has been to see the policy of confiscation and repression as successful in that it did take land out of Catholic hands, but misguided in that it left the native population sullen and resentful. I have already suggested that the new plantation was much less successful than expected. Although the change in land-ownership was accomplished, new settlers and Protestant tenants failed to arrive in sufficient numbers. Trade and political power became Protestant monopolies, but Catholics were not cleared from the walled towns or from the areas east of the Shannon.

Two questions now arise. Was the policy of confiscation and discrimination against Catholics misguided because unlikely to secure English rule in Ireland? Secondly, just how repressive was Cromwellian policy? The easy dismissal of Cromwellian policy rests on the assumption that all attempts to convert the Irish Catholics were foredoomed to failure. But the reason why Ireland was never brought under the religion, as well as the rule, of England has yet to be fully explained. One historian who has faced this difficult problem, Father Corish, suggested that in 1601 Catholicism might still have been overthrown in Ireland; by 1641 it was secure, thanks to the impact of the Counter-Reformation.[9] More recently Father Corish has stressed events after 1641, the struggles of the 1640s and the effects of the Cromwellian persecution, in identifying the Catholic faith with the fight of Ireland against England.[10] Clearly the use of Catholicism as an index of guilt in the 1650s made that faith the focus of nationalism and anti-English sentiment. Nevertheless there are two signs which suggest that Ireland, even in the 1650s, was not yet lost to Protestantism and that Cromwellian policy could have succeeded.

First, there were the conversions to Protestantism during the Interregnum. The sincerity of these changes was questioned, and in many cases they amounted to no more than occasional or nominal conformity. Yet the converts' sincerity mattered little so long as they were prepared to live peace-

[9] P. J. Corish, 'The reorganisation of the Irish Church, 1603–41', *Proceedings of the Irish Catholic Historical Committee* (1957), p. 14.

[10] P. J. Corish, 'The Origins of Catholic Nationalism', in *The history of Irish Catholicism*, ed. P. J. Corish, iii, fascicle 8 (Dublin and Sydney, 1968).

fully under English rule. These conversions were accomplished not by Protestant evangelization, but by punitive
measures which excluded Catholics from the possession of
land, from trade, and political power.

The second hopeful sign was the apparent moderation of
the initial repression: the laxity which allowed the return of
Catholic priests and schoolmasters and on which the Archbishop of Armagh commented in 1658. The changes were
slight, and there was no question of Catholics recovering their
lands or their privileges. It did, however, suggest that Henry
Cromwell might give the Catholics a tacit toleration. If he
did, the way would be open for co-operation between
moderate Catholics and the Cromwellian regime, similar to
the harmony between the Old English and the early Stuarts
before 1641. There was, then, this shift away from punitive
to conciliatory measures as the decade progressed. Hopeful as
this alteration was, it can be objected that conciliation could
not work as it had before 1641 because too much had
changed. The Catholic laity was now more interested in
regaining its lands and power than in securing toleration for
the practice of its religion; and concessions on those issues
could never be made by Henry Cromwell, since they were
equally unacceptable to the government in London and to his
Protestant supporters in Ireland.

It is doubtful if the later moves towards conciliation of the
Catholics would have worked. Was the earlier policy of
converting them also doomed? Had the harsh penalties on
the Catholics been accompanied by a vigorous effort at
evangelization, with care for instruction in Irish, it is possible
that conversions would have been much more numerous. This
policy was what the new English rulers had promised. Yet it
was not forthcoming. The reasons were the difficulty of
finding enough suitable ministers and of paying them, and
the theological and political controversies which turned the
Protestant community in on itself. Also there was confusion
how the native Irish should be treated. Especially in the early
years of the Interregnum there was reluctance to send
ministers to preach in Irish to the Catholics. When the need
of such efforts was appreciated, it was impossible to find
properly qualified preachers for this work. Attempts to

convert the Irish were negligible, and a unique opportunity when the incentives to abandon Catholicism were strong was forfeited. However the spirit of resistance was kept alive among the Catholics less by the ban on their religion (which in practice was evaded with increasing ease) than by the commercial and political discrimination against them.

The two other elements in policy were those provided by Ireland's governors before and after 1655. Earlier judgements on Fleetwood's government have been uniformly unfavourable, blaming him for sectarian strife and the political disaffection in the army and civil administration. Fleetwood was an unfortunate choice as lord deputy: he was popular only among the extremists who made him their tool. Much of the introspection of English policy and neglect of Ireland's needs resulted from his conduct. He obliged Henry Cromwell to dissipate his energies conciliating those whom Fleetwood had alienated. Yet is the harsh verdict on Fleetwood wholly justified? His period of government was when the English army radicals and Independents had greatest influence: since these were men of ideals committed to far-reaching reforms we should expect to see this reflected in policy in Ireland. Most of the important reforms and innovations — the substitution of government salaries for tithes, state payment for schoolmasters, the revival of the Munster presidency court, the act for the propagation of the Gospel — occurred between 1649 and 1652, and were the result of the Rump's or (more often) Oliver Cromwell's and Ireton's activity. Fleetwood was generally content to follow the policies already laid down, having conventional ideas on law reform and tithes. In general the members of the army and administration in Ireland until 1655 were more interested in English events and institutions, and as a result formulated no detailed proposals for reform in Ireland. Only gradually did those who acquired and settled on Irish lands concern themselves with their adopted country's wants. The main contribution of the administration in Dublin to policy between 1652 and 1655 was to support a harsh attitude towards the native Irish, and to defend their promiscuous transplantation to Connaught. This was a policy harmful to Irish economic interests and illustrated well their doctrinaire approach.

Henry Cromwell's arrival in 1655 ushered in new policies. However the completeness of the change must not be exaggerated: it took time for his approach to evolve in response to circumstances; moreover it was not until 1657 that he had power to enforce his wishes. Similarly we have to guard against too uncritical praise of his administration. In the past he has received encomiums because his attitude has been misunderstood. In particular it has been suggested that Henry Cromwell was sympathetic towards the restoration of Charles II: this showed most clearly in 1659, but (it is alleged) coloured the whole of his government. This view originated in Henry Cromwell's own actions after 1660, and especially in the picture he himself gave of his policy to secure a pardon. His explanations were accepted and he was well treated thanks to the support of his allies in Ireland in the 1650s (like Broghill and Worth) and, more important, the support of returning royalists (notably Ormonde and Clarendon).[11] The opinion of Henry Cromwell's supporters appeared in print: in the accounts of Clarendon, Borlase, and the Presbyterian minister Patrick Adair. According to Clarendon Henry Cromwell in Ireland 'by the frankness of his humour, and a general civility towards all, and very particularly obliging some, render'd himself gracious and popular to all sorts of people . . . .'[12] Henry Cromwell's cultivation of moderates and conservatives was contrasted with the disastrous effects of Fleetwood's government.[13] The one note of criticism found in these histories was the disappointment at Henry Cromwell's 'tame submission' to the Rump in 1659, instead of using his popularity among the Irish Protestants to defy the English authorities.[14] This tradition of favourable treatment was continued by Firth who recognized that when Henry Cromwell

came to Ireland he found it administered solely in the interest of one section of the colony, namely the last comers. The welfare of the older colonists was subordinated to theirs, and the opinions of the men born

11 H. Cromwell to Clarendon, 9 Apr. 1662: Brit. Mus., Sloane MS. 4159, f. 74; E. Worth to H. Cromwell, 6 June 1660: Huntingdon Record Office, 731 dd Bush, no. 145; R. W. Ramsey, *Henry Cromwell* (London, 1933), pp. 363–7.

12 Clarendon, *The history of the rebellion and civil wars in England* (Oxford, 1707), iii. 662.

13 Borlase, *The history of the execrable Irish rebellion*, p. 315.

14 Clarendon, *The history of the rebellion and the civil wars in England*, iii. 754.

and bred in Ireland were neglected and set aside in favour of officers who had been in the country three or four years. Henry Cromwell, however, governed Ireland in the interest of all classes of colonists and all sections of Protestants. In this respect he faithfully carried out the policy of his father.[15]

These evaluations raise three important questions: was Henry Cromwell little better than a crypto-royalist who paved the way for Charles II's restoration, even if at the crucial moment he shrank from coming out openly in the king's favour? Secondly, did he indeed govern Ireland 'in the interest of all classes of colonists and all sections of Protestants'? Finally, was this a policy that his father had originated? The picture of Henry Cromwell as a crypto-royalist is as unconvincing as the contemporary explanations of Worth's or Broghill's collaboration in similar terms. Henry Cromwell's main interest was in the secure establishment of his father's protectorate in Ireland, which meant creating solid support there and if necessary altering policies to achieve it; it also meant supporting those, notably the advocates of kingship, who offered ways of making the regime more stable in England. With Oliver Cromwell's death the chances of such stability lessened: increasingly it looked as if the protectorate in the person of his brother could not supply the necessary framework of order. Henry Cromwell was too committed to the Cromwellian protectorate to come out openly for an alternative in 1659; there is no reason to suppose that he viewed the unconditional restoration of Charles II with any more enthusiasm than did his political associates in Ireland. But once it had happened, then support had to be given.

Henry Cromwell's intention in 1655 had been to achieve a balance between the various sects, between the army and the civilian population, and between the Old Protestants and the newer settlers. This entailed increasing the influence of those disavowed by Fleetwood: the Independents and Presbyterians, the Old Protestants and the civilians. The unwillingness of the soldiery, the radicals, and the Baptists to accept a reduction of influence defeated the attempt at balancing. Henry Cromwell was forced into heavier dependence on his chosen allies. Thus by 1658 it was no longer

15 Firth, *The last years of the Protectorate*, ii. 174.

true that all the sects enjoyed an equal share of his favour: the Independents, the Baptists, and the Quakers had virtually none; army radicals, commonwealthsmen, and opponents of the protectorate were also excluded from influence. Thanks to the attitude of his confidants (his brother-in-law, John Reynolds; Petty, his secretary; and Lord Broghill) and his own inclinations, the Old Protestants settlers were deferred to more than the adventurers or the new settlers. There were sound political reasons for this policy: it was successful in giving the protectorate a secure foundation among the Protestants of Ireland. However Henry Cromwell's undisguised enthusiasm for the alliance damaged him in England, and ultimately undermined his political position.

Firth suggested that conciliation of the Old Protestants had begun with Oliver Cromwell. Certainly during his campaign of 1649–50 he offered concessions to the Protestants, especially in Munster, forcing Broghill to serve the new regime rather than retire to the continent and using other influential settlers like Sir William Fenton. Yet once the military crisis had passed and when Cromwell was no longer in Ireland his generosity towards the Old Protestants was rarely translated into action, and then only after much prompting. It cannot be denied that Oliver Cromwell saw the importance of having the Old Protestants' support, but was himself concerned to achieve this only in 1649–50. I have also shown that the policy of using the Presbyterians of Ulster started before Henry Cromwell's arrival. Clearly then there were precedents for a more generous treatment of the older planters before 1655. It was only after Henry Cromwell's arrival that this became a consistent policy, and indeed the main characteristic of his administration. He was committed to it not only for its political merits, but because of his personal friendship with several leading Old Protestants. Attacks on his policy, which he regarded as factious, made him cling to it more obstinately.

Apart from the gain of political support that the alliance brought, it advanced certain reforms. The co-operation of Worth and the Presbyterians of Ulster helped to re-establish religious order, and was the prelude to ecclesiastical reorganization which would strengthen the church, help to increase the supply of clergy, and allow the conversion of the Irish to be tackled. But there were losses: in religious freedom, and superficially with the restoration of tithes. Similarly the Old Protestants were interested in improving Protestant education, sat on the committee for the second college in Dublin, and even patronized the schemes of the Hartlib circle. By relying on the Old Protestants Henry Cromwell did not shut the door on reform, but made it more likely that the reforms would be cautious and better attuned to Ireland's needs.

Much of the marked difference between Fleetwood's and Henry Cromwell's governments came from the latter's association with the Old Protestants. There were other causes, notably the return of peace to Ireland. Peace made it possible and indeed necessary to restore more traditional forms of justice and to dismantle the temporary reforms. Peace may also have influenced the decision to restore municipal charters in 1656; to revive the commission of the peace; and to free trade from some of its restrictions in 1655. It is impossible to know how much direct responsibility Henry Cromwell had for these changes, or for the greater stability and prosperity. We can see that Henry Cromwell made good use of the return to normality, installing the Old Protestants in positions of national and local influence and thereby contributing to Ireland's political security if not to its growing prosperity.

It was with the problem peculiar to the Interregnum that Henry Cromwell's success was greatest, but transitory. The revolutionary and initially unpopular English regime was secured in Ireland. Less spectacular was progress with the more deep-rooted problem: how to Anglicize Ireland and to prevent any future revolt against England. Throughout the Interregnum the Cromwellians continued traditional methods of establishing English authority. With no new answers the Cromwellians relied instead on bringing greater vigour to the familiar policies. It is true that useful reforms in ecclesiastical organization (advocated before 1641) and of the law were accomplished; further ambitious improvements in education and the church were projected. Yet by 1660 the Protestant Gospel, English habits, language, and industries, were no more securely planted among the native population than they had been in 1640. The earlier neglect, of which the Cromwellians had loudly complained, had not been remedied. Indeed the gulf between Protestant rulers and the Catholics had widened: Catholics could no longer be appeased by toleration of their religion; they had now to recover their estates, their share of trade and of political power, before they would accept English rule.

The failure to redeem their promises was in part explained by lack of time and money: given more time Cromwellian achievements would have been more substantial. Another defect was that plans of reform devised in England were introduced into Ireland after 1649 and were often irrelevant to Irish conditions: only slowly did those with first-hand experience of the country gain influence over policy.

Although the protectorate was swept away in Ireland, all traces of its influence were not so easily effaced. Protestants were left owning the bulk of Irish land, and with monopolies of trade, local and national power. The Old Protestants had acquired unprecedented influence; the pre-eminence of Dublin among Irish towns had increased. Presbyterianism in Ulster, thanks to government support, had taken an ineradicable hold; other varieties of Protestant nonconformity had been introduced and would persist.

In other respects the policies of the Interregnum resembled those of the governments before 1641 and after 1660. Efforts had been made to strengthen the Protestant church, to make English education and law more effective, and to encourage English manufactures. Yet there had been disputes about how exactly this was to be done, and about what attitude towards the Irish should be adopted. Moreover the genuine concern of the administration in Dublin and of the Irish Protestants met with indifference or opposition in London, where different and less generous ideas of Ireland's needs prevailed. Once again the disadvantages of rule from England had appeared very clearly: it produced administrative neglect and inefficiency; it led to legislation which subordinated Ireland's interests to England's. These were familiar weaknesses of the Irish government: the Cromwellians had not surmounted them. The administration in Dublin was weakened by its key role in English domestic politics: the contending parties in England looked hopefully to their supporters in Dublin as possible sources of strength. This too was nothing new. Strafford's identification with the party of 'Thorough' had involved his Irish government in the attacks of 'Lady Mora' and of the 'country' party; after 1660 the Irish viceroyalty was again dragged into the contentions of the English court.[16]

The radical spirit which Oliver Cromwell and the English army promised to breathe into Irish affairs after 1649 was only briefly and fitfully felt. Instead, under Henry Cromwell, the Irish Protestants acquired an administration peculiarly sensitive to their interests. The character of the Protestant 'ascendancy' was largely formed in these years, and was the Cromwellians' enduring contribution to Ireland. Otherwise policy continued in its conventional pattern, occasionally improving on the record of the Stuarts and the Church of Ireland, more often falling short.

[16] J. C. Beckett, 'The Irish viceroyalty in the restoration period', *Trans. Royal Hist. Soc.*, 5th Ser. xx (1970); J. I. McGuire, 'Why was Ormond dismissed in 1669?', *Irish Historical Studies*, xviii (1973).

BIBLIOGRAPHY

I. GUIDES TO SOURCES

Abbott, T. K., *Catalogue of the manuscripts in the library of Trinity College Dublin* (Dublin, 1900).

Abbott, W. C., *A bibliography of Oliver Cromwell* (Cambridge, Mass., 1929).

Ainsworth, John, 'Reports on manuscripts in private collections' (typescripts in Nat. Lib. Ire.).

Alden, John, *Bibliographica Hibernica: additions and corrections to Wing* (Charlottesville, Va., 1955).

Catalogue of the Bradshaw collection of Irish books in the University Library Cambridge (Cambridge, 1916), 3 vols.

Catalogue of the pamphlets, books, newspapers and manuscripts relating to the Civil War . . . collected by George Thomason, 1640–1661 (London, 1908), 2 vols.

Dean, J., *Catalogue of the manuscripts in the Public Library of Armagh* (Dundalk, 1928).

Dix, E. R. McC., *Catalogue of early Dublin printed books 1601–1700* (Dublin, 1897–1912), 5 parts.

    'Pamphlets, books, etc., printed in Cork in the seventeenth century', *Proceedings of the Royal Irish Academy*, xxx, C, no. 3 (1912).

    and S.na Casaide, *List of books, pamphlets, etc., printed wholly or partly in Irish* (Dublin, 1905).

Eager, A. R., *A guide to Irish bibliographical material* (London, 1964).

Hayes, R. J., *Manuscript sources for the history of Irish civilization* (Boston, Mass., 1964), 11 vols.

Leslie, J. B., *Catalogue of manuscripts in possession of the Representative Church Body* (Dublin, 1938).

Love, H. W., *Records of the Archbishops of Armagh* (Dundalk, 1965).

McNeill, C., *Publications of Irish interest published by Irish authors on the continent of Europe prior to the eighteenth century* (Dublin, 1930).

    'Rawlinson Manuscripts classes C and D', *Analecta Hibernica*, ii (1931).

    'Reports on the Rawlinson collection of manuscripts', *Analecta Hibernica*, i (1930).

Ogle, O., *et. al.*, *Calendar of the Clarendon State Papers* (Oxford, 1869–1969), 5 vols.

O'Neill, T. P., *Sources of Irish local history* (Dublin, 1958).

Public Record Office of Ireland, *Reports of the Deputy Keeper*, especially 10th, 14th, 26th, 55th, and 56th.

Russell, C. W., and Prendergast, J. P., *The Carte MSS. in the Bodleian Library, Oxford. A report* (London, 1871).

Scott, J. R., and White, N. J. D., *Catalogue of the manuscripts remaining in Marsh's Library, Dublin* (Dublin, 1913).

Shirley, E.P., *Catalogue of the library at Lough Fea* (London, 1872).

Simington, R. C., 'Annesley collection, Co. Down', *Analecta Hibernica*, xvi (1946).

Walsh, M. O'N., Irish books printed abroad, 1475–1700: an interim checklist', *Irish Book*, ii (1963).

Whitley, W. T., *A Baptist bibliography* (London, 1916).

Wing, D., *Short title catalogue of books ... 1641—1700* (New York, 1945), 3 vols.

Wolf, E., *Check-list of books in the Library Company of Philadelphia* (Philadelphia, Pa., 1959).

Wood, H., 'The Public Records of Ireland before and after 1922', *Trans. Royal Hist. Soc.* xiii (1930).

II. MANUSCRIPTS

National Library of Wales, ABERYSTWYTH
  Deposit 409 B. Letters from Baptists in Ireland, printed in J. Ivimey, *History of the English Baptists*; and in B. R. White, *Association records of the Particular Baptists* part 2.
  MS. 11440 D. Letter book of Col. John Jones, partly printed in *Trans. Historic Society of Lancashire and Cheshire*, N.S. i.
Public Record Office of Northern Ireland, BELFAST
  D.562/1—2. 2 letters of Sir J. Clotworthy.
  D.1608. MSS. of Earl Castlestewart.
  D.1759/1A/1. Transcript of the minutes of the County Antrim Presbytery, 1654—8.
  T.707. Dean Dobbs's transcripts from the corporation records of Carrickfergus.
City Archives Office, BRISTOL
  City Deposition Books, 1654—7 and 1657—61.
Society of Merchant Venturers, BRISTOL
  Wharfage Books, i (1654—9) and ii (1659—66).
University Library, CAMBRIDGE
  Add. MS. 711. Notebook of Anthony Dopping.
  Baumgartner Papers. Strype correspondence; letters of S. and T. Bonnell.
Chatsworth House, CHATSWORTH, Derbyshire
  Lismore MSS. 28—31. Diaries and correspondence of 2nd earl of Cork.
City Record Office, CHESTER
  AB/2. Corporation minutes.
  CB/166. Protested bills.
  ML/2/32. Mayors' letters.
University College Library, CORK
  Transcript of the Cork Court of D'Oyer Hundred Book, 1656—1729.
Christian Brothers' School, Richmond St., DUBLIN
  Jennings's transcripts from the Commonwealth records formerly in P.R.O., Dublin.
  Jennings's transcripts of Waterford prerogative wills formerly in P.R.O., Dublin.
Genealogical Office, The Castle, DUBLIN
  MSS. 87, 96, 141, 177, 178. Genealogies and copies of wills, mainly of Dublin aldermen.
King's Inns, DUBLIN
  Black Book.
  MS. 27 iv. 97. 3 vols. of transcripts made by J. P. Prendergast from the Commonwealth records, formerly in P.R.O., Dublin.
Archbishop Narcissus Marsh's Library, DUBLIN
  MS. Z.3.1.1. Complaint against Provost Winter.
  MS. Z.3.2.17(2). Notes by D. Loftus on courts martial, c. 1651—3.
  MS. Z.3.5.28. Commonplace book of C. Williamson.
  MS. Z.4.2.11. Commonplace book of D. Loftus.
  MS. Z.4.4.8. Copies of R. Boyle's letters to N. Marsh about the Irish translation of the Bible.
  MS. Z.4.5.16. Letterbook of C. Williamson.
National Library of Ireland, DUBLIN
  MS. 32. Orrery correspondence, mainly after 1660.
  MS. 40. W. Domville's 'disquisition', July 1660.

MSS. 2322–6. Ormonde MSS.
MS. 2701. Photocopy of Annesley MSS. relating to Irish finances.
MS. 2745. Orders of Sir C. Coote, 1651–4.
MS. 2992. Trim corporation records.
MS. 4908. Clonmel Assize records, from 1663.
MSS. 6254, 6257. Rentals of 2nd earl of Cork's property.
MSS. 8642–4 Lane MSS.
MSS. II,959–61. Transcripts from the Commonwealth records formerly in P.R.O., Dublin.
MS. 12,813. Calendar of the Lismore MSS. at Chatsworth.
MSS. 13,177–13,224. Orrery MSS., formerly at Petworth.
MS. 14,910. Notebook of R. Southwell.
P.C. 30. Bowen MSS.
Oirechtas Library, The Dail, DUBLIN
MS. 3.G.12. Petty's reports as a commissioner for setting out lands.
Pearse St. Public Library, DUBLIN
Gilbert MS. 78. Charters and documents of the Merchant Guild of Dublin.
Gilbert MS. 80. Documents of the Dublin Tailors' Guild.
Gilbert MS. 219. Proceedings of the General Convention's commissioners, 1660.
Public Record Office, DUBLIN
1.a.53.55/56. Lodge's extracts from the Cromwellian Chancery rolls.
1.a.53.72. List of members of King's Inns, Dublin, since 1607.
MS. 2.3.25. Repertory of pleadings in Chancery, 1655–9.
MS. 473. Copy of Morrice's life of the 1st earl of Orrery.
MS. 2449. Collections relating to 1st earl of Orrery.
MS. 4974. Caulfield MSS., extracts from the Commonwealth records formerly in P.R.O., Dublin.
Ferguson MSS. ix, x, xii, xx. Extracts from Exchequer records formerly in P.R.O., Dublin.
Prerogative will-book, 1664–84.
Repertory, Cromwell's leases, Chancery, 1656–9.
Thrift abstracts 2337, 5165–90.
Thrift will 2829. Will of V. Gookin (copy).
Representative Church Body, DUBLIN
MS. J.7. Survey by E. Worth of the bishopric of Killaloe, 1661.
MS. Libr.14. Transcript of the vestry book of St. Katherine and St. James, Dublin, from 1657.
MS. Libr.20. Seymour MSS., extracts from the Commonwealth records formerly in P.R.O., Dublin.
MS. Libr.26. Transcripts of Inquisitions, Counties Down and Antrim, 1657.
MS. Libr.27. Transcripts of Inquisitions, Counties Armagh and Kildare, 1657.
MS. Libr.41. Leslie's succession lists for the diocese of Elphin.
MS. T.11. Notebook of Dr. H. Jones.
Royal Irish Academy, DUBLIN
MS. 12.0.13. White book of the Guild of St. Anne.
Trinity College, DUBLIN
Bursar's Book.
General Registry from 1626.
General Registry from 1639.
MS. A.6.13. Sermons of W. Lamb and H. Sankey, 1674.
MS. D.1.2. Library catalogue.
MS. F.2.1. Includes details of customs, 1658–61, and instructions of H. Cromwell to his agents in 1659.

MS. F.2.3. Includes depositions of A. Boate and J. Harding in 1643.
MS. F.3.18. Collections of Dr. H. Jones.
MS. F.4.16. Dr. H. Jones's notes on High Court of Justice, 1653–4.
MS. F.5.15. Notebook of C. Williamson.
MS. F.6.3. Notebook of Dr. S. Winter.
MS. 1.4.20a. Admissions Book.
MS. N.1.4a. Account book of W. Petty.
MS. N.2.3. Includes acts of Irish Convocation in 1661.
MS. V.1.20. Catalogue of manuscript benefactions.
MS. V.2.15. Barrett's history of Dublin University.
Mun. P/1/376. Draft of a bill to establish the second college at Dublin by Sir M. Eustace.
Mun. P/1/378a. Invitation to H. Cromwell to accept the chancellorship.

City Record Office, EXETER
DD 62700A. Dartmouth Adventurers for Irish lands.

County Record Office, EXETER
1508/Irish deeds. Courtney MSS.

The University Library, HARVARD
MS. 218.22 F. Letters to Orrery.

Public Library, HOVE
Autograph collection nos. 211–19. Pepys family letters.

Huntingdon and Peterborough Record Office, HUNTINGDON
731 dd Bush. Cromwell-Bush MSS., especially nos. 11–14, 17, 18, 144 and 145.

Municipal Archives, KILKENNY
White Book of Kilkenny.

British Museum, LONDON
Add. MS. 4816. Collections of 1st earl of Anglesey for a history of Ireland.
Add. MS. 5014. Instructions for Fleetwood and his council, 17 Aug. 1654.
Add. MS. 15,635. Entry book of Irish statutes staple from 1658.
Add. MS. 19,833. Transcript of Irish civil list of 1655.
Add. MS. 19,843. Entry book of Irish statutes staple, 1639–58.
Add. MS. 19,868. Roche MSS.
Add. MS. 29,960. Includes letter of Sir H. Waller, 1657.
Add. MS. 31,885. Fee book of Dr. T. Arthur.
Add. MS. 35,102. Day book of trustees for satisfying army arrears in Ireland, 1656–9.
Add. MS. 36,786. Includes petition of Ald. D. Hutchinson.
Add. MS. 43,724. Originals of correspondence printed in *Thurloe State Papers*.
Add. MS. 45,850. Includes letter of Broghill, 1660.
Egerton MS. 212. Extracts from the Commonwealth records formerly in P.R.O., Dublin.
Egerton MSS. 1761, 1762, 1779. Transcripts of the Commonwealth records formerly in P.R.O., Dublin.
Egerton MS. 2542. Includes Broghill's commission as lord president of Munster, 1660.
Egerton MS. 2648. Barrington MSS.
Harleian MS. 4784. Survey of Edward Roberts's Irish lands, 1659.
Lansdowne MSS. 821–3. Correspondence to H. Cromwell, 1655–9.
Lansdowne MS. 1228. Includes two petitions on Irish trade, Lord Chancellor Steele's advice to H. Cromwell, and the address of the Dublin convention of ministers of 1658.
Sloane MS. 427. Includes a letter of M. Symner.
Sloane MS. 972. Contract of Irish customs farmers, 1658.

Sloane MS. 1008. Borlase MSS.
Sloane MS. 1731 B. Journal of Jean de Cardonnel's voyage to Ireland in 1649.
Sloane MS. 4062. Includes letter of J. Price, Fellow of T.C.D., 1659.
Sloane MS. 4106. Includes letter of B. Worsley, 1653.
Sloane MS. 4159. Includes H. Cromwell's letter to Clarendon (copy), April
 1662.
Sloane MSS. 4165–6. Correspondence between England and Ireland, mostly
 printed in *Thurloe State Papers.*
Sloane MS. 4184. Appointment of R. Pepys, 1654.
Sloane MS. 4227. MS. of Morrice's life of Orrery.
Sloane MS. 4274. Includes letter of E. Worth, 1654.
Sloane MS. 4278. Includes letters of N. Brewster.
Sloane MS. 4460. Notes on Dr. S. Winter's life.
Stowe MS. 82. Annotated and interleaved edition of Borlase's *History.*
Stowe MS. 185. Includes instructions to E. Ludlow, 1659.
Dr. Williams' Library, LONDON
 Baxter letters.
Guildhall Library, LONDON
 MSS. 5561–2. Ironmongers' Company: Prime Warden accounts, 1658–62.
 MS. 7270. Fishmongers' Company: Irish lands.
 MS. 11,588/4. Grocers' Company: orders of the court of assistants, 1640–68.
 Uncatalogued. Christ's Hospital muniments, including a MS. 'Erasmus Smith
  Esqr. His booke relateing to his charityes in Ireland', and a box labelled
  'Erasmus Smith'.
Royal Society, LONDON
 Boyle letters, vols. i and vii.
 Boyle papers, viii, xxv, and xxviii.
 Classified papers (arithmetic), 1660–1740, i. R. Wood on infinite fractions.
 Council book.
 Journal book.
Sion College, LONDON
 MS. Arc. L.40.2/E.17. Minute book of the London provincial assembly,
  1647–60.
Society of Religious Friends, Euston Rd., LONDON
 Swarthmore MSS.
Chetham Library, MANCHESTER
 MS. collection relating to Ireland.
St. Patrick's College, MAYNOOTH
 Renehan MSS. ii. Bagwell's transcripts from the Commonwealth records
  formerly in P.R.O., Dublin.
Bodleian Library, OXFORD
 Carte MSS. There is in the library a MSS. catalogue, arranged chronologically, of
  this large collection. Vols. 21, 23, 30, 32, 45, 48, 59, 63, 67 contain
  important material.
 Clarendon state papers. Include letters of Orrery. Vols. 45 and 46 contain
  letters about A. Boate.
 MS. Firth c.5. Transcripts from the Commonwealth records formerly in P.R.O.,
  Dublin.
 Ralwinson MSS. Apart from the originals of the correspondence in *Thurloe
  State Papers,* see:
 A.13. Letters of Irish Baptists, 1654.
 A.14. Petition of native Irish against transplantation.
 A.37. Proposal of 'Church of Christ', Whitechapel to settle in Co. Wexford.

A.189. John Cook's reasons for refusing judicial office in Ireland in 1655.
A.208. Includes payments to the army and administration in Ireland.
B.508. Rent roll of houses in Irish towns confiscated after 1649.
D.830. Historical and theological collections of the Revd. John Crookshank, 1658–65.
D.1347. Letter of G. Marsden to S. Mather.
MS. St. Edmund Hall 16. Notebook of H. Dodwell, 1659.
Worcester College, OXFORD
Clarke MS. 52.
University Library, SHEFFIELD
Hartlib MSS., especially nos. vii(116), vii(123), viii, ix, xv, xxxiii, xlvii, lxii(45).
. Papers and correspondence of R. Child, S. Hartlib, W. Petty, M. Symner, R. Wood and B. Worsley.
Corporation Record Office, SOUTHAMPTON
DM 1/1. Correspondence of W. Molyneux and J. Flamsteed.
Somerset County Record Office, TAUNTON
C.1509: DD/Br/ely. Pym and Hales MSS.
Trevelyan MSS., box 57.
Municipal Archives, WATERFORD
Corporation records.
Houghton Library, The University, YALE
Osborn collection. Correspondence of W. Petty and S. Hartlib.

III. PRINTED SOURCES

Abbott, W. C., *The writings and speeches of Oliver Cromwell* (Cambridge, Mass., 1937–47), 4 vols.
An Asesssment for Ireland for three months . . . (Dublin, 1654).
Barclay, A. R., ed., 'Letters, etc., of early Friends', *The Friends' Library*, ed. W. Evans and T. Evans, ix (Philadelphia, Pa., 1847).
Berry, H. F., 'The Records of the Dublin Gild of Merchants, known as the Gild of Holy Trinity 1438–1671', *JRSAI* xxx (1900).
        ed., *The Registers of the Church of St. Michan, Dublin. 1636–1700*, Parish Register Society of Dublin, iii and viii (Dublin, 1907–9).
Berwick, E., ed., *Rawdon Papers* (London, 1819).
Blake, M. J., 'Galway Corporation Book B', *Journal of the Galway Archaeological and Historical Society*, v (1907–10).
Bolton, Robert, *A translation of the Charter and Statutes of Trinity College, Dublin* (Dublin, 1760).
The Works of the Honourable Robert Boyle, ed. T. Birch (London, 1744), 5 vols.
Burrows, M., ed., *The Register of the Visitors of the University of Oxford, 1647–58*, Camden Society, N.S. xix (London, 1881).
Diary of Thomas Burton, Esq., ed. J. T. Rutt (London, 1828), 4 vols.
Calendars of the State Papers, Domestic; Ireland; and Venetian.
Caulfield, R., ed., *The Council Book of the corporation of Kinsale* (Guildford, 1879).
        ed., *The Council Book of the corporation of the city of Cork* (Guildford, 1879).
        ed., *The Council Book of the corporation of Youghal* (Guildford, 1878).
        ed., *The Register of the Parish of Holy Trinity (Christ Church) Cork, July 1643–February 1668* (Cork, 1877).
'Commonwealth Records', *Archivium Hibernicum*, vi (1917), and vii (1918–21).
[Anthony Dopping], 'Remedies proposed for the Church of Ireland (1697)', ed. J. Brady, *Archivium Hibernicum*, xxii (1959).

Dunlop, R. T., *Ireland under the Commonwealth* (Manchester, 1913), 2 vols.
Ellison, C. C., ed., 'Bishop Dopping's Visitation Book, 1682–85', *Riocht na Midhe*, Records of the Meath Archaeological and Historical Society, iv (1971–).
'Extract from the papers of Sir Henry Butler ...', *Anthologia Hibernica*, i (Dublin, 1793).
Fincham, F. W. X., 'Letters conerrning Sir Maurice Eustace, Lord Chancellor of Ireland', *Eng. Hist. Rev.* xxv (1920).
Firth, C. H., ed., *The Clarke Papers*, iii and iv, Camden Society, N.S. lxi and lxii (1899, 1901).
    ed., 'Papers relating to Thomas Wentworth ... From the MSS. of Dr. William Knowler', *Camden Miscellany*, ix, Camden Society, N.S. liii (1895).
    and R. S. Rait, *Acts and Ordinances of the Interregnum 1642–60* (London, 1911), 3 vols.
Fitzmaurice, H. W. E. P., marquess of Lansdowne, *The Petty Papers* (London, 1927), 2 vols.
    The Petty-Southwell Correspondence (London, 1928).
Forbes, A. B., *Winthrop Papers, v, 1645–49*, Massachusetts Historical Society (Boston, Mass., 1947).
Gilbert, J. T. and Lady Gilbert, eds., *Calendar of the Ancient Records of Dublin* (Dublin, 1889–1944), 19 vols.
Gilbert, J. T., *Facsimiles of National Manuscripts of Ireland* (London, 1884), 4 vols.
Gogarty, T., ed., *Council Book of the corporation of Drogheda, i, 1649–1734* (Drogheda. 1915).
Hamilton, William, *The Hamilton Manuscripts*, ed. T. K. Lowry (Belfast, n.d.).
Hayes, Richard, ed., *The Register of Derry Cathedral (S. Columb's) ... 1642–1703*, Parish Register Society of Dublin, vii (Exeter and London, 1910).
Hill, George, ed., *The Montgomery Manuscripts* (Belfast, 1869).
Historical Manuscripts Commission,
    First Report, appendix (MSS. of corporations of Dublin, Cork, Kilkenny, Waterford, and Limerick).
    Second Report, appendix (Cromwell-Prescott MSS.).
    Tenth Report, appendix, part v (MSS. of Irish Jesuits, corporations of Waterford and Galway).
    Eleventh Report, appendix, part iii (MSS. of Southampton corporation).
    Twelfth Report, appendix, part ix (MSS. of Gloucester corporation).
    City of Exeter.
    De L'Isle and Dudley, vi.
    Egmont.
    Hastings, iv.
    Leyborne-Popham.
    Ormonde, i and ii, and new series.
    Portland, i.
    Various Collections, vi (Lord Brown and Oranmore).
Journal of the House of Commons [England].
Journal of the House of Commons of the kingdom of Ireland (Dublin, 1796–1800), 20 vols.
Journal of the House of Lords [England].
Journal of the House of Lords of the kingdom of Ireland (Dublin, 1779–1800), 8 vols.
Knowler, W., *Letters and dispatches of the earl of Strafforde* (London, 1739), 2 vols.
Lawlor, H. J., ed., *The Register of Provost Winter (Trinity College, Dublin), 1650–1660*, Parish Register Society of Dublin, iv (Exeter, 1907).

Lenihan, M., ed., 'The Fee-book of a physician of the 17th century', *Journal of the Kilkenny and S.E. Ireland Archaeological Society*, N.S. vi (1867).

Leslie, J. B., 'Inquisition concerning the parishes of County Louth 1658', *County Louth Archaeological Society Journal*, vii (1929).

MacGrath, K., 'Irish priests transported under the Commonwealth', *Archivium Hibernicum*, xiv (1949).

MacLysaght, E., *Calendar of the Orrery Papers*, Irish MSS. Comm. (Dublin, 1941).
    'Commonwealth State Accounts: Ireland, 1650–56', *Analecta Hibernica*, xv (Dublin, 1944).

McNeill, C., *The Tanner Letters*, Irish MSS. Comm. (Dublin, 1943).

'Manuscripts of the Old Corporation of Kinsale', *Analecta Hibernica*, xv (Dublin, 1944).

'Mather Papers', *Collections of the Massachusetts Historical Society*, 4th Ser. viii (1868).

Mayer, J., ed., 'Inedited letters of Cromwell, Colonel Jones, Bradshaw and other regicides', *Transactions of the Historic Society of Lancashire and Cheshire*, N.S. i (1860–1).

Millet, B., ed., 'Archbishop Edmund O'Reilly's report on the state of the Church in Ireland, 1662', *Collectanea Hibernica*, ii (1959).

Mills, James, ed., *The Registers of St. John the Evangelist, Dublin, 1619–1699*, Parish Register Society of Dublin, i (Dublin, 1906).

Milward, E., ed., *Collection of the State Letters of Roger Boyle, First Earl of Orrery* (London, 1742).

Mitchell, A. F. and Christie, J., *The Records of the commissioners of the General Assemblies of the Church of Scotland ... 1648 and 1649*, Scottish History Society, xxv (1896).

Moody, T. W., and Simms, J. G., eds., *The Bishopric of Derry and the Irish Society of London, 1602–1705, i, 1602–1670*, Irish MSS. Comm. (Dublin, 1966).

Moran, P. F., *Spicilegium Ossoriense* (Dublin, 1874–84), 3 vols.

Nickolls, J., *Original Letters and Papers of State addressed to Oliver Cromwell* (London, 1743).

Nuttall, G. F., *Early Quaker letters from the Swarthmore MSS. to 1660* (1952, reproduced from typewriting).

The Correspondence of John Owen, ed. P. Toon (Cambridge and London, 1970).

Peck, F., *Desiderata Curiosa* (London, 1779).

Pender, S., ed., *A 'Census' of Ireland, c. 1659*, Irish MSS. Comm. (Dublin, 1939).
    'Studies in Waterford History – x–lxi: the guilds of Waterford 1650–1700', *JCHAS* lviii–lxi (1953–6).
    'Studies in Waterford History – iii–ix: the old council books of the corporation of Waterford', *JCHAS* lii–lvii (1947–52).

Seymour, St. J. D., 'Family papers belonging to the Purcells of Loughmoe, Co. Tipperary', *Journal of the North Munster Archaeological Society*, iii (1913).

Shaw, W. A., ed., *Letters of denization and acts of naturalization for aliens in England and Ireland, 1603–1700*, Huguenot Society of London, xviii (Lymington, 1911).

Simington, R. C., ed., *The Civil Survey, 1654–56*, Irish MSS. Comm. (Dublin, 1931–).
    ed., *The Transplantation to Connacht, 1654–58*, Irish MSS. Comm. (Dublin, 1970).

Smith, W. J., *Herbert Correspondence*, Irish MSS. Comm. and Board of Celtic Studies (Dublin and Cardiff, 1963).

State Papers collected by Edward, earl of Clarendon, eds. R. Scrope and T. Monkhouse (Oxford, 1767–86), 3 vols.

The Statutes at large . . . Ireland (Dublin, 1786).

Steele, R., *Tudor and Stuart proclamations* (Oxford, 1910), 2 vols.

Stephen, W., ed., *Register of the consultations of the Ministers of Edinburgh, ii, 1657–60*, Scottish History Society, 3rd Ser. xvi (1930).

'Original letter of Bishop Jeremy Taylor on Theological Studies, *Irish Ecclesiastical Journal*, 102, no. v (1849).

A Collection of the State Papers of John Thurloe, ed. T. Birch (London, 1742), 7 vols.

Trevelyan, Sir W. C. and Trevelyan, Sir C. E., *Trevelyan Papers*, Camden Society, cv (1872).

The Whole Works of the Most Reverend James Ussher, ed. C. R. Elrington (Dublin, 1847–64), 17 vols.

Walsh, Reginald., ed., 'A letter of three Irish Franciscans in 1656', *Archivium Hibernicum*, ii (1913).

White, B. R., *Association Records of the Particular Baptists of England, Wales and Ireland to 1660*, part 2, The West Country and Ireland (London, 1973).

Winthrop, R. C., ed., *Correspondence of Hartlib, Haak, Oldenburg . . . with Governor Winthrop of Connecticut, 1661–72* (Boston, Mass., 1878).

Wood, Herbert, ed., *The Registers of S. Catherine, Dublin, 1636–1715*, Parish Register Society of Dublin, v (Exeter and London, 1908).

The Diary and Correspondence of Dr. John Worthington, ed. J. Crossley, Chetham Society, xiii (1847).

Young, R. M., ed., *The Town Book of the corporation of Belfast, 1613–1816* (Belfast, 1892).

IV. CONTEMPORARY AND NEAR-CONTEMPORARY WORKS

An Account of the Affairs in Ireland in reference to the late change in England (London, 1659).

An Account of the Chief Occurrences of Ireland . . . 22 February–27 February [1660], and *12 March–19 March* [1660] (Dublin, 1659[60]).

Adair, P., *A True Narrative of the rise and progress of the Presbyterian Church of Ireland 1623–70*, ed. W. D. Killen (Belfast, 1866).

The Agreement and Resolution of severall associated Ministers in the County of Corke . . . (Cork, 1657).

The Agreement and Resolution of the Ministers of Christ associated within the City of Dublin, and Province of Leinster . . . (Dublin, 1659).

Barrow, Humphrey, *The Relief of the Poore and advancement of learning proposed* (Dublin, 1656).

Baxter, Richard, *The Certainty of the Worlds of Spirits* (London, 1691).
    Reliquiae Baxterianae, ed. M. Sylvester (London, 1696).

Bedell, W., *The A.B.C., or the Institution of a Christian* (Dublin, 1631).

Belcamp, J. V., *Consilium et Votum pro Ordinando ac Stabilienda Hibernia* (London, 1651).

Bernard, N., *The Life and Death of . . . Dr. James Usher* (Dublin, 1656).

Blackwood, C., *Apostolicall Baptisme* (London, 1645).
    Expositions and Sermons . . . (London, 1659).
    An Exposition upon the ten first chapters (London, 1659).
    Some Pious Treatises (London, 1654).
    A Soul-searching Catechism (London, 1653).
    The Storming of Antichrist (London, 1644).

A Treatise concerning deniall of Christ (London, 1648).

A Treatise concerning repentance (London, 1653).

Blaughdone, B., *An Account of the Travels* ([London], 1691).

Boate, A., *The character of a trulie vertuous and pious woman* (Paris, 1651).

Observationes medicae de affectibus omissis (London, 1649).

Boate, A. and G., *Philosophia Naturalis Reformata* (Dublin, 1641).

Boate, G., *Irelands Naturall History* (London, 1652).

Bolton, Sir Richard, *A Iustice of Peace for Ireland* (Dublin, 1638).

Borlase, E., *The History of the execrable Irish Rebellion* (London, 1680).

Borr, C., *Disputationum practicarum de Historii Aegrorum: Decima-Nona. De caecitate* (Trajectum ad Rhenum, 1650).

The Works of the Most Reverend . . . John Bramhall, ed. J. Vesey (Dublin, 1676).

A Brief Historical Relation of the Life of Mr. John Livingston (n.p., 1727).

A Brief of Proceedings between S[i]r Hierom Sankey and Dr. William Petty (London, 1659).

Bridges, J., Warren, A., and Warren, E., *A Perfect Narrative* (London, 1660).

Burroughs, E., *The Memorable Works of a son of a son of thunder and consolation* ([London], 1672).

Burston, D., *Christs last call to his glorified Saints* (Dublin, 1666).

Εʼυϲγγελιοτη, ετι εʼʼγγελιϛοʼεγοϛ, *or the Evangelist yet Evangelizing* (Dublin, 1662).

Butler, J., *A Sermon Preached on the Sunday before Easter 1661*[2] (Cork, 1662).

Calamy, E., *The Nonconformists' Memorial*, ed. S. Palmer (London, 1802), 3 vols.

Calver, E., *Zions thankful echoes* (London, 1649).

Canne, J., *The Improvement of Mercy* (London, 1649).

Catalogus Librorum . . . Benjaminis Worsley, tum duorum aliorum (London, 1678).

Chambre, R. [Chambers], *Some Animadversions* (Dublin, 1659).

The Works of Stephen Charnock (London, 1684), 2 vols.

The Complaint of the boutefeu scorched in his own kindlings (London, 1649).

Constitutions and Canons Ecclesiasticall (Dublin, 1635).

Cook, J., *Monarchy no Creature of Gods making, etc.* (Waterford, 1651).

Redintegratio Amoris (London, 1647).

A True Relation of Mr. Iohn Cook's Passage by Sea (London, 1650[51]).

Cook, J., *Unum Necessarium: or the Poor Mans Case* (London, 1648).

The Vindication of the Professors and Profession of the Law (London, 1646).

What the Independents would have (London, 1647).

C[ooke], E., *Here is somthing of concernment in Ireland* (n.p., n.d., c. 1657).

Cox, Richard, *Hibernia Anglicana* (London, 1679).

Coxe, Sem., *Two Sermons Preached . . . before the honourable the General Convention of Ireland* (Dublin, 1660).

Davies, Sir John, *A Discoverie of the True Causes* (n.p., 1612).

A Declaration by the Presbytery at Bangor in Ireland, July 7. 1649 (n.p., 1649).

A Declaration Concerning the Fines to be imposed on the Delinquent English and Brittish Protestants of Munster (Dublin, 1655).

A Declaration For the Payment of Custom and Excize (Dublin, 1654).

A Declaration of Sir Charles Coot . . . (London, 1659[60]).

A Declaration of the Army in Ireland . . . Feb. 18 1659[60] (Dublin, 1659[60]).

A Declaration of the General Convention of Ireland . . . 8 of March 1659[60] (Dublin, 1659[60]).

A Declaration of the General Convention of Ireland, with the late proceedings there, newly brought over by a gentleman (London, 1660).

A Declaration of the Lord Broghill ... (London, 1660).

A Declaration of the Lord Deputy and Council for removing and preventing of some mistakes in government in Ireland (Dublin, 1655).

A Declaration of the Lord Lieutenant Generall of Ireland for setling the Protestant Religion (Cork, 1648).

A Declaration of the Lord Lieutenant of Ireland, For the undeceiving of deluded and seduced people (London, 1650).

A Declaration of the Protestant Clergie of the City of Dublin (Dublin, 1647).

A Discourse Concerning the Affaires of Ireland (London, 1650).

Discourses Political and Moral, of the Conveniency and Justice of Reserving some lands in Ireland towards satisfying the arrears and publique faith of England (n.p., n.d.).

Journal of the Life ... *of William Edmundson* (London, 1715).

Eyres, J., *The Church Sleeper Awakened* (London, 1659).

R.G.,[1] *A Copy of a letter from an Officer of the Army in Ireland* ... ([London, 1656?]).

Galanus, C., *Logica, seu Introductio in totam Aristotelis Philosophiam*, translated by D. Loftus (Dublin, 1657).

Gilbert, C., *The Blessed Peace-Maker and Christian Reconciler* (London, 1658).
   The Libertine School'd (London, 1657).
   A Pleasant Walk to Heaven (London, 1658).
   A Preservative against the Change of Religion (London, 1683).
   A Sovereign Antidote against sinful errors (London, 1658).

Gookin, V., *The Author and Case of Transplanting the Irish into Connaught Vindicated, from the unjust aspersion of Colonel Richard Laurence* (London, 1655).

[Gookin, V]., *The Great Case of Transplantation in Ireland Discussed* (London, 1655).

Hackett, T., *A Sermon preached before the Convocation of the Clergy in Ireland* ... (London, 1662).

Harcourt, D., *A New Remonstrance from Ireland* (London, 1643).

Harrison, T. *Threni Hibernici* (London, 1659).
   Topica Sacra (London, 1658).

Samuel Hartlib His Legacie, 2nd edition (London, 1652).

Heylyn, P., *Aerius Redivivus, or the History of the Presbyterians* (Oxford, 1670).

Hill, William, Διονυσιου Οικουμενη, Πεδικγκσι, *Dionysii orbis Descriptio* (London, 1658).

His Maiesties Directions for the ordering and settling of the Courts, and course of Iustice within his Kingdome of Ireland (Dublin, 1638). Also edited in *Analecta Hibernica*, xxvi (1970) by G. J. Hand and V. Treadwell.

Hodden, R., *The One Good Way of God* (London, 1661).

The Horrid Conspiracie of Such Impenitent Traytors as intended a New Rebellion in the Kingdom of Ireland (London, 1663).

The Humble Petition of the Officers Now Engaged for Ireland (London, 1649).

The Humble Petition of the Protestant Inhabitants of the Counties of Antrim, Downe, Tyrone, etc. (London, 1641).

Instructions to be duly observed by the Iudges of every respective Court of Iustice (Dublin, 1653).

[1] The identity of this author is discussed by J. G. A. Pocock, in 'James Harington and the Good Old Cause: a study in the ideological context of his writings', *Journal of British Studies*, x (1970), 34—6. The copy in T.C.D. bears the note, in a seventeenth-century hand, 'I take this letter to be penn'd by L. Gen[era]ll Ludlow.'

Irelands Ambition Taxed (London, 1659).

Irelands Excise (London, 1643).

Johnson, J., ᾽Εκλεμψιδ τωγ δικ᾽ιωυ, *or the Shining Forth of Righteousness* (London, 1680).

Jones, Henry, *A Remonstrance of Divers Remarkeable Passages concerning the Church and Kingdome of Ireland* (London, 1642).

    A Sermon of Antichrist (Dublin, 1676).

    A Sermon preach't before the Generall Convention of Ireland (London, 1660).

Kavanagh, S., ed., *Commentarius Rinuccinianus*, Irish MSS. Comm. (Dublin, 1932–49), 6 vols.

King, C. S., *A Great Archbishop of Dublin* (London, 1906).

Ladyman, S., *The Dangerous Rule* (London, 1658).

L[awrence], R., *Englands Great Interest in the Well Planting of Ireland with English People Discussed* (Dublin, 1656).

Lawrence, R., *The Interest of England in the Irish Transplantation Stated* (London, 1655).

    The Interest of Ireland in its Trade and Wealth Stated (Dublin, 1682).

Leslie, Henry, *A Discourse of Praying with the Spirit* (London, 1660).

A letter from Sir Hardress Waller . . . to Lieutenant General Ludlowe (London, 1660).

A letter sent from a Merchant of Dublin . . . to his friend in London (London, 1659[60]).

Loftus, D., *Liber psalmorum Davidis, ex Armenico idiomato in Latinum traductus* (Dublin, 1661).

Lord Henry Cromwels Speech in the House ([London], 1659).

Lord Inchiquins Queries to the Protestant Clergy of the Province of Munster (The Hague, 1649).

The Memoirs of Edmund Ludlow, ed. C. H. Firth (Oxford, 1894), 2 vols.

Lynch, John., *Cambrensis Eversus*, ed. Matthew Kelly (Dublin, 1848), 3 vols.

The Marquess of Ormonds Declaration (London, 1649).

Maxwell, R., *In Obitum Clarissimi Integerrimique Viri D. Richardi Pepys Armigeri* (Dublin, 1658[9]).

Mercurius Elencticus, 6–13 February 1648[9].

Morford, T., *The Baptist and Independent Churches (so called) set on fire* (London, 1660).

Morison, Maurice, *Threnodia Hiberno-Catholica* (Innsbruck, 1659).

Morris, Thomas, *A Sermon Preached at the funeral of the right honourable Roger Earl of Orrery* (London, 1681).

Murcot, J., *Saving Faith and Pride of Life Inconsistent* (London, 1656).

    Several Works (London, 1657).

A Necessary Representation of the Present Evills . . . by the Presbytery of Belfast (n.p., 1649).

The Autobiography of Henry Newcome, ed. R. Parkinson, Chetham Society, xxvi and xxvii (1852).

News from Ireland concerning the proceedings of the Presbytery in the County of Antrim in Ireland (London, 1650).

An Ordinance of the Commons assembled in Parliament for a Bill . . . Concerning the qualifications of the Knights, Citizens, and Burgesses who shall be admitted to sit in Parliament for the Kingdome of Ireland (Dublin, 1647).

Osborne, H., *A more exact way to delineate the plot of any spacious parcel of land* (Dublin, 1654).

Owen, J., *The Labouring Saints Dismission to Rest* (London, 1652).
   The Stedfastness of Promises and the Sinfulness of Staggering (London, 1650).
W. P., *A letter from Ireland to an honourable citizen of London* (n.p., [1660?]).
Parr, R., *The Life of . . . James Usher* (London, 1686).
Patient, T., *The Doctrine of Baptism* (London, 1654).
Perkins, W., *The Christian Doctrine*, translated by G. Daniel (Dublin, 1652).
'The petition of officers of the precincts of Dublin, Carlow, Wexford and Kilkenny', *Mercurius Politicus*, no. 251 (29 Mar.–5 Apr. 1655).
The Advice of W[illiam] P[etty] to Mr. Samuel Hartlib (London, 1648).
Petty, W., *The Discourse made before the Royal Society the 26 November 1674* (London, 1674).
Economic Writings of Sir William Petty, ed. C. H. Hull (Cambridge, 1899), 2 vols.
The History . . . of the Down Survey by Doctor William Petty, ed. T. Larcom, Irish Archaeological Society (Dublin, 1851).
Petty, W., *The political anatomy of Ireland* (London, 1691).
   Reflections on Some Persons and Things in Ireland (London, 1660).
   A Treatise of Taxes & Contributions (London, 1662).
'Philo-Jesus Philo-Carolus', *Lemmata Medititionum* (Dublin, 1672).
Pressick, G., *An Answer to Griffith Williams Lord Bishop of Ossorie* (n.p., n.d.).
   A breife relation of some of the most remarkable passages of the Anabaptists ([London], 1660?).
Proposals to the Adventurers for lands in Ireland (London, 1658).
Propositions approved of and granted by the Deputy-General of Ireland to Col. Richard Lawrence . . . (London, 1650[1]).
Reeve, John and Muggleton, L., *A Volume of Spiritual Epistles* (n.p., 1675).
Rogers, John, *Ohel or Beth-shemesh* (London, 1653).
   Sagrir (London, 1653).
Rules and Orders to be observed in the proceedings of causes in the High Court of Chancery in Ireland (Dublin, 1659).
M. S., *A discourse concerning the rebellion in Ireland* (n.p., 1642).
Salusbury, Thomas, *Mathematical Collections and Translations* (London, 1661).
S[heridan], W., *A Sermon Preach'd at the funeral of the right honourable Sir Maurice Eustace* (Dublin, 1665).
Shuckburgh, E. S., ed., *Two Biographies of William Bedell Bishop of Kilmore* (Cambridge, 1902).
Sicklemore, James, *To all the inhabitants of the town of Youghal, who are under the teachings of James Wood* (n.p., n.d.).
A Sober Vindication of Lt. Gen. Ludlow (London, 1660).
The Speeches and Prayers of some of the late King's Judges (London, 1660).
The Autobiography of the Rev. Devereux Spratt (London, 1886).
Stearne, J., *Animi Medela* (Dublin, 1658).
   Clarissimi Viri Adriani Heereboordi, Philosophiae Professoris Ordinarii, Disputationum de Concursu Examen (Dublin, 1660).
   De electione et reprobatione dissertatio (Dublin, 1662).
   Θανατολογια, *seu, De morte dissertatio* (Dublin, 1659).
Taylor, J., *A Sermon Preached at the Consecration of two Archbishops and ten Bishops . . .* (Dublin, 1661).
   A Sermon Preached . . . May 8. 1661 (London, 1661).
Teate, F., *Nathanael, or An Israelite Indeed* (London, 1657).
   The Soldiers Commission, Charge and Reward (London, 1658).
   The Uncharitable Informer Charitably Informed (Dublin, 1660).
Temple, John, *The Irish Rebellion* (London, 1646).

The Tryall and Condemnation of Mr. John Cooke (London, 1660).

W[arren?], E., *A Reply to the Answer of Lieutenant General Ludlow* (London, 1660).

J. W., *The Life and Death of . . . Dr. Samuel Winter* (London, 1671).

The Whole Works of Sir James Ware, ed. Walter Harris (Dublin, 1764), 2 vols.

Ware, Robert, *The Hunting of the Romish Fox* (Dublin, 1683).

Warren, E., *Calebs Inheritance in Canaan by Grace, not Works* (London, 1656).

[Wheeler, William], *To the Honorable Commissioners of Assessments* ([Cork, 1656]).

Whitelocke, B., *Memorials of the English Affairs* (Oxford, 1853), 4 vols.

Williams, Griffith, *Four Treatises* (London, 1667).

    The Persecution and Oppression . . . of John Bale . . . and of Gruffith Williams (London, 1664).

Williamson, C., *Panegyris in Excellentissimum Dominum Dominum Henricum Cromwellum* (Dublin, 1658).

Winter, S., *The Summe of Diverse Sermons* (Dublin, 1656).

Wolfe, D. M., ed., *Leveller Manifestoes of the Puritan Revolution* (New York, 1944).

Wood, A., *Athenae Oxonienses*, ed. P. Bliss (London, 1813–20), 4 vols.

W[ood], R., *The Times Mended* (London, 1681).

[Worth, E.], *Scripture Evidence for Baptizing the Children of Covenanters* (Cork, [1653]).

Worth, E., *The Servant Doing, and the Lord Blessing* (Dublin, 1658[9]).

Wright, William, *A Preparative to a Pacification betwixt the South and North Suburbs of Corke* ([Cork, 1656]).

V. LATER WORKS AND UNPUBLISHED THESES

Abernathy, G. R., 'Richard Baxter and the Cromwellian Church', *Huntington Library Quarterly*, xxiv (1961).

[Anderson, James], *A Genealogical History of the House of Yvery* (London, 1742), 2 vols.

Andrews, J. H., 'Notes on the historical geography of the Irish iron industry', *Irish Geography*, iii (1958).

Armstrong, J., 'An Appendix containing some account of the Presbyterian congregations in Dublin', in *Sermon: A Discourse on Presbyterian Ordination* (Dublin, 1829).

Aylmer, G. E., ed., *The Interregnum* (London, 1972).

Atkinson, E. D., *Dromore: an Ulster diocese* (Dundalk, 1925).

Ball, F. E., *The judges in Ireland, 1221–1921* (New York, 1926), 2 vols.

Barnard, T. C., 'The Hartlib Circle and the origins of the Dublin Philosophical Society', *Irish Historical Studies*, xix (1974).

    'Lord Broghill, Vincent Gookin and the Cork elections of 1659', *Eng. Hist. Rev.* lxxxviii (1973).

    'Planters and Policies in Cromwellian Ireland', *P. and P.* lxi (1973).

    'Miles Symner and the New Learning in seventeenth-century Ireland', *JRSAI* cii (1972).

    'The Purchase of Archbishop Ussher's library in 1657', *Long Room*, Bulletin of the Friends of Trinity College Dublin Library, iv (1971).

    'Trinity at Charles II's restoration in 1660', *Hermathena*, cix (1969).

Barry, J. G., 'The Cromwellian settlement of the County of Limerick', *Journal of the Limerick Field Club*, i (1897–1900).

Beckett, J. C., 'The Confederation of Kilkenny Reviewed', in *Historical Studies: II*, ed. M. Roberts (London, 1959).

'The Irish Viceroyalty in the Restoration Period', *Trans. Royal Hist. Soc.*, 5th Ser. xx (1971).

Protestant Dissent in Ireland, 1687–1780 (London, 1948).

Begley, J., *The Diocese of Limerick in the Sixteenth and Seventeenth Centuries* (Dublin, 1927).

Belcher, T. W., *Memoir of John Stearne* (Dublin, 1865).

Benn, G., *History of the town of Belfast* (Belfast, 1877–80), 2 vols.

Berry, H. F., 'History of the religious Gild of St. Anne ... 1430–1740', *Proceedings of the Royal Irish Academy*, xxv, C (1907).

'The Merchant Tailors' Gild ... 1418–1841', *JRSAI* xlviii (1918).

Besse, Joseph, *A Collection of the Sufferings of the People called Quakers* (London, 1753), 2 vols.

Bewley, E. T., 'Some notes on the Lowthers who held judicial office in Ireland in the seventeenth century', *Transactions, Cumberland and Westmorland Antiquarian and Archaeological Society*, N.S. ii (1902).

Blake, Martin J., *Blake Family Records 1600–1700* (London, 1905).

Blake, J. W., 'Transportation from Ireland to America, 1653–60', *Irish Historical Studies*, iii (1943).

Bolton, F. R., *The Caroline Tradition of the Church of Ireland* (London, 1958).

Bonn, M. J., *Die englische Kolonisation in Irland* (Stuttgart and Berlin, 1906), 2 vols.

Bossy, J., 'The Counter-Reformation and the people of Catholic Ireland, 1596–1641'. in *Historical Studies: VIII*, ed. T. D. Williams (Dublin, 1971).

Bottigheimer, K. S., 'Civil War in Ireland: the reality in Munster', *Emory University Quarterly* (1966).

'English Money and Irish Land: the "Adventurers" in the Cromwellian Settlement of Ireland', *Journal of British Studies*, vii (1967).

English Money and Irish Land (Oxford, 1971).

'The Restoration land settlement in Ireland: a structural view', *Irish Historical Studies*, xviii (1972).

Bowen, E., *Bowen's Court* (London, 1942).

Brady, J., 'The Irish Colleges in Europe and the Counter-Reformation', *Proceedings, Irish Catholic Historical Committee* (1957).

Brady, W. M., *Clerical and Parochial Records of Cork, Cloyne and Ross* (London, 1864), 3 vols.

Braithwaite, W. C., *The Beginnings of Quakerism* (London, 1912).

Brooks, E. St. J., 'Henry Nicholson: first lecturer in botany and the earliest Physic Garden', *Hermathena*, lxxxiv (1954).

Burke, J. B., *A Genealogical and Heraldic History of the Landed Gentry of Ireland*, 9th edition (London, 1899).

Burtchaell, G. D., *Members of Parliament for the county and city of Kilkenny* (Dublin, 1888).

and T. U. Sadleir, *Alumni Dublinenses* (Dublin, 1935).

Butler, W. F. T., *Confiscation in Irish history* (Dublin, 1917).

Butlin, R. A., 'The population of Dublin in the late seventeenth century', *Irish Geography*, v (1965).

G.E.C., *The Complete Peerage*, ed. V. Gibbs (London, 1910–).

J. C., 'Admiral Penn, William Penn and their descendants in Co. Cork', *JCHAS*, 2nd Ser. xiv (1901).

'Colonel Phaire, the regicide', *JCHAS*, 2nd Ser. xxi (1915).

Camody, W. P., *Lisburn Cathedral and its past Rectors* (Belfast, 1926).

Capp, B. S., *The Fifth Monarchy Men* (London, 1972).

Carré, A., *L'Influence des huguenots français en Irlande aux xviiᵉ et xviiiᵉ siècles* (Paris, 1937).

Carroll, K. L., *John Perrot: early Quaker schismatic*, Friends' Historical Society supplement no. 33 (London, 1971).

Carte, T., *Life of James, first Duke of Ormonde* (London, 1735–6), 3 vols.

Catterall, R. H. C., 'The failure of the Humble Petition and Advice', *American Historical Review*, ix (1903).

Clarke, A., *The Graces, 1625–41* (Dundalk, 1968).
    'Ireland and the General Crisis', *P. and P.* xlviii (1970).
    The Old English in Ireland, 1625–42 (London, 1966).
    'The policies of the "Old English" in Parliament, 1640–1', in *Historical Studies: V*, ed. J. L. McCracken (London, 1965).

Cole, A., 'The Quakers and the English Revolution', reprinted in *Crisis in Europe 1560–1660*, ed. T. Aston (London, 1965).

Coleman, J., 'Some early Waterford clerical authors', *Journal of the Waterford and S.E. of Ireland Archaeological Society*, vi (1900).

Coleman, R. V., *Roger Ludlow in Chancery* (Westport, Conn., 1934).

Comerford, M., *Collections relating to the Dioceses of Kildare and Leighlin* (Dublin, [1886]), 2 vols.

Coonan, T. L., *The Irish Catholic Confederacy and the Puritan Revolution* (Dublin, 1954).

Corcoran, T., *State policy in Irish education* (Dublin, 1916).

Corish, P. J., 'The Origins of Catholic Nationalism', fascicle 8 of *A History of Irish Catholicism*, iii, ed. P. J. Corish (Dublin, 1968).
    'Reorganization of the Irish Church, 1603–41', *Proceedings, Irish Catholic Historical Committee* (1957).

Costello, T. B., 'Trade tokens in the County of Galway in the seventeenth century', *Journal of the Galway Archaeological and Historical Society*, vii (1911–12).

Cotton, H., *Fasti Ecclesiae Hibernicae* (Dublin, 1845–78), 6 vols.

Cregan, D. F., 'The confederation of Kilkenny', in *The Irish Parliamentary Tradition*, ed. B. Farrell (Dublin, 1973).
    'The Confederation of Kilkenny: its organization, personnel and history', Ph.D., National University of Ireland, 1947.

Cullen, L. M., *Anglo-Irish Trade 1660–1800* (Manchester, 1968).
    An economic history of Ireland since 1660 (London, 1972).
    ed., *The formation of the Irish economy* (Cork, 1969).

Cusack, M. F., *A history of the kingdom of Kerry* (London, 1871).

Davies, G., *The Restoration of Charles II* (Oxford, 1955).

Dewhurst, K., 'The genesis of state medicine in Ireland', *The Irish Journal of Medical Science*, 6th Ser. ccclxviii (Aug. 1956).

Dickens, B., 'The Irish broadside of 1571 and Queen Elizabeth's types', *Transactions of the Cambridge Bibliographical Society*, i (1949).

Donaldson, A. G., *Some comparative aspects of Irish law* (Durham, N.C., 1957).

Douglas, J. M., 'Early Quakerism in Ireland', *Journal of the Friends' Historical Society*, xlviii (1956).

Duhigg, B. T., *History of the King's Inns, Dublin* (Dublin, 1805).

Dunlop, R. T., 'A note on the export trade of Ireland in 1641, 1665, and 1669', *Eng. Hist. Rev.* xxii (1907).
    'The Plantation of Leix and Offaly', *Eng. Hist. Rev.* vi (1891).
    'The Plantation of Munster, 1584–9', *Eng. Hist. Rev.* iii (1888).

Dwyer, P., *The Diocese of Killaloe from the Reformation to the close of the eighteenth century* (Dublin, 1878).

Edie, C. A., *The Irish cattle bills: a study in Restoration politics*, Transactions, American Philosophical Society, N.S. lx, part 2 (1970).

Edwards, R. D., 'The Irish Catholics and the Puritan Revolution', in *Father Luke Wadding commemorative volume*, ed. Franciscan Fathers (Dublin, 1957).

Egan, B., 'Notes on Propaganda Fide printing-press', *Collectanea Hibernica*, ii (1959).

Emery, F. V., 'Irish geography in the seventeenth century', *Irish Geography*, iii (1958).

Fahy, E. M., 'The Cork Goldsmiths' Company, 1657', *JCHAS* lviii (1953).

Ferrar, J., *The History of Limerick* (Limerick, 1787).

Firth, C. H., 'Account of money spent in the Cromwellian reconquest and settlement of Ireland', *Eng. Hist. Rev.* xiv (1899).

    Cromwell's Army, paperback edition (London, 1962).

    The Last Years of the Protectorate (London, 1909), 2 vols.

    and G. Davies, *A regimental history of Cromwell's army* (Oxford, 1940).

Fitzgerald, P., and McGregor, J. J., *The history, topography and antiquities of the county and city of Limerick* (Limerick, 1826), 2 vols.

Fitzmaurice, Lord Edmond, *The life of Sir William Petty, 1623–87* (London, 1895).

Foster, J., *Alumni Oxonienses, 1500–1714* (Oxford, 1891), 4 vols.

Frost, James, *The history and topography of County Clare* (Dublin, 1893).

Fuller, A., and Holms, T., *A Compendious View of some extraordinary sufferings of the people call'd Quakers* (Dublin, 1731), 3 vols.

Gale, P., *An Inquiry into the ancient corporate system of Ireland* (London, 1834).

Gardiner, S. R., *History of the Commonwealth and Protectorate* (London, 1903), 4 vols.

    'The transplantation to Connaught', *Eng. Hist. Rev.* xiv (1899).

Gimlette, T., *Huguenot settlers in Ireland* (n.p., 1888).

Gleeson, D. F., *The last lords of Ormond* (London, 1938).

    'An unpublished Cromwellian document', *North Munster Antiquarian Journal*, i (1936–9).

Goblet, Y. M., *La Transformation de la géographie politique d'Irlande au xviie siècle* (Paris, 1930), 2 vols.

Gorges, R., *The story of a family through eleven centuries . . . being a history of the family of Gorges* (Boston, Mass., 1944).

Gribbon, H. D., 'The Cork Church Book, 1653–1875', *Irish Baptist Historical Society Journal*, i (1968–9).

Guinness, H. S., 'Dublin Trade Gilds', *JRSAI* lii (1922).

Guizot, F. P. G., *History of Richard Cromwell and the Restoration of Charles II* (London, 1856), 2 vols.

Gwynn, A., 'Some notes on the history of the Book of Kells', *Irish Historical Studies*, ix (1954).

Hamilton, G. E., *An account of the honourable society of King's Inns, Dublin* (Dublin, 1915).

Hammerstein, H., 'Aspects of the continental education of Irish students in the reign of Queen Elizabeth I', in *Historical Studies; VIII*, ed. T. D. Williams (Dublin, 1971).

Hardacre, P. H., 'William Allen, Cromwellian Agitator and "Fanatic" ', *Baptist Quarterly*, xix (1962).

Hardiman, James, *The history of the town and county of Galway* (Dublin, 1820).

Hardinge, W. H., 'On circumstances attending the outbreak of the Civil War in Ireland on 23 Oct. 1641', *Transactions, Royal Irish Academy*, xxiv, Antiquities (1874).

'On manuscript, mapped and other townland surveys in Ireland . . . 1640—88', *Transactions, Royal Irish Academy*, xxiv, Antiquities (1873).

Hayes, R., 'Some old Limerick wills', *North Munster Antiquarian Journal*, i (1936—9).

Hayes-McCoy, G. A., 'Gaelic Society in Ireland in the late sixteenth century', in *Historical Studies: IV*, ed. G. A. Hayes-McCoy (London, 1963).

Hayman, S., 'The local coinage of Youghal', *Journal of the Kilkenny and S.E. of Ireland Archaeological Society*, N.S. iii (1858—9).

Hazlett, H., 'The financing of the British armies in Ireland, 1641—49', *Irish Historical Studies*, i (1938).

'The recruitment and organization of the Scottish army in Ulster', in *Essays in British and Irish History in Honour of James Eadie Todd*, ed. H. A. Cronne, T. W. Moody, and D. B. Quinn (London, 1941).

Healy, John, *History of the Diocese of Meath* (Dublin, 1908), 2 vols.

Hickson, M., *Ireland in the seventeenth century* (London, 1884), 2 vols.

Hill, C., *Economic problems of the Church* (Oxford, 1956).

God's Englishman (London, 1970).

Intellectual Origins of the English Revolution (Oxford, 1965).

'Propagating the Gospel', in *Historical Essays, 1600—1750*, eds. H. E. Bell and R. L. Ollard (London, 1963).

'Puritans and "the dark corners of the land" ', *Trans. Royal Hist. Soc.*, 5th Ser. xiii (1963).

Hill, George, *An historical account of the plantation in Ulster* (Belfast, 1877).

Hoppen, K. T., *The Common Scientist in the seventeenth century: a study of the Dublin Philosophical Society, 1683—1708* (London, 1970).

'The Dublin Philosophical Society and the New Learning in Ireland', *Irish Historical Studies*, xiv (1964).

'Queries for a seventeenth-century Natural History of Ireland', *The Irish Book*, ii (1963).

'The Royal Society and Ireland—William Molyneux, F.R.S., (1656—1698)', *Notes and Records of the Royal Society of London*, xviii (1963).

'The Royal Society and Ireland II', *Notes and Records of the Royal Society of London*, xx (1965).

Hore, P. H., *History of the town and county of Wexford* (London, 1900—11), 6 vols.

Hughes, J. L. J., *Patentee Officers, 1173—1826*, Irish Mss. Comm. (Dublin, 1960).

Hunter, R. J., 'Towns in the Ulster Plantation', *Studia Hibernica*, xi (1971).

Irwin, C. H., *A history of Presbyterianism in Dublin and the South and West of Ireland* (London, 1890).

Ivimey, J., *A History of the English Baptists* (London, 1811), 2 vols.

James, M., 'The political importance of the tithe controversy in the Puritan Revolution', *History*, N.S. xxvi (1941).

James, M. E., *Social problems and policy during the Puritan Revolution* (London, 1930).

Kearney, H. F., 'Ecclesiastical politics and the Counter-Reformation in Ireland, 1618—48', *Journal of Ecclesiastical History*, xi (1960).

'Richard Boyle, ironmaster', *JRSAI* lxxxiii (1953).

Scholars and Gentlemen (London, 1970).

Strafford in Ireland, 1633—41 (Manchester, 1959).

Kirkpatrick, James, *An historical essay upon the loyalty of Presbyterians* (n.p., 1713).

Kittredge, G. L., *Dr. Robert Child the Remonstrant* (Cambridge, 1919).

Knox, R. B., *James Ussher Archbishop of Armagh* (Cardiff, 1967).

Laffan, T., 'Fethard, Co. Tipperary: its charters and corporation records', *JRSAI* xxxvi (1906).

Lascelles, R., *Liber munerum publicorum Hiberniae* (London, 1824–30), 2 vols.

Lawlor, H. J., 'Primate Ussher's Library before 1641', *Proceedings of the Royal Irish Academy*, 3rd Ser. vi (1901).

Lenihan, M., *Limerick: its history and antiquities* (Dublin, 1886).

Leslie, J. B., *Ardfert and Aghadoe Clergy and Parishes* (Dublin, 1940).
    Armagh Clergy and Parishes (Dundalk, 1911).
    Clogher Clergy and Parishes (Enniskillen, 1929).
    Derry Clergy and Parishes (Enniskillen, 1937).
    Ferns Clergy and Parishes (Dublin, 1936).
    Ossory Clergy and Parishes (Enniskillen, 1933).
    Raphoe Clergy and Parishes (Enniskillen, 1940).

Lodge, J., *The Peerage of Ireland*, ed. M. Archdall (Dublin, 1789), 7 vols.

Lowe, J., 'Charles I and the Confederation of Kilkenny, 1643–49', *Irish Historical Studies*, xiv (1964–5).

Lynam, E. W., 'The Irish Character in Print, 1571–1923', *The Library*, iv (1924).

Lynch, K. M., *Roger Boyle, first Earl of Orrery* (Knoxville, Tenn., 1965).

MacCormack, J. R., 'The Irish Adventurers and the English Civil War', *Irish Historical Studies*, x (1956–7).

McCracken, E., 'Charcoal-burning ironworks in seventeenth and eighteenth century Ireland', *Ulster Journal of Archaeology*, xx (1957).
    The Irish woods since Tudor times (Newton Abbott, 1971).

McDowell, R. B., and Webb, D. A., 'Courses and teaching in Trinity College, Dublin, during the first 200 years', *Hermathena*, lxix (1947).

MacGillivray, R., 'Edmund Borlase, historian of the Irish Rebellion', *Studia Hibernica*, ix (1969).

Mackenzie, N., 'Sir Thomas Herbert of Tintern: a parliamentary royalist', *Bulletin of the Institute of Historical Research*, xxix (1956).

MacLysaght, E., *Irish life in the seventeenth century* (Cork, 1950).

McSkimin, S., *The History and Antiquities of the town of Carrickfergus*, ed. E. J. McCrum (Belfast, 1909).

Maddison, R. E. W., *The life of the honourable Robert Boyle, F.R.S.* (London, 1969).
    'Robert Boyle and the Irish Bible', *Bulletin of the John Rylands Library*, xli (1958).

Mahaffy, J. P., *An epoch in Irish history* (London, 1903).
    'The library of Trinity College, Dublin: the growth of a legend', *Hermathena*, xxviii (1903).

Mant, R., *History of the Church of Ireland from the Reformation to the Revolution* (London, 1840), 2 vols.

Mason, W. M., *The history and antiquities of the collegiate and cathedral church of St. Patrick* (Dublin, 1820).

Matthews, A. G., *Calamy Revised* (Oxford, 1934).
    Walker Revised (Oxford, 1948).

Millett, B., *The Irish Franciscans, 1651–1665*, Analecta Gregoriana, no. 129 (Rome, 1964).
    'Survival and Reorganization 1650–1695', fascicle 7 of *A History of Irish Catholicism*, iii, ed. P. J. Corish, (Dublin, 1968).

Moody, T. W., *The Londonderry plantation* (Belfast, 1937).

Moran, P. F., *Historical sketch of the persecutions suffered by the Catholics of Ireland under the rule of Cromwell and the Puritans* (Dublin, 1862).

Mullett, C. F., 'Sir William Petty on the plague', *Isis*, xxviii (1938).

Murdock, K. B., *Increase Mather* (Cambridge, Mass., 1925).
Murphy, J. A., 'The politics of the Munster Protestants, 1641—49', *JCHAS* lxxvi (1971).
Newark, F. H., 'Notes on Irish legal history', *Northern Ireland Legal Quarterly* vii (1947).
Niehaus, C. R., 'The issue of law reform in the Puritan Revolution', D.Phil., Harvard, 1960.
Nightingale, B., *The romance of Cuthbert Harrison* (Manchester and London, 1926).
Nourse, G. B., 'Law reform under the Commonwealth and Protectorate', *Law Quarterly Review*, lxxv (1959).
Nuttall, G. F., 'Presbyterians and Independents', *Journal of the Presbyterian Historical Society*, x (1952).
   Richard Baxter (London, 1965).
   Visible Saints (Oxford, 1957).
O'Brien, G., *The economic history of Ireland in the seventeenth century* (Dublin, 1919).
O'Brien, J. J., 'Commonwealth schemes for the Advancement of Learning', *British Journal of Educational Studies*, xvi (1968).
   'Samuel Hartlib's influence on Robert Boyle's scientific development', *Annals of Science*, xxi (1965), 2 parts.
O'Donoghue, F., 'Parliament in Ireland under Charles II', M.A., University College, Dublin, 1970.
O'Fiaich, T., 'Edmund O'Reilly, Archbishop of Armagh, 1657—69', in *Father Luke Wadding*, ed. Franciscan Fathers (Dublin, 1957).
O'Grady, H., *Strafford and Ireland* (Dublin, 1923), 2 vols.
O'Hart, J., *Irish landed gentry when Cromwell came to Ireland* (Dublin, 1883).
O'Sullivan, M. D., *Old Galway* (Cambridge, 1942).
O'Sullivan, W., 'The donor of the Book of Kells', *Irish Historical Studies*, xi (1958—9).
   'The library before Kinsale', *Annual Bulletin of Friends of the Library of Trinity College Dublin* (1952).
   'Ussher as a collector of manuscripts', *Hermathena*, lxxxviii (1956).
Pearson, J. B., 'The corporation of Exeter estate in Ireland, 1654—56', *Report and Transactions of the Devonshire Association*, xliv (1912).
Pender, S., *Waterford Merchants Abroad* (Tralee, 1964).
Pepys, W. C., *Genealogy of the Pepys Family, 1273—1887* (London, 1887).
Perry, J. H., *Roger Ludlowe* (Fairport, 1914).
Phillips, W. A., ed., *History of the Church of Ireland* (London, 1933), 3 vols.
Blessed Oliver Plunket Historical Studies (Dublin, 1937).
Power, P., *A bishop of the penal times* (Cork, 1932).
Prendergast, J. P., 'The clearing of Kilkenny, Anno 1654', *Journal of the Kilkenny and S.E. of Ireland Archaeological Society*, N.S. iii (1860—1).
   The Cromwellian settlement of Ireland, 3rd edition (London, 1870).
Purver, M., *The Royal Society: concept and creation* (London, 1967).
Quane, M., 'The Abbey School, Tipperary', *JCHAS* lxv (1960).
   'Charleville endowed school', *JRSAI* lxxxviii (1958).
   'Drogheda Grammar School', *County Louth Archaeological Society Journal*, xv (1963).
   'The diocesan schools, 1570—1870', *JCHAS* lxvi (1961).
   'Preston endowed school, Navan', *Riocht na Midhe*, Records of the Meath Archaeological and Historical Society, iv (1968).
Quinn, D. B., *The Elizabethans and the Irish* (Ithaca, N.Y., 1966).
   'The Munster plantation: problems and opportunities', *JCHAS* lxxi (1966).

Ramsey, R. W., *Henry Cromwell* (London, 1933).
Henry Ireton (London, 1949).
Ranger, T. O., 'The career of Richard Boyle, first Earl of Cork, in Ireland, 1588–1643', D.Phil., Oxford, 1959.
'Strafford in Ireland: a revaluation', reprinted in *Crisis in Europe 1560–1660*, ed. T. Aston (London, 1965).
Reid, J. S., *History of the Presbyterian Church in Ireland* ed. W. D. Killen (Belfast, 1867), 3 vols.
Rennison, W. H., *Succession list of the bishops, cathedral and parochial clergy of the Dioceses of Waterford and Lismore* ([Waterford, 1920]).
Richards, T., *A history of the Puritan Movement in Wales, 1639–53* (London, 1920).
Religious developments in Wales (1654–1662) (London, 1923).
Richardson, J., *A short history of the attempts . . . to convert the Popish Natives of Ireland* (London, 1712).
Roberts, S. C., 'The quest for Faithful Teate', *Times Literary Supplement*, 19 Apr. 1941.
Rogers, E., *Some account of the life and opinions of a Fifth Monarchy Man* (London, 1867).
Ronan, M. V., *Erasmus Smith endowment* (Dublin, 1937).
Sadleir, T. U., and Watson, Helen M., 'A record of 17th century *Alumni'*, *Hermathena*, lxxxix (1957).
Salusbury, T., *Mathematical Collections and Translations*, ed. Stillman Drake (London and Los Angeles, 1967).
Scott, Hew, *Fasti Ecclesiae Scoticanae*, 2nd edition (Edinburgh, 1928), 7 vols.
Scott, W. R., 'Members for Ireland in the Parliaments of the Protectorate', *JRSAI*, 5th Ser. iii (1893).
Seymour, St. J. D., *The Puritans in Ireland 1647–1661* (Oxford, 1921).
Samuel Winter (Dublin, 1941), reprinted from *Church of Ireland Gazette*, 5 Sept. 1941.
Shaw, F., 'Irish Medical Men and Philosophers', in *Seven Centuries of Irish Learning, 1000–1700*, ed. B. O'Cuiv (Dublin, 1961).
Shaw, W. A., *A History of the English Church during the Civil Wars and under the Commonwealth* (London, 1900), 2 vols.
Shirren, A. J., ' "Colonel Zanchy" and Charles Fleetwood', *Notes and Queries*, cxcviii (1953).
Sibley, J. L., *Biographical sketches of graduates of Harvard University . . . I (1642–58)* (Cambridge, Mass., 1873).
Simms, J. G., 'The Civil Survey 1654–6', *Irish Historical Studies*, ix (1955).
'Dublin in 1685', *Irish Historical Studies*, xiv (1965).
Jacobite Ireland (London, 1969).
The Williamite confiscation in Ireland, 1690–1703 (London, 1956).
'Sir Thomas Molyneux, Bart., M.D., F.R.S.', *Dublin University Review*, xviii (1841).
Stawell, G. D., *A Quantock Family* (Taunton, 1910).
Stearns, R. P., *The Strenuous Puritan: Hugh Peter, 1598–1660* (Urbana, Ill., 1954).
Stephens, W. B., 'The overseas trade of Chester in the early seventeenth century', *Transactions, Historic Society of Lancashire and Cheshire*, cxx (1968).
Stokes, G. T., *Some Worthies of the Irish Church* (London, 1900).
Stranks, C. J., *The Life and Writings of Jeremy Taylor* (London, 1952).
Strauss, E., *Sir William Petty: portrait of a genius* (London, 1954).
Stubbs, W. C., 'Finglas, County Dublin, Vestry Books', *JRSAI* xlvi (1917).
Swan, J. P., 'The Justices of the Peace for the County of Wexford', *JRSAI*, 5th Ser. iv (1894).

Swanzy, H. B., *Succession lists of the Diocese of Dromore*, ed. J. B. Leslie (Belfast, 1933).

—— and Leslie, J. B., *Biographical succession lists of the clergy of the Diocese of Down* (Enniskillen, 1936).

Synge, E., *A brief account of the laws now in force* (Dublin, 1723).

Taylor, E. G. R., *Mathematical Practitioners on Tudor and Stuart England* (Cambridge, 1954).

Taylor, J. H., *Roger Ludlow the colonial lawmaker* (New York and London, 1900).

Tenison, C. M., 'Cork M.P.s, 1559–1800', *JCHAS*, N.S. i (1895).

Treadwell, V., 'The Irish Court of Wards under James I', *Irish Historical Studies*, xii (1960).

Trevor-Roper, H. R., *Religion, the Reformation and social change* (London, 1967).

Turnbull, G. H., *Hartlib, Comenius and Dury* (London, 1947).

—— 'Oliver Cromwell's College at Durham', *Research Review*, Institute of Education, University of Durham, iii (1952).

—— 'Robert Child', *Transactions of the Colonial Society of Massachusetts*, xxxviii (1959).

—— 'Samuel Hartlib's influence on the early history of the Royal Society', *Notes and Records of the Royal Society of London*, x (1953).

Underdown, D., 'Civil War In Ireland: commentary', *Emory University Quarterly* (1966).

—— *Pride's Purge* (Oxford, 1971).

Urwick, W., *The early history of Trinity College, Dublin, 1591–1660* (London, 1892).

Veall, D., *The popular movement for law reform, 1640–1660* (Oxford, 1970).

Venn, J., and Venn, J. A., *Alumni Cantabrigenses* (Cambridge, 1922), 4 vols.

Vincent, W. A. L., *The State and School Education, 1640–1660* (London, 1950).

Walsh, T. J., 'Compulsory Irish in France', *JCHAS* lviii (1953).

Warren, Thomas, *A history and genealogy of the Warren family* (n.p., 1902).

Webb, J. F., *Municipal government in Ireland* (Dublin, 1918).

Webb, J. J., *The Guilds of Dublin* (Dublin, 1929).

Webster, C., 'Decimalization under Cromwell', *Nature*, ccxxix, 12 Feb. 1971.

—— 'English medical reformers of the Puritan Revolution: a background to the "Society of Chymical Physitians" ', *Ambix*, xiv (1967).

—— 'Henry More and Descartes: some new sources', *British Journal for the History of Science*, iv (1969).

—— 'New light on the Invisible College', *Trans. Royal Hist. Soc.*, 5th Ser. xxiv (1974).

—— 'The origins of the Royal Society', in *History of Science*, vi, ed. A. C. Crombie and M. A. Hoskin (Cambridge, 1968).

—— ed., *Samuel Hartlib and the Advancement of Learning* (Cambridge, 1969).

Webster, C. A., *The Diocese of Cork* (Cork, 1920).

—— *The Diocese of Ross* (Cork, 1936).

Welply, W. H., 'Colonel Robert Phaire, "regicide" ', *Notes and Queries*, 12th Ser. xii (1923).

Westropp, M. S. D., 'Glassmaking in Ireland', *Proceedings of the Royal Irish Academy*, xxix, C, no. 3 (1911).

White, B. R., 'The organization of the Particular Baptists, 1644–1660', *Journal of Ecclesiastical History*, xvii (1966).

—— 'Thomas Patient in England and Ireland', *Irish Baptist Historical Society Journal*, ii (1969–70).

White, J. D., 'Extracts from original wills formerly preserved in the consistorial office, Cashel ...', *Journal, Kilkenny and S.E. of Ireland Archaeological Society*, N.S. ii (1858–9).

Whitley, W. T., 'The plantation of Ireland and the early Baptist churches', *Baptist Quarterly*, N.S. i (1922–3).

Whitmore, J. B., 'Dr. Worsley being dead', *Notes and Queries*, clxxxv (1943).

Widdess, J. D. H., *A History of the Royal College of Physicians of Ireland, 1654–1963* (Edinburgh and London, 1963).

Wight, T., and Rutty, J., *A history of the rise and progress of the people called Quakers in Ireland* (Dublin, 1751).

Witherow, T., *Historical and literary memorials of Presbyterianism in Ireland* (Belfast, 1879).

Wood, H., 'Sir William Petty and his Kerry estate', *JRSAI*, 7th, Ser. iv (1934).

Wood-Martin, W. G., *History of Sligo, County and Town* (Dublin, 1889).

Woodward, D., 'The overseas trade of Chester, 1600–1650', *Transactions, Historic Society of Lancashire and Cheshire*, cxxii (1971).

Woolrych, A. H., 'The Good Old Cause and the fall of the Protectorate', *Cambridge Historical Journal*, xiii (1957).

Young, R. M., *Historical notices of old Belfast* (Belfast, 1896).

INDEX

Abbey Boyle, Co. Roscommon, 65 n, 75; King family of, 215

Abbott, Col. Daniel, 39

Abbott, W. C., 262

Accountant-General of Ireland, *see* Wood, Robert

Adair, Partrick, Presbyterian minister, 133 n, 300

Adams, Major Thomas, mayor of Kilkenny, 66 n

Adrian, Sir Hubert, 85–6

adultery, penalized, 76, 148, 258; practised, 110 n

Adventurers for Irish lands, 27, 36, 41, 60–2, 132 n, 186, 215, 234, 286, 293; and education, 186, 190

Albury, Surrey, 223

Aldeburgh, Suffolk, 59 n

alehouses, 40, 76, 154

Allen, Adjutant-General William, and religion, 103, 104, 105, 108, 111; and law, 288

almshouses, 75, 208 n

America, ministers from, 138, 139, 145; propagation of the gospel in, 191; settlers from invited to Galway, 56, 58–9 n; settlers from invited to Waterford, 53; settlers from and Trinity College, Dublin, 204; William Steele and, 116 n; mentioned, 47, 57, 101, 222, 289

Amersham, Bucks., 131 n

Amiraut, Paul, minister, 143 n

Amsterdam, compared in size with Dublin, 78 n; connections with Dublin, 86

anatomy, studied, 217, 238

Anglesey, first earl of, *see* Annesley, Arthur

Annesley, Arthur, first earl of Anglesey, justice of the peace, 290 n; M.P., 8; and the new learning, 216, 247; trustee of Dublin's second college, 209

Antrim, County

churches in, 169; commission of the peace, 291; ecclesiastical incomes in, 166; ecclesiastical livings in, 162; lay patronage, 150; parochial reorganization, 163, 164; schools, 188, 191; value of confiscated tithes, 155 n

Antrim, town
college proposed in, 190

Antwerp, Irish press of, 178

apothecaries, 86 n

apprentices, Catholics debarred as, 68; laws regulating, 74

Aran Island, Co. Donegal, 192 n

Ardagh, diocese of, no school in, 184

Aristotle, 209, 217, 222, 243

Armagh, Catholic archbishop of, *see* O'Reilly, Edmund

Armagh, Protestant archbishop of, *see* Bramhall, John, and Ussher, James

Armagh, county
ecclesiastical incomes in, 166; ecclesiastical livings in, 162; parochial reorganization, 163, 164; schools in, 188; tithes in, 157; value of confiscated tithes, 155 n

Armagh, town
school, 188; university proposed, 206

army, in England, 13, 14, 16, 104–5, 158, 293; and law reform, 279

army, in Ireland, chief engineer of, *see* Symner, Miles; and commission of the peace, 290–1; cost of, 26, 78, 80, 81; disbanding of, 26, 106; doctors, 219, 241–2, 246; and Fleetwood, 299; lands for, 36, 61; and the law, 258, 289, 292; and law reform, 254, 255–6, 261; opposes Henry Cromwell, 21, 106, 301–2; provisioning of, 82; and Quakers, 109–11; and religion, 91, 98–100, 102–6, 139; and Ussher's library, 211; mentioned, 27, 30, 32, 38, 214, 215, 293

Arrowsmith, John, 145

Arthur, Capt. John, Mayor of Wexford, 59 n

Arthur, Dr. Thomas, 241

Ashe, Luke, alderman of Derry, 64 n

Ashe, St. George, 78 n, 246

assessment, 27, 28–9, 258
astrology, 237, 248
astronomy, 228, 238, 239–40
atheism, reported in Co. Cork, 109 n, 110 n
Athenry, friars of, 179 n
Atherdee, Co. Louth, school proposed, 188
Athlone, court at, 274, 275, 277
Athy, Co. Kildare, 83
Attorney-General of Ireland, see Basill, William
Auditor-General of Ireland, see Roberts, Edward
Axtell, Col. Daniel, Baptist, 101, 103 n, 105, 108; governor of Kilkenny, 66; vandal?, 170

Bacon, Francis, first Lord Verulam and Viscount St. Albans, 92, 216
Bagshaw, Sir Edward, justice of the peace, 290 n
Baines, Edward, minister, 130 n, 133 n, 136 n, 137 n, 139, 140, 142–3
Baker, George, Protestant bishop of Waterford, 141
Baker, Capt. John, 149
Baltimore, Co. Cork, schoolmaster at, 189
Banagher, King's Co., 185
Bandon, Co. Cork, 75; Baptists in, 102; school in, 185, 189
Bangor, Co. Down, school in, 185, 188
banks, discussed, 244
Baptists, in Ireland, 57, 62, 65, 66, 119, 120, 125, 126, 129, 131, 132–3, 135, 144, 145, 147, 149, 152, 159, 170, 219, 221, 232, 288, 291 n, 301–2; criticized by English Baptists, 107 n; praise Ussher, 92; rise and fall, 98–109, 111–12, 114, 115–16; and second college, 210
Barnstaple, Devon, 46
Barrow, Col. Robert, Baptist, 103, 108
Barry, Sir James, proposed as judge, 281 n, 282 n
Barton, William, London clothier, 41, 58
Basill, William, attorney-general, 199 n, 208 n, 281 n, 290
Baxter, Richard, 120, 145; and Lord Orrery, 134 n

Becher, Henry, 205 n
Beck, Gabriel, 230
Beckett, J. C., 296
Bedell, William, Bishop of Kilmore, 91, 173, 177, 178, 215, 238; as provost of Trinity College, Dublin, 174, 200
beef, exports, 33, 36
Belfast, church in, 170; corporation, 62, 64; vicar, 141
Belfast, precinct of, tithes in, 158
Bellingham, Daniel, Dublin alderman, 83
Benburb, battle of, 9
Bence, Alexander, 58
Bernard, Nicholas, 92 n
Bigoe, Philip, 39
Birr, King's Co., glassworks, 39
Bisse, John, recorder of Dublin, 88 n, 192 n, 281 n, 282 n, 288, 290
Blackwood, Christopher, minister, 101–2, 103 n, 108
Bladen, Thomas, minister, 143 n
Bladen, William, Dublin alderman and printer, 83 n
Boate, Arnold, 214, 225, 235, 237, 241
Boate, Gerard, 214–15, 216, 241; his Naturall History, 214–15, 229, 234–7, 239
Bohemia, refugees from invited to Ireland, 57, 234
Bolton, Lancs., 82 n
Bolton, Sir Edward, 281, 282, 290 n
Bolton, Sir Richard, 281 n; praises Common Law, 252
Bonnell, James, 246
Bordeaux, 46, 241
Borlase, Edmund, 295, 300
Boroughs, English, 67
Boroughs, Irish, Catholics expelled from, 68, 297; and education, 190; guilds in, 13, 72–4; New Rules for, 69 n; official policy towards, 13, ch. IV; power and religion in, 67–71, 172; property in, 28, 51–2; restored, 120, 259, 303
Borr, Cornelius, 248
Bowen, Col. Henry, atheist, 109 n
Boyle, Katherine, Lady Ranelagh, 194, 216, 236, 243, 247
Boyle, Michael, dean of Cloyne, 273–4
Boyle, Richard, first earl of Cork, 36, 37, 283; and schools, 185

Boyle, Richard, second earl of Cork, 29, 38, 66 n, 149 n, 161 n; justice of the peace, 291; lay patron, 150; and Munster presidency court, 273–4, 277; and new learning, 247; praises Richard Pepys, 284; religious practices of, 151

Boyle, Robert, 173, 179, 191, 214, 216, 217, 219, 223, 231, 236, 238, 239, 245, 247

Boyle, Roger, first lord Broghill and earl of Orrery, career in 1640s, 7, 8–9, 301; career in 1650s, 294–5; and Henry Cromwell, 22, 23, 302; and Invisible College, 216; and G. Lowther, 283; and Munster presidency, 270, 271; and new learning, 231, 233, 243, 247; and religion, 118, 134 n; and schools, 193; Scottish policy of, 123; mentioned, 70 n, 134, 149 n

Boyle, family, 22 n

Brabazon, Edward, second earl of Meath, 150

Bramhall, John, Protestant bishop of Derry and archbishop of Armagh, 91, 92–3, 122, 154, 173, 177

brass, export of, 33

Bray, vicars of, 94

Brehon law, 249–50

Brenan, John, catholic bishop of Waterford, 55

Brereton, John, schoolmaster, 129 n

brewing, 40–1

Brewster, Francis, M.P., 141 n

Brewster, Nathanael, minister, 136 n, 137 n, 138, 139, 141, 289

Briscoe, Michael, minister, 136 n, 137, 141

Bridges, Col. John, 145, 205, 208 n, 210 n

Bristol, Coopers' Co. of, 34–5, 43; and Irish fisheries, 34–5, 43; and Irish trade, 32 n, 36, 37, 38, 41–2, 43–4, 46; and Waterford, 54; mentioned, 77

Broghill, Lord, see Boyle, Roger

Brooke, Sir William, 19 n

Browne, Geoffrey, 70 n

Browne, Sir Valentine, 205 n

Brün, J., see Unmussig, John

building, 36; see also, Church buildings

Burbidge, Leics., 262

Burke, Edmund, a late friar, 175 n

Burke, Ulick, first marquess of Clanricarde, 295

Burston, Daniel, minister, 120 n, 143

Burton, William, dissenting minister and Dublin graduate, 205 n

Bury, William, Irish councillor, 20, 22; Presbyterianism of, 22 n

Butler, Elizabeth, successively countess, marchioness and duchess of Ormonde, 29

Butler, James, first duke of Ormonde, career in 1640s, 5, 6, 7, 9; and Church of Ireland, 94 n; and Henry Cromwell, 300; and second college at Dublin, 211; mentioned, 71, 84, 118, 141, 181, 256

butter, 33

Caen, 216

Calais, 53

Calvinism, 93, 100

Cambridge University, 127, 130, 137, 222, 242, 285; statutes of, 200; King's College, 189 n; Magdalene College, 268; Trinity College, 202

Campanella, Tommaso, 217

canons, ecclesiastical, see Ireland: Church of Ireland

Capell, Arthur, first earl of Essex, 78 n, 88, 211; and Francis Roberts, 141 n, 211 n

Carey, Edward, offered judicial office in Ireland, 281, 282

Carey, George, alderman of Derry, 64 n

Carey, James, convert from Catholicism, 175 n

Carlow, County, 230; confiscated houses in, 51 n

Carney, Richard, mathematician and ? astrologer, 248

Carpenter, Nathanael, 213–14, 215

Carrickfergus, Co. Antrim, corporation of, 62, 64, 73; guilds in, 73; religion in, 102, 122, 124 n, 136; trade of, 46, 73

Carteret, Philip, 288

Carwardine, Walter, 271 n, 273, 274

Carysfort, Co. Wicklow, 185

Cashel, dean of, see Williamson, Caesar

Cashel, charter restored, 63; schoolmaster at, 189 n

Catholics in Ireland, *see* Ireland: Catholics
cattle, 33, 36, 47, 48
Caulfield, Thomas, 288
Cavan, County, value of confiscated tithes in, 155 n
Cawdron, George, mayor of Waterford, 66 n
Chambers, John, minister, 102 n
Chambers, Robert, minister, 136 n, 137, 143, 192 n; preaches in Irish, 175–6
Chancery, Irish, *see* Ireland: Court of Chancery
Chapell, William, provost of Trinity College, Dublin, 174, 201, 203
Charlemont, Co. Armagh, minister at, 162
Charles I, 3–5, 6–7, 8, 85 n, 93, 118, 131, 253, 254, 262, 281; household of, 66 n; trial of, 262, 276, 285
Charles II, 9, 24, 32, 52, 69, 84, 87, 109, 122, 141, 142, 247, 272, 300, 301; prayed for, 121, 125; and second college in Dublin, 211; and E. Smith schools, 192
Charnock, Stephen, minister, 117, 133 n, 136, 137, 139; plots, 143
Cheshire, 59, 193; and Trinity College, Dublin, 205
Chester, 142; and Irish trade, 42, 59 n
Chichester, Sir Arthur, first earl of Donegall, 162, 190
Child, Dr. Robert, 206 n, 216, 222–3, 226 n, 235–6, 237, 239, 240, 247
Christ's Hospital, 191, 245
Church buildings, 90, 95, 135, 168–71
Clanricarde, marquess of, *see* Burke, Ulick
Clare, County, confiscated houses in, 51 n; confiscated tithes in, 155 n
Clarke, Robert, minister, 108 n
Cliffe, William, Dublin alderman, 83 n
Clonfert, Co. Galway, university proposed, 206
Clonmel, Co. Tipperary, assizes at, 142 n, Baptists in, 102; houses in, 51 n; minister at, 131 n, 136
cloth manufacture, 31–2, 38, 41, 83, 87
Clotworthy, Sir John, first Viscount Massereene, and education, 190; F.R.S., 247; and Invisible College,

216; justice of the peace, 291; lay impropriator, 162; lay patron, 150; M.P., 6, 8; religious views, 92 n, 124, 126 n, 127 n
Cloyne, dean of, *see* Boyle, Michael
Cobham estates, 19 n
Cock, George, 261 n
Coffey, Thomas, minister, 143 n
coinage, 42, 47–8, 224
Cokely, Thomas, 271 n
Coleraine, Co. Derry, schoolmaster at, 189 n
Colvill, Dr. Alexander, 163
Comenius, Jan Amos, 185, 215
Commission for the propagation of the Gospel in the North, 96
Commission for the propagation of the Gospel in Wales, 96; in South Wales, 145
Commission of the peace, in Ireland, 76, 83, 103, 110, 132, 147–8, 149–50, 221, 249, 258, 259, 289–91, 303
Commissioners for the administration of justice; in 1655, 257 n; in Dublin, 257; in Leinster, 257, 281, 290; in Munster, 274; instructions for, 278; mentioned, 284
Commissioners for almshouses and hospitals, 75, 208 n
Commissioners for probate of wills, 83, 259, 288 n
Commissioners, revenue, 29, 83, 144–5, 258–9, 278
Commissioners to inquire into church resources (1657), 161–4, 187
Commissioners to try Irish rebels, 259
Committee for approbation of ministers, in Dublin, 146, 147, 150; in London, 145, 146, 148; in Munster, 148–50
Committees to regulate fees, 253
Committee to visit Irish schools (1656), 197
Common Law, praised, 252, 254–5, 267; reform of, 255, 267
Common Prayer Book, 94, 96, 97, 139, 151, 177, 179, 198
Comptroller-general of the Irish revenue, *see* Wood, Robert
Connaught, plantation in, 1; presidential court and lord president, 24, 89, 251, 270, 272, *see also* Coote, Sir

Charles; provision of justice in, 257, 258; rebellion in, 5; transplantation of Catholics to, 10–12, 277, 293; mentioned, 41

Connecticut, 289

Connor, dean and chapter of, 162

Convention, General, see Ireland: Convention of

Convention, Dublin (1658), 117–22, 126–9, 147–8, 157, 158

Convocation, see Ireland: Church of Ireland

Conway, Edward, 3rd Viscount Conway and Killultagh, first earl of Conway, 162

Cook, Isaac, 262, 265

Cook, John, and law reform, 266–7, 275, 278, 280; chief justice of Munster, 268–74, 277, 278, 280; proposes reforms, 264–7, 275; refuses office, 274–5, but later accepts, 281 n; religious views, 263–4, 274; trustee of Trinity College, Dublin, 199 n; mentioned, 14, 149, 255, 256, 257, 261–3, 281, 282, 288, 290, 291–2

Cooke, Sir Walsingham, justice of the peace, 290 n

Coote, Sir Charles, first earl of Mountrath, alderman of Derry, 64 n; mayor of Galway, 65; justice of the peace, 290 n; lord president of Connaught, 270 n, 272; and religion, 134; mentioned, 24, 38, 55

Corbet, Miles, parliamentary commissioner in Dublin and Irish councillor, 20, 22, 23, 281, 282, 283; said to be in debt, 286 n; as an Irish judge, 285–7, 288; and religion, 101, 119 n, 283

Corish, P. J., 297

Cork, association of ministers, 117, 120–2, 140–1, 143, 177

Cork, assizes at, 274; Baptists in, 102, 149; cathedral chapter in, 118 n; charter of, 63; Christ Church, 169; confiscated property in, 52; corporation of, 64; ecclesiastical patronage in, 152; governor of, 110, see also Phaire, Robert; guilds of, 73; Quakers in, 110, 112; St. Stephen's Hospital, 151; schoolmaster in, 189; trade of, 34, 46

Cork, County, atheists in, 109 n; commission of peace for, 291; confiscated houses in, 51 n; confiscated tithes in, 155 n; High Sheriff, 58 n; ministers in, 129, 140; Protestant nonconformists in, 129 n; Quakers in, 109–10; mentioned, 36, 241

Cork, dean of, see Hackett, Thomas; and Worth, Edward

Cork, earl of, see Boyle, Richard

Cork, precinct, 75; doctor in, 241; revenue commissioners for, 29 n

Cork, Cloyne and Ross, diocese, 165; incomes of clergy in, 166; inquisitions into former lands of, 161 n; schools in, 184

Corporations, municipal, see Boroughs

coshering, 76

Cottingham, Yorks., 203 n

Council of the North, 271

Council of Trade, England, 220

Counter-Reformation, 3, 154, 182, 184–5, 297

Court of Chief Place, see Ireland: Court of Common Pleas

Court of Common Pleas, see Ireland: Court of Common Pleas

Court of Exchequer, see Ireland: Court of Exchequer

Court of Wards, England, 286

Court of Wards, see Ireland: Court of Wards

Coventry, Warks., 99

Cowley, Joshua, 202

Coxe, Samuel, minister, 125 n, 131 n, 133 n, 136 n, 137 n, 138, 140, 142

Cremer, Balthazar, 86 n

Cremer, Thomas, 86 n

Cremer, Tobias, 86 n

Croke, Charles, 131 n

Cromwell, Bridget, see Fleetwood, Bridget

Cromwell, Henry, appointment, 20–3; and the Baptists, 105–9; and the Catholics, 181, 298; Chancellor of Trinity College, Dublin, 114; chaplains of, 14, 88, 117, 136, 192, 210, 233; character, 21; and the commission of the peace, 290–1; and doctors, 241; and Dublin, 81; and education, 193, 196; and the Independents, 112-17, 129; and the Irish, 174, 193; and judges, 282, 284; and the law, 259, 292; and Anthony Morgan, 223; and Munster, 119–22, 127–30; and the new learning, 225–6, 231–3, 243; opposition to, 20–2, 106–8, 160, 232, 286; and the plot of 1663, 143 n; policy, 105–6, 114–5, 233, 293, 294, 299, 300–3, 305; praised, 295, 300; and provincial government, 272, 276; and the Quakers, 109–11; and religion, 130–2, 135, 139, 140, 145, 146, 148, 150, 153, 157, 159, 161, 164, 177; and second college in Dublin, 206–7, 208, 211, 212; secretary to, 218–9, see also Petty, William; thought to favour Charles II, 300, 301; trustee of Trinity College, Dublin, 199 n; and Ulster, 122–6, 302; and Ussher's library, 211–12; and Robert Wood, 224, 236; and Benjamin Worsley, 221–2; mentioned, 25, 26, 28, 29, 30–1, 33, 35, 42, 43, 44–5, 47, 48–9, 56, 62–3, 64, 73, 84, 209, 230, 245

Cromwell, Oliver, and advancement of learning, 230; attitudes towards Ireland, 11–12, 293, 294, 299, 301, 302, 305; death of, 22, 128, 301; and Ireland in 1649, 9–10, 17, 18–19, 20–1; and the Irish Catholics, 172, 178, 180; and the law, 255, 256, 262, 263, 265, 267–71, 273, 275, 291, 294; praised by Froude, 296; and propagation of the Gospel, 96–7, 198, 212, 294; and the second college at Dublin, 207; and Trinity College, Dublin, 201; mentioned, 13, 16, 25, 34, 53, 55, 57, 58, 59, 63, 96, 100, 105–6, 114, 127, 138, 145, 148, 158, 159

Cromwell, Richard, 21, 22, 301
Cudworth, Ralph, 199 n
Currer, William, 241, 242, 247
Customs, 27, 28, 29–30, 33, 34, 37, 44–6, 244; farm of, 45, 47, 59, 80; petty customs, 83

Dalway, Capt. John, mayor of Carrick-fergus, 64 n
Daniel, Godfrey, minister, 178, 179
Daniel, William, archbishop of Tuam, 178 n
Darcy, Patrick, 2, 252

Dartmouth, Devon, 58 n
Davies, Sir John, 184
Davies, Sir Paul, 209
debt, law of, 253, 267, 269–70, 271, 273, 274, 278–9, 292
Derry, bishop of, see King, William
Derry, County, value of confiscated lands in, 155 n
Derry, precinct, 124; ministers in supported by tithes, 158
Derry, town, assizes at, 277; charter restored, 63; church in, 170; college proposed at, 211 n; corporation of, 64; justices of the peace in, 76; school at, 185
Descartes, René 216, 217
Desminières, John, 85
Desminières, Lewis, 85, 86
Desminières, Robert, 85 n
Dingle, Co. Kerry, 46
Diodati, Jean, Genevan theologian, 262
Dionysius, Periegesis of, 196
Directory of Worship, 95, 178, 179–80
doctors, 75, 196, 240–2, 288; in the army, 241, 248; Irish, 240–1, 248
Dod, Paul, mayor of Galway, 65 n, 104 n
Dodson, William, customs farmer, 45 n
Dodwell, Henry, 243 n
Donegal, County, value of confiscated tithes in, 155 n
Donegall, earl of, see Chichester, Sir Arthur
Donnellan, James, 257, 281, 282, 290 n
Donnellan, Nehemiah, archbishop of Tuam, 282 n
Douai, 179
Down, County, commission of peace, 291; ecclesiastical incomes in, 166; ecclesiastical livings in, 162; lands in, 58 n; lay patronage in, 150 n; schools in, 188; tithes in, 157; value of confiscated tithes, 155 n
Down, dean and chapter, 162
Down, school at, 188
Down, and Connor, bishop of, see Leslie, Henry
Down survey, see land surveys
Draper, John, minister, 102 n, 108 n
Drebbel, Cornelius, 217
dress, reform of, 12, 40, 76

Drogheda, Co. Louth, Catholics in, 68; guilds of, 73; mayor of, 67; minister in, 136; E. Smith school in, 192, 203

Dromore, dean and chapter of, 162; diocese of, 165

drunkenness, 40, 76, 148, 196, 208

Drury, John, 45 n

Dublin, city
  almshouses, 75
  books published in, 214, 228
  brewing, 40
  Castle, 23, 211
  Catholics in, 68, 69, 79; Catholic priests in, 181
  Christ Church cathedral, 77, 99—100, 102, 165, 170, 197; see also Golborne, John
  College of Physicians, 242, 248
  Commission of the peace for, 221 n, 258, 290
  Cork House, 207, 211, 243
  corporation, 62, 63, 68, 69, 72, 77—89, 99—100, 113, 174; aldermen, 290; common council, 78, 79; mayor, 67, 290
  coup in, December 1659, 23, 66 n 133
  doctors in, 196, 218
  education in, 190, 195—6, 197
  fisheries, 34
  and government policy, 77—89
  guilds of, 72, 73, 79, 83; Brewers' Guild, 40; Goldsmiths' Company, 86 n; Merchant Guild, 45, 72—3, 80, 82, 84, 85 n, 152; St. Audeon's Guild, 84 n, 152
  hospitals, 75, 214, 241—2
  judges in, 257, 274, 277
  King's Inns, 77, 136, 251, 278, 282, 288; John Cook enters, 263 n
  latitude established, 240
  merchants of, 27, 72—3, 77—89; merchant staple of, 73
  office of address proposed, 238
  physic garden proposed, 239
  poor relief in, 75
  population of, 77, 78
  printing in, 214, 228 n
  recorder of, see Bisse, John
  religion in, 83, 87—8, 93, 95, 99—100, 124—5, 128—9, 131—3, 136; association of ministers, 128—9; Baptists in, 101, 102, 105,

109; conversion of the Irish in, 175—6; episcopalians in, 152; number of ministers in, 165; Protestant nonconformity in, 87—8, 142—3
  Royal Society in proposed, 247
  St. Audeon's, 152, 169
  St. Bride's, 176
  St. John's, 84 n, 169
  St. Katherine's, 125, 131 n, 169
  St. Michael's, 152
  St. Michan's, 152
  St. Nicholas's, 81, 83, 99—100, 152
  St. Patrick's Cathedral, 77, 165; school of, 195, 197
  Schools in, 185, 186, 194—8; proposed Lord Protector's school, 195
  scientists there in 1653, 223
  second college to be established, 31, 92, 175, 183, 186, 206—11, 212, 243, 303
  ships of, 42, 79
  Smithfields, 142
  trade of, 46, 72, 73, 77, 85, 88—9; pre-eminence of, 304

Dublin, County, confiscated property in, 51 n; conversions of Catholics in, 180; High Sheriff of, 83

Dublin, protestant diocese of, 165; clerical incomes in, 166; supports school, 184

Dublin Philosophical Society, 209, 213, 226, 237, 244—8

Dublin, precinct, revenue commissioners for, 29 n; number of ministers in, 165

Dublin, Trinity College, 31, 77, 97, 100, 113, 118, 137, 143, 165, 173—5, 183, 186, 191, 193, 195, 206, 209, 225; chancellor, 114; curriculum, 243; fellows, 192 n, 201—4; foundation, 184; and government policy, 198—206; and Irish, 173—5, 178 n; and medicine, 242; and the new learning, 213, 240; professor of mathematics, 227—8, 244, 246, see also Symner, Miles; provost, 112, 133, 201, see also Winter, Samuel; and Chapell, William; revenues of, 199—200; scholarships at, 191; schoolmasters and, 189, 197; statutes, 200—1; trustees, 198—200; undergraduate numbers, 204—5;

undergraduates' origins, 204–5; undergraduates' schools, 197; and Ussher's library, 211; vice-chancellor of, *see* Jones, Henry; Benjamin Worsley enters, 219

du Moulin, Dr. Peter, the younger, 151 n

Dungan, Thomas, 257, 281, 282, 290 n

Dungannon, Co. Tyrone, school at, 190

Dungarvan, Co. Waterford, fisheries, 34

Dunkirk, 16

Dunlop, Robert, 296

Durham, university proposed, 207–8, 224

Durham, County, 138

Dury, John, 215, 231

Dutch, *see* Netherlands

East Anglia, ministers from in Ireland, 138

Easthorp, Reuben, minister, 136, 137 n, 138, 139, 141 n

Eaton, Samuel, 139

Eccleston, Richard, 230, 232

Edinburgh, Broghill's contacts in, 134 n

Education, 12, 13, ch. VII, 213, 293, 303, 304; of Irish, 174–5

Edwards, Dr. Jonathan, minister and master in chancery, 288

Edwards, R. D., 171–2

Elizabeth, I, 173, 177

Elphin, dean of, *see* Synge, Edward

Elwyn, John, alderman of Derry, 64 n

engagement, *see* oath of engagement

England, subsidizes Ireland, 27; trade with Ireland, 31, 34, 47, 48

England: Church of England, 90; Canons of 1604, 93

Commonwealth, 9, 11; oath of engagement to, 67–8, 148

Council of State, and Ireland's government, 17, 18, 20 n, 107, 293; and advancement of learning, 226, 231; and education, 187; and the law, 260, 281; negligent, 294; preachers to, 138, 147, and tithes, 159; and Ussher's library, 211–12

Council of State (1660), 270

Protectorate, 11, 13, 18; how to establish in Ireland, 114–15; opposed in Ireland, 104–6, 115, 121

Enniscorthy, Co. Wexford, ironworks, 38

Erasmus, Desiderius, 241 n

Essex, earl of, *see* Capell, Arthur

Eton College, 223

Eustace, Sir Maurice, and schools, 193; and the second college in Dublin, 207, 209

Evans, Thomas, alderman of Dublin, 84 n

Evans, Capt. Thomas, mayor of Kilkenny, 66 n

Everard, Nicholas, 71 n

Exchequer, Court of, English, barons of, 284, 285

Exchequer, Court of, Irish, *see* Ireland: Court of Exchequer

excise, 27, 28, 33, 39, 41, 45–6

exports, 32–4, 35–6, 42, 47, 89

Eyres, John, mayor of Galway, 57 n

Eyres, Joseph, minister, 119 n, 120, 121, 127 n, 139, 143 n, 149–50

famine, 76

Fennell, Dr. Gerald, 248

Fenton, Sir William, 118, 149, 271 n, 302

Fermanagh, County, value of confiscated tithes in, 155 n

Fethard, Co. Tipperary, charter and corporation of, 71 n

Fifth Monarchists, 101, 105, 132; and the law, 255, 265, 267

Finglas, Co. Dublin, 197

Firth, Sir Charles, 296, 300–1, 302

fish, 33, 34–5, 44, 59

Fitzsimons, Philemon, minister, 176 n

Flanders, 219; settlers from, 57 n

Fleetwood, Bridget, (née Cromwell), 102 n

Fleetwood, Charles, chaplain, 136; and the government of Ireland, 16, 18, 20–1, 25, 26, 62, 80, 81, 293, 294, 299, 300, 301, 303; and the law, 255, 260, 261, 281, 282; religious views of, 100–1, 105–6, 119, 264; and tithes, 155 n, 158–9; mentioned, 60, 110, 113, 135, 145, 153, 232, 285, 286

Foulke, Bartholomew, master in chancery, 288

Fountain, James, doctor, 248

Foy, Dr. Nathanael, bishop of Waterford, 167

France, trade with Ireland, 35, 46, 89
Franecker, university of, 241
free trade, wanted, 71, 80
Froude, J. A., 296

Galen, 217, 241
Galilei, Galileo, 240
Galway, County, confiscated property in, 51 n
Galway, town, Baptists in, 57, 102, 103–4, 108 n; confiscated property in, 52; corporation of, 64, 65, 103–4; minister in, 136; re-settlement of, 53, 55–7, 58–9 n; school in, 191, 192; trade of, 46, 57 n; mentioned, 32
Geer, Laurence de, 58, 59
Geer, Louis de, 58
Geissen, 86 n
Geneva, 262
Gilbert, Claudius, minister, 131 n, 136, 137 n, 139, 140, 141, 149 n
Glamorgan, earl of, see Somerset, Edward
Glasgow, university, 137
glass-making, 38–9
Gloucester, property in Ireland, 56
grain, 37, 42, 44, 46, 76
Grantham, Lincs., 20
Greek, to be taught, 184, 187, 195; degree requirement at Trinity College, Dublin, 200; masters skilled in, 189, 196
Goddard, Jonathan, 199 n
Goldborne, John, schoolmaster, 195, 197
Goodwin, Robert, Irish councillor, 19, 22, 23
Goodwin, Thomas, president of Magdalen College, Oxford, 145, 200, 233
Gookin, Vincent, 149, 220
Gorges, Dr. Robert, clerk to the Irish council, 208 n, 210
Graffan, Hugh, convert from Catholicism, 175 n
Greatrakes, Valentine, 273
Greg, John, Presbyterian minister, 124
Grey, Enoch, minister, 136 n, 137 n, 138 n, 141
guilds, trading, 13, 72–4, see also boroughs

Haarlem, 87 n

Hackett, Thomas, dean of Cork (1660), 118, 130 n, 143
Halley, Edmond, 229
Halsey, William, 274, 288; chief justice of Munster, 288 n; justice of the peace, 290 n
Hamilton, James, 2nd Viscount Clandeboy and first earl of Clanbrassil, 123, 151 n, 162, 185, 188 n, 215
Hammond, Robert, short-lived Irish councillor, 19
Harding, Dr. John, 119 n, 149, 199, 210
Harrison, Major-General Thomas, 101
Harrison, Thomas, minister, 14, 88, 117, 136, 137 n, 138, 139, 140 n, 142, 147 n, 192, 233
Hart, John, Presbyterian minister, 124
Hartlib, Samuel, 190, 206, 213, 214–5, 216, 217, 219, 222, 223, 224, 229–38, 239, 240, 247; and Boate's Naturall History, 234–7; death, 237; quest for an income, 233–4
Hartwell, Capt. William, mayor of Limerick, 65 n
Harvard, university, 137, 138
Hatfield, Ridgely, Dublin alderman, 45, 192 n
Hawkins, William, 58
Heaton, Richard, botanist, 247
Heavens, John, 54 n
Hebrew, to be taught, 187, 195; degree requirement, 200
Helmont, J. B. van, 217
Henry II, 249
Henry VIII, 173
Herbert, Edward, 3rd Lord Herbert of Cherbury, 145
Herbert, Sir Thomas, 205
Hevelius, Johannes, 239
Hewson, Col. John, 99, 103 n, 145, 146, 147 n
Hickes, John, 205–6
hides, 33, 35, 36, 39–40, 42
Hill, Col. Arthur, 151, 222, 247, 291
Hill, William, schoolmaster, 189, 196–8, 205 n, 212
Hoare, Mr., 273
Hobbes, Thomas, 217
Hodden, Major Richard, governor of Kinsale, 110

Hodder, John, mayor of Cork, 149
Hoegarden, Abraham van, 58–60
Hoegarden, Isaac van, 58
Holdsworth, W. S., 249
holidays, superstitious, to be suppressed, 76; observed, 151 n
Holland, see Netherlands
Hooke, Robert, 229
Hooke, Thomas, Dublin alderman, 81–4, 85 n, 147 n, 176, 192 n
Hoppen, K. T., 246
hospitals, 75, 214, 241–2; in London, 230
Houghton, John, mayor of Waterford, 66 n
Hoven, Garret van den, 86
Hoven, Peter van den, 86
Howell, Roger, 84
Hoy, Sir John, justice of the peace, 290 n, 291 n
Hoyle, Nathanael, 202–3
Huguenots, invited to Ireland, 57; in Dublin, 85–8
Hull, Yorks., 230
Hunt, John, minister, 103 n
Hurd, Lt. Col. Humphrey, mayor of Galway, 65
husbandry, 223, 235, 238; Legacy of Husbandry, 235
Hutchinson, Daniel, Dublin alderman, 41, 81, 83, 84, 115; justice of the peace, 290, 291 n; treasurer of E. Smith schools, 192 n
Hutchinson, Edward, minister, 102 n, 142 n
Huygens, Christiaan, 240
Hyde, Edward, first earl of Clarendon, on Henry Cromwell, 300; on Ireland, 295; on Irish judges, 287; mentioned, 134 n

imports, 35, 89
Inchiquin, Lord, see O'Brien, Morrough
Independents, religious, and Henry Cromwell, 14, 108, 112–17, 120, 121, 299, 301–2; in Dublin, 84 n, 87–8, 125; in England, 114, 116, 121, 132; and the law, 261, 272; ministers, 140; and preaching in Irish, 135; and the second college, 210; and tithes, 126–7, 158; and Trinity College, Dublin, 201, 203;

vet ministers, 147-8; mentioned, 98–9, 104, 131, 132–3, 262–3
industry, 12, 37–8, 83, 87, 293, 296; little established, 303–4
Ingoldsby, Henry, governor and mayor of Limerick, 65
instrument-makers, 227
Invisible College, 216, 219
IRELAND:
Catholics of,
to be transplanted, 10–11, 165, 172, 277, 299; clergy, 5–6, 76, 175, 177–8; combatted, 94; in Connaught, 171, 176; converted to Protestantism, 180–1, 297–8; and corporations, 64–5, 67–71, 79, 80; and Henry Cromwell, 108, 296–9; deported to West Indies, 47; in Dublin, 79, 80; and education, 184–5, 193, 194, 213; generosity towards, 11-12, 298; in 1660, 134; intellectual influence, 213; laws against, 172; and the law, 256, 277; merchants, 50, 52, 54–5, 57 n, 60; not won over, 303–4; and Parliament, 2 n, 69–71; policy towards, 12, 36, 296–9; and poor relief, 75; racially inferior, 12; rebel, 2–6, 9, 10; share of land, 11; and trade, 73, 74; Trinity College, Dublin, to combat, 198; Ussher's views on, 92; their worship illegal, 172
protestant Church of Ireland,
Canons of 1615, 93; Canons of 1634, 93, 173, 177, 184; and the Catholics, 171, 175–7; compared with the Cromwellian church, 305; Convocation, 166; Henry Cromwell's attitude towards, 116; and education, 183–4, 186–7, 192, 193; in 1660, 129, 134; and the Irish language, 175–7; lands of, 75; lay patronage, 150–1, 153–4, 155, 161; ministers, 94, 95, 97; ministers act as schoolmasters, 189; number of ministers, 165–6; poverty of, 167–8; and reform, 135; its revenues, 155, 161; W. Steele's attitude towards, 116; Trinity College, Dublin, and, 198, 202; weaknesses of, 182; mentioned, 90–1, 92–4, 97, 131, 137, 143, 154, 225; see also, Church Buildings; Common Prayer Book

Confederation of Kilkenny, 4–6, 8–9; lawyers and, 252

constitutional position, 26, 29, 70, 98, 280; unsatisfactoriness of, 304–5

Convention (1660), 22 n, 24, 26, 29, 49, 84, 133, 248 n, 288 n; and the law, 287; Protestant ascendancy in, 71 n; removes Provost Winter, 201; and the second college in Dublin, 211

Council (1654–9), 18–23, 52, 56, 116, 147, 231, 232, 234, 284–5, 286, 294; clerk to, 218, *see also* Gorges, Dr. Robert, *and* Petty, William; and education, 187, 206; meetings, 285; quorum of, 22 n salary of members, 277

Council of trade, 49, 244

Courts leet, baron and of pie powder, 289

Court of Castle Chamber, 252

Court of Chancery, 63, 161, 234, 250–1, 253, 256, 260, 267, 283, 285; decentralization of, 279–80; irregularities in, 287; masters in chancery, 279–80, 288; placed in commission, 260; reform of, 279, 285, 292

Court of Claims, 286, 288

Court of Common Pleas, 250; to be suppressed, 260; judges in, 281, 282, 283

Court of Exchequer, 67, 250, 260, 283, 287; judges in, 281 n

Court of High Commission, 252

Court of King's Bench, 250

Court of Upper Bench, formerly King's Bench, 260; judges in, 275, 281 n, 282, 283; suppression suggested, 283

Lord Justices, 5

Parliament, 5–7, 50, 59, 60, 71, 84, 163, 174, 244, 252, 283; Catholics and, 69–71; lawyers in, 252; restoration wanted, 29

Parliamentary Commissioners (1650–4 and 1659), 17, 144, 156, 172, 227, 257, 259–60, 294; chaplain to, 99, 117; and the law, 278; and provincial government, 272; salaries of, 17 n, secretary to, 220

plantations, 10, 11, 30, 60, 61

Privy Council, 69 n, 209, 211

statutes, 250, 263

trade, 16, 72; character of, 34–42, 43; free trade, 32; regulated, 31–4; volume, 42–7

Ireton, Henry, 17, 25, 104, 149, 172 n, 269, 271, 272, 291, 293, 299; suspicious of Broghill and Coote, 272 n; trustee of Trinity College, Dublin, 199 n

Irish language, 3, 76, 90–1, 171–2, 173–80, 298, 304; failure to extirpate, 303–4; interpreters, 277; Irish Bible, 177, 178–9; and the law, 277; preaching in, 174, 176 n; Trinity College, Dublin, and, 173, 174

Irish people, civilization of, 234; conversion, 171–82, 296, 302–3; customs, 235; education of, 187, 188, 191, 193–4, 206–7; guilt of, 293–4; and religion, 91, 102, 129, 135

iron, 37, 38

Isle of Man, and Trinity College, Dublin, 204

James I, 70, 173, 249

James II, 69, 248

Jenner, Thomas, minister, 138

Jeonar, Capt. John, mayor of Kilkenny, 66 n

Jephson, William, 6, 8

Jessop, William, 230

Jesuits, 179, 216

Johnson, ?John, 238

Johnston of Wariston, Sir Archibald, 104

Jones, Dr. Ambrose, 143 n, 244

Jones, Dr. Henry, 161 n, 166, 173, 178–9, 192, 233, 234, 244, 247, 295; and the second college, 210; trustee of Trinity College, Dublin, 199; and Ussher's library, 211

Jones, Col. John, parliamentary commissioner in Ireland, 14, 17, 23, 101, 272 n

Jones, Sir Theophilus, 211, 290 n

juries, 254

justices of the peace, *see* Commission of the peace

Kells, Book of, 211

Kempson, Col. Nicholas, 111 n

Kent, 222

Kerr, Patrick, Presbyterian minister, 84 n

Kerry, County, Baptists in, 108 n; confiscated property in, 51 n; confiscated tithes in, 155 n; lands in, 228 n; law in, 257; minister for, 145

Kildare, archdeacon of, *see* Travers, Joseph

Kildare, bishop of, *see* Jones, Dr. Ambrose

Kildare, County, churches in, 169; commission of the peace for, 291; confiscated property in, 51 n; parochial livings in, 162; parochial reorganization, 163, 164; schools in, 188; tithes in, 157; unauthorized ministers in, 163

Kilkenny, County, confiscated property in, 51 n; mentioned, 123, 167, 230

Kilkenny, town, Baptists in, 101–2, 103, 170; charter restored, 63; corporation of, 64, 66, 169; education in, 190; guilds of, 73; new academy there mentioned, 206 n; new college of physicians proposed there, 248; St. Canice's cathedral, 169

Killaloe, bishop of, *see* Worth, Edward, *and* Rider, John

Killaloe, diocese of, incomes of ministers, 165

Kilmore, bishop of, *see* Bedell, William, *and* Maxwell, Robert

Kilrush, Co. Clare, 58

King, Edward, 215

King, Gabriel, mayor of Galway, 65 n

King, Ralph, alderman of Derry, 64 n

King, Sir Robert, 24, 147 n, 199, 215, 225, 290 n

King, William, successively bishop of Derry and Archbishop of Dublin, 167, 173, 188–9, 211 n, 240

King's County, confiscated property in, 51 n; glassmaking in, 39

Kinsale, Co. Cork, archdeacon of, 143; Baptists in, 102; corporation, 64; ecclesiastical patronage, 152; governor, 110; Quakers in, 110; schoolmaster, 189

Knight, James, minister, 103 n, 108 n

Ladyman, Samuel, minister, 127 n, 131 n, 136 n, 137 n, 139, 140, 141

Lamb, William, Baptist preacher, 109

Lambert, John, 17, 218

Lancashire, and Trinity College, Dublin, 205

lands, forfeited, 27; price of, 60

land surveys, 218–9, 220, 225, 226–9, 245; Down survey, 218, 226, 227

La Rochelle, 46, 53

Latin, to be taught, 183–4, 187, 195; and the law, 266; masters skilled in, 189, 196

Laud, William, archbishop of Canterbury, chancellor of Trinity College, Dublin, 200; ecclesiastical policy, 92, 139; mentioned, 263

Lawrence, Col. Richard, 53, 66 n, 101, 103 n, 146, 147 n

lead, 39

leather, 33

Leckey, William, 203

Leghorn, 46

Leinster, association of ministers, 128–9; clergy in, 128–9; commissioners for the administration of justice, 257, 281, 290; commission of the peace, 258, 290

Leitrim, County, confiscated property in, 51 n; confiscated tithes in, 155 n; education in, 194

Leslie, Henry, bishop of Down and Connor, 151

Leyden, 87, 214, 216, 222, 248 n

Lifford, Co. Donegal, 185

Lilburn, John, 262

Limerick, County, confiscated property in, 51 n; confiscated tithes in, 155 n; lands in, 228 n

Limerick, diocese, clerical incomes in, 166; lands for Hartlib, 234; no Irish preachers in, 176 n; school in, 184; mentioned, 151 n, 165

Limerick, town, archdeacon of, *see* Ladyman, Samuel; Baptists in, 102, 103 n, 108 n; charter of, 63; confiscated property in, 52; continental trade of, 65 n; corporation, 64, 65; ministers in, 131 n, 136, 139; Quakers in, 111 n; schoolmasters in, 189 n; university proposed, 206; mentioned, 6, 32, 51

Lincolnshire, 20

linen, 38, 41–2, 89

Lisburn, Co. Antrim, 222–3, 235, 247;

school, 190, trade, 46
Lismore, Co. Waterford, 22 n; castle, 38; school, 185
Liverpool, 56
Livingstone, John, Presbyterian minister, 124—5, 130, 136 n, 137 n, 140
Lloyd, Jenkin, 96—7, 145; trustee of Trinity College, Dublin, 198, 199 n
Loftus, Dr. Dudley, 209, 259, 288
Loftus, Nicholas, justice of the peace, 290 n
London, Baptists in, 101; College of Physicians, 242; Gresham's College, 217; Inns of Court, 251, Gray's Inn, 262, 288 n; Inner Temple, 289; Lincoln's Inn, 285; Middle Temple, 284; Irish Society, 58, 63; merchants of, 41, 56, 220; ministers from in Ireland, 117, 138; population, 77 n; Presbyterians, 121, 127; recorder of, see Steele, William; Royal Society, 209, 244, 245, 247; Savoy conference, 128; Savoy and Ely House hospitals, 230; trade, 46, 82
Longford, County, confiscated property in, 51 n; confiscated tithes, 155 n
Louth, County, churches in, 169; confiscated property in, 51 n; judge in, 288 n; parishes, 162; parochial reorganization, 163; schools of, 188; tithes in, 157
Louvain, Irish press at, 178
Love, John, biographer of Orrery, 295 n
Lowther, Sir Gerald, 281, 282—3, 290 n
Ludlow, Edmund, parliamentary commissioner in Ireland, 17, 18, 101, 111 n, 262, 286, 289
Ludlow, Roger, 288—9
Lull, Ramon, 241 n
Lyndon, Capt. Roger, mayor of Carrickfergus, 64 n

Mallow, Co. Cork, court at, 275; schoolmaster in, 189
manners, reformation of, 40, 76, 258
Market Deeping, Lincs., 82 n
Markham, Col. Henry, 23, 139

Marsden, Gamaliel, 140, 203 n
Marsden, Jeremiah, 140
Marsden, Josiah, 140
Marsden, Ralph, 140
Marseilles, 35, 46
Marten, Sir Henry, 11
Maryborough, Queen's Co., 103
Massachusetts, 61—2, 289
Massareene, Viscount, see Clotworthy, John
mathematics, 217, 223—4, 225, 240, 244, 245, 246, 248; professor of, 208, 225, 227—8, see also Symner, Miles
Mather, Samuel, minister, 117 n, 136 n, 137 n, 138, 142, 192 n
Matthews, Lt. John, mayor of Galway, 65 n, 104 n
Maxwell, Robert, bishop of Kilmore, 284
Mayo, County, confiscated property in, 51 n; confiscated tithes in, 155 n
maypoles, 76
Meath, bishop of, see Jones, Dr. Henry, and Ussher, James
Meath, county, confiscated property in, 51 n; confiscated tithes, 156 n; parochial reorganization in, 163, 164; unauthorized ministers in, 163; value of livings in, 162
Meath, diocese of, churches in, 168—9, 170; Irish preachers in, 176 n; parochial unions in, 167
Meath, earl of, see Brabazon, Edward
medicine, 75, 153, 196, 214, 216, 218, 223, 238, 240—2, 245
Mercator, 240
Meredith, Sir Robert, 291 n
Mersenne, Marin, 217
Mexico, 53
Middelburg, 46
Milton, John, 215
Minehead, Somerset, 38
ministers of religion, average salaries, 166; catechize, 189; character, 135—44; control of, 144—50, 150—4; numbers, 165—6, 181; payment, 26, 136, 298; teach, 183, 189; and Trinity College, Dublin, 198; mentioned, 94, 208, 288
Molyneux, Adam, 246
Molyneux, Samuel, 246
Molyneux, William, 229, 237, 240, 245—7

Monaghan, County, value of confiscated tithes in, 155 n

Monmouth rebellion, 206

Monro, Major-General Robert, 7, 122

Montagu, Edward, first earl of Sandwich, 284

Montgomery, Hugh, 3rd Viscount Montgomery of the Ards and first earl of Mount Alexander, 122, 123, 132, 162

Morgan, Major Anthony, 210, 216, 223, 225, 237, 238, 243, 244

Morrice, Thomas, customs farmer, 45 n

Morris, Capt. William, 111 n

Mosaic law, rejected by John Cook, 265; wanted, 255

Mountrath, earl of, see Coote, Sir Charles

Muggletonians, 111 n

Municipal corporations, see boroughs

Munster, army in, 109–10, 119; boroughs of, 64; chancery in, 279; clergy in, 112, 115, 153; commissioners for the administration of justice in, 274; Oliver Cromwell and, 302; and education, 185, 189; lay impropriation in, 155; plantation of, 1; Quakers in, 109–10, 119; rebellion in, 5; and religion, 92–3, 99, 109–10, 112, 118–22, 128–9, 134, 144, 151; and Trinity College, Dublin, 205; war in, 7–8, 118

Munster, presidency
chief justice, 256, see also Cook, John, and Halsey, William; Oliver Cromwell and, 267–8, 275, 299; lord president, 17, 89, 271, see also Boyle, Roger; presidential court, 251, 256, 257, 262–76, 278, 279, 292, 294, 299; dismantled, 270; fees in, 269; irregularities, 287; powers, 270; proceedings, 272–4, 277; salaries in, 268–9

Murcot, John, minister, 140, 147 n

Naas, Co. Kildare, Baptists in, 103, 152

Nantes, 53

natural philosophy, professor of, 208

Navigation Act, 47, 220

Naylor, Robert, dean of Limerick, 151 n

Netherlands, merchants of, 56; schools of, 197–8; settlers from, 57–8, 235;

settlers from in Dublin, 85–8; trade with Ireland, 33, 34, 46; workers from, 39 n; B. Worsley and, 219, 220

Newcastle upon Tyne, 84

New Ross, Co. Wexford, 103

Newry, Co. Down, 248 n

Newtown, Co. Down, 288 n

Noble, Thomas, 54 n

Noel, Martin, 35, 59, 60

Norbury, Robert, minister, 203 n

Norfolk, 138, 145, 285

Norman Yoke, 269

Norwich, 77

Nye, Philip, 145, 147

oath for mayors, 67

oath of abjuration, 172, 174, 180, 181, 187, 293

oath of allegiance, 69 n

oath of engagement to the English Commonwealth, 67–8, 148

oath of supremacy, 69 n, 70–1

oath to the Protectorate, 68

oats, 36

O'Brien, Henry, 6th earl of Thomond, 208

O'Brien, Morrough, 6th Lord Inchiquin and first earl of Inchiquin, 7–8, 9, 110 n, 118

O'Neill, Owen Rowe, 5, 9

ordination, 120, 127, 131

O'Reilly, Edmund, Catholic archbishop of Armagh, 180, 298

Ormonde, duke of, see Butler, James

Orrery, earl of, see Boyle, Roger

Osborne, Henry, 228–9, 240

Osborne, Henry, alderman of Derry, 64 n

Ossory, Bishop of, see Williams, Griffith, 131

Ossory, dean of, 66 n

Ostend, 53

Oughtred, William, 223

Owen, John, Dean of Christ Church, Oxford, 96–7, 98, 99, 121, 145, 233; trustee of Trinity College, Dublin, 198, 199 n, 200

Owen, Maurice, schoolmaster, 189 n

Oxford, experimental science club in, 210, 217, 224; university of, 127, 130, 137, 223, 224, 242; its statutes, 200; All Souls College, 198 n, 199 n; Brasenose College, 203, 217; Christ

Church, 189 n, 199 n; Corpus Christi College, 139; Jesus College, 199 n; Lincoln College, 224, 244; Merton College, 196, 199 n; New College, 139; Wadham College, 262; mentioned, 131

Padua, 222
Paracelsus, 217, 237; praised by B. Worsley, 222 n
Paris, 78 n
parishes, to be reorganized, 90, 95, 126, 127, 135, 157, 160–2, 163, 166, 167 n, 170–1, 187; to be retained, 127, 133; and their schools, 183, 187
Parliament, English
  1628, 285
  1640 (Short Parliament), 19 n, 285
  1640–53 (Long Parliament), 3, 4–5, 6–8, 59 n, 93, 95, 96, 98, 113, 156, 168, 198, 209, 219, 220, 221, 257, 271, 285, 293, 294, 299, 300; and the government of Ireland, 13, 16–18, 23, 27; and Irish policy, 10, 293; and religion in Ireland, 98, 161, 168; its committee of examinations, 286
  1653 (Barebone's Parliament), 13, 158, 168, 255; and the settlement of Ireland, 293
  1654, and the law, 260
  1656–7, 28-9, 83, 158, 172, 293
  1659, 158, 233
Parsons, Sir Richard, 39, 215
Parsons, Sir William, 39, 215
Partridge, Nathanael, minister, 100 n, 136, 137, 141
Patient, Thomas, minister, 101–2, 138, 146
Pell, John, 217
Pepys, Richard, Irish councillor, 19, 22, 23, 101, 259, 282, 284, 286–7, 288, 290 n; his political and religious opinions, 283–4, 286–7
Perkins, William, 178, 179
Peter, Hugh, 96–7, 121, 145, 160; on the law, 255; on tithes, 155 n
Petty, William, 22, 48–9, 78, 108, 197–8, 204, 207, 210, 216, 221, 222, 225, 226–8, 231–3, 235, 236, 237, 238–9, 241, 243, 245–6, 302; early career, 216–19; career after 1660, 245, 248; and the Dublin

Philosophical Society, 246–7; on Ireland, 269 n; on Irish judges, 287; and medical reform, 241–2; his profits, 228 n; ridicules Worsley, 220 n
Phaire, Col. Robert, 38, 110, 149, 274
Pierce, Robert, schoolmaster, 189 n
Pine, Mr., 273
pipestaves, 35, 36, 42
Pitt, Simon, alderman of Derry, 64 n
piracy, 48
plague, 57 n, 74, 76, 78, 104
Plunkett, Capt. and Mrs., 272–3
poor relief, 74–6, 242
pork, 33, 35
Portland, earl of, see Weston, Jerome
Portumna, Co. Galway, 124
potash, 39
Poynings' law, 2, 280
Presbyterianism, to be introduced into Ireland, 95; enthusiasm for in 1660, 134; Solemn League and Covenant, 7, 9, 122
Presbyterians, cultivated, 14; efforts to accommodate, 130; favoured by Henry Cromwell, 108, 117, 140, 302; in Cork, 120; in Dublin, 131; in London, 121, 127, 128, 140, 146; in Ulster, 122–6, 128, 132, 137, 156, 190, 243, 302, 304; mentioned, 1, 6, 7, 10, 64, 92, 129, 209, 301
Preston, Hugh, 82 n
Preston, John, Dublin alderman, 81, 82, 83, 192 n, 193
Preston, General Thomas, 5
Prettie, Col. Henry, 38, 39, 103 n
Price, John, 203 n
price regulation, 40, 74
printing, in Dublin, 214, 228; in Irish, 173, 177–80
Protestantism, to be spread in Ireland, 12, ch. V, 135, 181–2, 215, 234, 293, 298; lack of success, 303–4; ordinance (1650) to propagate, 96, 186, 195, 198, 206, 207, 294, 299
Protestant nonconformists in Ireland, 38, 88, 93, 98, 126, 129 n, 137, 141–3, 304; Orrery wants comprehension for them, 134 n; and the schools, 193, 203
Protestants of Ireland, ascendancy gained, 297, 304; and corporations, 64; and Henry Cromwell, 14, 16, 114–5, 300–3, 305; and Oliver

Cromwell, 302; and education, 187, 303; as judges, 282, 288; as justices of the peace, 290–1; their lands, 27; and the law, 251, 252, 258, 269, 273–4, 276, 277, 280, 284; and politics, 3, 6–8, 10, 14, 69–71, 118–19, 130, 133, 134, 294–5, 298; and religion, 92–4; and taxation, 29, 30
Providence Island Company, 138
public health, 74, 75
Pym, John, 5

Quakers, 109–112, 119, 132, 149, 159, 302
Queen's County, Baptist in, 108 n; confiscated property in, 51 n, mentioned, 221

Rand, James, 230, 232
Ranelagh, Lady, see Boyle, Katherine
Ranters, 99, 110
Rathmines, battle of, 9
Rawdon, George, 151, 190, 291
Reading, John, 288
rebellion of 1641, 2–6, 10–13, 90–1, 191, 211, 283; destroys churches, 169; predicted by Ussher, 92
receiver-general of revenue in Ireland, see Wood, Robert
Redman, Major Daniel, 139
Reeves, W., 249
Reformation, the, 90
restoration of Charles II, 24, 78, 129, 133, 243
revenue, see assessment, customs, excise
Reynolds, John, 302
Rheims, university, 241
Richards, Andrew, mayor of Waterford, 66 n
Richardson, John, bishop of Ardagh, 215
Richardson, John, 173
Richardson, Thomas, Dublin alderman, 83 n
Rider, John, bishop of Killaloe, 176
Rinuccini, Giovanni Battista, 6
Riverius, Lazarius, 196
Roberts, Edward, 190, 192 n, 208 n, 210
Roberts, Francis, minister, 117, 124, 130, 136, 137 n, 138, 140, 141, 210, 211 n

Roche, Jordan, Limerick alderman, 65 n
Rogers, John, minister, 99–100, 103, 105, 132, 136 n, 137 n, 138 n, 155 n, 158
Rome, 262; Irish printing press at, 178 n
Roscommon, County, confiscated property in, 51 n; confiscated tithes, 155 n
Ross, Co. Wexford, charter of, 63; trade, 46
Rotterdam, 56
Rouen, 46, 85 n
Rouse, Jacob, minister, 130 n
Row, Peter, minister, 103 n, 108 n
royalism, in Munster, 121; in Ulster, 125
Royal Society of London, see London: Royal Society
Royle, Thomas, adulterous atheist, 110 n
Rushworth, John, 230

Sadler, John, 231, 267–8
Sadler, Col. Thomas, 103
St. John, Oliver, 92 n
St. Malo, 53
St. Sebastian, 53
salt, 59; excise on, 28, 34
Salusbury, Thomas, 240
Salwey, Richard, 17
Sandwich, earl of, see Montagu, Edward
Sankey, Col. Hierome, 103 n, 107 n, 109, 147 n, 192 n, 210, 219, 231, 232, 233
Santhy, John, 281 n, 288
Saunders, Francis, 203 n
Savage, Abraham, 149 n
schoolmasters, appointed by the state, 186–7; character of, 189; number, 188; salaries of, 187–8, 191, 195, 196 n, 197; unauthorized, 189; mentioned, 183, 190, 213–4, 299
schoolmistresses, 188, 189; salaries, 187
schools, Catholic, 184–5, 194; curriculum, 191; diocesan, 183–4, 186; grammar schools, 186, 187, inquiries into, 187, 197; lands to support, 186–7; schemes for, 190–4; E. Smith schools, 191–4; in Ulster,

185–6; for wards, 186, 214; see also Dublin: schools

Schoute, Theodore, 86

Scobell, Henry, 230

Scotland, army trom, 5, 7; and the Irish fisheries, 34; law in, 250, 278; Parliament of, 7; Presbyterian church of, 122–3, 124, 134 n, 145–6, 263; settlers from in Ireland, 1, 5, 7, 64, 122, 235; and trade with Ireland, 33; universities, 137, 189, 205

Scott, Joseph, 192 n, 203

Shakerley, Jeremy, 229

Shaw, John, 192 n

sheep, 32, 47, 76

Sherard, Hope, minister, 138

sheriffs, abuses of, 254, 278

Sherlock, Sir John, justice of the peace, 290 n

shipping, 35, 36, 42, 43, 46, 79

Shropshire, and Trinity College, Dublin, 205

Sidney, Philip, Viscount Lisle, 7, 8, 99, 220

silver, 39

Sligo, County, confiscated property in, 51 n; confiscated tithes in, 155 n

Sligo, town, E. Smith school, 191

Smith, Erasmus, London alderman, 190–4

Smith, William, chaplain to Lord Cork, 151 n

Smith, William, Dublin alderman, 84

Smith, Zephaniah, minister, 142 n

smuggling, 31–2

soap, 39

Socinianism, 221

Solemn League and Covenant, see Presbyterianism

Somerset, Edward, 11th earl of Glamorgan and second marquess of Worcester, 6

Sondes, William, 291 n

Southwell, Robert, 247

Spain, trade with, 46, 55, 57 n, 89; war with, 16

Stampe, Timothy, 38

staple, 32

Staplehurst, Kent, 102

Stapleton, Robert, trustee of Trinity College, Dublin, 198 n

Stearne, John, 202, 242, 248

steel, 39

Steele, William, Irish councillor and

lord chancellor, career, 19–20, 22, 282, 283, 284–5; and law reform, 261, 279, 285; and religion, 115–17, 126, 146–7, 148, 153, 158; salary of, 277, 285 n; and trial of Charles I, 262, 285; mentioned, 231, 291

Stopford, Capt. James, 208 n

Stowell, Jonas, minister, 143

Strabane, Co. Tyrone, school in, 190

Strickland, Walter, 220

Stubbers, Col. Peter, mayor of Galway, 65

Sudbury, Suffolk, 19 n

Sulliard, Sankey, Dublin alderman, 86

Suffolk, 19

Sutton Coldfield, Warks., 196

Sweden, 220

Sydenham, Richard, 230

Symner, Miles, 176 n, 210, 211–12, 215, 216, 224–5, 227–8, 234, 236, 237, 238, 239, 243, 244, 246, 247

Synge, Edward, dean of Elphin, 151 n

tallow, 33, 35, 42

Tandy, Philip, minister, 102 n

Taylor, Jeremy, 132, 151, 202

Taylor, Timothy, minister, 136, 137 n, 140, 142

Teate, Faithful, 131 n, 136, 137, 140, 141 n

Teate, Joseph, 88

Temple, Sir John, 147 n

Thomlinson, Matthew, Irish councillor, 19, 22, 23, 119 n; and law reform, 261

Thomond, earl of, see O'Brien, Henry

Thurloe, John, 107, 109

Tighe, Richard, 41, 81–2, 83, 291 n; treasurer of E. Smith schools, 192 n

Tighe, William, 82 n

timber, 33, 36, 40

Tipperary, County, confiscated property in, 51 n; confiscated tithes in, 155 n; lands in, 59 n; mines in, 39; school in, 191, 192

Tipperary, palatinate court of, 251, 279–80, 288

tithes, 27, 30, 125, 126, 127, 133, 153–60, 167, 190, 197, 283, 299, 303; yield of, 156, 161

tobacco, 47, 170

Tollet, George, 246

trades, history of, 232

Travers, Joseph, 202, 203, 204
treason, law of, 258, 280
treasurer, deputy, *see* Hutchinson, Daniel
Trent, Council of, 184
Trim, Co. Meath, Baptists in, 103, 133; Catholics in, 68; corporation of, 68, 133
Tuam, archbishop of, *see* Daniel, William, *and* Donnellan, Nehemiah
Tuam, Co. Galway, M.P. for, 70 n
Tyrone, County, education in, 188–9; value of confiscated tithes in, 155 n

Ulster, agricultural improvement in, 239; bishops in, 131; boroughs of, 64; Catholics in, 181; church in, 144, 148, 151; confiscated property in, 51 n; Henry Cromwell and, 115, 117, 134; education in, 185–6, 188–9, 190, 205; episcopalians in, 123; law in, 256, 257, 258, 279; lay impropriation in, 155; plantation in, 1, 95, 185; population, 126; Presbyterians in, 92, 122–6, 128, 129, 140–1, 153, 156, 158, 159; Quakers in, 112; rebellion in, 4, 5; trade of, 36, 42, 46; transplantation from, 123; war in, 7
Underwood, Richard, 152 n
Universal Character, 238
Unmussig, Dr. John, 241
Ussher, Dr. James, successively bishop of Meath and archbishop of Armagh, 91–2, 94 n, 163, 241, 242; his library, 92, 207, 211, 212, 225, 243; and the new learning, 213–14, 215, 225
Utrecht, 85 n

vagrancy, 74–5, 76
Vane, Sir Henry, the younger, 220, 221
Veel, Edward, 203 n
Venables, Robert, 199 n
Vernon, Capt. John, Baptist, 103, 105, 108, 111
Verschoyle, William, 86
Vesey, Thomas, minister, 143 n
Virginia, 151 n, 220

Wale, Edward, minister, 127 n, 136, 137 n, 138 n, 140, 141

Wales, 32, 225; needs compared with Ireland's, 95 n; propagation of the Gospel in, 96, 98, 160, 168, 179; and Trinity College, Dublin, 204, 205
Waller, Edward, 149 n
Waller, Sir Hardress, 6, 7, 24, 139, 147 n
Wallis, John, 245
Wallis, Major Peter, 110 n, 149 n
Walwyn, William, 11
Wandesford, Christopher, 253
Ward, Dr. Seth, 242
wards, 186, 193–4, 214; *see also* Ireland: Court of Wards
Ware, Sir James, 209–10
Warren, Abel, mayor of Kilkenny, 66 n
Waterford, Catholic bishop, *see* Brenan, John
Waterford, Protestant bishop, *see* Baker, George, *and* Foy, Nathanael
Waterford, County, confiscated property in, 51 n; confiscated tithes in, 155 n; justices of the peace, 150, 291; mentioned, 54, 123
Waterford, diocese of, schools in, 184
Waterford, town, Baptists in, 101–2, 103; Catholics in, 68; charter restored, 63; church in, 169; confiscated property in, 52; corporation, 64, 66, 68; education in, 190; fisheries, 34; freemen, 73–4; merchants of, 52–3; ministers in, 127 n, 136; recorder, 275 n, *see* Cook, John; resettlement, 53–5, 66; mentioned, 51, 141
Waterhouse, Dr. Joseph, 242
Watts, Thomas, mayor of Waterford, 66 n
Weaver, John, parliamentary, commissioner in Ireland, 17, 18, 23, 84 n, 113, 115–16, 126 139, 259
Webb, William, 39, 227
Webbe, Ezekiel, minister, 143 n
Webster, Charles, 216
weights and measures, 40, 74
Wentworth, Thomas, first earl of Strafford, and the council of the north, 271; and Ireland, 1–4, 6, 12, 16, 24, 44, 92, 122, 154, 283, 305; and the law, 252, 253–4, 263, 271, 276, 278; and the new learning, 214, 215, 219
Westenra, Derrick, 86
Westenra, Warner, 86

West Indies, 47, 55, 74–5
West Kirby, Cheshire, 139
Westmeath, County, confiscated property in, 51 n; confiscated tithes in, 155 n
Weston, Jerome, 2nd earl of Portland, 271
Wetherell, Mr., 149 n
Wexford, County, commission of the peace for, 104 n, 290; confiscated property in, 51 n; confiscated tithes in, 155 n
Wexford, town; Baptists in, 102; charter restored, 63; fishing trade of, 34, 35, 59; schoolmaster in, 129 n; sea captains of, 52; mentioned, 51
wheat, 36
Whitehall, Robert, schoolmaster, 189 n
Whitelocke, Bulstrode, 78 n, 198, 220
Whitelocke, James, 198 n, 199 n
Wicklow, County, confiscated property in, 51 n; conversions of Catholics in, 180; High Sheriff of, 83
Wilkinson, John, minister, 143 n
Wilkinson, Capt. Robert, 111 n
Wilkinson, Thomas, minister, 146 n, 147 n
Williams, Griffith, bishop of Ossory, 131, 285
Williamson, Caesar, 202
Willoughby, Dr. Charles, 78 n
Wilson, Capt. Ralph, mayor of Limerick, 65 n
Winchester, St. Cross hospital, 263
Winter, Josias, 203
Winter, Dr. Samuel, career, 81, 83, 99–100, 112–17, 118, 120, 121, 126–7, 129, 132, 133, 136, 137 n, 138, 139, 140, 141, 147 n, 158, 192, attacked, 201–2; congregation of, 152 n; and the Irish, 174; out of favour, 210; as provost of Trinity

College, Dublin, 199–200, 201–5; salary of, 136 n, 138 n
Winter, Samuel, the younger, 203
women, preaching in Dublin, 140 n
Wood, Anthony, 196, 197
Wood, James, minister, 192 n
Wood, Robert, 48–9, 207, 210, 216, 223–4, 233, 236, 237, 239, 240, 243–6, 284
wool, 31–4, 41, 48, 76
Wootton, Henry, minister, 136 n, 137 n, 138 n, 140 n, 141, 147 n, 192 n
workhouses, 75
Worsley, Benjamin, 48, 197–8, 210, 214–17, 219–22, 225, 227, 228, 230–3, 235, 236, 237, 239, 241, 243, 244; ideas of, 222; and political opposition, 221; salary of, 228 n
Worth, Dr. Edward, dean of Cork and bishop of Killaloe, 118–22, 125, 126–30, 133, 140, 141, 143, 147, 149, 151–3, 156, 159, 177, 243–4, 284, 300–2; ancestry, 140 n; as bishop of Killaloe, 167; founds a school, 193; and the second college, 210; his wife a Quaker, 120 n
Wybrants, Daniel, 85, 86
Wybrants, Daniel, the younger, 85
Wybrants, Peter, 85, 86
Wyke, Andrew, minister, 99

Yarmouth, Suffolk, 285
Yarner, Abraham, 248
Yarwell, William, mayor of Limerick, 65 n
Yorkshire, and Trinity College, Dublin, 205
Youghal, Co. Cork, corporation of, 62, 64; fisheries of, 34; minister in, 192 n; school at, 185